MW01274905

Christian Churches in Dahomey-Benin

Studies of Religion in Africa

Supplements to the Journal of Religion in Africa

Edited by

Paul Gifford

School of Oriental and African Studies, London

VOLUME 31

Christian Churches in Dahomey-Benin

A study of their socio-political role

by

Patrick Claffey

BRILL

LEIDEN • BOSTON
2007

On the cover: The Jar, Symbol of the Nation
A modern version of the holed water jar, at the entrance to Bohicon, 6 km east of
Abomey. The jar became a symbol of the nation under Gezò, who explained it as
follows: *Our freedom is like a jar full of holes, which cannot hold water. If all the
sons and daughters of this nation can block one hole the jar will hold the water.*
It has been assimilated into the political symbolic lexicon of modern Benin as a
symbol of unity and co-operation.

ISBN 10: 90 04 15572 4
ISBN 13: 978 90 04 15572 5

© Copyright 2007 by Koninklijke Brill NV, Leiden, The Netherlands.
Koninklijke Brill NV incorporates the imprints Brill, Hotei Publishing,
IDC Publishers, Martinus Nijhoff Publishers and VSP.

PRINTED IN THE NETHERLANDS

CONTENTS

ACKNOWLEDGEMENTS

While many people have contributed to this book it is impossible to mention them all by name. Some debts, however, have to be acknowledged and I am very happy to do so.

I am particularly indebted to Professor Donal Cruise-O'Brien and Professor J.D.Y. Peel of the School of Oriental and African Studies, London, and Dr Richard Banégas of the Sorbonne, Paris, for their helpful remarks on the thesis that has become this book. I am also grateful to my research assistant Yvon de Souza (Cotonou), as well as my colleagues Dr Jane Soothill (SOAS), Dr Vincent Foucher and Dr Cédric Mayrargue Foucher (Sciences Politiques, Bordeaux) for their advice and encouragement. The weaknesses in this work are entirely my own.

The historical research involved in this work was one of the most enjoyable parts. I am very grateful to Fr Martin Kavanagh, of the Société des Missions Africaines (Rome), and his predecessor P. Bernard Favier, Paris, for facilitating my use of the SMA archives, and to the staff of the SOAS special collection, which includes the invaluable archive of the Wesleyan Methodist Missionary Society. Propaganda Fide in Lyon and Le Service Protestant de Mission in Paris were helpful in providing further archival materials.

In Benin, I am grateful to the Director of the Centre Béninois pour la Recherche Scientifique, Professeur Fatiou Toukourou, and the Director of the Département de Recherche en Sciences Humaines et Sociales, in Porto Novo, Monsieur Domingo. I am particularly grateful to Frs Barthelemy Adoukonou, Raymond Bernard Goudjo, Michel l'Hostis and Paul Quillet, Pierre Legendre and Pastor Kä Mana, all of whom contributed helpful information, insights and comments at various stages of my research.

For practical reasons it would be impossible to mention the many people I met in the Christian Churches and movements in Benin, bishops, priests and pastors, but also the faithful who were always more than willing to share their experiences as *Chrétiens béninois*. I am very grateful to all of them.

My thanks go to my SVD colleagues Michael Joyce, Michael Egan, Gunther Gessinger, Romano Gentili and Joseph Kallanchira for their hospitality at various times in the research and writing. I am grateful to the Society of the Divine Word for allowing me the time and providing the financial support necessary for this project.

While most of the missionaries I mention in this book lived in the south of Dahomey-Benin, I grew attached to *le Nord* over the thirteen years I lived there. It became an important part of my interior landscape. This was a privileged view into the lives of people through the medium of their own language that has marked my life indelibly. My thanks to the many people I came to know and admire there.

Finally my thanks to my editor at Brill, Paul Gifford, for his advice at all stages of this work.

Dublin, 11 April 2006

CHAPTER ONE

INTRODUCTION

Personal perspectives—Africa 1977–1999

This book probably had its starting point in Donal Cruise O'Brien's office in October 1999. Coming to the School of Oriental and African Studies (SOAS) as a mature student to do an MA in African Christianity after a career of almost twenty-five years in West Africa certainly made the question "What are you doing here?" seem quite reasonable, and it was one I had asked myself several times. By that stage, however, I had a fairly clear idea of what I wanted. My time at SOAS was an attempt to make sense of much of what I have lived through in Africa over the previous years, and also, an attempt to come to an understanding of both my own role in it and that of the institution I had served, the Catholic Church.[1] Obviously, exposure to the world of academic research broadened this considerably over time to an interest in the wider question being investigated by Paul Gifford and others of the role of the different forms of Christianity in social change in Africa. After so long, working within this was to be a step back to look at the wider picture.

I feel that what I bring to this work above all is the experience of living and working mostly *en bas*, insofar as an expatriate involved in development work and with access to considerable resources can ever really be *en bas*, in a rural part of West Africa in a period, 1977–2002, when so much changed. At the same time, it is important to situate this work in the larger regional picture, and indeed the whole African picture during that period. In socio-political terms it was a sombre time during which the last hopes born in the period of independence had faded, while many new ones flickered, most to die even more quickly. Ghana, the beacon under Nkrumah, where I first

---

[1] The author worked as a missionary in Togo (1977–1986) and in Benin (1987–2002). He also had responsibilities for missions in other parts of Africa (1990–1997). This work involved language research and an active involvement in development work, as well as pastoral ministry.

arrived in 1977, spent a few weeks and have visited regularly since, was already being described as a failed state and certainly looked like one then, even to a newcomer. I spent much of my early years in Togo getting supplies to my colleagues in Ghana at a time when even the most basic commodities were absent. Cars came across the border to have new tyres fitted and were loaded with the necessities of mission work, cement, iron sheets, as well as the necessities of life, coffee, sugar, condensed milk and the occasional bit of French cheese. The *Cedi* was worthless and payment was arranged through accounts in Europe or the United States. This was the period when the celebrated *Kalabule* in the so-called parallel economy, a major source of capital accumulation in Ghana's conditions of extreme crisis and brutal recession, was invented.

Within two years Flight Lt. J.J. Rawlings had led his first coup and the cross-border transactions closed down for some time at least. This event was of some importance in what I have come to understand as the near collapse of a large part of West Africa. I have now come to view it as the first thread to be pulled, and it eventually led to the unravelling of the fragile political weave of post-colonial West Africa. It was the beginning of the end of the *ancien regime*. The graduates of the LSE and the French *écoles d'administration*, as well as the braided former Sandhurst and Saint Cyr cadets who had been rushed into place to prepare for the inevitable new independence paradigm, ended up being seen as having betrayed the dream of a better life in an independent Africa. Rawlings became the firebrand model for younger officers, and even ambitious NCOs, like Samuel Doe in Liberia (1980), Thomas Sankara and Blaise Campaoré in Upper Volta (1983), and Valentine Strasser in Sierra Leone (1992). Lean, mean and revolutionary, Rawlings was apparently determined to make a break with the past, not without an eye to Muammar al-Qaddafi and the even more frightening and bloody Mengistu Haile Mariam. While Rawlings withdrew from the revolutionary brink when he introduced Structural Adjustment Programmes (SAPs) under International Monetary Fund (IMF) supervision in 1983, instability spread ineluctably through Upper Volta (despite Campaoré's neo-liberal *volte-face*), Liberia, Sierra Leone, until finally history and its own inherent political fragility caught up with Ivory Coast. A model of post-colonial co-operation, good management and political stability during the long reign of Felix Houphouët-Boigny (1905?–1993), one of the last remaining political links with the colonial period, the descent of Ivory Coast into chaos following a coup at Christmas 1999 (a favoured time of year for West African political upheaval) and the more recent escalation of violent anti-French rhetoric could hardly have been predicted. The result of all this has been regional stagnation and often, as in the case of Liberia, Sierra Leone and now Ivory Coast, chaos and apparently unbridled anarchy. Refugees, often amputees, roam from one country to another, while the small arms introduced over the years, going back to Sankara's 'hot' revolutionary regime in Burkina Faso, are moved on from one conflict to another. These become *lethal weapons* in the hands of thousands of juvenile Rambos and Commander Kick Butts, now celebrated in grim photography.[2] The Nigerian colossus, meanwhile, has taken on the role of sometimes peacekeeper while it struggles to find its own way out of stagnation.

My first real experience of an African state came during eight years in Togo during the height of the Eyadema regime (1977–1986). It was from this time that I began to look seriously at the question of religion and politics in Africa and more particularly the role of the churches. Here I had the experience of an extremely strong national security state, as well as a highly developed personality cult, inspired in great part by Mobutu's Zaire. The Churches, like all other institutions, had been assimilated into what Toulabor has described as "*un œcuménisme Eyademistique*", even providing theological justifications for the regime.[3] One bishop described himself to me in medieval terms, and with some irritation, as "*l'évêque de la cour*". Here I found myself to be very much a participant observer as a reluctant walk-on actor in the 'shows' of state, the political performances the Eyadema regime used so successfully to keep itself omnipresent in the lives of the Togolese people. Like others in my position, on 13 January each year, the anniversary of the regime's accession to power, I was obliged to lead public prayers for *Le Guide du Togo Nouveau* either in the local football stadium or *La Maison du Peuple*. Here Catholics, Protestants and Muslims, somewhat embarrassed thurifers, lined up, one after the other, in front of the local politico-administrative and traditional authorities,

---

[2] See Paul Richards, *Fighting for the Rain Forest: War, Youth and Resources in Sierra Leone*, Oxford: James Currey, 1996.

[3] See Comi Toulabor, 'Monseigneur Dosseh, Archevêque de Lomé', *Politique Africaine*, 35, 1989, 68–76. See also Comi Toulabor, *Le Togo sous Éyadéma*, Paris: Karthala, 1986.

essentially to praise and pray for Eyadema and the perpetuation in
power of his regime. *"Eyadema toujours au pouvoir"* the *groupes-
choc* sang, though not without a little derision at times. I eventually enjoyed using scriptures and texts that were slightly subversive
during these services. Isaiah 10: 24–27 was a particular favourite:

> *My people who live in Zion*
> *Do not be afraid of Assyria!*
> *He may raise the club against you*
> *but in a very short time*
> *the retribution will come to an end,*
> *and my anger will destroy them.*
> *Yahweh Sabaoth will brandish a whip at him…*
> *When that day comes,*
> *his burden will fall from your shoulders,*
> *and his yoke from your neck,*
> *and the yoke will be destroyed.*

It was more derision than subverion and certainly not subversive
enough to find myself in gaol or, more probably after a few days,
on a plane back to Europe, as had happened to one of my predecessors who had reacted to what he saw as an instrumentalisation of
the Church by the regime. My own response was hardly liberation
theology, but it was contestation of a sort, expressing frustration with
both the regime and what I considered to be a sycophantic Church.
In those heady days of *Eyademisme*, I had little audience apart from
one or two politicised *lycéens* who enjoyed seeing how closely I
could sail to danger without falling foul of the regime. There were
one or two explanatory visits to the *préfet*, who simply asked me,
albeit indirectly, to be careful. This was as much for his sake as for
mine since this was the local arena and his job as the '*représentant
du pouvoir central*' was to keep the show on the road. Having to
expel me would have been a messy business.

Part of my later work allowed me to travel quite extensively
and to see first-hand other African states. I watched with interest
Rawlings' Ghana over twenty years and multiple phases, arap-Moi's
Kenya, the complexities of Nigeria, the decline and fall of Mobutu
in the former Zaire, as well as Togo's eventual decline into a state
of stagnation from about 1993. This was a very sombre picture and
certainly gave food for thought on the nature of state and society
in Africa. Three incidents above all marked me during this period.
The first occurred in Ghana at the height of the Rawlings' revolution

in 1980–1981. Having asked a customs official at a remote border crossing in northern Ghana whether it was lawful for him to confiscate my passport and detain me for apparently no reason, he replied: "This is a revolution, *I am the law*". I had no real answer, or at least none that would not have made a bad situation worse. The second involved driving, unwittingly, into a riot in Lomé (Togo) and finding myself stopped at knifepoint, only to be released minutes later for the price of a beer, and led out of the chaos through the backstreets by a helpful taxi-driver. When I told a police officer of the incident his reply was: "*Monsieur, voyons, c'est votre démocratie-là qui fait ça*". The final incident was more of an impression. I sat in Kinshasa's N'Djili Airport in April 1997, witness to what has now been described as 'the criminalisation of the state in Africa' as I watched for several hours unmarked planes spirit away large, unidentifiable cargoes to unknown destinations. During these death throes of his kleptocracy-become-"felonious state,"[4] the former *Timonier National*, Mobutu Sese Seko Koko Ngbendu Wa Za Banga ('The all-powerful warrior who, because of his endurance and inflexible will to win, will go from conquest to conquest, leaving fire in his wake'), was holed up in Gbadolite, dying and looking for a way out of the 'fire in his wake'. Here again, the region had imploded in the years following the atrocities in Rwanda and Burundi in 1993–1994 to become the quagmire it has been ever since.

These were situations that were laden with premonitions of chaos, glimpses into a Hobbesian nightmare world that I could hardly have imagined. I still occasionally have a nightmare that involves an imagined encounter with the late General Eyadema at the Commissariat de Police in Lomé, or of being stuck in N'Djili Airport or that remote Tatale border-post pleading for my passport. These were certainly dramatic illustrations of the fragility of the states within which I found myself, and indeed much of Africa, at that time and now. The sense of crisis was widespread. Africa, if there was *an* Africa, was, to borrow the words of V.S. Naipaul speaking of India, "a wounded civilisation",[5] perhaps even dying.

---

[4] Jean-François Bayart, Stephen Ellis, Béatrice Hibou, *The Criminalization of the State in Africa*, Oxford: James Currey, 1999.
[5] V.S. Naipaul, *India: A Wounded Civilisation*, London: Random House, 1997.

In Christian theology several theologians were already looking at ideas of contestation and liberation and the need to conquer "[anthropological] pauperisation through a new cultural foundation of Africa as a cultural entity".[6] Clearly the situation was serious. The Congolese theologian, Kä Mana, like many others, was wondering if Africa was not "going to die".[7] He pleaded for a reconstruction of the continent, with the Christian myth as a starting point for the imagining of a new utopia.[8] He was seeking "a coherent schema in which the 'images of the world' might constitute a force, a breath, a dynamic of pregnant symbols and vital representations capable of mobilising the energies of the peoples of Africa in order to invent the future".[9]

But there were some bright spots, including a visit to South Africa in April 1994. A new dawn, one hoped, but there are clouds on the post-apartheid horizon.[10] Here the Churches had played an important role following the publication of the celebrated *Kairos Document*. By the time I reached Benin in 1987, the Marxist-Leninist *Parti Révolutionnaire de la République Populaire du Bénin* (PRPB) regime had entered its terminal period. However, there was the birth of hope with the apparently successful *Conférence Nationale des Forces Vives de la Nation* (CNFVN) and the transition to a democratic system of government. This was perhaps a democracy "at the minimalist end of the spectrum... a rough and ready version",[11] but it was one that saw the country out of a very difficult impasse. It survives down to the present, however haltingly, as a *nouveau contrat social béninois*. Given the possible bloody alternatives, this was a considerable achievement of which the Béninois are still proud and which they are reluctant to compromise. This impressive political show, a national *palabre*, transmitted live on radio and television, was the first of a number of similar experiments, in many of which the Churches played an

---

[6] Engelbert Mveng, *L'Afrique dans l'Eglise. Paroles d'un croyant*, Paris: L'Harmattan, 1986, in Kä Mana, *Théologie africaine pour temps de crise: Christianisme et reconstruction de l'Afrique*, Paris: Karthala, 1993, 41.

[7] See Stephen Smith, *Négrologie: Comment L'Afrique meurt*, Paris: Calman Levy, 2003.

[8] Kä Mana, *L'Afrique va-t-elle mourir?: essai d'éthique politique*, Paris: Karthala, 1993.

[9] Kä Mana, *La Nouvelle Evangélisation en Afrique*, Paris: Karthala, 2000, 21.

[10] See Peter Vale, *Whatever happened to the post-apartheid moment?*, London: CIIR, 2004.

[11] J. Wiseman, (ed.), *Democracy and Political Change in Sub-Saharan Africa*, London: Routledge, 1995, 220.

important and very visible role, most notably in Zaire, the Republic
of Congo and Togo. In no case, however, apart from Benin and Mali
(where the Churches were not involved), has the result been durable,
and in most cases it was a total failure from the outset.

The Wider Picture

The emergence of Churches as socio-political actors was not a phenomenon confined to Benin. While religious institutions, particularly
in Western Europe, had been in a process of withdrawal from public
space since the Enlightenment, by the 1980s there appeared to be
resurgence, at least in parts of the world. Religion had apparently
"left its assigned place in the private sphere...and thrust itself into
the public arena of moral and political contestation"[12] as part of a
broader civil society. From 1976, both *Time* and *Newsweek* had begun
to take note of the evangelical phenomenon, naming 1976 "the year
of the evangelicals" in the United States.[13] In 1979 both Pope John
Paul II and the Ayatollah Khomeini stepped on to the world stage,
both with a very political message that had real consequences for
the regimes they clearly contested.[14] By 1990 Kepel was speaking of
La revanche de Dieu, as he noted the reassertion of Islam, Judaism,
Hinduism and Christianity in public space. Huntington saw religion
as an important factor in 'the third wave' which might lead to wider
democratisation at the end of the twentieth century.[15]

While Catholicism was performing its very public role and
operating in the field of 'high politics' in seeking social and political change,[16] it was suggested, most notably by Martin and, more
tentatively, by Stoll, that something else might also be going on
at a more popular, grassroots level. It was around this time that

---

[12] José Casanova, *Public religions in the modern world*, Chicago: UCP, 1994, 3.
[13] Gilles Kepel, *La revanche de Dieu: Chrétiens, Juifs et Musulmans à la recon-
quête du monde*, Paris: Seuil, 1991, 165.
[14] Samuel Huntington, *The Clash of Civilisations and the Remaking of World
Order*, London: Simon and Schuster, 114.
[15] Samuel Huntington, *The Third Wave: Democratisation in the Late Twentieth
Century*, Norman, OK: University of Oklahoma Press, 1991.
[16] George Weigel, "Roman Catholicism in the Age of John Paul II," in Peter Berger
(ed.), *The Desecularisation of the World*, Cambridge: Eerdmans, 1999, 19–35.

the fire of evangelical Protestantism had begun to make a deep impression in Latin America and in Asia. Stoll wondered if Latin America might be "turning Protestant", while Martin too spoke of "a vast volcanic eruption in Catholic Latin America".[17] They speculated that the Pentecostal phenomenon might carry something of the Weberian "Protestant ethic and the spirit of capitalism" and so become a significant factor in bringing about social change. This would not happen through revolution and contestation, which in something of a spirit of social quietism, Evangelicals most often eschew, but rather through a *process* of socialisation in the new spaces created by the Churches. There would be a filtering down of the Protestant ethic to create the spirit of capitalism, which would reconfigure Latin America and lead it out of under-development into modernity. Stoll writes:

> ...the secret may be the foundation of Pentecostal Churches in homes and families rather than workplaces. Where a proletariat are not brought together in large factories, where the poor instead are forced to become shrewd petty traders in order to survive, the household could be considered the basic unit of social struggle.[18]

These Churches, Martin argues, "represent the creation of autonomous spiritual space *over against* comprehensive systems",[19] tracing Pentecostalism through America back to its English Methodist roots, claiming that within these spaces all kinds of things can happen that can lead to deep and lasting social and political change.

Stoll is tentative, even sceptical, but presents as a possible scenario the role of Pentecostal Churches in bringing about change. In his view evangelicals reach the poor in ways that liberation theology, because it is the theology of "religious professionals with professional interests", has failed to do. Pentecostals, he suggests, think and act in a way that is closer to the way of poor people, taking into account their religious imagination and social organisation. Unlike liberation groups, they do not dismiss popular religiosity in favour of social analysis

---

[17] David Stoll, *Is Latin America Turning Protestant? The Politics of Evangelical Growth*, Berkeley: CUP, 1990; David Martin, *Tongues of Fire: The Explosion of Protestantism in Latin America*, Oxford: Blackwell, 1990; David Martin, *Pentecostalism: The World their Parish*, London: Blackwell, 2002.

[18] Stoll, *Is Latin America*, 318.

[19] David Martin (1990), *Tongues of Fire: The Explosion of Protestantism in Latin America*, Oxford: Blackwell, 7.

and indeed have a large dose of "magical power" discourse that has a strong appeal on a grassroots level. Pentecostalism, he concludes, "comes out of the heart of the struggle for personal survival, from core issues of health and reproduction hedged about with beliefs in the supernatural".

The second way Pentecostals may be effective, Stoll claims, is in providing "a model in their ability to organise relatively stable, expanding structures, with a definite capacity for adapting to changing conditions". This obviously holds great attractions in a world that is changing so fast and where traditional, more local social structures, including the nation-state as Giddens noted, have come under increasing pressure from globalising forces.[20]

Lastly, "Pentecostals provide an interesting model [in] their relation to an oppressive social order...They conform to outer restraints yet maintain a degree of independence", they live comfortably in a world where 'yes' is not really 'yes', 'no' is not always 'no', and everything comes back to survival. This is, of course, the prevailing situation in many of the societies where this form of Christianity appears to be most successful, Latin America, sub-Saharan Africa, parts of Asia and amongst struggling minorities and marginalised groups in other parts of the world.

Stoll posits his hope, rather than his belief, on three observations: that these Churches are already playing a role in the self-imagining of new groups in heterogeneous urban settings; that despite their apparent indifference to politics, Pentecostal Churches often become "marshalling grounds" for the entry of new actors into political life; and finally, that these Churches "are attempting to build new moral communities". In addition to this, they appear to have access to elites who are "crucial to any claim to moralise the present social order". Citing Brusco, Stoll speculates on the influence of these Churches on gender and family relationships, wondering whether "the impact of born-again religion on gender roles could have implications for the socialisation of children, patterns of authority in the household, conceivably even for public morality and the political culture".[21] If even a part of all of this were to be true, then it would certainly

---

[20] Anthony Giddens, *The Consequences of Modernity*, Cambridge, 1990, 65.
[21] Martin, *Tongues*, 312–321. See also Elizabeth E. Brusco, *The Reformation of Machismo: Evangelical Conversion and Gender in Colombia*, Texas: UTP, 1995.

represent significant social change in Latin America where *machismo* appears to be an important feature of family relationships.

Martin is even more enthusiastic, claiming that liberation theology had run into the sand to be replaced by Pentecostalism as the religion of the Latin American poor. More recently he has extended the scope of his assertion to Pentecostalism worldwide, including Africa. Basing his thesis heavily on materials provided by Marshall and Meyer, he claims:

> To be born again is to have the power to "construct a space" for freedom and dignity, and to exercise authority by prayer, by exorcism and by averting misfortune.
>
> The reorganisation of a chaotic moral field enables Pentecostals to participate in popular discontent with government. Most born-again Christians do not bribe officials or even tolerate such behaviour, and they also articulate an indirect critique of state-sponsored violence and the operations of the fraternities. They wrestle against the principalities and powers, and that means spiritual and satanic wickedness in high places, i.e. big and evil men. They are armed with countervailing power and their struggle on the spiritual level is all of a piece with their refusal to "play the game". There are signs that this spiritual contest with corruption and with violence and lack of accountability of the powerful may grow into a more institutional participation in politics...Clearly this cannot be a homogeneous movement precisely because Evangelicals express different sets of interests in their opposition to corrupt elements in the social order. Nevertheless, they are part of self-conscious regulation "in an ongoing process of social transformation.[22]

Martin's thesis is that Pentecostalism has "replicated Methodism" and that its socio-economic and political effects in Latin America and in Africa will be similar to those it is claimed it led to in Great Britain and in the United States. He is enthusiastic about its transforming effect on the situation of oppressed groups and particularly women, even calling it "a women's movement".[23] The Pentecostal emphasis on "betterment, self-discipline, aspirations and hard work" which are "the first harsh phase of modernisation" will, he claims, eventually propel other parts of the world into modernity. I am not so sure about all of this. While it is true that the Churches in Benin have a socio-political

---

[22] David Martin (2002), *Pentecostalism: The World their Parish*, Oxford: Blackwell, 140–141.

[23] Martin, *Pentecostalism*, 169.

relevance, I would find it difficult to share Martin's optimism and my fieldwork revealed little that corresponds to his thesis.

Churches and socio-political change in Africa—a brief look at the literature

Writing of religion and politics in Africa, Bayart notes that it is "because the religious field is a locus of social change that it is simultaneously a field of political recomposition". Whatever their relationship to the colonial enterprise, the Churches were agents for social change if only through their involvement in education or their negative comment on the society they encountered. Religion, Bayart asserts, "can contribute to the invention of modernity", pointing to the role of both the Catholic and Protestant Churches "in the inculcation of new economic values and in the expansion of the capitalist world economy in the nineteenth and early twentieth centuries".[24] Mazrui points to their role in education and the provision of a particular humanitarian and universalist political discourse that favoured the birth of nationalism.[25] This of course refers specifically to the mainline historical Churches and we shall look at this in Chapter VI. Africans, however, had long since begun to experiment with their own forms of Christianity. This development was also intimately connected with social change and thus was not without political consequences. Africa has been producing its own prophets and its own responses to African questions for a long time. These were new "arguments of image",[26] however incomprehensible they might sometimes have seemed to the outsider. It has, then, long been obvious that Christian Churches had a definite socio-political significance.

Ranger has reviewed religious movements extensively in East, Central, Southern, and, to a lesser extent, Western Africa, looking at the possible socio-political implications across a wide range. Speaking of early African religious movements, he notes: "even if

---

[24] Jean-François Bayart, *Religion et modernité politique en Afrique noire*, Paris: Karthala, 1993, 302–307.
[25] Ali Mazrui, *Political Values and the Educated Class in Africa*, London: Heinemann, 1978, 153–154.
[26] James Fernandez, 'African Religious Movements', *Annual Review of Anthropology*, 7, 1978, 228–229.

they were not unequivocally anti-colonial they constituted a form of politics".[27] It is my view that this holds good for all the later religious movements as well. While they may not always be involved in overt contestation and it may be difficult to pin down a clear causal connection between religious movements and socio-political change, they do indeed constitute a form of politics, if only because, as I point out in Chapter VI, they can be 'exit options', places to go to sulk and hide away from an intrusive or even dangerous state. While it would be an error to reduce religious movements to the purely political, it is true to say that their existence is in itself a political statement. They can indeed constitute a challenge to states today just as much as Harris, Oschoffa or Kimbangu did to both the Belgian and French colonial administrations. This can be said to be the case if only because religious imaginary and religious movements of any kind are extremely difficult to predict or control. Linden writing of colonial Rwanda, for example, recounts the fears of a Belgian Catholic administrator at the idea of Protestant education handing out "a spiritual food which revolutionises their way of thinking, creates anarchy…and gives rise to extreme individualism".[28] For a colonial *administration* which, above all, wanted its subjects to be docile, the problems arising out of such a change would have been very serious indeed. A fundamental part of my thesis is that many of the Churches today continue to constitute a commentary upon the state and society within which they find themselves and an attempt, however vain it may seem to positivists, to *imagine* it, or at least *hope* that it might be *otherwise*.

West Africa presents very different historical characteristics from both East and Southern Africa and this is inevitably reflected in the development of religious movements. The most important of these is surely the fact that it never had a real settler community that in some way laid a special claim to the Christian myth, although a European monopoly of access to the Christian myth was also contested here, particularly in the Aladura and similar movements. My fieldwork in the Celestial Church of Christ (CCC) confirms that, to some extent, this continues to be the case. On the other hand, West Africa presents

---

[27] Terence O. Ranger, 'Religious Movements and Politics in Sub-Saharan Africa', *African Studies Review*, 29 (2), 1986, 4.
[28] Ian Linden, *Church and Revolution in Rwanda*, London: Heinemann, 1977, 156.

many of the same elements as other part of the sub-Saharan Africa: the presence of the historical Churches, African Instituted Churches from the early part of the twentieth century, post-war Evangelical development, as well as more recent Pentecostal and charismatic movements. I shall attempt to look across this spectrum.

There has been an important literature on this area. Aladura was an early focus of attention.[29] More significantly for this work, however, Peel continued to research the socio-political significance of Christianity in Nigeria, looking historically at the role of religious encounter in the creation of Yoruba identity. This authoritative work was published after I had started this research but its influence on its direction has been considerable. In religious terms, as I shall show in Chapter III, Danxomɛ owed much to old Yorubaland.[30] In political terms, as we shall see in Chapter II, Danxomɛ was a constant threat, its historical nemesis. Peel's work pointed in the direction of more historical research than I had perhaps anticipated. This task was facilitated by my reading of Bernard Salvaing's very useful study of the missionary encounter with this part of Africa in the nineteenth century.[31] This led me to the Wesleyan Methodist Missionary Society archive (WMMS), now fortunately housed at SOAS. This historical line of inquiry was also greatly helped by the work of Christiane Roussé-Grosseau and Martine Balard, who examined the "cultural shock" involved for French Catholic missionaries in this encounter and how they came to cope-or not cope-with it.[32] This led to the archives of the Société des Missions Africaines in Rome.

The tentative moves toward democratisation in Africa in the early 1990s gave rise to a considerable literature examining the role of the Churches in this process and in the wider political context. Gifford looked at the Churches in the democratisation processes in an edited

---

[29] H.W. Turner, *History of an Independent African church: The Church of the Lord (Aladura)*, Oxford: Clarendon, 1967; H.W. Turner, *Religious Innovation in Africa: Collected Essays on New Religious Movements*, Boston: G.K. Hall, 1979; J.D.Y Peel, *Aladura: A Religious Movement Among the Yoruba*, London: OUP, 1968.

[30] J.D.Y. Peel, *Religious Encounter and the Making of the Yoruba*, Bloomington: Indiana Press, 2001.

[31] Bernard Salvaing, *Les missionnaires et la rencontre de l'Afrique au XIX siècle: Côte des Esclaves et pays Yoruba*, Paris: L'Harmattan, 1994.

[32] Christiane Roussé-Grosseau, *Mission catholique et choc des modèles culturels en Afrique: l'exemple du Dahomey, 1861–1928*, Paris: L'Harmattan, 1992; Martine Balard, *Mission catholique et culture vodoun: l'œuvre de Francis Aupiais (1877–1945)*, Perpignan: PU, 1998.

volume, and more generally at their "public role".[33] It was also during this time that there was a surge of interest in what was coming
to be seen as the 'Pentecostalism explosion' in Africa as part of a
wider transnational phenomenon, as well as its role in the political
imaginary. Here Gifford has made an important contribution to West
African studies with two monographs looking at Liberia and, more
recently, Ghana.[34] Based on extensive fieldwork, he contests the more
starry-eyed view of Pentecostalism taken by Martin, although he does
acknowledge that these Churches are not "static" and he sees in a figure
like Mensa Otabil the development of some kind of social critique.
While acknowledging that they may contribute to the maintenance
of a certain social cohesion and "peaceability", as Martin suggests,
Gifford has little time for the idea that they contribute in any meaningful way to the "reform of culture". Even in their understanding
of "peaceability", he argues, they play the game of those in power,
and thus in dulling the public debate that is essential to a working
democracy. As we shall see in this book, in speaking of 'peace' there
can be the implied threat of impending chaos. Peace does not always
mean real peace but the simple absence of the turmoil that might
follow change. Better, then, to keep the peace. Gifford is equally
dismissive of their role in gender issues, the understanding of success,
the inculcation of democratic values, the building of social capital
or trust, and the work ethic, all at the core of Martin's argument.
Whatever the situation in Latin America, Gifford's argument is that
this is not what is going on in Ghana. While I agree with what he
says to some degree, and certainly do not agree with Martin's speculation, I feel he may be underestimating the importance of the question
of peace and social cohesion for the people in the pews (or plastic
seats). This is especially so in the light of the traumas of the whole
continent over the past decade. My underlying analysis is of Africa
as very fragile, ready to implode at any moment in almost any part
of the continent. Liberia is at the centre of the present West African
tragedy, while Ghana lies just on the fringes, and Ivory Coast has
already been dragged in. Conflict is clearly contagious in contiguous

---

[33] Paul Gifford (ed.), *The Christian Churches and the Democratisation of Africa*,
Leiden: Brill, 1995; Paul Gifford, *African Christianity: Its Public Role*, London:
Hurst, 1998.
[34] Paul Gifford, *Christianity and Politics in Doe's Liberia*, Cambridge: CUP, 1993;
Paul Gifford, *Ghana's New Christianity*, London: Hurst, 2004.

regions. I believe, and hope to show, that this is also the 'analysis' of many of the people I have met across grassroots Christianity, and that it serves to explain much of what goes on at this level. Democratic values, the work ethic, rational bureaucracy and the spirit of capitalism are all very fine, but they can be left until later when the immediate search is for refuge and protection in a world threatened by what Corten, in a very sombre analysis of Haiti, has described as *"la misère-désolation"*.[35] This fragility of West African society is the theoretical basis of much of my analysis, and I shall look at it in more detail presently.

Until recently, little research had been done on Christianity in modern Benin. De Surgy attributes this, in part at least, "to the positivist heritage overseeing the development of 'religious sciences' in France, which was both secular and anticlerical, as well as a reductionist Marxist ideology".[36] It was assumed that the *République laïc* inherited from the colonial period would endure without question. However, a remarkable growth of Christian Churches in the liberalised space created by the CNFVN began to ask some questions that needed answers and opened up a new field of research. De Surgy produced three ethnographic works, including a detailed and very sympathetic study of the Celestial Church of Christ (CCC), the first major study of this Church, now one of the biggest in the region. He has also written two critical studies of Pentecostal Churches and their African derivatives, as well as an essay on Pentecostalism and the political imaginary.[37]

Perhaps partly because of the country's reputation as "the home of Vodún", but also because of President Kérékou's well-known flirtation with different forms of religious experience, there has been literature on this aspect of African politics in Benin.[38] The liberalisation

---

[35] André Corten, *Misère, religion et politique en Haiti*, Paris: Karthala, 2001, 34.
[36] Albert de Surgy, *L'Eglise du Christianisme Céleste: Un exemple d'Eglise prophétique au Bénin*, Paris: Karthala, 2001.
[37] Albert de Surgy, *Le phénomène pentecôtiste en Afrique noire: Le cas béninois* Paris: L'Harmattan, 2001; *Syncrétisme chrétien et rigueur anti-pentecôtiste en Afrique noire occidentale—Le cas béninois* Paris: L'Harmattan, 2003; "Le choix du monde spirituel comme espace public Albert de Surgy", in A. Corten & A. Mary (eds), *Imaginaries politiques et pentecôtismes*, Paris: Karthala, 2000.
[38] See Ulrike Sulikowski, "Eating the flesh, eating the soul: Reflections on politics sorcery and vodun in contemporary Benin", in J.-P. Chrétien *et al.* (eds), *L'invention religieuse en Afrique. Histoire et religion en Afrique noire*. Paris: Karthala, 1993, 379–392; Cedric Mayrargue, *Religions et changement politique au Bénin*, Mémoire de

of public space was to favour all religions and, as we shall see in
Chapter 4, the apparent rehabilitation of the Vodún enlivened debate
considerably.

Anthropological fragility and the fear of 'misère-désolation'

Probably because of my experience living in Benin, this book took on
a broader and more narrative form than might have been the case for a
younger author. The reason for this was my desire to understand the historical reasons for many of the observations I had made about Béninois
society and the tensions that appeared to bedevil it and hobble its development. The overall impression was of a society ill at ease with itself,
often marked by deep suspicions, and of a State that had experienced
great difficulties in imagining itself as a State, and making a claim
on the affections and loyalty of its people in the forty years of its
independent existence.

The book is divided into two major sections. The first is historical and anthropological as I examine the traditional kingdom and
the place of religion, the Vodún, in its politics. It is my contention
that the *Weltanschauung* that produced the Vodún still underlies
Benin today and informs the religious imaginary of the Béninois.
In the final chapter of this section, I examine what I have come
to see as the unassumed memory of Danxomε in modern Benin,
this narrative of pride and suspicion, which appears to haunt the
modern state and explain many of its difficulties. In the second
section, I look at the role of the Christian Churches across a wide
denominational spectrum, historically in relation to the kingdom,
in the creation of colonial Dahomey, and in the modern state
where they continue to play a very visible role. While much has
changed, there are also continuities here which I shall examine.

Donal Cruise O'Brien refers to "the emotional texture of the state"
as a requisite for legitimacy, and this is what I set out to examine
in the first section. It did not seem to me enough to decry colonialism, neo-colonialism and, more recently, globalisation as obstacles to

---

DEA "Etudes Africaines", CEAN, Bordeaux, 1994; Camille Strandsbjerg, "Kérékou,
God and the Ancestors: Religion and the conception of political power in Bénin",
African Affairs, 99, 2000, 395–414.

development, though I have no doubt all of these are indeed factors in the country's difficulties. My observations, however, led me to believe that the problems were much deeper and were woven in to the very fabric, the texture, of what I often refer to as Danxomε-Benin, in recognition of the inextricable links between the historical kingdom and the modern state. I was encouraged in this direction by a conversation I had with the Béninois priest and intellectual, Barthelemy Adoukonou, in May 1999, and by later conversations with Raymond-Bernard Goudjo, Roger Gbégnonvi, Paulin Hountondji, my research assistant Yvon de Souza and other Béninois intellectuals. I have also used what I have called in my field notes *remarques trottoir*, the throwaway remarks and commentaries on everyday life by *les petites gens*, the stuff of fieldwork that can reveal so much of the texture of any society.

It was during these conversations that the question of history came up, and particularly the problems posed by "the wounds of the past".[39] It has been suggested that I may have had Germany in mind when dealing with this subject. This is partially true and Germany was certainly referred to with admiration by several of my interlocutors in Benin as the example of a country that had risen above its historical memories in great part by openly acknowledging them and coming to terms with them, however painful that process may have been. However, I was also looking at a case closer to home for me. My own country, Ireland, has been undergoing a process of historical revision in recent years as it seeks to break out of the cycle of violence and the political stalemate that has marred it since independence in 1922, and particularly over the last thirty years. Here it has also been a question of memories and coming to terms with history. The so-called revisionist historians such as Foster and Ferriter, referring to an even earlier school, have examined the grand Irish historical narratives, the 1798 Rising, the Famine, the Celtic Revival, Easter 1916, and both the earlier and later 'Troubles', questioning our long-held assumptions in order to get a new view of our history.[40] In so

---

[39] See Edouard Adè, "Les fidèles laïcs et la politique au Bénin", in *Une Expérience Africaine de l'Inculturation, (III Politique et Développement)* Sillon Noir, Cotonou, 1992, 62.

[40] See Colm Toibin and Diarmid Ferriter, *The Irish Famine: A Documentary*, New York St Martins Press, 1999; Roy Foster, *The Irish Story*, London: Allen Lane, 2001.

doing, they have tampered with the myths, as W.B Yeats had already done in his poem *Easter 1916*, when he dared ask whether the Rising of that fateful year had not been "needless death after all", a death out of which "a terrible beauty is born". They argue that emotion and an unthinking anti-Englishness have skewed our understanding of our history and of our relationship to the world. Conor Cruise O'Brien and Kevin Myers, amongst others, have taken this up in a more polemical style in both *The Irish Independent* and *The Irish Times*, causing more than a little irritation in the process. These writers have attempted to deconstruct and revise what they perceive as the historical myths that lie at the root of many of our contemporary problems, particularly in relation to the violence that has been such a feature of life in Northern Ireland. Both have dared to question the 1916 Rising—the foundation myth of the Republic, its heroes and the war that followed. This sacralisation of violence, during Easter Week, with its loaded religious imagery, was calculated for maximum effect. The consequences, they would argue, have been devastating as the event is invoked to legitimate ongoing violence, with the Provisional IRA claiming to be the inheritor of this sacralised and very bloody tradition. The question for both Ireland and Benin is to what extent the past is determining the present, or, even more negatively, to what extent the present is is its prisoner? The other question that begs to be asked it to what he extent we really understand that past.

Danxomε, as we shall see in Chapter 2, was constructed as a very dark place both in the eyes of those who visited it, the early travellers, the missionaries, the putative anthropologists and eventually by the people who make up the modern state and who see it as casting an enduring historical shadow. Born in response to the Transatlantic Slave Trade, Danxomε had indeed a tragic past that certainly requires attention. Adè speaks in Freudian terms of "the dangers of an ill-assumed history", adding that it is important for Béninois society to acknowledge and assume its history, since "the wounded memory [is] dangerous for the Other",[41] as, indeed, it is damaging for the Self. This problem has been acknowledged in the research of the *Sillon Noir*, a socio-anthropological research group founded by Adoukonou, which provided me with the theoretical concept which underlies the

---

[41] Adè, *Les fidèles laïcs*, 63.

whole of this book, that of the anthropological fragility (*fragilité anthropologique*) of Béninois society.

This concept needs further examination here. Adè outlines three facts which he sees as symptomatic of this condition: the role played by the kingdom of Danxomε in the Slave Trade; the observation by French philosopher Emmanuel Mounier in the 1920s that the Béninois intelligentsia were capable of the best and the worst of things, the infamous *nivellement par le bas* which is inimical to all development, and which Adè sees as having been borne out in the third symptom: the chaotic political instability of the country after independence leading to ten *coups d'état* in twelve years (1960–1972) and the eventual imposition of a totalitarian Marxist-Leninist regime. There is here, he concludes, concrete evidence of anthropological fragility that requires examination.[42] At the root of this, he places the question of the Transatlantic Slave Trade, which I examine in some detail in Chapter II. Adoukonou notes that while until 1434 the West had no direct contact with deepest Africa, Gil Eanes passing Cape Bojador was the moment when sub-Saharan Africa entered into history, when it was 'discovered'. It was the beginning of the encounter with the West and also the start of the most extreme alienation, as, in less than a century, human beings became no more than *ebony*, a commodity to be traded, as Césaire puts it, "like English linen sheets or Irish salted meat".[43] Philosophy, including that of the Enlightenment, remained blind to this development or even justified it, "reified religion" did little better, and politics was the centre of this complicity.[44] In Smith's words: "The history of Africa, in its relations with the outside world, is a long trauma: the slave trade, colonisation, apartheid as a pathological racism, globalisation and a new humiliation of the black person…".[45] In Adè's view, the healing of the wounds left by this history, hatred and fatalism, can only be achieved when it is fully assumed by *all* of those historically involved. It is a history, however, which is often denied, simply because it is so emotionally charged,

[42] Adè, *Les fidèles*, 63–64.
[43] Aimé Césaire, *Cahier d'un retour au pays natal*, Paris: Presence Africaine, 1983, 38–39.
[44] Adè, *Les fidèles*, 65. See also Laënnec Hurbon, *Pour une sociologie d'Haiti au 21ème siècle*, Paris: Karthala, 2001, 27–33 on the *Code Noir*, Louis XIV's 1685 legislation governing the laws of slavery, which he notes was almost totally overlooked by the philosophers of the Enlightenment and supported by the Church.
[45] Smith, *Négrologie*, 82.

as I show in Chapter 4. He points out that the modern Béninois was *not* the victim: "we were not the ones who were chained and tortured in the sugar and coffee plantations". This is attested to by the Creole expression reported by Laënnec Hurbon: "*Depi lan Ginen, nèg ryai nèg*" ("Going back to Guinea, the Negro has hated the Negro").[46] The Béninois must, Adè says, reduce the distance that separates him from his history in order to really confront it and be reconciled both to the real African victims and to the European Other in whose crime he has been an accomplice.

At the centre of this lies the responsibility of Africa itself in the tragedy:

> It was the Black who delivered his brother sold into slavery and it was the White who martyred the slave...[The] fact is that the millions of slaves sold and chained in the New World were not only the captives of Western wars. We need to have the historical courage to acknowledge that we have a large part of the responsibility in this sinister event.[47]

Adè notes that when one examines closely the political instability of the independent state in the early years, as well as the years of the militaro-Marxist dictatorship, one sees the ethnic tensions and the individual thirst for power. Above all, however, he notes "the fragility of interpersonal relations resulting from a false relationship with the world". This is the result of a history in which the kingdom of Danxomε, accomplice in the Slave Trade, was founded upon "a transgression of the laws of friendship and hospitality and by the collapse of fraternity", effectively the destruction of the old *Ebi* system, which we shall look at later in this Chapter.[48] Danxomε was a compromise built upon this collapse into "a war of all against all", though *compromise* is hardly a word one would use in speaking of the new hegemonic polity that came to be reputed for its violence. The very constitution of Danxomε was predicated on violence and its growth was assured "by the impulsion of the same violence" which led to a delimiting of fraternity and

---

[46] See Laënnec Hurbon, *Les mystères du vaudou*, Paris: Gallimard, 1993, 21.

[47] Adè, *Les Fidèles*, 66.

[48] See Robin Law, *The Kingdom of Allada*, Leiden: Brill, 1997, 61 for a discussion of the *Ebi* social system of Allada, which Dahomey was to reject. Also I.A. Akinjogbin, *Dahomey and it neighbours 1708–1818*, Cambridge: Cambridge University Press, 1967, 14–17. Social relations in the old *Ebi* system had been based on the sense of the sacred, maintained by the *souvenir de l'être cher*, the common ancestor. These values were, however, destroyed through manipulation to increase the power of the absolute monarch.

the clan and the imposition of slavery and domination, the *gànhúnŭ* which was the mark of the kingdom. This is examined in Chapter 2, with the Hundred Years' War, the Thirty Years' War, Restoration England and Hobbes' *Leviathan*, as well as more recent European history, all hovering in the background to remind us that extreme political violence is not unique to Danxomɛ.

"[This implosion of the old order led to a situation] whereby one could sell blood brothers simply because they did not belong to the royal circle".[49] Adè claims to see the continuation of this in politics in the modern era, when the brother can be sold for the benefit not of the nation but of the political party that has taken on an ethnic profile. It is not so much, he asserts "that there is a resurgence of interethnic combat but rather a perverse functionalisation of the ethnic conscience and a dangerous manipulation of the rancours of the past".[50] What are often identified as ethnic categories are really the vestiges of defunct political entities, "the nationalisms within nationalisms", the primordial entities of "competing traditions gathered accidentally into concocted political frameworks rather than organically evolving civilisations".[51] In the presence of such competing tensions, a state community is difficult to imagine.

This is not unique to Benin but it does explain its tripartite politics. This was essentially, as we shall see, a game of *Danxomɛ vs the Rest*, which has marred the country since the inception of modern politics and continues to feature today. As Adè points out, even these ethnic regional cleavages, remnants of long-disappeared polities, are fictions that left to themselves would not hold together. But they are not left alone and the embers are often stoked for political ends. The difficulty, he concludes, is that the Béninois has real "difficulty in living with the difference that is proper to each human person" and this undermines any possibility of living in fraternity. This "particular pathos" is then transferred to the political field and "given various masks according to the conjuncture",[52] while the texture of society is put under increased strain. The national consciousness of the traditional

---

[49] Adè, *Les Fidèles*, 67.
[50] Adè, *Les Fidèles*, 68.
[51] Clifford Geertz, *The Interpretation of Cultures*, London: Fontana, 1993 edition, chs. 9–10. Geertz refers specifically to the case of Asante within modern Ghana (p. 273).
[52] Adè, *Les Fidèles*, 70.

kingdoms, Adè points out, was in fact a very negative "position by opposition", which led to constant wars and continues to cause political tension. This was very different from the old *Ebi* system. These *Ebi* values were, however, destroyed through manipulation by the political powers, the cult of the king replacing *l'être cher*, in order to create "a national conscience by opposition", and this is being reproduced today. In Adè's view, this anthropological fragility is at the heart of the political tension, but with the difference that there is no national consciousness but rather the unbridled pursuit of individual interests in the cultural vacuum and free-for-all created by the disappearance of the old order and the imposition of a half-baked or even botched modernity. But, one must ask, is there a longing here for the "old, eternal"[53] Africa, an Eden violently annihilated? Did this idealised pre-colonial *Ebi* world ever exist? One is certainly entitled to ask the question. Naipaul remarks that "Africa lives its past like a dream of purity, the past as a religion."[54] This is something that is not uncommon in countries struggling to come to terms with their history, as my Irish experience and several variants of attempted Celtic revivals testify. Smith notes the tendency to idealise the past and the demonisation of everything that has happened to the continent since "its forced entry into the universal". But Adè's analysis, as a Béninois intellectual, certainly has serious implications for state and society.

Hurbon, writing of Haiti, speaks of *la crise du lien social*, to describe the shredded social fabric of a country where the common bonds that should hold it together appear to have been completely lost and the texture of society almost completely destroyed. The Danxomε and Haiti narratives are intertwined from their tragic starting point in the transatlantic slave trade, down through the Vodún or Haitian *lwa*, to the commonalties one finds between Haitian *Creole* of Port-au-Prince and *le petit français* of Cotonou. Hurbon notes that "the influence of the Fòn of Dahomey, together with the Yoruba of Nigeria, is preponderant and serves as a unifying base for an ensemble of cultural practices transplanted to the island by the slaves". It is not surprising then that there may be similarities in the problems encountered. In Hurbon's view, Haiti is still determined by "the memory of the slave trade" and the collapse in values that this engendered. Haiti repro-

---

[53] Naipaul, *India*, 3.
[54] V.S. Naipaul, in Smith, *Négrologie*, 82.

duced the chaos of the Slave Coast, perhaps even in aggravated form
since there was a more total loss of social references. Dailey notes
that "Haiti remains in the grip of an archaic past, and its crippling
social and economic legacy...Its political culture is atavistic". Its
governments have been consistently autocratic, not to say despotic,
marked by chronic instability and extreme violence, whether of the
Duvalierist Tonton Macoute or the more recent *Chimères*, the thugs
who reign over the desolation.[55] Like Adè, Hurbon sees the same
psychological need to deal with "this past [...] so that it does not
serve as a source of resentment, a means of blackmail or an excuse
to hide from every law".[56]

This Creole proverb describes it well: "*Konstitusyon se papye, bayon-
het se feh*" (The constitution is paper, a bayonet is iron). A former
Mayor of Port-au-Prince says hopelessly: "Anarchy is overwhelming us".[57] This is Graham Greene's "nightmare republic".[58] Hurbon
describes a scenario that is much feared in Benin. Haiti, in his view,
is mired in this past and the social chaos it created. This is the reason
for its failure and also for the recourse to the religious as a safe space,
a place of refuge, in the flight from a state that has been predatory
since its inception, in its West African 'pre-history' in Danxomε and
in Haiti itself. It is inhabited by the victims of predation, some of
who gained a monopoly of the occult forces they brought with them,
the Vodún, to become predators themselves. Apparently described by
Mother Theresa as "the fifth world", it is a paradigmatic failed state
going back two centuries to its birth in the Bois de Caïman.[59] Fatton
describes the government of the country in the terminal period of the
Aristide regime as "babbling with catastrophe and nearing the abyss".[60]
A Haitian economist says: "It's like a jungle here. People believe
the government is so irrational it could do anything".[61] It is fair for

---

[55] Peter Dailey, Haiti: The Fall of the House of Aristide, *The New York Review
of Books*, 50, 4, 2003.
[56] Hurbon, *Sociologie*, 14.
[57] Dailey, *Haiti*.
[58] See Graham Greene, *The Comedians*, London: Penguin, 1991.
[59] See Peter Hallward, 'Option Zero in Haiti', *New Left Review*, 27, 2004,
23–47.
[60] Roger Fatton, *Haiti's Predatory Republic: The Unending Transition to Democracy*,
New York: Rienner, 2002, in Peter Dailey, 'Haiti's Betrayal', *New York Review of
Books*, 50, 5, 2003.
[61] Michael Norton, "Haitians Withdrawing U.S. Dollars", Associated Press, 16
October 2002, in Dailey *Haiti's Betraya*.

the denizens of this state to conclude that "*L'état mange toujours*" and the first victims of its voracious appetite are its own citizens. A recent poll found that 67% of its population would flee.[62] This is a modern form of the *marronnage*, the centrifugal flight from the state in all its forms to primordial communities in the hills built around the Vodún, that has been a feature of Haiti since its foundation.[63] It is hardly surprising then to find Hurbon speaking specifically of the growth of Pentecostalism in the following terms:

> One can ask oneself if the Pentecostal public space is not conceived essentially on the basis of the imaginary of witchcraft. In other words, only the Church herself, that is the assembly, can offer a haven of protection against a world understood as totally hostile, and in some sense an intermediate space which serves both as a private and as a public sphere, in the sense that the individual can allow himself to freely express the sufferings of his daily life and at the same time find a certain fusion with the pentecostal community, his new family. Can we say that we are witnessing here a *marronnage* (that is to say a flight) from the political?[64]

In discussing Haiti, Corten uses Hannah Arendt's term "desolation"[65] to construct his own depressing concept of *la misère-désolation* to describe a situation that is beyond poverty. For Arendt, twentieth-century modernity was marked by the emergence of human superfluousness, the permanent possibility of homelessness, statelessness as a global condition. Her greatest fear was that the extreme superfluousness of the human person as expressed in the creation of the death camps, once considered an aberration, might, under the conditions of totalitarianism and imperialism, become the norm. Given the situation in Haiti, the unimaginable human destitution, the apparent cheapness of human life, the flight from the country without any consideration of the risks or for the future, one can see how Corten found the expression depressingly meaningful. He concludes that *la misère-désolation* is "the destruction of all private life by filth, promiscuity, physical weakness and fear. The conditions of life are such that human dignity

---

[62] Dailey, *Haiti.*
[63] See Laënnec Hurbon, *Culture et dictature en Haïti: l'imaginaire sous contrôle,* Paris: L'Harmattan, 1978, 34. Also R.S. Price, *Maroon Society,* New York: Doubleday, 1973.
[64] Hurbon, *Sociologie,* 241.
[65] See Hannah Arendt, *Le système totalitaire,* Paris: Seuil, 1951.

cannot survive....It is a question of open air concentration camps".[66] Inspired by Arendt, the Hungarian writer Imre Kertész speaks of the *Etre sans destin*. The ambiguity is no doubt intentional, it can mean "to be without a destiny" but also "a being without a destiny", a captive of hopelessness.[67] In this scenario, life is indeed likely to be nasty, brutish or short. If this is the emotional texture of the state, flight must seem like a sensible option. In his election campaign in 1990, Jean Bertrand Aristide apparently confirmed Corten's analysis in setting his goal as "changing conditions in Haiti from misery to poverty with dignity".[68]

I would hesitate to speak of Benin in such stark terms, since many social structures do still have substance and meaning in the lives of people and, while there is undoubtedly much poverty, people for the most part live with great dignity. The state does have some purchase on the imagination and has gained again the loyalty of its people based on the symbolic capital created by the CNFVN. I feel, however, that the whole of West Africa has this image of Haiti as its worst nightmare. This might not be so alarming if the reality had stayed in Haiti, far away, but it is increasingly a reality closer to home, in Liberia, Sierra Leone, Ivory Coast and Togo from where refugees from the brutal reality of a predatory state flood over the border seeking shelter. Some of the people living in the poorer areas of Accra, Lomé, Cotonou and, perhaps above all, the chaotic megacity of Lagos may well see life in terms of *misère-désolation*. This is well expressed in the popular Nigerian song *Sweet Mother*:

> When I dey sick, my mother go cry, cry, cry,
> she go say instead when I go die make she die.
>
> O, she go beg God,
> "God help me, God help, my pikin oh."
>
> If I no sleep, my mother no go sleep,
> if I no chop, my mother no go chop, she no dey tire oh.
> Sweet mother I no go forget you,
> for the suffer wey you suffer for me.[69]

---

[66] Corten, *Misère*, 34.
[67] Imre Kertész, *Etre sans destin*, Paris: Collection 10/18 Domaine Etranger, 2002.
[68] Norton, *Haitians Withdrawing*.
[69] From song lyrics by Prince Nico Mbarga, 1976.

The song was said to be a Nigerian national anthem in the expression it gives to people's feelings and indeed it has echoed around West Africa.[70] There is the feeling that the world is indeed fragile, life is precarious and the demon of destruction is just being held at bay. There are demons from within and, increasingly, demons from without that nobody seems to know how to control, and the threat of a certain *misère-désolation*. It appears to me that this, rather than the Protestant ethic and the spirit of capitalism, is what popular religiosity in Benin is all about, as I try to show in my final chapter.

In an essay entitled "The religious effects of culture: nationalism", Hart cites Quentin Skinner's *The Foundation of Modern Political Thought* to suggest that political modernity in Europe, the state and the nation-state, were born in the political ferment of the Renaissance and Reformation age and the religious wars that followed:

> On Skinner's view, the state is what 'happened' when Europeans found themselves drowning in their own blood for religious reasons. The absolutist claims of the state usurped and displaced the absolutism of Christian convictions, the *imperium* of the state displacing the *imperium* of the Church.[71]

In effect, the state had to be strong to contain the warring forces within it and impose order and, ironically, religious enthusiasm led to the secularisation. What I am suggesting here is a similar process but somehow in reverse. The weakness of states such as Haiti in the most extreme case, and Benin and other states in West Africa to a lesser degree, creates a situation allowing Churches to emerge, providing, however tentatively, the space for some semblance of an ordered life, and some *hope*, however ephemeral.

It was this analysis, then, that led me back to look at Danxomε and the origins of the modern state of Benin. I needed to know what kind of place it was and why it continues to exercise the hold it does. The first part of the book is taken up with this investigation, and the political and religious system upon which it was built. This was done through research in a substantial literature, starting with the early travellers down to more modern historiography. It concludes

---

[70] See Ogunyemi, Chikwenye Okonjo, *Africa Wo/Man Palava: The Nigerian Novel by Women*, (WCS) Women in Culture and Society Series, 1998, 287.

[71] In William D. Hart, *Edward Said and the Religious Effects of Culture*, Cambridge: CUP, 2000, 48. See also Quentin Skinner, *The Foundations of Modern Political Thought*, Cambridge: CUP, 1978.

with an examination of how it continues to be perceived in the popular imagination and how it still pervades the political process at all levels. This analysis was based on interviews and conversation recorded in the course of my fieldwork, but also older anecdotal evidence recollected from my years of living in Benin. While I am not completely pessimistic about modern Benin, and feel that some progress has been made in the past decade, I am very aware of its inherent fragility and the constant strains upon the social fabric. There are worrying signs of political atavism in the failure to renew political elites and create the socio-economic dynamism that would give the country some hope of improving its position as one of the poorest in the world. While the spiral may not be downward there is an *"immobilisme"*[72] or stagnation that can lead to frustration, which places further strains on society.

In the second part of the book I look at the role of the Churches, both historically and in modern Benin. For historical reasons the Catholic Church plays a large part here. As I show in Chapter 5, it had staked its claim on the new state even before it came into being, and indeed played some role in its inception. From the colonial period, largely through its role in education, it established a relationship with the socio-political elite that has endured, with the expected highs and lows, down to the present day. Despite the development of other Christian groups, and a strong Muslim presence, it remains one of the most substantial institutions operating within the state. Its discretion and political acumen keep it above the political fray, while allowing it to maintain a place in national life and make a contribution to national debates. Since the CNFVN it has come to be perceived, and certainly perceives itself, as a guarantor of the new political dispensation, while also being somewhat discouraged by what it sees as a lack of real progress on vital issues touching the lives of the people.[73] It has become increasingly aware of the importance of its social doctrine and has sought to use it, as Goudjo puts it, as a "springboard" for the establishment of a new socio-political discourse based on its own scholastic principles. This discourse, and its application in Benin, will be critically examined on the basis of my own reading of the social

---

[72] Alexis Azonwakin, "Bénin: toujours l'immobilisme", *Fraternité*, 651; 30/07/02, 4.
[73] Mgr I. de Souza, 'L'Afrique est déçue par la démocratie' (Interview), *Jeune Afrique* 1836, 13–19 March 1996, 30.

doctrine. This part of my work was, of course, greatly facilitated by
my first-hand experience of the Catholic Church in Benin and my
own past role in it, as well as my contacts with significant actors in
its development both historically and in the present.

I also had considerable contact with the Methodist Church (Synod)
in Cotonou and Porto-Novo.[74] While the Church is relatively small
in numbers, its strength in education has given it an important voice
in socio-political matters and several of its members play prominent
public roles. It maintains good co-operative relations with the Catholic
Church.

Parallel to this level of Christianity, however, one finds what I have
called here *le Christianisme béninois*. This is examined in some detail
in Chapter 7, since it is here I feel one hears *la voix du menu peuple*
and the most authentic commentary on state, society and Christianity.
For this work I chose and regularly visited a number of Churches
that I felt, with my work with the Catholic and Methodist Churches,
completed an accurate reflection of the spectrum of *le Christianisme
béninois*. These were the Celestial Church of Christ, Christian Action
Faith Ministries, Winners' Chapel, Freedom Tabernacle, Assemblies
of God, Union des Eglises Evangéliques du Bénin, and the Eglise
de la Sagesse de Dieu en Christ. These were all in the Protestant
section. But I also did research in the Catholic Charismatic Renewal
Movement (CCRM) and the form of popular Catholicism I found
represented in two large urban parishes in Cotonou: Paroisse Saint
Michel in the centre of the capital, and Paroisse Sacré Cœur in the
quartier populaire of Akpakpa. This research provided the material
for my final chapter. Here I was asking myself: "Why do people
come here? What are they looking for? What is this all saying?" As I
show, the responses can be somewhat alarming. While it is not quite
Haiti, one does find here significant indicators of the anthropological
fragility I have dealt with above. While not perhaps *marronnage*,
the Churches at this level are 'exit options' and safe spaces, 'Rock',
'Shield', 'Stronghold' and 'Refuge', to borrow the scriptural terms;
from within which people look out at state and society and try perhaps to imagine them *otherwise*.

---

[74] The Methodist church in Benin has had several splits. The 'Synode' branch is
the one that is internationally recognised.

Languages and orthography

ARCEB (Action pour la Recherche de la Croissance des Eglises au Bénin) identifies forty-seven ethnic groups within the Republic of Benin, speaking a similar number of dialects or even distinct languages. I have had the opportunity to learn one of these languages to a point of relative fluency, and to gather what I consider to be the social smatterings of a few others, enough for greetings as well as a few of the more common expressions which indicate a certain familiarity with the milieu. These were all languages of the north, however, and they were of relatively little direct use in my research, most of which took place in the south. I feel, however, that familiarity with any African language gives a certain familiarity with the *langage* or *patois* in either French or English that one hears in the street and was the *lingua franca* of many of the Churches. The Fòn and the people of the Ajă-Fòn cluster, however, constitute more than three-fifths of the total population and Fòngbè is the predominant language of the south. I was very ably assisted in dealing with both Fòngbè and Gunbè, as well as with other matters, by my research assistant, Yvon de Souza.

The orthography posed some problems and in this book I have adapted it again. Whenever possible, I used the work of Segurola and Rassinoux.[75] Many Béninois scholars, however, use an improvised orthography with few diacritics, which is far from stable. When referring to older texts, therefore, since I lack the knowledge to adjust them properly, I simply keep them as they are.

In writing of the historical kingdom of Danxomɛ, I have used this spelling not for simple reasons of orthography but, more importantly, to distinguish it from Dahomey, both the colonial and independent polity, which was a completely different state, whatever the historical continuities. I have also insisted upon this orthography when speaking of the Vodún. Although there are established spellings in both French and English these vary enormously. I also feel the Vodún has been the subject of much misapprehension and even caricature and should be seen here as something uniquely Fòn, to be known

---

[75] Basilio Segurola and Jean Rassinoux, *Dictionnaire Fon-Français*, Madrid: SMA, 2000; Jean Rassinoux, *Dictionnaire Français-Fon*, Madrid: SMA, 2001.

on its own terms and not confused with the popular understanding
or misunderstanding.

I faced something of a dilemma in dealing with a large amount
of material in French. The question arose as to whether it should be
left in French, on the assumption that the readers would know that
language, or whether to translate it into English. This was more than
a simple technical consideration since I felt that some of this material, from both French and Béninois sources, was very colourful and
would inevitably lose in translation. I am thinking here particularly
of some of the early missionary texts which were written very much
in the language of their time which I was reluctant to sacrifice. For
the most part, however, pragmatism won out and I translated the
texts with a few exceptions, which I have maintained in the original
because of their particular *saveur*. I have also maintained some expressions I acquired in the French academic literature, which makes up a
significant part of the work. I have maintained the Fòngbè proverbs
and other materials in a similar way.

The use of interviews

A large part of my fieldwork was taken up with interviews, most
of which have been transcribed. However, a lot of my material also
comes from what one colleague described as 'common room' conversations with colleagues in Benin. In fact these were an important
source in coming to understand the country and its history. But as I
have underlined in my text, much of this history remains tendentious,
leading to the sharpest of divisions. I do not wish to contribute to the
tension in any way, so I have decided that any interviews will only
be dated. Any remarks already in the public forum are, of course,
fully attributed.

Photographs, maps and other appendices

I have tried to use photographs, my own and other people's, some
recent and some historical, to provide an overall impression of the
country as well as to illustrate some specific points. These are set
out in two separate sections in the text.

I have provided basic political and socio-economic data on the country in résumé form, compiled from several web sources. This can be found in the appendices. I have also included a small number of historical documents in this section.

CHAPTER TWO

DANXOMƐ—A NARRATIVE OF PRIDE AND SUSPICION

Beware and take care in the Bight of Benin,
One came out where a thousand went in.
(Anon)

Composing a state—the historical origins of the Republic of Benin

The modern Republic of Benin is an amalgam of several very distinct historical entities. These entities continue to subsist within the modern state and have meaning both for their subjects and for those to whom they represent the socio-cultural and political *other*. Long after they have ceased to exist as independent polities, they continue to play a role in shaping modern Benin, or, perhaps more accurately, in the difficulties that modern Benin has in taking on a stable political shape.

The north-eastern Borgou department, largely co-extensive with the politically loose, feudal, Bariba kingdom, lies along the old caravan routes, stretching across the border into present-day Nigeria and to the sahelian north. A northern kingdom, it has been influenced by its position on the northern trade routes and a significant Fulani population. The north-western Atakora department brings together several small, acephelous groups. No single entity here has emerged with any strength. But since the development of modern political activity in Benin, following the 1944 Brazzaville Conference, the Atakora has aligned itself with the Borgou in a well-documented northern alliance,[1] which endures to the present day.

The south-east of the country is mainly composed of Yoruba speaking peoples. They have traditionally looked to the Bariba in the north or to the Ouémé, and to the Kingdom of Porto Novo, which has its origins in the seventeenth-century kingdom of Aladà, with a strong influence from Nigeria. These areas have lined up consistently behind their own

---

[1] Martin Staniland, "The three party system in Dahomey: I, 1946–56", *Journal of African History*, XIV, 2, 1973, 306–308.

regional candidates in all modern political activity down to the present day, driving deals of political expediency with the other two entities at various times.

The remaining departments of the Mono and the Atlantique and the Plateaux cover much of the small kingdoms of Xwedá, Aladà, and what was eventually to become, from the early part of the eighteenth century, the hegemonic kingdom of DanxomƐ, with its centre in AgbŏmƐ. All have, however, retained their very distinctive and separate character and presence in the political field. Of all of these polities, however, the traditional kingdom of DanxomƐ (literally, in the belly of the Vodún Dàn), with its centre at AgbŏmƐ (literally, inside the rampart), was, and remains, of central importance in the modern state.

Colonial Dahomey was dated from the defeat of the traditional kingdom, under Gbɛhanzın, by General Dodds in 1892. The choice of Dahomey as the name for the new colony was in itself significant. Le Hérissé, setting it apart in almost biblical terms, noted that it was indeed "worthy of holding the first place among the tribes, its neighbours, henceforth brought together under the civilising authority of France".[2] In the eyes of the colonial power, the vanquished DanxomƐ took on something of an almost mythical quality, and AgbŏmƐ was to be 'the heart' of the new colony. The political organisation, Le Hérissé says, was "really extraordinary for a black country". The kings were not just brutal despots but had also given the country a "strongly hierarchical administration, a permanent army and embryonic judicial and customs services". This was almost modernity in comparison with Porto-Novo and Borgou, and certainly far beyond the stateless societies of the Atakora, the disparaged *Somba*. Le Hérissé saw in DanxomƐ both a glorious victory for France and the cornerstone upon which the colonial edifice could be built.

The transatlantic slave trade brought tremendous pressure to bear on the societies of the Guinea coast. The the European traders vied among themselves and sought monopolies with the local powers and by the early seventeenth century the evidence suggests a Hobbesian scenario of a 'war of all against all' in the attempt to satisfy demand of the slave factories on the coast. DanxomƐ, like Asante, emerged early in the eighteenth century as a response to the growing chaos, having

---

[2] A. Le Hérissé, *L'Ancien Royaume du Dahomey*, Paris, 1911, 1.

succeeded in defeating the small kingdoms of Xwedá and Aladà.[3]
Aladà, the dominant power at the time, was a weak state, lacking the
structures and coercive power necessary to control the situation. In the
period 1690–1724, Xwedá was in conflict both internally and with Aladà
to which it was subject.[4] In this situation, it is hardly surprising that
what emerged was an excessively strong state, and one which, by the
eighteenth century, presented "a consistent picture [...] characterised by
three principal elements: militarism, brutality (especially the practice
of human sacrifice), and despotism in government".[5] However, the
simple fact was that "Danxomɛ... was eventually able to restore order
in the region, because it was organised on radically different principles;
"its political structure was highly centralised, its kings raising their
authority on military conquest rather than dynastic right, and enjoying
effectively unlimited autocratic power".[6] This was a Hobbesian solution
to a Hobbesian problem.

The nature of the Danxomɛ has been the subject of a heated debate.
In the simplest terms, this has been between those, particularly the early
historians, who saw it in the bluntest terms of militarism, brutality, and
despotism, and those, such as Akinjogbin, who attempted to revise this
picture in presenting some of the more positive aspects of the kingdom
and its political system. Law has provided much of the recent historical
material. What is clear from all the material is that Danxomɛ was a
very distinctive polity. What is of particular interest to this thesis is
the fact that the debate about the nature of the kingdom continues to
rage, not just in the academy but very much in both the popular and
political debates within the modern Republic of Benin.

Wilks has argued that "there is no difficulty in discerning Greater
Asante as the precursor of the country we know as Ghana".[7] The purpose
of this chapter is to examine the kingdom of Danxomɛ in order to see
its role in the formation of the future state of Dahomey/Benin. What is

---

[3] Robin Law, "Dahomey and the Slave Trade: Reflections on the historiography
of the rise of Dahomey", *Journal of African History*, 1986, XXII, ii, 241–242.

[4] Robin Law, "The common people were divided: Monarchy, aristocracy and
political factionalism in the kingdom of Whydah, 1671–1727", *International Journal
of African Historical Studies*, 1990, 23, 201–229.

[5] Law, "Dahomey and the Slave Trade", 247.

[6] Robin Law (1997), *The Kingdom Of Allada*, Leiden: School of Asian, African,
and Amerindian Studies, 65.

[7] Ivor Wilks, *One Nation, Many Histories: Ghana Past and Present*, Aggrey-
Fraser-Guggisberg Memorial Lectures 1995, Accra, 1996, 41.

its place in the popular imagination and to what extent has the myth and history of the vanished kingdom influenced contemporary perceptions and political discourse? It is my contention that this unresolved question plays a large part in the apparent fragility of the modern state. Goudjo affirms that, for the peoples surrounding the old kingdom of Danxomɛ, "the wounds [caused by the slave trade] remain as repressed memories, maintained by legends and myths that sacralise a reality that is perhaps less dramatic". For a citizen of northern Benin *everybody* from the south is a Dahomean.[8] Echoing both Hurbon's analysis of Haiti and Adè's reading of Benin, which I referred to in the introduction, he asserts that these "repressed memories", deeply embedded in the collective conscience of the Béninois people, have implications for the construction of the modern state, social cohesion, and aspirations to national unity, particularly in times of social and political stress. At the same time, they help to explain the role of the Christian Churches as 'exit options' in a society where the social bonds appear so tenuous, as well as the continuous emphasis on peace and social cohesion that has marked the discourse of the Churches themselves.

The Atlantic slave trade and the rise of Danxomɛ

> *Et ce pays cria pendant des siècles que nous sommes des bêtes brutes;*
> *que les pulsations de l'humanité s'arrêtent aux portes de la négrerie;*
> *que nous sommes un fumier ambulant hideusement prometteur de cannes*
> *tendres et de coton soyeux et l'on nous marquait au fer rouge et nous*
> *dormions dans nos excréments et l'on nous vendait sur les places et*
> *l'aune de drap anglais et la viande salée d'Irlande coûtaient moins*
> *chers que nous...*[9]

The Atlantic slave trade remains a contentious, if often repressed, issue underlying national debate in Benin. The social impact of the trade has been the subject of much debate. Polanyi depicts it, in economic terms as part of "an archaic economy".[10] A less academic and more emotive

---

[8] Raymond B. Goudjo, *La liberté en démocratie: L'éthique sociale et la réalité politique en Afrique*, Frankfurt/Paris: Peter Lang/Presses Universitaires Européennes, 1997, 129.

[9] Césaire, 38–39.

[10] Karl Polanyi, *Dahomey and the Slave Trade: An Analysis of an Archaic Economy*, in collaboration with Abraham Rotstein, London: University of Washington Press, 1966.

division of views, however, would be between those who see the trade as little more than a historical blip, with little or no social or demographic effect,[11] due to some extent at least to population pressure,[12] and those who see it as 'a radical break in the history of Africa...[And] a major influence in transforming African society',[13] with ongoing effects down to the present time.

All the evidence indicates that in most of Africa the Atlantic slave trade peaked at the beginning of the eighteenth century and went into decline with the rise of abolitionism and the onset of the Napoleonic wars. But in Danxomε it continued, at least in clandestine form, until 1870. There is some discussion about the exact figures involved. *The Encyclopaedia Britannica* is at the lowest end of the scale, with estimates of 9,710,000 slaves arriving in the Americas out of the 11,640,000 thought to have left the whole of Africa. Quenum gives more radical statistics, claiming the unlikely figure of up to the 30 million slaves from the Slave Coast alone.[14] Lovejoy's estimate of around 12 million arriving in the Americas appears to have a more widespread acceptance.[15]

Over half the slaves are estimated to have come from western Africa, north of the Equator, while 35% came from the Slave Coast.[16] Law estimates that Aladà alone was exporting up to 15,000 slaves a year during the 1690s. Manning calculates that 1,215,700 slaves were taken from the Ajă area, covering Danxomε's military sphere of influence, between the 1640s and the 1860s.[17] The population of the area at that time was well under half a million, from an estimated high of 462,000

[11] David Eltis, "Economic Growth and the Ending of the Transatlantic Slave Trade", New York, 1987, 77, in Paul E. Lovejoy, 'The impact of the Atlantic slave trade on Africa: a review of the literature', *Journal of African History*, 30, 1989, 365–394.

[12] *Encyclopaedia Britannica*: CD-Rom, 1999.

[13] Paul E. Lovejoy, 'The Impact of the Atlantic slave trade on Africa: a review of the literature', *Journal of African History*, 30, 1989, 365.

[14] Alphonse Quenum, *Les Eglises chrétiennes et la traite atlantique du XVe au XIXe siècle*, Paris, 1993, 285.

[15] There is documentation for 27,000 voyages, 66–75% of the total (Robin Law, *Individualising the Transatlantic Slave Trade: the Biography of Mohammah Gardo Baquaqua of Djougou (1854)*, lecture to the Royal Historical Society, London, 30 April 2001).

[16] Lovejoy shows that 33.5% of the slaves exported by French traders in the eighteenth century, a total of 351,240, were from the Bight of Benin. Further, of these, in the period 1721–97, 43.2% were of Ewe-Fon origin (Lovejoy, *The Impact*, 373–380). Law lends support to this thesis (see Law, *The Kingdom*, 85–89).

[17] Patrick Manning, *Slavery, Colonialism and Economic Growth in Dahomey, 1640–1960*, Cambridge: CUP, 1982.

in 1670–1690 to a low of 267,000 from 1780–1810. The trade reached clearly catastrophic proportions in the period 1700–1720 when, in a figure that corresponds roughly to Law's estimates, an estimated 297,500 people were exported, representing an annual average of 3.7% of the population. At its height, these statistics would be the equivalent of almost 2 million people a year leaving the United Kingdom. It was estimated that in 1846 the trade was worth $50,000 or £10,400 per annum to the kingdom.[18] It seems reasonable to conclude with Manning that, in comparison with the other polities in the area, DanxomƐ was exceptional in its dependence on and participation in the Atlantic trade.[19]

The statistics are surely enough to rebut minimalist theory and were certainly enough to create a nightmare, which still retains a strong grip on the collective imagination. This emotive, and little studied, historical issue remains at the heart of the debate about DanxomƐ. The more negative interpretation, in early pre-colonial sources[20] and colonial administrators Le Herissé and Dunglas,[21] presents it as a kingdom built on predation while its apologists, notably Akinjogbin, see it rather as a victim of European pressure for slaves, which had originally sought to put an end to the trade.[22]

The perspective of the sources is in question here, particularly Snelgrave, Norris and Dalzel as early traders with a vested interest, and later, Le Herissé and Dunglas who relied heavily on these sources and were themselves members of the colonial establishment. Akinjogbin argues that "neither the eighteenth century slave captains, nor Agaja's diplomatic utterances, nor yet the popular 'textbook' oral traditions collected almost two centuries later can point to a correct assessment of Agaja's motives for invading the coastal Ajă kingdoms". He asserts

---

[18] Winniet to Grey, 12 May 1847, C.O. 96/11, no. 42 in Paul Ellingworth, "Christianity and Politics in Dahomey", *Journal of African History*, v, 2, 1964, 210.

[19] Manning, *Slavery*, 343.

[20] See William Snelgrave, *A New Account of Some Parts of Guinea*, London, 1734/1971. Robert Norris, *Memoirs of the Reign of Bossa Ahadee, King of Dahomey*, London, 1789/1968; Archibald Dalzel, *The History of Dahomey—an Inland Kingdom*, London, 1793/1967.

[21] Edouard Dunglas, 'Contribution à l'histoire du Moyen Dahomey', *Etudes Dahoméennes*, XIX, 1957, 90.

[22] Akinjogbin, *Dahomey*, 68–109; Eleni Coundouriotis, *Claiming History: Colonialism, Ethnography, and the Novel*, New York: CUP, 1999: 45–72. See also John C. Yoder, "Fly and elephant parties: political polarisation in Dahomey, 1840–1870", *Journal of African History*, XV, iii, 1974, 417–432.

that the motive was primarily "to sweep away the traditional political system" and, secondarily, "to restrict and eventually stop the slave trade, which had been the cause of the breakdown of the traditional system in Ajă, and to substitute other 'legitimate' items of trade between Europe and the new kingdom of Dahomey".[23] These views, however, have been contested by those who hold that, despite their anti-abolitionist agenda, the observations of the early slavers still have validity and that the origins of the kingdom may well have been, as Forbes suggested "a banditti",[24] an observation which met with Burton's approval,[25] a gang of bandits rather than "the highly-principled and far-seeing Ajă" suggested by Akinjogbin.[26]

The problem, from my point of view, is not one of distributing blame or seeking rehabilitation but rather that of understanding the ongoing impact of the trade in Benin today. As Geertz points out:

> the political processes of all nations are wider and deeper than the formal institutions designed to regulate them; some of the most critical decisions concerning the directions of public life are not made in parliaments and presidiums; they are made in the unformalised realms of what Durkheim called "the collective conscience".[27]

The question for us is to what extent both the slave trade and the kingdom of Danxomε remain as factors informing the collective conscience and thus the imagining of the modern state.

The imaginary construction of Dahomey

Wherefore I am a great king,
And waste the world in vain,
Because man hath not other power,
Save that in dealing death for dower,
He may forget it for an hour
To remember it again.[28]

---

[23] Akinjogbin, *Dahomey*, 77.
[24] Frederick Forbes, *Dahomey and the Dahomeans*, 2 vols, London, 1851 (Cass 1966), vol. 1,19.
[25] David Ross, "European models and West African History: further comments on the recent historiography of Dahomey", *History in Africa*, 10, 1983, 263.
[26] Akinjogbin, *Dahomey*, 203.
[27] Clifford Geertz, "The politics of meaning", in *The Interpretation of Cultures*, London: Fontana, 1973/1993, 316.
[28] G.K. Chesterton, *Ballad of the White Horse*, Book III.

Thinking back to my own boyhood images of Danxomε, and doing an informal check among a few friends and colleagues, leaves me in little doubt that there exists a very definite and overwhelmingly negative image of the traditional kingdom of Danxomε and indeed its post-colonial republican successor. This is confirmed by the entry on the kingdom in the *Encyclopaedia Britannica*, which reads:

> Dahomey was a despotic and militaristic kingdom…The king's authority was buttressed by an elaborate cult of the deceased kings of the dynasty, who were honoured by the offering of human sacrifices at yearly public ceremonies (the "annual customs").[29]

In a recent biography of the travel writer Bruce Chatwin, Nicholas Shakespeare writes: "The kings of Dahomey, practitioners of human as well as of animal sacrifice, hunted their victims in season, like pheasants."[30] Chatwin himself provides us with a striking fictional description of the slave trade at Xwedá in the early eighteenth century:

> The King went to war in January and the chain-gangs started reaching Ouidah towards the end of March.
> The captives were numb with fright and exhaustion. They had seen their homes burned and their chiefs slaughtered. Iron collars chafed their necks. Their backs were striped purple with welts; and when they saw the white man's ships, they knew they were going to be eaten.[31]

In these three texts we have what had become the image of Danxomε, and what became something of a nineteenth-century stereotype for many African kingdoms: despotic, militaristic, predatory and sanguinary in the cause of its own power. It can well be concluded, "few places have been as completely demonised by European travellers as Dahomey".[32] Building on the Dahomean literature, many other African polities were presented as "phantasmagoric landscapes of death",[33] Hobbesian kingdoms of darkness, plunged in depravity, preying on their innocent neighbours to satisfy the apparently inexhaustible demand for slaves

---

[29] *Encyclopaedia Britannica*, CD-ROM.
[30] Nicholas Shakespeare, *Bruce Chatwin*, London: Vintage, 2000, 324.
[31] Bruce Chatwin, *The Viceroy of Ouidah*, London: Vintage, 1980, 56.
[32] Eleni Coundouriotis, (1999) *Claiming History: Colonialism, ethnography, and the novel*, New York: CUP, 1999, 46.
[33] Ibid., 64. See also "The kingdom of darkness [as set forth in the Scriptures] is nothing else but a confederacy of deceivers, that to obtain dominion over men in this present world, endeavour by dark, and erroneous doctrines, to extinguish in them the light, both of nature, and of the gospel; and so disprepare them for the kingdom of God to come." Thomas Hobbes, *Leviathan*, Part V, Ch. XLIV, Section 333.

in the transatlantic trade, as well as victims for sacrifice to underpin their power. Coundouriotis has argued that:

> Burton's authoritative explanation of Dahomean culture as exclusively sacrificial facilitated the consumption of Danxomε as an economic resource directly or a cultural symbol for the depravity of the African in general that it could be deployed to justify imperialist interventions in other areas of Africa.[34]

It came to be seen, as the missionaries and the colonial authorities would put it, as a place in need of *redemption* or, in terms that satisfy both *laïc* and cleric, a *civilising mission*.

Danxomε, like Asante, darkly fascinated the early travellers and its colonisers. There is an abundant literature, of varying quality, providing valuable information on the kingdom. Our image of Danxomε has been constructed from several, often layered and interdependant sources, which require examination in order to understand the construction of the wider narrative.

The early European travel narratives

The early travellers, slave captains and merchants—Bosman,[35] Snelgrave, Lambe,[36] Norris, and, most notably, Dalzel—as well as the committed abolitionist Atkins[37] provide us with the earliest European literature on the kingdom. These narratives are often rich in the spectacular, the bizarre and the most horrendous aspects of the life they witnessed. Polanyi writes:

> The Dahomey of the eighteenth and nineteenth century British travellers was the home of the Amazon army, a fighting force unparalleled since Herodotus' semi-mythical Scythia; a pyramid of skulls, evidence of human sacrifice demanded by the duties of ancestor worship; and to some extent, of religious cannibalism...[38]

---

[34] Coundouriotis, 63.

[35] William Bosman, *A New and Accurate Description of the Coast of Guinea*, London, 1705/1967.

[36] Bulfinch Lambe, 'Abomey, 27 Nov 1724', in William Smith, *A New Voyage to Guinea*, London 1744/1967.

[37] John Atkins, *A Voyage to Guinea, Brazil and the West Indies in His Majesty's ships 'The Swallow' and 'Weymouth'*, London, 1735/1970.

[38] Karl Polanyi, *Dahomey and the Slave Trade*, London: University of Washington Press, 1966, xxii.

Whatever one thinks of them, several of the sources were in fact "exceptionally well informed on Dahomean affairs".[39] They provide much valuable information on the organisation and nature of the Dahomean state and have a place in the historical record. One of the earliest, for instance, by the quaintly named English adventurer Bulfinch Lambe,[40] left a first-hand account of the fall of Aladà to DanxomƐ in 1727, the only written record of the event. A later refutation of this account by Skertchly is in itself interesting and illustrates the problem of all of the Dahomean narratives. Skertchly dismisses Lambe's narrative as "being the imaginative description of a man paralysed by fear. He whines and groans in a manner disgraceful to any man…"[41]

There are, however, several difficulties with these accounts. Law has pointed out that they are largely "cannibalistic", with later accounts drawing generously on earlier ones and reinforcing their impact, as well as feeding into the later ones, such as Herskovits' anthropological studies.[42] Even a cursory look at the most influential of these early accounts—Dalzel's *History of Dahomey*, for instance—will show that he drew extensively on Barbot, as well as Bosman, Snelgrave, and Norris. Herskovits and, much later, Saulnier used Burton, Skertchly and Forbes.[43]

At the same time, much attention needs to be paid to the perspective and agenda of the authors, and, as in all literature, the question of what sells.[44] Fage notes that Dalzel's text is "as much a pro slave-trade tract

---

[39] Law, *Dahomey and the Slave Trade*, 243.

[40] Marion Johnson, 'Bulfinch Lambe and the Emperor of Pawpaw: a Footnote to Agaja and the Slave Trade', *History in Africa*, 1978, 5, 345–350, and Robin Law, "Further Light on Bulfinch Lambe and the 'Emperor of Pawpaw': King Agaja of Dahomey's Letter to King George of England, 1726", *History of Africa* 17, 1990, 211–215.

[41] J.A. Skertchly, *Dahomey as it is; being a narrative of eight months residence in that country, with a full account of the notorious annual customs, and the social and religious institutions of the Fons: also an appendix on the Ashantee, and a glossary of Dahomean words and titles. Ills and sketches by the author*, London: Chapman & Hall, 1875.

[42] Law, *Dahomey and the Slave Trade*, 238. See Melville J. Herskovits, *Dahomey: an Ancient West African Kingdom*, Evanston: NUP, 1938; Melville J. and Frances S. Herskovits, *Dahomean Narrative*, Evanston, 1958.

[43] Jean Barbot, *'Description des côtes d'Afrique'* unpublished 1688 ms, in Public Record Office, London: (Adm.7 830), II Partie, 136; Pierre Saulnier, *Le Meurtre du Vodon Dan*, Madrid: SMA, 2002.

[44] Finkelstein suggests that Blackwood substantially amended the journal of Speke's travels in order to project the image of the 'dark continent' and to promote imperial ambitions. See David Finkelstein, *The House of Blackwood: Author-Publisher*

as it is a history".[45] Law points out that Danxomε came to be known to
the outside world during the debate on "the morality of the slave trade,
and eighteeth-century perceptions of Dahomey were clearly coloured by
the controversies between Abolitionists or Anti-abolitionists".[46] These
narratives have, however, served to provide the data for our imaginary
construction, a kind of historical *bricolage*, of Danxomε.

In a comment that is consistent with my experience in Benin, and
is fundamental to my thesis, Law states that "the issues raised in these
eighteenth-century debates continue to feature in historical discussion
in Danxomε down to the present, so that current debates reproduce to
a surprising degree contemporary polemics over the slave trade".[47] To
this can be added the even more emotive question of human sacrifice,
which, in my experience, is also a feature of rumour, and both public and
private debate, down to the present.[48] Law affirms that in the eighteenth
century Danxomε had overshadowed Benin (Nigeria) as the major
practitioner of human sacrifice in West Africa, adding that "the scale
of the...sacrifice in Dahomey was enormous".[49] Certainly the overall
impression left by these early sources cast the die in which the image of
Danxomε was moulded.

The most influential was Dalzel's *History of Dahomy*. Dalzel, a slave
captain, had time on his hands, as well as an interest, which led him to
write a *history.*[50] The work claims a certain academic *gravitas* precisely
as a *history*. In his introduction to the 1967 Cass edition, J.D. Fage
noted that "despite his pro-slave trade bias...[Dalzel] was no mean
historian of Dahomey..."[51] Perhaps the most significant passage in the
History is king Adahoonzou's[52] "speech, upon hearing what had passed

---

Relations in the Victorian Era, University Park: Pennsylvania State University, 2002.

[45] J.D. Fage, "Introduction", in Dalzel, *History*, 9.
[46] Law, *Dahomey and the Slave Trade*, 243.
[47] Law, *Dahomey and the Slave Trade*, 243.
[48] See Sulikowski, "Eating the flesh, eating the soul".
[49] Law suggests that "the annual slaughter in Dahomey....must have run into several hundreds". Robin Law, "Human sacrifice in pre-colonial Africa", *African Affairs* 1985, 84, 68.
[50] See I.A. Akinjogbin, "Archibald Dalzel: Slave Trader and Historian of Dahomey", *Journal of Africa History*, VII, 1966, 67–78.
[51] Fage, *Introduction*, 22.
[52] Adandozan (reigned 1797–1818). He was the most controversial of the kings considered as a usurper and was banished from the tradition. He attempted several unpopular reforms which would have diminished the powers of the priestly class.

in England upon the subject of the Slave-trade".[53] In the speech the king effectively defends himself from what had become the most negative perceptions of his kingdom. In his introductory remarks, he professes his admiration for the white man, but makes an immediate distinction between white and black people, "whose whole disposition differs as much from that of the whites, as their colour". Not only is there a difference in skin colour but there is also an important distinction to be made "in the quality of their minds". In addition to this there is the great geographical distinction to be made between England, a mere island, and Danxomɛ, which finds itself on a great continent,

> hemmed in [...] speaking different languages [thus being obliged] by the sharpness of our swords, to defend ourselves from their incursions, and punish the depredations they make on us. Such conduct is productive of incessant war.

The king rejects the allegation that he goes to war simply to provide for the slave trade, rejecting the idea of a "reformation, as you call it, in the manners of the blacks", as was being proposed by English abolitionists. With dark diplomacy he points out that in order to impose this "reformation",

> a great many must be put to death, and numerous cruelties must be committed, which we do not find to have been the practice of the whites: besides, that this would militate against the very principle which is professed by those who wish to bring about a reformation.

The obvious conclusion, though not stated, is that it is better then to leave things unchanged.

The king goes on to argue that the slave-trade was not undertaken "for the sake of procuring wherewithal to purchase your commodities", giving deeper reasons which had to do with the nature of Danxomɛ itself:

> I, who have not long been master of this country, have, without thinking of the market, killed many thousands, and I shall kill many thousands more. When policy or justice requires that men be put to death, neither silk, nor coral, nor brandy, nor cowries, can be accepted as substitutes for the blood that ought to be spilt for example sake. Besides, if white

---

He was also reputed to have wanted to extend the slave trade and human sacrifices to include members of the nobility.

[53] Dalzel: 217–219.

men chuse [sic] to remain at home, and no longer visit this country for
the same purpose that has usually brought them hither, will black men
cease to make war? I answer, by no means. And if there be no ships for
their captives, what will become of them? I answer for you, they will
be put to death...God made war for all the world; and every kingdom,
large or small, has practised it more or less, though perhaps in a manner
unlike, and upon different principles. Did Weebaigah sell slaves? No,
his prisoners were all killed to a man. What else could he have done
with them? Was he to let them remain in his country, to cut the throat
of his subjects? This would have been a wretched policy indeed, which,
had it been adopted, the Dahomean name would have long ago been
extinguished, instead of becoming, as it is at this day, the terror of the
surrounding nations.

Adahoonzou offers this defence of his kingdom and its policies because
he is "hurt" by the malicious representation of Danxomɛ, "in books,
which never die", as a kingdom which lives simply on the slave trade:
"alledging [sic], that we sell our wives and children for the sake of
procuring a few kegs of brandy".

The king is stout in his own defence, and Dalzel is clearly anxious
that he should be so. The king finds it "extraordinary for a parcel of
men with long heads, to sit down in England, and frame laws for us
and pretend to dictate how we live". The king concludes, obviously
to Dalzel's approval, that they have been the victims of a propaganda
campaign by jealous opponents who have "vilified both black and
white traders" alike. Adahoonzou then goes on to an analysis of the
Grand Customs,[54] which were certainly the most notorious feature of
the country in the later literature. For the king they are simply a part
of the way he rules, instruments of power.[55] He freely acknowledges
that he kills people in the Customs but for *raisons d'état*:

> I kill them; but do I ever insist on being paid for them? Some heads I
> order to be placed at my door; others to be strewed about the marketplace,

---

[54] Burton provides a definition of these events. "The word 'custom' is used to
signify the cost or charges paid to the King at a certain season in the year. It is borrowed by us from our predecessors on the West Africa Coast—the old French—who
wrote coûtume, and the Portuguese costume, meaning habit or usage. The Grand
Customs are performed only after the death of a king. They excel the annual rites
in splendour and in bloodshed, for which reason the successor defers them till he
has become sufficiently wealthy" (Burton, 200).

[55] See Aguessy, *Du mode de l'existence*, Ch. V for a treatment of this subject.
Aguessy accepts that the customs were in fact an essential tool for the reinforcement
of state power and prestige. He notes that the purpose of the wars was in fact to
feed the Customs (278).

that people may stumble upon them when they little expect such a sight. This gives grandeur to my Customs, far beyond the display of fine things which I buy. This makes my enemies fear me, and gives me a name in the bush. Besides, if I should neglect this indispensable duty, would my ancestors suffer me to live? Would they not trouble me night and day, and say, that I sent nobody to serve them; that I was only solicitous of my own name and forgetful of my ancestors.[56]

The king goes on to explain that white men simply do not understand these customs, which will continue "to be made, as long as black men continue to possess their own country". Those who are sold into slavery, he notes, are indeed even happy, since they conclude: "We shall continue to drink water…white men will not kill us; and we may even avoid punishment, by serving our new masters with fidelity".[57]

This is certainly a most remarkable text, spoken ostensibly by a Dahomean king, and it could reasonably be said to have been at the origin of the construction of the image of Danxomɛ. But accounts such as this also created problems for their European successors, following the suppression of the slave trade, since they provided evidence of clear European complaisance, if not outright complicity, in many of the more horrific rituals so offensive to Victorian sensibilities, and appeared to contradict the philanthropic aspirations of empire. They provided compelling evidence not only for the more gruesome activities of the Dahomean court, but also for the fact that "the British had been very much implicated in Dahomey's culture of violence",[58] often participating in the Customs with obvious amusement. In Dalzel's narrative, Adahoonzou himself initiated the process of the *othering* of the Dahomean. The literature which was to follow, building upon this earlier material and reinforcing it, was part of the progressive othering of the slave trade and Danxomɛ but also a distancing of the British from any kind of complicity in either.

The Victorian administrators and 'discoverers'

The evidence makes it clear that Danxomɛ was reluctant to renounce the slave trade.[59] Law notes that "in Dahomey…the critical decade in

---

[56] Dalzel, 220–221.
[57] Dalzel, 220–221.
[58] Coundouriotis, 47.
[59] Polanyi's thesis was contested by Peukert who argues that in fact "the Atlantic

the decline of the slave trade was as late as the 1850s..."[60] and the palm-oil trade developed haltingly. This led to numerous missions by British delegations to Agbɔmɛ, from Duncan's visit in 1845 to Burton's consulate in 1861–1864. The object of these visits is well illustrated in correspondence between the British Foreign Secretary, Lord Palmerston, and Gezò in 1848–1849.[61]

Letter from the kingdom of Dahomey to Her Majesty Queen Victoria
Abomey, November 3, 1848

The King of Dahomey presents his best compliments to the Queen of England. The presents which she has sent him are very acceptable, and are good for his face.[62]

When Governor Winniet visited the King, the King told him that he must consult his people before he could give a final answer about the Slave Trade. He cannot see that he and his people can do without it. It is from the Slave Trade that he derives his principal revenue. This he has explained in along palaver to Mr Cruickshank. He begs the Queen of England to put a stop to the slave trade everywhere else, and allow him to continue it.

The King is anxious that the Queen of England should send a Governor to Whydah Fort, in order that he pay have an opportunity of seeing the manner in which the King governs his people.

The King also begs the Queen to make a law that no ships be allowed to trade at any place near his dominions lower down the coast than Whydah, as by means of trading vessels the people are getting rich, and withstanding his authority. He wishes all factories for palm-oil removed from Badagary, Porto Novo, Agado, and Lagos, as the trade that is now

---

slave trade formed only a very small part of the national income..." and seeks to "destroy once and for all the image of Dahomey as primarily a slave trading kingdom" (Marion Johnson, "Polanyi, Peukert and the political economy of Dahomey", *Journal of African History*, 21, 1980, 395). Law concludes that "though the early kings of Dahomey had themselves been major contributors to and profiteers [from the trade] their ultimate triumph [in stabilising the state]...was no doubt widely welcome for the relative peace which it promised (Law, *Dahomey and the Slave Trade*, 267).

[60] Robin Law, "The transition from the Slave Trade to 'Legitimate' Commerce", *Studies in the World History of Slavery, Abolition and Emancipation*, I, 1, 1996, 5.

[61] The most influential of the Kings of Dahomey, reigned 1818–1858 following liberation from Oyo in 1823. Much admired today amongst people from his area and those who wish to see the kingdom in a more positive light. It is of interest to note that Honorat Aguessy, in his 1970 doctoral thesis *Du Monde de l'existence de l'Etat sous Guézo* (1818–1858) (Thèse d'Etat, Paris-Sorbonne—BIU Centrale, Cote TMC 4823, microfiche), stretched the reign of the hero-king by one year to 1859, thus allowing him to attain forty-one years of reign. The figure forty one has arcane significance for the Fon, being the figure of perfection, four cords of ten beads, plus one.

[62] Tim Coates, (Editor) *King Guezo of Dahomey*, 1850–52 [Collected Correspondence], London: The Stationery Office, 2001, 13–14.

done at these places can be done at Whydah, and the King would then receive his duties, and be able to keep these people in subjection; and also in the event of his attacking these places he would not run the risk of injuring Englishmen or their property.

He hopes the Queen will send him some good Tower guns and blunderbusses, and plenty of them, to enable him to make war. He also uses much cowries, and wishes the queen's subjects to bring plenty of them to Whydah to make trade. He wishes to see plenty of Englishmen making trade at Whydah.

The King has spoken all his mind to Mr Cruickshank, who can explain what is fit for the King and his country. He begs the Queen of England to continue his good friend, as he likes Englishmen more than any other people.[63]

Gezò's letter is a fascinating document quite different from Dalzel's attempted interpetation of Adahoonzou's thinking. One can surmise that it was probably written from his own dictation, probably by a European trader lacking Dalzel's education.[64] It offers us an interesting insight into Guezo's position. Offering presents to Queen Victoria, he is anxious to present himself as a good ruler, although he finds it impossible to suppress the slave trade since "he cannot see that he and his people can do without it". While he is in favour of it being suppressed elsewhere, he feels that Danxomε should have an 'exit clause' and he presses Her Majesty's Navy to assist him in establishing a trade monopoly and political hegemony in the region. He deftly plays the geopolitical game, stating that "he likes Englishmen more than any other people". Not surprisingly, Palmerston's reply seeks to bring the king a little further in his concessions on the slave trade.

Viscount Palmerston to the King of Dahomey
Foreign Office, May 29, 1849

The Queen of Great Britain and Ireland, my Sovereign, commands me to acknowledge receipt of your letter dated the 3rd of November, which I have laid before Her Majesty, and to thank you for your friendly assurances. The British Government is glad to find that you wish the Slave Trade to be put an end to in all places beyond the limits of your territories, because that wish on your part shows that you are sensible of the bad nature of the Trade.

With regard to your own dominions, you may be quite certain that if you would stop the Slave Trade, your revenue and the profits of

---

[63] Coates, 13–14.
[64] See Johnson, "*Bulfinch Lambe*"; Law, *Further Light*, dealing with Lambe's role as a scribe and emissary for the king of Dahomey.

your people would not be diminished but would very shortly be much increased; for it is well known that agriculture and commerce are more useful and advantageous than the stealing and selling of men, women, and children...

I avail myself of the return of Mr Duncan, whose appointment as Vice-Consul in your dominions I have notified to you in another letter of this days date, to send to you a few articles of British manufacture, which Mr. Duncan informed me you had expressed a desire to have, and which Mr Duncan will deliver to you as a present from Her Majesty's Government.[65]

Despite the dissimilarities of style, Gezò's logic is similar to that of his predecessor Adahoonzou. Qualms about the morality of the slave trade, he reasons, are a 'white man's palaver' and he has the more pressing reality of his own power to deal with. This was to be the tenor of relations for the following years and into the reign of Glɛlé. As Palmerston states in his reply, British policy, following the suppression of the slave trade, was the promotion of agriculture and commerce. Although Gezò and Glɛlé developed the cultivation of palm oil, Danxomɛ seems to have been less than enthusiastic about agriculture, probably for both "ideological" and "material" reasons. The Dahomean elite "was an essentially warrior class...The shift to commercial agriculture was seen as incompatible with this traditional warrior ethos, and threatened to undermine the legitimacy and authority of the Dahomean State".[66] In practical terms, it meant that once Danxomɛ had taken the agricultural option, it became impossible to deploy able bodies to execute a war or as slaves for the remaining transatlantic trade.

There is an interesting contrast here with Asante, and certainly a clue as to why Asante has survived to a much greater degree than Danxomɛ. Wilks underlines the fundamental importance of agriculture in Asante, stating that:

the economy of Asante...was not one based upon slave-trading for export purposes...Slaves were in fact of crucial importance to the Asante economy not so much for the export trade as for satisfying the labour requirements of agriculture and industry.[67]

---

[65] Coates, *King Guezo*, 12.
[66] See Law, "The transition", 5.
[67] Ivor Wilks, *Asante in the nineteenth century*, Cambridge: CUP, 1975, 80; 176–178.

Asante, unlike Danxomɛ, had both gold[68] and kola nuts to trade, and this required intensive labour investment, making the export of slaves subject to local agricultural and industrial production. The blockade of the transatlantic trade in the early nineteenth century was not nearly as damaging for Asante as it was for Danxomɛ.

In contrast with Danxomɛ, Asante, despite its fine soldiers, was not a society "with any strong commitment to the use of military means in pursuit of its ends".[69] There were both martial and mercantile factions in Asante, whereas my reading of the Danxomɛ literature reveals no presence of the latter, probably because there was so little to actually trade. Danxomɛ was outside the sub-Saharan trade routes, which passed well to the north through Borgou, as well as the Islamic influences that accompanied this trade.[70] In fact, Danxomɛ was defined to a great extent by contact with the Atlantic trade.

Lacking the wealth of Asante, and weighed down by a martial tradition, Danxomɛ saw little economic choice but to pursue the slave trade to the bitter end. This led to flurries of diplomatic activity, with highs and lows, as the Dahomeans failed to come to terms with the change in the attitude of the Europeans who had previously been so eager for trade, as Palmerston expressed it, of such a "bad nature". Duncan began what was to become the sensationalisation of the kingdom, with the Annual Customs as a centrepiece of horror. By the middle of the nineteenth century Danxomɛ had acquired "the most 'sinister' reputation as a place of savagery where purportedly ritual killings ('sacrifices') by the thousands were annual events".[71] In a review of this literature,

---

[68] British takings from the Asante goldfields in the mid nineteenth century were 50,000 oz per annum. However, "this quantity, and that taken by the Dutch, must be presumed...to have represented a comparatively small proportion of the total production" (ibid., 193).

[69] Ibid., 83.

[70] There is evidence that demonstrates the influence of Muslims in Asante, particularly in foreign policy whereas the king of Danxomé was described as Kaffar ben al Koufar, the infidel of infidels (Wilks, *Asante*, 259; 310–312).

[71] Coundouriotis, 46. Although there are several references to these killings, which undoubtedly took place, it is impossible to establish reliable statistics for the numbers involved (Ibid., 178). The literature often refers to thousands but this may be highly impressionistic in accounts often written several years after the event. Snelgrave refers to 4,000 victims but this figure confuses victims of both a war and the rituals (in Robin Law, "'My head belongs to the king': On the political and ritual significance of decapitation in pre-colonial Dahomey", *Journal of African History*, 30, 1989, 401). Burton, who did not witness the killings himself, reports earlier sources having

Coundouriotis, using an analysis of the graphic plates accompanying
the various texts, shows how there is a gradual withdrawal of the British
from the scene of these bloody events. They move from the apparent
enjoyment of the spectacle by earlier travellers, illustrated in Dalzel, to
a much more squeamish approach by the Victorian visitors in Forbes.
In Forbes they are represented only by three Union Jacks in the distance
with no sign of any white face on the scene.

In his journal for 31 May 1849, Forbes gives us his own account
of the Customs:

> If I were to conclude the history of this day's Customs here, I should
> merely remark that there might be a policy in making appear munificence
> the distribution of a sum of money,[72] that if doled out to each individually,
> would prove a miserable pittance, although it tended much to debase the
> minds of this people, if that were possible. But what follows is almost
> too revolting to be recorded.
>
> As if by general consent, and evincing a slight dawning of decency,
> hardly to be expected from these truly barbarians, silence reigned, and
> when broken, the eunuchs would strike a metal instrument each was
> supplied with, to enforce it, sounding the knell of eleven unfortunate
> human beings, whose only crime known to their persecutors was that they
> belonged to a nation Dahomey has warred against, Attahpam.[73] Out of
> fourteen now brought upon the platform, we, the unworthy instruments of
> Providence, succeeded in saving the lives of three. Lashed as described
> in yesterday's journal, except that only four were in boats, the remainder
> in baskets, these unfortunates gagged, met the gaze of their enemies
> with a firmness perfectly astonishing—not a sign was breathed. One
> cowardly villain put his hands to the eyes of a victim, who say with his
> head down, to feel for moisture; finding none, he drew upon himself the
> ridicule of his hellish coadjutors. Ten of these human offerings to the
> vitiated appetite of his soldiers, and the alligator and cat, were guarded
> by the male soldiers, and to the right of the King; four to the left were
> guarded by women.
>
> Being commanded into the presence, the King asked if we wished to
> be present at the sacrifice; with horror we declined, and begged to be
> allowed to save a few by purchasing. After a little hesitation, we were
> asked which we would have; I claimed the first and last of the ten, while
> Mr Beecroft claimed the nearest of the four, and 100 dollars being stated
> as the price, was gladly accepted. In all my life I never saw such coolness

---

said that "not less than 500 men, women and children fell 'victims to revenge and
ostentation, under the show of piety." (Burton, *Mission*, 200).

[72] This refers to the distribution of gifts by the King to the people, which was an
essential part of the Customs and an underlying element of Dahomian stability.

[73] Atakpamé, now in neighbouring Togo.

so near death: the most attentive ear could not have caught the breath of a single sigh—it did not look reality, yet it soon proved fearfully so.

Retiring to our seats the King insisted on our viewing the place of sacrifice. Immediately under the Royal canopy were six or seven executioners armed with large knives, grinning horribly; the mob now armed with clubs and branches, yelled furiously, calling upon the King to "feed them—they were hungry".

Scarcely had we reached our seats, when a demoniac yelling, caused us to look back. The King was showing the immolations to his people, and now they were raised over the heads of their carriers, while the Monarch made a speech to the soldiers, telling them that these were the prisoners from Attahpam, he called their names. The Charchar[74] left at the same time with ourselves, but Ignacio and Antonio da Souza remained spectators.

The unfortunate being nearest the King, stripped of his clothes, was now placed on end on the parapet, the King giving the upper part of the boat an impetus, a descent of twelve feet stunned the victim, and before animation could return, the head was off; the body, beaten by the mob, was dragged by the heels to a pit at a little distance, and there left prey to wolves and vultures.

After the third the King retired; not so the slave merchants. When all was over, at 3pm, we were permitted to retire. At the foot of the ladder in the boats and baskets lay the bleeding heads.

It is my duty to describe; I leave exposition to the reader.[75]

This is certainly important as it can be said to have become the stereotypical image of DanxomƐ, and Forbes' book was widely read. Versions of this scene of horror and state violence were part of history, whether ancient or more recent. Tyburn or Revolutionary France come to mind, but this was DanxomƐ and not Europe. Let us then look in this passage at some of the ideas the book popularised and the image it created.

The underlying image is of the king of DanxomƐ as a despot, overseeing a "debase(d), truly barbarian" people, made mindless by depravity, and easily bought for "a miserable pittance". The kingdom preys on its weaker neighbours in search of "human offerings" culled "to satisfy the vitiated appetite of his soldiers, and the alligator and cat". The scene "did not look reality" but he finds himself to be part of it, seeing the place of "sacrifice" and encountering the monstrous

---

[74] The King's representative at the slave port of Ouidah, the viceroy of Ouidah.
[75] Extracts in King Guézo of Dahomey, 1950–1952: the Abolition of the Slave Trade on the West Coast of Africa, London: the Stationery Office, 2001, 65–66.

"executioners and their hellish coadjutors, armed with large knives" and "grinning horribly". The mob, which engages in "demoniac yelling", is depicted as baying for blood as they call upon the King to "feed them— they were hungry". Following the "immolations", the bodies "beaten by the mob" are "dragged by the heels to a pit and there left prey to wolves and vultures".[76] It was a scene of some horror and Forbes was clearly shocked. His presentation of his own role is of equal interest and almost missionary in tone. He and his party were "the unworthy instruments of Providence" who had "with horror declined to be present at the sacrifice" but who had "begged to be allowed to save a few by purchasing".

Burton notes, with some disdain, that Forbes "writes feelingly".[77] His text was, in any case, important in fixing the image of Danxomɛ in the popular imagination. His *Dahomey and the Dahomeans* was an important reference for many, including Burton, in the years that followed. The book was widely read by, among others, young missionaries in training in the latter part of the nineteenth century, thus forming their idea of Danxomɛ in particular.[78]

Because of his subsequent celebrity, Burton's two-volume work *A Mission to Gelele, King of Dahome* (1893) eventually replaced Forbes. Newbury's introduction to the 1966 edition of this work is damning for Burton: "His writings reveal his great weakness and his great strength. Superstitious, irascible, pseudo-scientific, he stands out as one of the mid-Victorian anthropologists who sought answers to questions they were already convinced about. The major question posed by the age was whether Africans could be considered part of the human race". Burton really had little doubt in his answer to this and goes about showing his contempt through the use of "phrenology, anatomy, potted history, linguistics, and current affairs (the slave trade was sometimes a wonderful red herring)".[79]

---

[76] The scavenger *Necrosyrtes monachus*. From the Greek *necrosyrtes*—'agent(s) acting together at a corpse'. Its inclusion in this scene and in both Freeman's (Thomas B. Freeman, *The Journal of various visits to the kingdoms of Ashanti, Aku and Dahomey*, London, 1844/1968) and Skertchly's plates, heightens the effect of horror considerably. (Note: since Freeman's journals appeared in the Wesleyan Missionary Notices over a period of three years, 1840–1843, with an edited version published in 1844, all references will indicate the year, i.e. *Freeman, Journal*, 1844.)

[77] Burton, *Mission*, 201.

[78] Salvaing, *Les missionnaires*, 97.

[79] Newbury, Introduction to Burton, *Mission*, 38.

In his reporting of the Customs, Burton, on principle, removes himself from the scene, which he says began "early on the Day of the Innocents".[80] Coundouriotis observes that in not attending, he "gives us the most extreme and paradoxical example of the absent witness".[81] Burton's depiction of DanxomƐ, however, is damning, beginning with his treatment of the King himself and the adulation he receives from his entourage:

> All gave the ruler that full feed of flattery which his soul loves. He may be said to breathe an atmosphere of adulation, which intoxicates him. The wildest assertions, the falsest protestations, the most ridiculous compliments, the ultra-Hibernian 'blarney'—are all swallowed in the bottomless pit of poor human vanity, and midnight will often see him engaged in what ought to be a very nauseous occupation.[82]

Although Burton refuses to attend the So-sin Custom, he renders the sacrifices diffuse; they are implied everywhere in his representation of DanxomƐ. For Burton the sacrifices are "an integral part of the ambience of Dahomey".[83] His own account sets the tone: "During the night, at times, the deep sound of the death-drum and the loud report of a musket informed us that some mortal spirit had fled."[84] Having been left to cool his heels for two months at the residence at Cana, 10 km south-east of AgbŏmƐ, Burton was eventually received at the palace. Here he presented his message to the king regarding the "forbidden themes at the Court of Dahome",[85] the slave trade and human sacrifices. GlƐlƐ's reply, as reported by Burton and echoing his predecessors, is typical of the impasse that had been reached on both points:

> the slave trade was an ancestral custom, established by white men, to whom they would sell all they wanted: to the English, who, after greatly encouraging the export, had lately turned against, palm oil and 'tree wool'; to the Portuguese, slaves. That a single article would not defray such expenses as those which I had witnessed. Moreover, that the customs of his kingdom compelled him to make war, and that unless he sold him he must slay his captive, which England, perhaps, would like even less...
>
> Upon the second subject of human sacrifice, Gelele declared that he slew only malefactors and war captives, who, if they could, would do

---

[80] Childermas, 28 December; cf. Matthew 2: 16–18.
[81] Coundouriotis, 59.
[82] Burton, *Mission*, 213.
[83] Coundouriotis, 60.
[84] Burton, *Mission*, 1893 edition, Vol 2: 18, in Coundouriotis, 59.
[85] Burton, *Mission*, 343.

the same; that his own subjects were never victims; that in the accounts reported by 'mutual' enemies there had been, as he had told Captain Wilmot, a gross numerical exaggeration...

Burton's reply took the form of a homily and what he clearly saw as a severe dressing down:

> When asked for my reply, I submitted, in Jeremy Bentham's words, that the worst use to which he could put a man was to kill him; that Dahome wanted not deaths, but births, and that subjects followed the religion of their prince. It was, therefore, incumbent upon him to reduce the number of his sacrifices, and to spare his visitors the disgusting spectacle of nude and mutilated corpses, hanging for two or three days in the sun; moreover, that until such barbarity should be changed I should advise all Englishmen, who dislike 'tickling of the liver', to avoid his Court at Customs' time. The King has never heard so much truth in his life: he did not accept my plain speaking without 'stirring of the mind', nor could I expect it. The Rev. Mr Bernasko thanked me aloud, and all around understood the expression.[86]

This certainly illustrates the divide that had established itself between the two sides. Rev. Peter Bernasko, who regularly accompanied British delegations to Agbŏmɛ,[87] does not share Burton's recollection or interpretation of the events. This hapless man, working under the terms of the native pastorate,[88] incurred the disdain of Borghero, Burton and later of Skertchly. Bernasko, however, had an equally dim view of the great Burton. Reporting in a letter to the Methodist Missionary Office, he writes "the commissioner... did not go to Dahomey with any patient heart",[89] and he believed Burton's arrogant attitude was largely responsible for the failure of the talks with Glɛlé.

In any case, Burton came to the conclusion that Danxomɛ, an "effluvium", was inseparable from human sacrifice to the point that

[86] Burton, *Mission*, 344–345.

[87] Fr. Francis Borghero notes this in his journal for 3 December 1862. He is sceptical and feels that the English have "illusions", remarking that the simple name of England will not be enough to bring about a change in "secular mores" (Francis Borghero, *Journal de Francis Borghero premier missionnaire du Dahomey (1861–1865): Sa vie, son journal (1860–1864) la relation de 1863*, Paris: Karthala, 1997, 118).

[88] See Jehu. J. Hanciles, "Anatomy of an experiment: the Sierra Leone Native Pastorate", *Missiology*, XXIX (1), 2000, 63–64.

[89] In Colin W. Newbury, *The West African Slave Coast and its Rulers: European Trade Administration among Yoruba and Adja Speaking People of Southwest Nigeria, Southern Dahomey and Togo*, Oxford: Greenwood Press, 1961, 2. Skertchly also notes that Burton had left a bad impression (Skertchly, *Dahomey*, 303).

"to abolish human sacrifice is to abolish Dahomey".[90] He concluded: "Britain should minimise its ties with West Africa. The slave trade had so demoralised the people that they were beyond help".[91] He writes:

> Finally, the present King is for the present committed to them; he rose to power by the goodwill of the reactionary party, and upon it he depends. There is a report that his grandsire Agongoro (Wheenoowhew) was poisoned because he showed a propensity to Christianity, and the greatest despots in Yoruba are easily told to 'go to sleep', or were presented with the parrot's eggs. Gelele, I am persuaded, could not abolish human sacrifice if he would; and he would not if he could. The interference of strangers will cause more secrecy, and more decorum in practice; but the remedy must come from the people themselves.[92]

In order to follow this part of the process of demonisation and 'othering' through, we must take a very brief look at one remaining and rather obscure figure. Rev. J.A. Skertchly, a Victorian entomologist in the very English curate-naturalist tradition, found himself held under conditions of "polite imprisonment"[93] in DanxomƐ for eight months.[94] Prevented from collecting, Skertchly applied his powers of observation to the local scene, leaving what the travel writer Bruce Chatwin has described "one of the surrealist books of all time".[95]

The title in itself is of interest, as *Dahomey as it is*...seeks to affirm Skertchly's empirical objectivity as a kind of social Darwinist. In his preface he states that DanxomƐ has been "effectually 'tabooed' to Europeans"[96] who rarely visit it. He is critical of the "exaggerated accounts [which] have been published" and his own intention therefore is to portray DanxomƐ "as it is" and "the negro as he is". Skertchly has little time for liberal whimpering on the plight of black people. "The civilisation and education of the Negro is all very well" but he is intent on portraying the country *as it really is*, in the hope that at "the conclusion of the campaign the eyes of our countrymen will be opened to the fallacy of attempting to make 'silk purses from sows ears'".[97]

---

[90] Burton, *Mission*, Vol 2, 17.
[91] Fawn M. Brodie, *The Devil Drives: A life of Sir Richard Burton*, New York: Norton, 1967, 209.
[92] Burton, *Mission*, 235–236.
[93] Skertchly, *Dahomey*, viii.
[94] Apparently to assist the King with some guns he had acquired. He says he was well treated but was very restricted in his movements and not allowed to do any collecting (Skertchly, *Dahomey*, ix–x).
[95] Shakespeare, 62.
[96] Skertchly, *Dahomey*, viii.
[97] Ibid., xi–xii.

Coundouriotis correctly notes that "his posture is that of a disaffected, objective observer, yet his prose belies him"[98] and the book is in fact an ugly little pamphlet. He does not even pretend to have attended the Customs, which he sees as no more than executions, or religious manifestations:[99] "not one whit more barbarous that the suttee of the Hindoo, and far less so than the incarceration of an unwilling maiden within the loathsome walls of a Popish nunnery."[100] However, despite his protests of empirical neutrality, "he emphasises the ritualistic display of bodies and describes Dahomey as a land littered with exposed corpses".[101] His plate illustrating the So-Sin ritual victims is a graphic illustration of this:

> A few yards to the north we come upon the first victim, a fine stalwart fellow, suspended by the ankles and knees to the crosspole of one of the gallows. His arms hung limp, and the eyes were staring with a glassy look, while his mouth was pegged open, as were all others. This was done to show that in death they repented of their crimes, and wished to warn the people in the market against falling under the king's just displeasure. All were stark naked, and showed no signs of life, save the mutilation before mentioned [genital mutilation], and a slow drip, drip of dark coloured blood from the mouths and nostrils, and the fractured occupits, showed that the had been killed by the knobbed club.[102]

In Coundouriotis' view, Skertchly represents the final point in this process of demonisation. The British have been completely removed from the scene. What is left is a scene of utter horror occupied only by Dahomeans, with two women walking to market or returning from their farms, apparently unconcerned by the sight of three suspended corpses, outside the walls of the palace, with the ever-present vultures perched on the cruciform gallows. This represents Danxomε as almost at the centre of the heart of darkness.

---

[98] Coundouriotis, 61.
[99] Ibid., 193.
[100] Ibid., 237.
[101] Coundouriotis, 61.
[102] Skertchly, *Dahomey*, 240.

The early missionaries

There had been attempts at a Christian missionary presence in Danxomɛ dating back to the seventeenth century.[103] However, the first more enduring presence came following the visit of Wesleyan missionary, Thomas Birch Freeman, in 1843. Freeman was apparently a tolerant and mild-mannered man, little given to condemnation, who became quite friendly with Gezò and other African leaders he met.[104] However, his first impressions of Agbŏmɛ start with an image that could well have been the basis of the plate in Skertchly referred to above, with the cruciform gallows and the ubiquitous "turkey buzzards". He comments simply: "It was a frightful sight".[105]

Freeman, like all early evangelical missionaries, was preoccupied by the violence and savagery and "gloried in describing them".[106] The above scene is quite typical and his apparent nonchalance, in describing the victim as a criminal punished for his "obnoxious" crimes, does little to diminish the effect. Significantly, one of only two plates in Freeman's published account is also an image of "human sacrifice" and almost inevitably includes "two or three turkey-buzzards".

Both the slave trade and what he saw as the "moral desolation" of Danxomɛ preoccupied Freeman. Writing in a letter ten years later, following another visit before the Custom, he notes:

> The platform was erected, *pro tempore*, for the occasion, in the great market place, whence human victims were to be thrown headlong for torture among an excited and infuriated populace; and in this work of moral desolation and ruin *all* seemed to be busily engaged. It is true, there were no painful, disgusting exhibitions of human suffering during our visit; but we nevertheless felt that we were indeed in regions of darkness, on the confines of the shadow of death.[107]

The missionaries who expressed their desire to "give a death-blow to its existence" soon vilified Danxomɛ as "this sink of iniquity".[108] In the

---

[103] See Robin Law, "Religion, trade and politics on the 'Slave Coast': Roman Catholic missions in Allada and Whydah in the seventeenth century", *Journal of Religion in Africa* 21 (1), 1991, 47.

[104] Thomas B. Freeman, *The Journal of various visits to the kingdoms of Ashanti, Aku and Dahomey*, London: 1844/1968, 255.

[105] Freeman, *Journal* (1844), 255.

[106] Wright, "Introduction", xxxv.

[107] Freeman, 'Letter', Cape-Coast, 12 August 1854, *WMN*, 1854, 176.

[108] Henry Wharton, Letter, Akrah, 16 August 1854, *WMN*, 1854, 173.

following years, the reports coming out of Danxomɛ were increasingly
alarming, leading the *Wesleyan Missionary Notices* to publish material
which it saw as "supplying authentic information as to the crimes and
miseries of Heathenism". The account, from Henry Wharton in the
Gold Coast, was certainly the most sensationalised, speaking of "a
great pit [that] has been dug, which is to contain human blood enough
to float a canoe".[109]

This was the view of Danxomɛ that came to prevail among the
missionaries, drawing them into the colonial project that was developing.
It was certain the view of Francis Borghero, now known as the first
Catholic missionary of Danxomɛ, whom we shall look at him in more
detail in Chapter 5.

There was clearly a great amount of interdependence among all of
the above sources, the early sources informing the later ones, with these
reinforcing the images created by their predecessors. As I have shown,
these were all produced in popular form, whether as travel books or as
mission propaganda, and all contributed to the darkly negative European
construction of Danxomɛ. This construction, as we shall see, has to
some degree been assumed by many of its own people, particularly in
the Christian Churches.

The bas-reliefs of the Royal Palaces of Abomey

The above were all European sources. But we have one significant
African source, quite apart from oral tradition and folk history. Les
Palais Royaux were declared a UNESCO World Heritage site in 1985,
and they have since been receiving extensive ongoing restoration. The
site continues to attract a certain number of visitors who, like the early
travellers, seem to be fascinated by the gore: the blood mixed into the
walls, the skulls supporting the throne, and the hundreds of victims
said to have been buried with the different kings. The palaces remain a
controversial landmark as well as a historical question mark in modern
Benin.

The bas-reliefs on the palace walls are one of the most striking
features. These have had several restorations, starting in the 1920s and

---

[109] *WMN*, 1860, 158; 160.

continuing down to the present.[110] Lévy Bruhl notes that it is rare to find in West Africa "historical documents of incontestable authenticity, coming from the natives themselves".[111] Here, he states, "the Kings of DanxomƐ inscribed the history of their reign". Béninois historian Nondichao Bachalou affirms that "the bas-reliefs are our only *written* history."[112] Ranier and Piqué suggest that "these sacred places continue to exercise a powerful influence... These sites are not just material places and buildings... but the place of a living tradition [...] a unique visual repertory of Fòn history and culture".[113]

Coundouriotis strongly contests the historicity of the bas-reliefs, pointing out that, in the process of colonial restoration, there was an adulteration of the works. However, she concedes that this "adulteration should be considered an aspect of their history".[114] What is of interest to me, however, is the acknowledgement that the bas-reliefs are not "stable texts". It is precisely this that gives them their importance and power as part of the imagining of DanxomƐ since they were, and are, "aides to the transmission of oral history... [which] reinforced the collective memory of the community".[115]

The fact today, of course, is that they are not being read solely by members of the Fòn "community", but by anybody who chooses to visit the site. They are thus subject to different interpretations and serve to reinforce the collective memory of other communities who may not see in them the record of a glorious past. They are an essential part of the various imaginings of DanxomƐ. The bas-reliefs include some very striking scenes of violence. These scenes refer to the wars executed against the neighbouring states, with a particular emphasis on the Yoruba. It is clear to me that not only did they serve to reinforce the collective memory of the community that originally created them, or participated in their restoration, they also, albeit unwittingly, served as an illustration of the earlier European Dahomean narratives, and continue to inform the imagining of DanxomƐ today, for better or for

---

[110] See George E. Waterlot, *Les bas-reliefs des bâtiments royaux d'Abomey (Dahomey)*, Paris: Institut d'Ethnologie, 1926; Francesca Piqué and Leslie H. Rainier, *Les Bas-reliefs d'Abomey: L'Histoire racontée sur les murs*, Cotonou: Flamboyant/ Paul Getty Trust, 1999.

[111] Waterlot, *Les bas-reliefs*, v.

[112] Piqué and Rainier, *Les bas-reliefs*, 3 (emphasis mine).

[113] Ibid., 4.

[114] Coundouriotis, 84–89.

[115] Ibid., 88.

worse. Visiting the site several years ago with two Béninois students, both Nagot, we were particularly interested in the bas-reliefs relating to their own historical narrative. I had read Waterlot, giving his interpretation to the students of a number of war scenes from the Palace of Glɛlɛ́ at Agbŏmɛ and a representation in memory of the Amazons showing a wife of the king killing a Nagot and disembowelling him. I was interrupted by the guide, however, who asked me not to explain the bas-reliefs, not because he contested Waterlot's interpretation but rather *"pour ne pas exciter l'esprit des jeunes et raviver les tensions tribales du passé"*. It was certainly a telling testimony to the emotive power of the bas-reliefs.

Colonial Dahomean Literature in French

Danxomɛ, which took pride in being known as *le quartier latin de l'Afrique*, has produced several distinguished writers down to the present time.[116] As in all literatures, this corpus also looked to the past for inspiration and indeed started as a type of ethnography, inspired largely by the Catholic priest Francis Aupiais, whom we shall look at in a later chapter. The best known of the early writers was Paul Hazoumé (1889–1980), a schoolteacher and self-taught ethnographer who, along with Aupiais and Maurice Delafosse, initiated in Danxomɛ the rehabilitation of black culture, particularly in the short-lived journal *La Reconnaissance Africaine*.[117]

Alladaye, writing a doctoral thesis in France at the height of the Marxist revolution in Benin, is dismissive of the Catholic-educated elites, of whom Paul Hazoumé was certainly one of the best known, describing them as "culturally alienated".[118] In his introduction to the English translation of one of Hazoumé's two major works, the novel *Dogucimi* (1938),[119] published in 1990, the translator Richard Bjornson sees something more complex. He admits that Hazoumé's "scenes of extraordinary cruelty do not depict traditional Africa in a

[116] See Adrien Huannou, *La littérature béninoise de langue française*, Paris: Karthala, 1984.
[117] SMA, 3H50, Le mouvement intellectuel indigène de M. Delafosse.
[118] Jérome C. Alladayec, *Les Missionnaires Catholiques au Dahomey à l'époque coloniale 1905–1957*, (Thèse), Paris, 1978, 175.
[119] Hazoumé's other major work is *Le Pacte du Sang*, Paris: Institut d'Ethnologie, 1937.

particularly favourable light", and he acknowledges the critics who have "admonished Hazoumé for pandering to a European taste for the exotic."[120] Where Hazoumé appears to me to be important, however, is in the fact that his work expresses the ambivalence of the modern Béninois in his attitude to the historical DanxomƐ. He "viewed the historical DanxomƐ with a mixture of admiration and moral repugnance".[121] In the heroine of his novel *Dogucimi*, Hazoumé creates "a character who embodies its highest ideals and then places this character in dramatic conflict with a corrupt society that merely pays lip service to them". Hazoumé manages to present the religious nature of the people in their submission to the king, while also portraying Gezò, the "Father and Mother of the People" and "The Master of the World", as a victim of tradition and unable to change it. At the same, however, according to the novel, these most brutal ritual practices were being contested even from within DanxomƐ and to Gezò's face.[122]

Hazoumé was not himself DanxomƐnu, but rather from Porto-Novo with which DanxomƐ was usually in a state of conflict. Like many Africans of his day, however, he was searching for materials from which the new state could be imagined, and DanxomƐ, as a powerful historical entity and the cornerstone of the new colony, had to be taken into consideration. Hazoumé, like his mentor Aupiais, admired "the nobility, the courage, the deeply religious sense of life, and the highly successful administration"[123] of the kingdom but found it impossible to overlook the more horrific aspects of its history. Bjornson observes that Hazoumé was "psychologically and emotionally incapable of portraying [DanxomƐ] in wholly negative terms".[124] Neither, however, could be bring himself to defend it.

In a pamphlet celebrating the life of Mgr Steinmetz, Hazoumé lent support to the more horrific vision of DanxomƐ as a slave state and a sanguinary tyranny, dismissing Gbéhazin as a dethroned despot, reproaching the people of DanxomƐ for their servile acceptance of an unjust system. [125] Like Steinmetz and the other missionaries, Hazoumé came to the conclusion that DanxomƐ was, at best, a culture that had

---

[120] Richard Bjornson, 'Introduction', in Paul Hazoumé, *Dugucimi*, Washington: Three Continents Press, 1990, xvii.

[121] Ibid., xviii.

[122] See *Dogucimi*, 112 for an illustration of this.

[123] Bjornson, "Introduction", in Paul Hazoumé, *Dugucimi*, Washington: Three Continents Press, 1990, xix.

[124] Ibid.

[125] Paul Hazoumé, *50 ans d'apostolat, Mgr. Steinmetz*, Lomé, 1942.

gone seriously wrong, it was a social aberration. From here it was but a short step to concluding that it was a society in need of redemption and the *mission civilisatrice*, Christian and republican values, the credentials of modernity. It was more complex, however, and Coundouriotis gives a positive appreciation of Hazoumé. He sees *Dogucimi* as "resistant history...not merely in opposition to colonial rule but in an attempt to define a national identity against the hegemonic notions of tradition."[126] It was, in a manner of speaking, an attempt to re-imagine Danxomε in a new way.

With Hazoumé, we have, in a manner of speaking, come full circle, as an African writer takes on the narrative started in the early travel literature.[127] Because of his ethnic origin, he recounts the Danxomε narrative as something of an outsider. He struggles to free himself from the earlier versions but he never fully succeeds. Peel states that until the publication of Johnson's *History of the Yorubas* (1921), the Yoruba had little sense of themselves as a people. This was "the earliest important source of information for pre-colonial Yoruba history" and "gave the notion of a Yoruba people real historical substance by making them the subject of a powerful story of growth, decline, and recovery".[128] I would suggest that Dahomean narrative, in its cumulative effect, played a similar but very *negative* role in the imagining of Danxomε as the type for the rule of darkness. It certainly left little in terms of symbolic capital with which to imagine the future of a nation. This image has endured and, as we shall see, weighs upon what has become the Republic of Benin today. There have been significant efforts to rehabilitate Danxomε and, indeed, more recent anthropology and historiography have often seemed like an effort to understand, explain, justify and, even occasionally, excuse Danxomε in order to free it from the weight of its past. On the ground, however, the past remains largely occulted, a *non-dit* posing great problems for the imagining of the modern state and the building of its future. To borrow the expression of Geertz, it remains "this fine-spun and lovingly conserved texture of pride and suspicion and we must somehow contrive to weave it into the fabric of modern politics".[129] This is not a uniquely Béninois problem. It is the

---

[126] Coundouriotis, 98.

[127] See Huannou, *La Littérature*, 99–113 for a treatment of how later writers view Dahomean society and the kingdom.

[128] Peel, *Encounter*, 45.

[129] Clifford Geertz, *Old Societies, New States: the Quest for Modernity in Africa and Asia*, New Delhi: Amerind, 1963/1971, 119.

problem of any society with historical shadows and problems of national identity, from Ireland to the countries of the former Soviet bloc. Facing its history and building a national identity is no less a problem for the modern Béninois than it is for other peoples. It is, however, precisely in this situation of tension, doubt and often considerable suspicion that the Churches attempt to play a role, at least in assuring some kind of reconciliation and social cohesion and perhaps in providing elements of the symbolic capital necessary for the attempt at constructing a new narrative and re-imagining the nation.

CHAPTER THREE

DANXOMƐ KASUDU:[1]
VODÚN AND THE FOUNDATION OF DANXOMƐ

> If the world of Vodún and the world of the ancestors hold together, then
> Danxomɛ will not be broken.[2]

Like Danxomɛ itself, Vodún has a special place in the popular imagining
of Africa, evoking the mysterious, the arcane, the occult and something
that is more than a little frightening. Mention of it is tinged with
apprehension and the idea that one is tampering with unknown force
one may not control. The etymological origins have been lost but, in
the Fòn language, Vodún "evokes the idea of mystery and designates
that which has its origins in the divine".[3] The popular perception has
taken it much further, stressing "spells and necromancy", "charm",
"voodoo…to bewitch by or as if by means of voodoo: hex".[4]

Geschiere has noted the difficulties many aspects of African religions
pose for Western scholars who try to fix them in rigid categories.[5] The
scholar struggles for neat definitions, which almost invariably refuse to
come, in discussion with interlocutors that are often interspersed with
remarks such as "*C'est ça, mais ce n'est pas ça*" or "*Oui, c'est un Vodún
mais ce n'est pas vraiment un Vodún aussi*". The description of Vodún,
by the Danxomɛnù, as a "closed calabash", accessible only to the
Vodúnù, the priests, and, to a lesser extent, to the Vodúnsì, the followers
or literally "the wives of the Vodún", offers little encouragement. From
my research and experience, it is certainly clear that Vodún remains a
closed calabash, reserved to the initiated, esoteric almost by definition,[6]
and presenting considerable difficulties of access for scholars.

---

[1] Danxomé the Closed Calabash.
[2] In Barthelemy Adoukonou, "Une Nouvelle Sortie d'Egypte" in Adoukonou (ed.), *Une Expérience*, 148.
[3] Segurola and Rassinoux, *Dictionnaire*, 469.
[4] Merriam Webster Dictionary, CD-Rom.
[5] Peter Geschiere, *Sorcellerie et Politique en Afrique*, Paris: Karthala, 1995, 35.
[6] Adoukonou, who defines Vodun as an *esoteric* form of reason, makes the following distinctions between this form of human reason and that which he calls *exoteric*: "L'exotérisme serait propre à la raison diaphane, disponible à toutes les intelligences capables. L'ésotérisme se signale comme raison arcane, réservée et accessible par voie d'initiation," (Adoukonou, *Nouvelle Sortie*, 145).

Most scholarly accounts have been constructed largely on the basis of information from the early travellers cited in the previous chapter, the local ethnologists and collectors of the early twentieth century, and some converts and other sources who gave information to missionary/ scholars like Steinmetz, Aupiais and Parrinder, administrator/scholars such as Le Hérissé and particularly Maupoil, as well as to later academic researchers, most notably Herskovits and the photographer and ethnographer Pierre Verger.[7] As stated in the previous chapter, all of these contributed some important data, even if the interpretation was skewed by other considerations. However, as with the data dealing with DanxomƐ itself, it is cannibalistic and often difficult to assess. It is frequently contested, often in defence of the mystery itself, and on the basis that the sources[8] were working on the principle of "*Yovó hwenuxo*", that "these are stories for white man",[9] and were, at best, sparing on detail, thus assuring that the calabash remained hermetically sealed.

I have, therefore, relied on six secondary sources to guide my research and questioning: Maupoil's study of divination, which provides us with an outline of the religious world of the Fòn, as well as studying the central question of Fá divination; Verger's comparative work on the Orisha and Vodún[10] both in Africa and in Bahia; Glélé's studies of the rise of the kingdom of DanxomƐ[11] and the birth of the modern state,[12] which look at the political aspects of Vodún, past and present; several works by Adoukonou,[13] which seek to give an interpretation of this

[7] Bernard Maupoil, *La Géomancie à l'ancienne Côte des Esclaves*, Paris: Institut d'Ethnologie, 1943; Melville J. Herskovits, *Dahomey: an ancient West African Kingdom*, Evanston: NUP, 1938; Pierre Verger, *Notes sur le culte des Orisa et Vodun: à Bahia, la Baie de tous les Saints, au Brésil et à l'ancienne Côte des Esclaves en Afrique*, Dakar: IFAN, 1957.

[8] See Maurice A. Glélé, *Le Danxomé: du Pouvoir Aja à la Nation Fon*, Paris: Nubia, 1974, 25. Glélé questions the reliability of Herskovits' principal informer.

[9] See Olabiyi Babalola J. Gai, "The Path is Open: The Herskovits Legacy" from *African Narrative Analysis and Beyond*, PAS Working Papers No. 5, 1999 for a critical evaluation of Herskovits' methodology.

[10] Verger, *Notes*.

[11] Glélé, *Le Danxomé*.

[12] Maurice A. Glélé, *La naissance d'un état noir: L'évolution politique et constitutionnel du Danxomé de la colonisation à nos jours*, Paris: Librarie Générale de Droit et de la Jurisprudence, 1969.

[13] Barthélémy Adoukonou, *Jalons pour une théologie africaine*, Paris: Editions Lethielleux, 1979; *Vodun sacré ou violence*, Université Descartes, Paris, 1989; *Vodún, Démocratie et Pluralisme Religieux*, Cotonou, Sillon Noir, 1993.

world and its meaning, while at the same time looking at its implications
for modern Benin; Aguessy[14] who looks particularly at Vodún Lɛgbà;
and cross references to Peel's recent work on the Yoruba.[15]

The perspectives of these works are very different in several ways.
Maupoil comes from the tradition of the administrator/scholar, with the
post-colonial limitations that this implies, but in a very short period
of only two years in Abomey and Porto-Novo, he did provide an
exemplary work which retains its value today. Verger spent a lifetime
studying both the slave trade and Vodún, bringing together important
data, and his excellent photographs are of immense value. Peel provides
comparative perspective, much information on the wider Yoruba-Fòn
cluster, and how the Orisha were perceived and explained by the early
missionaries. Glélé, Aguessy and Adoukonou provide a very different
perspective. All are Béninois scholars, in politics and jurisprudence,
social anthropology and theology. Glélé and Adoukonou are committed
Christians, and both belong to princely Abomey families: Glélé to that
of his illustrious nineteenth-century namesake, Glɛlé, and Adoukonou to
the family of Agongló, whom he claims was the first king of Abomey
to "open the path" for Christianity. Aguessy is director of l'Institut de
Développement et d'Echanges Endogènes (IDEE), Ouidah, pursuing
research into *les savoirs endogènes*. He is staunch in his defence of
Danxomɛ and has written an authoritative study of Lɛgbà.[16]

These perspectives are essential to this work, since not only do they
offer useful insights into what might be going on inside the calabash,
they also reveal the polemic which often surrounds Vodún and its place
today. From my research, I shall try to show that Vodún still plays an
important role in what has become the modern Republic of Benin, as a
religious reference in the way power is perceived, and in the tensions
that underlie the wider society.[17]

---

[14] See particularly Honorat Aguessy, "La divinité Legba et la dynamique du panthéon
vodû au Danxomé", *Cahiers des Religions Africaines*, 7, 1970; *Les religions africaines
comme source et valeur de civilisation*, Paris: Présence Africaine 1972; *Essai sur le
mythe Lêgba*, (Thèse), Paris, Sorbonne, 1973.

[15] Peel, *Encounter*.

[16] See Paulin J. Hountondji, *Les savoirs endogènes: pistes pour une recherche*,
Paris: Karthala, 1994; Honorat Aguessy, *Du mode d'existence de l'Etat sous Guezo
1818–1825*, (Thèse), Paris, Sorbonne, 1970; Honorat Aguessy, "Le Dan-Homê du
XIXe siècle était-il une société esclavagiste?", in *Revue française d'études africaines*,
50, 1970, 71–91.

[17] Karola Elwert-Kretschmer, "Vodun et contrôle social au village", *Politique
Africaine*, 59, 1995, 102–119.

It is not my ambition to penetrate this world. At the same time, I have no doubt that Vodún is an essential key to understanding the historical kingdom of DanxomƐ, as well as providing important elements of the religious logic underlying modern Benin, both as religion relates to the individual, and as it relates to society and the state. It is essential, then, that we look at elements of this that can provide us with some guidelines. So I shall attempt to look at Vodún on two levels: first of all how it relates to the individual person and helps to form her religious world; but also how it relates to state and society as a religious institution penetrating deeply into DanxomƐ society, and serving as an essential support for the historical monarchy and leaving imaginary vestiges that are still important today.

The Origins and Nature of Vodún

Although the people who created DanxomƐ came from Tado, to the west, they drew much of their religious inspiration from the east, old Yorubaland, the "*oikoumene* where Ile-Ifa carried prestige and there was a diffusion of cults such as Ifa and Ogoun".[18] Maupoil suggests that for the Fòn, Ife was not just a simple administrative unit, but rather a "holy city", a "mystical fatherland", home of the great creator god, "from which emanates the whole mystery of the world and his coming into the world".[19] Aguessy affirms that for the Fòn "the world was created at Ife" with Odoudoua as god and king. Every Bokónò, or diviner of Fà, who dies will return to Ife, the source of his life and his credibility.[20] Adoukonou notes, however, that there is a tension in the relationship, with the Yoruba seen as holding a formidable spiritual power, while the Fòn hold a political power which "while it may not be the most detestable is still the most hated".[21] In other words, DanxomƐ sought to build its political power on a Yoruba religious base.

The religious influence of Yorubaland in DanxomƐ-Bénin is not then a recent phenomenon, although, as we shall see in our examination of the modern Christian Churches, it certainly continues down to the present day. On the other hand, Vodún itself has spread far afield, on

---

[18] Peel, *Encounter*, 28.
[19] Maupoil, *Géomancie*, 32ff.
[20] Aguessy, *Essai*, 188.
[21] Adoukonou, *Vodun sacré*, 511.

the slave ships to the Caribbean and Brazil, while the freed Brazilian slaves made the return journey to influence Danxomɛ-Bénin and the forms of Christianity which developed there.

Definitions of Vodún are difficult to come by. Segurola and Rassinoux provide a useful working version, describing it as:

> every manifestation of strength or intelligence…a mysterious thing demanding a cult. [It acts] for good and evil in the world. The principal aim of the cult is to capture for one's benefit the mysterious forces through admiration, love and fear.[22]

Maupoil takes an etymological approach, but finds little that is convincing, stating that it simply signifies "that which is mysterious, independently of time and place, thus that which is divine in origin". Somebody who dies becomes a Vodún, but this does not mean that he/she will be adored. He concludes that translating the expression Vodún "as a divinity is then exact, but it gives only one sense of the word, which seems the least imprecise, and closest to our [European] mentality". While the Vodún is certainly a divinity of the other world, it is also closely linked to the human world as "a tie of solidarity". The Vodún and humans are "complementary", with humans feeding and maintaining the strength of the Vodún through their offerings. The relationship is marked, however, by a certain resentment at the cost on the part of humans, but also by social constraint and "the fear of divine reprisals and the confidence they have in the efficacy of a relationship with the unknowable. If one ceased completely adoring a Vodún, its name would disappear".[23]

Adoukonou rejects a polytheistic approach, with the implied notion of a *deus otiosus* and a pantheon of more active lower deities. He links the Vodún more firmly to the human world, stating that one must take into consideration the whole Fòn representation of each person as coming to eschatological self-realisation in his/her Vodún.

> The Vodún is the way in which each person lives the anticipation of his end…He is the entelechy[24] of the Gbé too. It is given to each individual to be a Vodún and to become one.[25]

---

[22] Segurola and Rassinoux, *Dictionnaire*, 469.

[23] Maupoil, *Géomancie* 52–57.

[24] This reflects Adoukonou's scholastic background and an essentially Catholic theological reading of the Vodun. Entelechy (Greek, *entelecheia*): that which realises what is otherwise merely potential. It is intimately connected with Aristotle's distinction between matter and form, or the potential and the actual.

[25] Adoukonou, *Jalons*, 305.

Akpowena, an eminent Lɛgbànù,[26] reported by Aguessy, is quite clear when he states:

> In effect, every living being ends up dying and transforming itself into a Vodún. In one sense there is no Vodún, only beings who transform themselves into Vodún.[27]

These examples serve to illustrate the ambivalence of the Vodún, as it comes into being and as it moves between the top and the bottom end of the calabash, the Gbɛ́, the human and the divine (see Appendices 2–3), negotiating, and holding together the world order.

Gbɛ́, Sɛ́ and the Vodún pantheon

Before looking at the Vodún, it is important to have a clear idea of Gbɛ́. For the Danxomɛnù, Gbɛ́ was the universe itself—life, existence, the world, providence, and God. In a sense, it was the largest calabash, within which one found Danxomɛ itself,[28] which for the Danxomɛnù was almost co-extensive with the natural world, before arriving at the kernel, Vodún-tò, the world of the Vodún, and Kúyito-tò, the world of the ancestors. As the proverb quoted in the title to this chapter indicates, it was this alliance of the Vodún and the Kúyito that held Danxomɛ together. The Vodún Dàn is often represented as the Vodún who holds the Gbɛ́ together, negotiating between the sky and the earth, encircling it with his body, as his tail comes back to his mouth. The Vodún themselves are in constant movement at the heart of Gbɛ́, negotiating the contingencies of the human Sɛ́, that vital principle of human life, Sɛ́gbó, the spirit, the destiny, and the fate of every human being in its relation to Mãwu, the other Vodún, the Kúyito-tò, *and* within him/herself.

> *This life where we have awoken*
> *is a thing of mystery.*
> *Man has a Sɛ́, the wild animal has a Sɛ́*
> *The bird has a Sɛ́, the tree has a Sɛ́.*
> *And all of the Sɛ́, who knows them?*

---

[26] Priest of the deity Lɛgbà.

[27] Honorat Aguessy, *Corpus en Langue Fô sur le mythe Lɛgbà*, tome II, (Thèse), Paris, Sorbonne, 1974, 15.

[28] The calabash is also used to describe several of the kingdoms that make up the modern Benin e.g. Porto Novo, Allada, as well as Danxomɛ itself. See Jacques Le Cornec, *La Calebasse Dahoméenne ou Les Errances du Bénin*, Paris, 2000, 29.

It is Mǎwu Gbɛ́ who is their Sɛ́.
And the diviner Gêdêgbɛ́
is the Sɛ́ of Danxomɛ.[29]

Only slightly more prosaically, Adoukonou notes that Gbɛ́ is nature and culture, as well as the dialectic between the two and, ultimately, the visibility of *Sɛ́* the creator and his work of creation.[30] Ségbó is the Sɛ́ of Gbɛ́, the totality of what exists and its vital principle. It is an overwhelmingly religious view of the universe, and there is little reason to think that it has essentially changed.

Given the depth of the attachment to Ife, it is hardly surprising to find that the major Orisha of the Yoruba pantheon reoccur in the Vodṹn. The temptation for all outsiders, most notably the missionaries, has always been to try to fix the pantheon in a way they find comprehensible. However, as Peel has pointed out, "God was neither as definite, unchanging and uniform", or as "distinct from the Orisha", as the missionaries or the scholars might have liked.[31] Aguessy notes that to study the "progressive organisation of the Danxomɛ pantheon is to evoke the socio-political history of [the] country",[32] which means it is a narrative of movement, change, invention, and often, improvisation, as it moves from Yorubaland to Danxomɛ, and within Danxomɛ itself. Let us look briefly at this pantheon.

Mǎwu-Lisà, are the creator couple. Mǎwu, the female partner, "characterised by gentleness, joy, freshness, wisdom, maturity" and assisted by the Vodṹn Dàn, is charged with the ordering of the natural world. Lisà, the male partner, the Vodṹn of force and fire, "characterised by strength, robustness, heat, work, and youth",[33] assisted by Gʋ, takes charge of the ordering of humans. Mǎwu was adopted by the earliest missionaries as the local name for the Christian God, while Lisà, thought by some to be her partner and others to be her son, came to be taken, for a brief period, as the figure of Jesus Christ. This appears to have its origins in the misunderstandings involved in the first Catholic pamphlet, *Doctrina Christiana*, prepared by the Capuchins in 1658 for

---

[29] From the Fon original in Adoukonou, *Vodun sacré*, 476.
[30] Ibid., 42.
[31] Peel, *Encounter*, 116–117.
[32] Aguessy, *Divinité*, 90.
[33] Ibid., 91.

DanxomƐ,[34] compounded by later missionary interpretations.[35] There is, however, also evidence that the king, attracted by monotheism,[36] which would provide a certain legitimisation for his increased personal power, also encouraged this development, though it was discouraged by the Vodúnnò,[37] worried no doubt about their own place within the structure. In any case, Măwu has emerged as supreme, while Lisà, has drifted progressively into the category of the less important Vodúnnò.

Aguessy points out that the Vodún pantheon is essentially architectonic. It is a structure and a genealogy in which each Vodún "lives its dependence in relation to a significant major who is the demiurge, the creator couple Măwu-Lisà".[38] While Măwu has emerged as the supreme sky god, and perhaps something of a *deus otiosus*, although this is contested,[39] there exists a lower level of several deities that occupy a space between earth and sky, between Măwu-Lisà, and their creation. They often act as intermediaries, each with particular responsibilities, often apparently composites, taking on the attributes of other Vodún, and extremely complex in their relationship to each other.

The following are among the major Vodún: Xεbyoso commands the skies, the Vodún of "atmospheric phenomena perceptible to man";[40] the Vodún of thunder "commands the earth in its relations with man";[41] Sakpatá is responsible for plague-like illnesses, most notably of smallpox; Agbè commands the sea. Agε, a Vodún born of the union of Măwu and Lisà is honoured with them—the hunter, it is sometimes represented as a chameleon, commanding the forest and caring for the animals. Dàn is the serpent/rainbow, the Vodún of stability, power and prosperity, moving between the ocean, the forest and the sky,[42] giving

---

[34] Henri Labouret, Paul Rivet, *Le Royaume d'Ardra et son évangélisation au XVIIe siècle*, Paris: Institut d'Ethnologie, 1929, 18.

[35] Protestant missionaries tended to avoid these terms for God, though, as we shall see later, both Protestants and Catholics used the same terms for the devil.

[36] Adoukonou argues that there was a process of indigenous theological reflection; at this time which was leading to a more transcendent notion of the deities and to a more ethical religion. This, he claims, was ignored, (*Vodun sacré*, 563–564).

[37] Finn Fugelstad, "Quelques réflexions sur l'histoire et les institutions de l'ancien Royaume du Dahomey et ses voisins", *Bulletin de l'IFAN*, Série B, XXXIX, iii, 1977, 507. See also Law, "Religion, trade and politics".

[38] Aguessy, *Divinité*, 92.

[39] Adoukonou, *Jalons*, 305.

[40] Aguessy, *Divinité*, 91.

[41] Maupoil, *Géomancie*, 72.

[42] See Saulnier, *Le Meutre* for an examination of the popular narratives concerning this *Vodun*.

his name to the kingdom "in the belly of Dàn". He links earth and
sky, holding the Gbέ together. Gŭ, "the strength of his parents" Măwu
and Lisà, is the Vodún of untilled land, iron, and war, introduced by
Agongló following a war with the Mahí. Djo represents "the invisibility
of the Vodún",[43] with overtones of the Hebrew *ruah*, "the breath that
envelops the universe". Gbădù is said to be the most esoteric of the
cults, who "possesses all the Fá" and is symbolised by the calabashes
containing mysterious objects.[44]

Aguessy has categorised six of these Vodún as the highest in the
pantheon, charged with the direction of the universe: Xεbyoso, Sakpatá,
Agbè, Agε, Gŭ, Djo. But he makes it clear that there are several variants in the names, and in the hierarchical order in different cultural
groups within Danxomε, which take into account local socio-political
considerations.[45] An illustration of this might be the case of Gŭ who
becomes dominant where there are smiths or in states of social strife, or
Agé where there are hunters, thus changing the order. It is also evident
that this hierarchy of high Vodún does not exhaust the pantheon, and
that below it there is an almost infinite number of lesser clan Vodún,
personal Vodún for every Danxomεnù, lapsed Vodún and imported cults
readily adopted and adapted in Danxomε, and indeed modern Benin.
Atigali, a witch-hunting cult, for example, was imported from Ghana
and has become widespread amongst the Ajă and the Dassa. Even more
widely known is the cult of the sea goddess Mamiwátá.[46] The latter is
a particularly interesting example of the kind of religious assimilation
and improvisation that has been a feature of Danxomε. A new image
of Mamiwátá based on a German print of an exotic female snake
charmer became popular at the end of the nineteenth century. Around
1955, large numbers of this print were reprinted in India for distribution
in Africa. These were very popular and resulted in some elements of
Hinduism being incorporated in Mamiwátá rituals. Densu—Mamiwátá's
male counterpart—also finds his origin in a popular Hindu print and
has become part of a cult on the coast. The presence of many Indian
traders, their success in business, and the belief that Indians possess

---

[43] Aguessy, *Divinité*, 92.
[44] Maupoil, *Géomancie* 84–85. Segurola and Rassinoux, *Dictionnaire* (202) note that
Gbadu is a sign of the Fá whose possessor is greatly feared because of the misfortune
he can bring.
[45] Aguessy, *Divinité*, 92.
[46] *Mamiwátá* a local water goddess worshipped by the Ibibio, Ijaw, and Igbo speaking
peoples of south-eastern Nigeria. It was rendered to me as *mammyaita*.

occult powers, as well as the previous existence of a water goddess cult, perhaps from Brazil or Haiti, caused the popularity of Mamiwátá to flourish.

> Nowadays a highly complex cult has developed around Mamiwátá, with rituals and dances in which elements from Christianity, Hinduism, Buddhism and even astrology can be found. Mamiwátá is associated with wealth and beauty...Mamiwátá embodies the link between both cosmic worlds.[47]

This is hardly surprising since Danxomɛ has always welcomed new cults. There is an "extraordinary multiplication" of the Vodún and at the same time of shrines and cults. This is marked by "a complex fluidity where the different forces of the universe are distributed amongst the divinities",[48] creating an extraordinarily complex pantheon of specialised deities, full of variants, determined largely by the socio-political needs of Danxomɛ itself. Aguessy notes that the number of Vodún on earth and in the skies "will never exhaust the catalogue of real or possible Vodún". In fact, there will be as many Vodún as there are people, and this dependence of the Vodún on its human reception is well expressed in the Fòn proverbs, with which Durkheim would hardly disagree:

> For the Vodún to exist it must be welcomed. It is man who creates the sacred.[49]

In my own fieldwork it became clear that Vodún was the lattice upon which the fragile Danxomɛ society and the state itself were constructed. There is a continuous proliferation of the divine in a society that is marked at every crossroads by a Vodún. This is made all the more intense by the density of population in the southern part of the country as compared to the north. According to a 1986 report, there were 213 inhabitants per square kilometre in the Atlantique Prefecture, falling off, as one moves northwards to the open savannah, to only 9.6 inhabitants per square kilometre in the Borgou.[50] Since the number of Vodún is in direct relation to the population, it is not difficult to see that this creates

---

[47] Ineke Eisenburger (ed.), *Geest en Kracht: Vodun uit West Africa*, Bergen Dal: Afrika Museum 1996, 139.

[48] Aguessy, *Divinité*, 90.

[49] In Maximin Massi, "Le Vodun et le pouvoir monarchique dans l'ancien royaume du Danxomé", *La Voix de St Gall*, 64, 1993, 23–34, 25.

[50] See Institut National de la Statistique et de l'Analyse Ecomonique, *Seminaire National de Dissemination des resultats des enquetes nationales demographiques au Bénin entre 1979–1983*, Cotonou, 1986.

an intensely religious landscape and a rapidly expanding religious demography. In the course of my research, it became very clear to me that this, and the social disruption and inevitable pressures and tensions of urban dwelling in the developing world, acted in large part as an explanation both for the great expansion of Churches and the roadside signs indicating their presence. Put simply, this was a space to be filled either by the Vodún, the Muslim or the Christian God, and all were staking their claim to the land as shrines, temples, mosques, chapels, churches, healers and miracle workers in all shapes and forms offering solutions to all kinds of problems were planted throughout the country.[51] As an illustration of this, I did a simple survey of the 28km stretch of road between the Godomey Circle and the entrance to Ouidah, on the main artery from Cotonou to the Togolese border. This revealed twenty-four *Celestial Church of Christ* communities, a ratio of 0.85 communities per kilometre. When the sample was reduced to just the first 10km, in the very densely populated suburbs of the city, this rose to 1.8 churches per kilometre. This sample was for the CCC alone, which claims to have 1,000 such churches throughout Benin.[52] The sample could be repeated elsewhere with largely similar results. Another example would be the northern road from Parakou, to Djougou. This is a rural stretch of some 100km, with over thirty Christian chapels and churches of various denominations strategically placed and dominating some twenty villages in the first 50km. They are largely replaced by mosques on the second leg of the journey, reflecting intense efforts and often competitive responses by all religious groups. This is repeated and intensified with increased urbanisation throughout the country but is more obvious in the densely populated south.

Lɛgbà—the Vodún of the Age of Confusion

It is the thought that is in the depths of the belly of every man that is Lɛgbà.[53]

[51] See Guillaume Badufle, *Dynamiques religieuses et urbanisation dans les campagnes de l'entre-deux villes Cotonou/Porot-Novo, Sud-Bénin (L'axe Djeregbé-Porto-Novo)* Mémoire de maîtrise de géographie, Université de Caen, 1999.
[52] Interview, Porto-Novo, 20 July 2002.
[53] Aguessy, *Essai*, 318.

Despite the fluidity and the complexity of the pantheon described so far, the above deities represent a certain structure and stability. They are predictable and follow only the orders of those to whom they are allied and in whose interests they act. They have their responsibilities, each having her/his domain in the management of the Gbɛ and they are both stable and reliable. However, one essential element is missing from this pantheon, which represents in many ways just the opposite. Adoukonou states that, within this architectonic pantheon, there is also a "movement that is unpredictable, that cannot be assigned to one place, a figure of human liberty, of desire, of the continuous desire in human to go beyond".[54] Lɛgbà is the trickster Vodún and the youngest of the offspring of Mǎwu-Lisà, *le puiné*,[55] credited with provoking "accidents, public and private calamities, quarrels, dissension and misunderstandings".[56] "Every aspect of Lɛgbà is an anger. And the great Lɛgbà is the anger of God."[57] He is the hidden companion of all of us, pushing us to be unreasonable, capricious and unpredictable. One old Bokonù describes his character saying: "Lɛgbà is a being that while doing evil veils it in good, and while doing good veils it in evil."[58] He is a Vodún without a fixed domain, described by another Bokonù as "the great pauper" but omnipresent.[59] Aguessy states that he is "the Vodún who has had nothing shared with him, or rather who received as his share nothingness".[60] By virtue of this fact, however, he is the Vodún that is free to roam and to play "the delicate and dramatic role of intermediary between the different Vodún, between the Vodún and humans, and between humans". He is "mediator of the gods, the dynamic principle of life and unrequited desire".[61] He is the messenger of the Vodún, the guardian of temples, houses and towns. He is the anger of other Vodún and other people, with a character that is mischievous, sensitive, violent, irascible, clever, vulgar, vain, and indecent.[62] He is the Vodún of alterity.[63] It can be said that he is part of the pantheon of Mǎwu-Lisà

---

[54] Adoukonou, *Nouvelle Sortie*, 149.
[55] Aguessy, *Divinité*, 93.
[56] Verger, *Notes*, 109.
[57] Maupoil, *Géomancie*, 83.
[58] Aguessy, *Corpus*, 117.
[59] "Le grand indigent" in Aguessy, *Corpus*, 203; 267.
[60] Original text: "qui n'eut rien en partage ou, plutôt reçut en partage (le) 'rien.'"
[61] Aguessy, *Essai*, 5; Joseph Ki-Zerbo, *L'Histoire de l'Afrique*, Paris, 1972, in Adoukonou, *Jalons*, 58.
[62] Verger, *Notes*, 109.
[63] Adoukonou, *Nouvelle Sortie*, 151.

precisely to contest its structural stability. To use a popular Béninois expression, he is a *pagailleur* (someone who is slightly anarchic, likes confusion but with a certain good humour). It is no doubt for this reason that Aguessy claims he is the most popular of the Vodún, inspiring amongst the Danxomɛnù "not fear but affection", because, in the end, he is the closest to themselves.[64] He is the most human, "neither completely good, nor completely bad; he works for good as well as evil, the faithful messenger of those who send him and make him offerings",[65] even standing up for humans in their debates with Vodún but still maintaining "the control and the mastery of the channels of communication in the divine world".[66]

It may well be for this reason that Lɛgbà was literally demonised by the Christian missionaries throughout the whole area,[67] and remains one of the more controversial Vodún down to the present. He was stigmatised by the missionaries as "wicked, perverse, abject, hatred, and opposition to the goodness, the purity, the elevation and the love of God".[68] It has been suggested that in Haiti he was replaced in popular devotion by St. Anthony the Hermit[69] or perhaps St Michael the Archangel. I would contend that the St Anthony here is more likely to have been the Portuguese St Anthony of Padua (1195–1231), whose reputation amongst traditional Catholics for finding lost objects, and perhaps even losing them in the first place, certainly suggests the trickster. This saint has reappeared in popular Catholic iconography in Benin, quite possible through Brazilian influence.

One Lɛgbànù notes that all the ills of the world are ascribed to Lɛgbà, "even those for which he is not responsible".[70] He is the reality of everyday life with its vicissitudes, its growing uncertainties and frustrations, and its harshness. He continues to be invoked and, indeed, as I shall suggest further on, he might well be called the Vodún of the present Age of Confusion.

---

[64] Aguessy, *Divinité*, 94.
[65] Verger, *Notes*, 109.
[66] See Aguessy, *Divinité*, 93.
[67] See Maupoil, *Géomancie*, 75. See also Peel, *Encounter*, 260, 263–64, 303, 366.
[68] Verger, *Notes*, 109.
[69] Maupoil, *Géomancie*, 59. The cult of St. Anthony of Padua is very developed in Catholic parishes in southern Ghana, with the adherents meeting at 4am each Tuesday (Fr Michael Egan, personal communication).
[70] Aguessy, *Corpus*, t. II, 267.

Fá—Visions and Dreams

> Whoever is seeking the truth, let him go to see Fá. He is called Fá, the only principal that can reveal the truth of the great Sɛ.[71]

At the centre of Vodún, one finds Fá, a divination cult, practised throughout the *oikoumene*. It was introduced in Danxomɛ during the reign of Gezò. Maupoil proposes an Arabic etymology,[72] coming via Nigeria, while Peel confirms its distant origins in Arab divination and sand-writing.[73] Is Fá a Vodún? The diviners themselves, in the language that frustrates the researcher, affirm simply that *"Fá est comme un Vodún"*. He resembles a Vodún to the extent that he is unknowable, but there are many characteristics he does not share with the Vodún: he does not take possession of his followers, cause them to go into trance, or frighten them.[74] For Verger, Ifa is *"le porte- parole d'Orunmila"*, and the other Orisha,[75] while Aguessy states that he is *"la parole du créateur"*.[76] In Adoukonou's Christological hermeneutic, he is the *xojoxo*, literally "the word that begets the word".[77] This in some way resembles the Johanine *Logos-Theos* (John 1: 1) which takes the Old Testament view of the Word or Wisdom of God as having been present with God before the world existed and revealed God to the world. John sees this Word-Wisdom in the powers of Jesus.

What is clear is that Fá, because of the special relationship to Mӑwu and to the other Vodún, plays a central role in the organisation and running of the Gbɛ. Fá is "the linchpin of the religious system".[78] It could be said that Lɛgbà is the *alter*-Fá. Fá represents reliability, even rigidity,[79] in the face of Lɛgbà's caprice. It is Fá who helps the Danxomɛnù in coming to terms with her/his Sɛ. The proverb cited above indicates the personal nature of Fá, encouraging the person who consults the oracle to first of all consult her own conscience. Fá is the oracle that accompanies the person on all the stages of her life: prenatal Fá of pregnancy (*Adogbo-Fá*), childhood (*Fá alo dokpo*), adolescence (*Fá*

---

[71] From the Fon original in Adoukonou, *Violence sacré*, 443.
[72] Maupoil, *Géomancie*, 5, footnote 1.
[73] Peel, *Encounter*, 115.
[74] Maupoil, *Géomancie* 10.
[75] Verger, *Notes*, 568.
[76] Aguessy, *Divinité*, 80–90.
[77] Adoukonou, *Jalons*, 290.
[78] Peel, *Encounter*, 115.
[79] Aguessy, *Divinité*, 80–90.

alowe), and into adulthood (*Fá yiyi*), when the person receives her personal Fá.[80] This process continues up to death when the word of life is fulfilled, *Xó ó fó*, the person's Sέ is realised, "Fá is destroyed and...Lεgbà broken".[81]

The professional of Fá, the diviner, is known as the Bokonù. Unlike the other cults, where the Vodúnnò are often female, the Bokonù is almost always male. He is sometimes called the Gbέwedoto, or the one who transmits the message of life. In Maupoil's view, this illustrates how the Bokonù place themselves in the politico-religious hierarchy, seeing themselves as "comparable to the priests of the highest god". His role is clearly at the centre of society and state. A senior Bokonù states that his function is to be "the father of all that lives on earth, of kings and their subjects, of parents and their children". His calling is a vocation in the religious sense, and dependent upon his moral and spiritual qualities, since he must neither kill, steal or commit adultery, and "he must act as a father, and therefore as a benefactor".[82]

As we have seen above, the Danxomεnù has an extremely difficult world to negotiate. It is both rigid and at the same time unpredictable, a world marked by existential *angst*, and it cannot be negotiated alone. The public role of the Bokonù is to be available to people who suffer in this situation. "Using the oracle, he must tell the whole truth to those whole consult him, pray for them and lead to the sacred forest those for whom the moment has come to receive a revelation of their Fá, and make the necessary sacrifices. He is the interpreter and the intermediary of Fá, who is the word of the creator. Without him the transmission of the will of Mãwu cannot happen. He is the one through whom Vodúnnò themselves ask for the healing of physical or moral ailments. He heals both body and soul". His respect in society is based on his role as diviner, sacrificial priest, the one who delivers prescriptions for medicines and charms; he is a doctor and quite often a pharmacist.[83] In terms of the religious hierarchy, he is the key figure and I suggest that he provides the model for many of the preachers who are emerging in *le Christianisme béninois*, many of whom, as we shall see, also have their origins in the same *oikumene*.

---

[80] Maupoil gives a slightly different definition and names to the stages: childhood (*Fa-kűñ-we*), adolesence (*Fa-si-se*), adulthood (*Fa-ti-te*), 271–332.

[81] Adoukonou, *Jalons*, 291.

[82] Maupoil, *Géomancie*, 113–116.

[83] Ibid.

We can look for interpretations on two levels: that of the anthro-pologist, and then on a more intimate, existential level, that of the Danxomɛnù themselves. In the first sense, this appears to be a confirma-tion of Durkheim when he declares that "religion is first and foremost a system of ideas by means of which individuals imagine the society of which they are members and the obscure yet intimate relations they have with it".[84] Aguessy writes of Fá: "It takes into account the per-manent need for man to mark out places in the order of things and in society."[85] Horton's view of African religion as essentially a question of explanation, prediction and control also springs to mind.[86]

For Peel the essence of Fá in nineteenth century Yorubaland was that it was, in Horton's sense, "a cult of control". It is, he states, "funda-mentally concerned with reconciling the far and the near; not merely heaven and earth, but also sacred presence and the messy actuality of the Age of Confusion in which outsiders and their religions were a growing presence".[87] The present age in West Africa hardly seems less confused than the nineteenth century, and Fá, as well as other deities—and often several together, certainly continues to be invoked in an effort to make sense out of it. As with all peoples, the Béninois perspective on the world is multi-faceted: they look out on the wider world but also back into a world that is closer to home. Adoukonou speaks of the fascination of people coming from "an esoteric, arcane, and initiate dominated Africa... for the purest products of transparent (exoteric) critical reason: science and technology".[88] They live in the present, with an eye to the future, but also to the past and to their own history. One of the most interesting observations of my fieldwork was to note the rapid expansion in the number of internet cafés and their use by Béninois youth. Computer screens, as well as cable TV, are becoming a new eye on the world and all it has to offer, stretching its frontiers and creating aspirations, even if much of it remains inacces-sible to the average Béninois. However, the closer one gets to home, the grimmer things become, inevitably creating tensions. A growth rate of about 5% may seem impressive but is less so when one considers

---

[84] Emile Durkheim, *The Elementary Forms of Religious Life*, New York: Free Press, 1995, 227.
[85] Aguessy, *Divinité*, 90.
[86] See Robin Horton, "African Conversion", *Africa*, 4, 1971, 85–108.
[87] Peel, *Encounter*, 115.
[88] Adoukonou, *Nouvelle Sortie*, 145.

the tiny base it builds upon, leaving Benin one of the fifteen poorest countries in the world.[89]

In between those two worlds there is an enormous area of tension, uncertainty and confusion, as well as frustrated aspirations to a certain kind of materialistic modernity of consumption. This is particularly the case for already alienated urban youth, or rural youth fleeing to urban centres. A college student in the course of my research described his generation as "cursed"; and his life as "blocked" by the occult forces of his tradition.[90] Rational means had failed to liberate him, or had not been tried, so this leaves the almost inevitable recourse to the imaginary "*les techniques du sacré*"[91] and a charismatic pastor who prayed over him. This narrative could be repeated a 1,000 times and the recourse to the invisible is perhaps the most striking characteristic of Béninois society today. The theologian Kä Mana, in an interview, takes it even further, however:

> Yes... it is a recourse to the invisible, but in the most terrible way because this mentality is inserted into the most visible relationships... The IMF has become a kind of invisible also, from which we are expecting miraculous answers... [But without] mobilising the citizens on their real capacity for inventiveness and the possibility of reorganising society for progress.[92]

International financial institutions may seem like capricious and unpredictable forces, eluding the power of the Vodún and the interventions of Fá, but they affect the Sé of every Béninois.

A second important observation was that of the great increase in the number of refugees[93] present in Benin's already crowded and little-structured capital, Cotonou. The evidence of this is clear all over Cotonou, particularly in the *buvettes*, the small beer bars, but also in many of the Churches, where refugees often make up a significant percentage of the congregations. Many of these, especially the men, often with amputated limbs, bear gruesome testimony to the horrors they have fled to seek refuge in a country that is ill equipped to succour them.

---

[89] "Le Bénin classé 158ème pays selon le rapport IDH 2002 du PNUD", *Le Républicain*, 406, 20 July 2002.

[90] Interview, 9 September 2002.

[91] Coquery-Vidrovitch, *Afrique Noire*, 237.

[92] Interview at the CEROS Institute, Porto Novo, 13 June 2002.

[93] Officially 4,600 mainly from the Great Lakes region, Togo and Nigeria (UNHCR Mid-Year Progress Report 2001). A report from the UN, dated 5 July 2005, puts the number of Togolese refugees alone at 34,000; following recent events in Togo, it is almost certainly much more, (http://www.un.org/apps/news/story.asp?NewsID=14407 &Cr=togo&Cr1=).

As we have seen in the previous chapter, Benin has a long and pain-ful history. As in all states, it is the past and its remembrance that give shape to the present in both the positive and the negative sense. These grim reminders of the realities in other parts of Africa, not always dis-tant, certainly touch Béninois deeply. They are aware of the inherent fragility of their own state and society, and the historical sparks that can be fanned to violence by contrary socio-political winds. Could it be said that in our time DanxomƐ, like much of Africa, has become LƐgbàxomƐ, the dominion of uncertainty and impending chaos? Which-ever way one looks, it appears that LƐgbà is ever present: he could be called the Vodún of the Age of Confusion, but certainly also of the Age of Globalisation and an Africa in ever-deepening crisis.

Although Fá continues to exist only in what Maupoil considered a decadent form, for most Beninois, of whatever social status, it is unthinkable that any decision could be taken without consulting the oracle. Like a good Bokonù, Maupoil seems prescient when he writes:

> Fá survives beyond itself. The conquest precipitated its fate, and, when the last Bokonù will have passed away, who will be able to recall ancient times and put a brake on the impudence of the youth, it will no doubt go through some other strange metamorphosis.[94]

There have indeed been strange metamorphoses. Fr. Paul-Henri Dupuis, who spent his retirement in a small southern village studying Vodún cults says that authentic Fá is now practised in only a very small number of remote villages.[95] It appears to me, however, that, as Maupoil pre-dicted, the Bokonù, Vodún, and Fá, as well as other aspects of traditional religion, provide the inspiration for much that has developed across the range of Christian Churches we shall be looking at in the second part of this work.[96] In fact, SƐ remains the major preoccupation, and many of these Churches have developed a discourse of *destiny*, preached by the new Bokonù, the *powerful men of God*, to meet it.

We must move on to another level, however: that of the modern Béninois and the existential meaning of Fá for the people who live with it. "*Je voudrai être rationaliste*," Paulin Hountondji apparently tells

---

[94] Maupoil, *Géomancie*, xi.
[95] Interview, 8 May 2002.
[96] See Ludovic Kosse Akiloulou, *Le Syncretisme Religieux: Le cas du Christianisme Céleste comme contribution à l'étude de la philosophie religieuse*, Memoire de maî-trise, UNB, 1994.

his students, but the conditional tense is clear. Fá, and the logic that underlies it, remain a reality: in the life of most Béninois. Hountondji in his person somehow illustrates the reality: deeply African, an eminent philosopher, a respected teacher, former revolutionary apologist,[97] democratic activist, government minister and still vice-president of the Methodist Church (Synod), sometimes affectionately known as "the Methodist pope", he attempts to juggle all of these realities. He also casts his eye speculatively to the tradition in a search for endogenous answers to Béninois questions.[98]

For Congolese Lutheran theologian Kä Mana, the real function of African theology "is to know whether Christ is for Africa an opportunity or a risk". He affirms that he is a wonderful opportunity but also emphasises the need for Africa to question Christ, or even "to recreate Christ, and for Christ to recreate Africa".[99] The investigation of the meaning and implications of Fá, then, or the questions raised by people like Hountondji or Aguessy, far from being an arcane debate between scholars, is a live debate in Benin. This was illustrated by a series of articles in the national newspaper *La Nation* in 2001, with the participants debating whether Jesus Christ had been initiated in Fá or whether he was above him.[100] There is an ongoing debate with the tradition, a need to go forward but not to abandon the past, and it is in this debate, particularly on the occult, that one comes closest to the religious spirit of the Fòn themselves.

It appears to me that Adoukonou goes very close to the centre of the spirit of the Fòn when he claims that central to the Fòn experience of life and religion is the need to build his power, *accroître sa puissance*. He writes: "The Fòn experience [...] is centred on the increase of power through listening to the *xójòxó*, a listening that makes us grow and allows us to grow".[101] The sense of life itself, Gbέ, is the increase of vital power, the development of the Sέ. Adoukonou says that the

---

[97] See Paulin J. Hountondji, *Libertés: contribution a la Revolution Dahomeenne*, Cotonou, 1973.

[98] Hountondji, *Les savoirs*.

[99] Kä Mana, *Théologie africaine*, 39.

[100] Moïse Adekambi "Le Christ Jésus, unitié du Fà? Quelle question!!!" *La Nation*, 2669, 31 January 2001; Dotou J. Segla, "Le Christ Jésus au delà du Fà", *La Nation* 31, 2678, 2679, 14–15 Feburary 2001. Also Brice C. Ouinsou, "Quel visage donnez-vous au Fils de Dieu?", *La Nation* 2 691, 10 March 2001.

[101] Adoukonou, *Jalons* 291. *Xójòxó*: "the word that is really word, an important word" (Segurola and Rassinoux, *Dictionnaire*, 511).

Danxomɛnù sees "the truth of being" not as "clarity" and "light" but rather as "the power of fecundity". The Fòn experience of God is the experience of "a fecund God" and a God that is infinitely generous.

> For the Fòn to be a creature is to be engendered, to have an origin, an anteriority. All of life is a process of engendering, of birth which underlines the diverse initiations to Fá...[102]

Here, he suggests, is something fundamental to the whole Fòn philosophy, the concepts of power and fecundity. As evidence, far removed from Adoukonou's complex reflections on his culture and back to *le trottoir*, one can simply examine the Guinness advertising hoarding on the streets of Cotonou: *Guinness...et la Puissance est en vous* reads the text beside the profile of a very virile and *puissant* man. It is a theme that reoccurs frequently in the discourse of the Béninois and nowhere more than in their Churches, as we shall see in Chapter 6, as life itself is a battle for *Hlònhlón* (potency), and *kúngbígbá* (fecundity).

Having achieved this, the desire is above all to *prosper*, another key term of many Churches, as we shall see. Here again we have recourse to the semantic content of certain important and popular concepts in the languages, in this case those of *Gbédudu*, an expression that is common in the south, and *Alǎfíà* which is more widely used right across West Africa. *Gbédudu* in the literal sense means 'to eat life' in the same way as one 'eats a market' or 'eats Christmas'. It is to enjoy life to the full, *to prosper*. *Gbédudu* expresses the plenitude of life, a holistic idea of well-being and prosperity, and it is something to which every Béninois aspires, as this interlocutor, a bank manager, expressed it:

> Prosperity is an ensemble...from the life that God gives you, to health...it is not necessarily money...the well-being of your family, the people around you, and the rayonnement you create for the people round you. It's all of that. If you see a person you will know whether he is prosperous or miserable...[103]

In this he ties fecundity and prosperity together in mentioning its essential elements: *life, material wealth in money, the family* and the projection of this (*le rayonnement*) into society. It is, in fact, a very clear definition of all that gives substance and meaning to Gbé.

---

[102] Adoukonou, *Jalons*, 291.
[103] Interview, 13 June 2002.

Alăfìà, probably a morphological derivation of *Lafia* (Haoussa), takes us out of historical Danxomɛ, but it is more commonly used both in Benin and elsewhere. It is generally used in two ways: most commonly as the reply to a greeting, indicating a satisfactory state of health. It also has the wider sense indicating a lessening of difficulties, the end of suffering, well-being, satisfaction, everything that works well and progresses. It was in this way that the first inhabitants of new villages often used it to name their new home as, for instance, in many villages called Alafìàrou. These were to be places of peace, prosperity and happiness, but also hinted at a past from which the inhabitants had fled that was less peaceful, prosperous and happy.[104]

It may be tempting to see all of this in terms of arcane semiotics. However, the terms remain in current use and can be said to reflect the aspirations of all Béninois. In my own earlier research on language in northern Togo and in northern Benin, the word occurred very often in Churches and always in the way described above. In *Lokpa* the expression *Alăfìà* was usually explicated by synonyms such as *laŋhɛɛsɔlɛ* (repose of the heart), *laŋhʊlʊmlɛ* (whiteness of the heart, as opposed to redness of the heart, signifying anger), *lʊtʊ kʊlʊmtʊ* (one belly) signifying social harmony, and extended to *ta, na ta piya, ta icatɛ na yılaa tɔna* (to us, our children, our village and all people). It was certainly the most common aspiration in prayer in any of the communities I visited. However, these aspirations were not just on a personal level but also in terms of public policy. A government policy document in 2000, attempting to set out long-term socio-economic planning up to 2025, stated clearly that the deepest aspirations of Béninois were "social, individual and collective well-being". This is then defined precisely as *Alăfìà*, "health, peace and prosperity", as opposed to another Hausa term *Wahala*, meaning suffering, struggle, and a more general wretchedness, which it accepts may seem more realistic.[105] The personal aspirations of the Béninois are usually not separated from those of the society in which he lives. However, as we shall see, many of the newer Churches do, in fact, tend towards a strong emphasis on individual success and on the rejection of the family as

---

[104] Source Documents of the CTP/NLTPS, recherche socio-anthropologique sur *Alafia*, Parakou Mai in Ministère d'Etat Chargé de la Coordination de l'Action Gouvernamentale/PNUD *Bénin 2025: Alafia: Etudes Nationales de Perspectives à long terme*, Cotonou: 2000.
[105] Ibid., 101–104.

an obstacle and even an enemy. This in itself is a significant element of social change, whatever one thinks of it.

Vodún and the monarchy

Thus far we have looked at Vodún as it applies to the lives of individuals in their search for meaning and security. However, Vodún was, perhaps above all, a state religion, intimately linked to, even "convergent with"[106] the whole structure of the monarchy and the state. The basis of the religion was the cult of the kings themselves, who, as they moved further from the world they had lived in, became themselves Vodún. Law, who is critical of Akinjogbin's secular interpretation, places religion at the centre of Danxomɛnù political ideology. He notes that "in Dahomey, as in pre-colonial Africa more generally, it was primarily through manipulation and control of religious institutions and beliefs that the state sought legitimacy."[107] There was always a question about the legitimacy of Danxomɛnù monarchy, and it struggled to rid itself of its image of being "Royal Usurpers".[108] While it succeeded in imposing itself militarily and in terms of political organisation upon the peoples it conquered, it also required ideological legitimacy, and this was found in the cult of the ancestors. Law points out that the cult of the ancestor kings, marked by the latterly notorious Grand Customs, provided this.

> [The] institution of the Annual Customs would obviously have made sense as an attempt to buttress Agaja's disputable legitimacy, by advertising his devotion to the cult of his predecessors. Alternatively, however, the institution of the Annual Customs would make equal sense in the 1730s, as a response to the crisis of royal authority which followed the conquest of the coastal area.[109]

M.A. Glélé affirms that "it is the cult of the kings that binds the community, making of it a nation living in union for and by the king".[110]

---

[106] Aguessy, *Du mode*, 214ff.

[107] See Law, *My head*, also, Fugelstad, *Quelques réflexions*.

[108] Robin Law, "History and legitimacy: aspects of the use of the past in pre-colonial Dahomey", *History in Africa*, XV, 1988: 439.

[109] Robin Law, "Ideologies of Royal Power: the dissolution and reconstruction of royal power on the slave coast", *Africa*, LVIII, iii, 1987, 326.

[110] Glélé, *Le Danxomé*, 169, my emphasis.

Although not himself a god, the king did have a sacral character and initially the royalty had a double politico-religious character emanating from the ancestors. In effect, the king carried their mystical force within his person.[111] "The socio-political order, by its transcendent character, brought one to recognise in the figure of the king an epiphany of the sacred", "an eminent figure of the sacred in front of whom all the Vodún were called to genuflect".[112] The king was the *summa potestas*,[113] the *Sémɛdó* (the master of the world), *ainó* (the eminent master of the earth), *dokunno* (the master and possessor of all riches), *jɛ xóxó* (the master of the pearls). He was even the Sɛ́—life and destiny itself.[114] After his death he would himself become an ancestor and eventually, in the course of time and as he receded from living memory, a Vodún. Under Huégbaja, the first strong ruler of the kingdom, however, a definite separation of powers, or at least of roles, took place.

Weber suggests that the obligations of religion pose some problems for martial classes and feudal lords,[115] and Agbɔ̆mɛ is an interesting illustration of this point. Glélé, based on his fieldwork amongst members of the royal family, suggests that Huégbaja accepted the separation of powers because the royal cult of Agasú[116] involved "imperatives of purity and righteousness which were incompatible with politics or 'the art of holding together a country and governing men".[117] With Machiavellian logic,[118] Glélé's informer tells him that politics is about "perjury, ruse, the will to dominate, war", adding: "You see, we cannot avoid being *louche*; the king cannot walk in a straight line, and do things in a righteous way".[119] It is difficult to know to what extent these remarks were genuine and to what extent Glélé was influenced by his reading

---

[111] Ibid., 65, 67.

[112] Adoukonou in Massi, *Le Vodun*, 29.

[113] The highest level of power in comparison, for instance, to the *plenam et sufficiatem potestatem* (full and sufficient power) accorded to the medièval "model parliament" of 1295 by Edward I. See John B. Morrall, *Political Thought in Medieval Times*, Toronto: UTP 1980, 63.

[114] See Glélé, *Le Danxomé*, 67.

[115] Max Weber, *The Sociology of Religion*, Boston: Beacon Press, 1991, 85–90.

[116] See Verger, *Notes*, 550 for a brief description of this *Vodún* who is central to the foundation myth of Danxomé.

[117] Glélé, *Le Danxomé*, 65.

[118] "The fact is that a man who wants to act virtuously in every way necessarily comes to grief among so many who are not virtuous. Therefore if a prince wants to maintain his rule he must be prepared not to be virtuous, and to make use of this or not according to need." Niccolo Machiavelli, *The Prince*, London: Penguin, 2003, 50.

[119] Glélé, *Le Danxomé*, 65.

of European political classics and his desire to interpret Dahomey in this light, but there are certainly echoes of Machiavelli here.

One of Adoukonou's informants confirmed that a king could not but be unjust and therefore he needed "the expiation of the high-priest of Agasừ called Daxo at Hwawe Gbennu". Adoukonou observes that DanxomƐ was built, in fact, on both "the betrayal of and fidelity to the sacred law of friendship between contractual partners for life and death".[120]

This is a very significant piece of ethnography, since it appears to me to go to the heart of DanxomƐ itself, underlining both the nature of the politics for which DanxomƐ still has a reputation, and the whole concept of power. It is worth looking at both in a little more detail. One of my interlocutors in the course of my research made the following remark on what he described as *la diplomatie aboméenne*, remarking on its ruthless subtlety, while noting that ironically the name Adou-konou is itself a commentary on this: "To translate it one would say *adʊ kò nǔ bo kuin kuin do xomƐ* which means: the teeth are laughing, but there is rancour in the belly." This interpretation was confirmed by several other sources and certainly forms part of the perception of AgbɔmƐ. This reputation for duplicity for *raison d'état* has continued to be central to the reputation of DanxomƐ and, as we shall see in the next chapter, is the reason it continues to experience difficulties in the modern state.

There is equally a specific concept of power, *gànhúnǔ*. In one of the rooms of the palaces at AgbɔmƐ, one finds it explicitly stated in the following proverb that is the essence of the political philosophy of kingdom: "*E dada Sέ vi do ahi o, e do no ni ho jè, hakin, je a, e doni lo gàhúnǔ wa*" (In sending his son to the market, the king does not ask him to bring back salt but the power of domination). An etymological analysis of the term *gànhúnǔ* is quite revealing. It can be constructed as follows: *gǎn* means chief, master, director, patron, superior power and potency from which, for example, we find the following example *dʊ gǎn nú mƐ* (literally, to eat a person's power signifying domination and vanquishing an opponent or enemy in a game or at war). This leads quite logically to *yɪ gǎn jǐ* (literally, to take on the power or ascend to the throne, to become chief or king).[121]

---

[120] Adoukonou, *Vodun sacré*, 558.
[121] Segurola and Rassinoux, *Dictionnaire* 178–179.

Many, though not all, Béninois are of the opinion that the Machia-vellian political ruse and a Hobbesian vision of *gànhúnŭ*, as a levia-than monarchic power, were at the heart of the political philosophy of Danxomε. This certainly appears in the motto of the kings. Gezò, under his totem, the buffalo, declares: "*The powerful buffalo traverses the country and nothing can stop him*", while Glεlέ declares, "*The lion claims to sow terror amongst his enemies from the moment he cuts his first teeth*", and Gbεhanzın boasts, "*I am a shark, I shall not abandon one inch of my kingdom*". There is certainly evidence that for somebody like Adoukonou, and other intellectuals, the philosophy of *gànhúnŭ* poses important questions about the nature of Danxomε itself. "I know Germany well", one intellectual stated, going even further in the polemic, "I studied there and Agbŏmε also sends me back to the idea of Hitler. I ask myself if there was not a strong resemblance, or even worse, between Agbŏmε and the Third Reich". Of course, histori-cally we are dealing with two very different things and this is tricky territory to tread upon. What is significant, however, is the discourse and how Agbŏmε itself has come to be perceived as an absolutist state, the revival of which is still very much feared.

The logic underlying the separation of the religious and the political is quite clearly illustrated. But all *gànhúnŭ*, secular and divine, ulti-mately comes back to the king, and religion was of great interest to the kingdom. The priests, however, continued to pose some problems. The kings did indeed need expiation for their sins but how did this affect their relationship to the priesthood? Weber again points out that warrior classes are little inclined towards concepts such as

> sin, salvation and religious humility [and indeed] they appeared reprehen-
> sible to their honour. To accept a religion that works with such conceptions
> and to genuflect before the prophet or priest would appear plebeian and
> dishonourable to any martial hero or noble person.[122]

Indeed, and, as we saw in the previous chapter, Danxomε was above all martial, and its heroes were no more inclined to bend the knee than others of their ilk. But like Henry II and other monarchs, they needed these "troublesome priests", for like their lowest subjects they also needed expiation as well as intercession to keep the gods on side.

---

[122] Weber, *Sociology*, 85.

Huégbaja (c. 1645–1685) delegated religious functions to the priests, but under the strict authority of the king and overseen by the Minister for Vodún cult, the Ajăxo. Maupoil describes the role of the diviners and the priests as follows:

> A role, sometimes mysterious, to the degree that the diviner, for the peril-ous honours of the court, knew how to tie, even subordinate, his religious strength to the temporal interests of the monarchy and the people. Always a delicate role of confidant and counsellor—at times protected, at times exposed by his functions and by the past as a counsellor who was listened to but always controlled.[123]

Aguessy describes it as "co-operation through subordination" of the religious to the political, without questions.[124] Henry would, no doubt, have admired this way of handling, if not quite ridding himself of, these "troublesome priests".[125]

Not alone did Danxomɛ develop an important royal cult; it also accu-mulated other deities and cults as part of the booty of its innumerable raids and wars. When the kings came from war, not only did they bring back booty and women, but also divinities. This was primarily a strategy for the integration of conquered peoples. The essential content of the *Tò* (kingdom), as Adoukonou explains it, was *acɛkpikpà* (to command, govern), and central to this was *acɛ* (power), which had its source in the Vodún.[126] After a period of vetting, the kings incorporated their new deities into the Vodún pantheon, putting them to work, so to speak, for the cause of Danxomɛ—expansion and domination. Having subjugated their deities, the people followed, eventually becoming Danxomɛnù. It was the kings of Agbŏmɛ who installed all of the Vodún that were to be found in the kingdom.[127] Adoukonou describes the edification of the kingdom in the following terms:

> The peaceable coexistence of the Ako under a law of hospitality—each Ako being tied to the invisible Creator by the Toxwiyo [common ancestor]—saw itself replaced by a law of constraint and violence. While some emigrated [...] Others were displaced from their Tò, with their belongings and their titular Vodún, with which the King of Abomey entered into the race to

---

[123] Maupoil, *Géomancie*, xii.
[124] Aguessy, *Du mode*, 214.
[125] See T.S. Eliot, *Murder in the Cathedral*, London: Faber, 1965.
[126] "Un ordonnancement, un ensemble de choses…un village, un pays" (Adoukonou, *Vodun sacrée*, 548).
[127] Maupoil, *Géomancie*, 65–66.

take his place in the royal city (Tò) and into the new political order whose ambition was not less than to acquire an international surface. This is how, little by little, Dahomey was built.

Those who did not submit made up the raw material of the "triangular commerce" so tragically renowned until there was a change in the international conscience which, under Gezò, brought about the replacement of the slave trade by the cultivation of palm oil.[128]

This was, of course, a high-risk strategy and required complete control. It was always possible that the followers of any of these Vodún would have visions and dreams that contested the authority of the monarchy and pose a threat to its existence. It was in order to counter this threat that the kings created a form of caesaro-papism, "subjecting the altars to the throne".[129] The whole system was based primarily on the royal cults, with the loyalty of the priests, assured through royal patronage. All the foreign Vodún, including Mǎwu-Lisà, were subject to the priests of Agasu and Zomadónu, both royal cults. It was through this creation of the subaltern as a channel to the superior Vodún that Danxomɛ created a state religion, an architectonic structure, which was an almost perfect replication of its own complex political institutions. There was a hierarchical structuring of the entire pantheon subordinated to Toxósú Zomadónu, in exactly the same way as the chiefs of the minor Tò, were subject to the Abomɛ-tò, thus creating Danxomɛ.

Vodún, on all levels, became a complex system of socio-political control, spreading to all corners of society, a great lattice upon which society and state were constructed and maintained. It held control over the lives of individual Danxomɛnù whose Sɛ́ was determined by Fá, and who was allied to an individual Vodún. There was a Lɛgbà at the entrance to every household and a Vodún at every crossroads, marking out Danxomɛ and dominating it. It went even further than this, however, in the formation of what can be considered to be a religious police, not in the sense of doctrinal surveillance, but in the form of quite overt socio-political control, leading Aguessy to speak of the installation in the kingdom of "a veritable system of mutual surveillance" with the active involvement of the religious institutions requiring almost total obedience and submission.[130] This took the form of particular cults,

[128] Adoukonou, *Vodun sacré*, 559.
[129] Maupoil, *Géomancie*, 65–66.
[130] Aguessy, *Du mode*, 196, 199, 206.

with very striking public manifestations performed by several societies charged with the organisation of the cult. The following are the most common: Egún,[131] Gɛlédɛ́ and Zàngbètó, (see Appendix 3b).

These public cults are now often broadcast on television. This is partly a cultural representation, showing "*les richesses culturelles du Bénin*", but it is by no means exclusively that. They are, in fact, every bit as mysterious as that of the cathode-ray tube or the Pentium chip that has allowed these images to be transmitted. This is, perhaps, the perfect illustration of the encounter between the arcane and the scientific observed by Adoukonou and noted earlier in this chapter.

In analysing the history of Danxomɛ and the nature of the kingdom, one is struck by the ambiguity and the moral complexity of the history. One reader of an earlier version of this text observed that in many ways Danxomɛ had been on the way to being a modern state in terms of Hobbes' understanding of the state as absolute:

> it appeareth plainly, to my understanding, both from reason, and Scripture, that the sovereign power, whether placed in one man, as in monarchy, or in one assembly of men, as in popular or aristocratic commonwealths, is as great, as possibly men can be imagined to make it. And though of so unlimited a power, men may fancy many evil consequences, yet the consequences of the want of it, which is perpetual war of every man against his neighbour are much worse.[132]

Speaking in very Hobbesian terms, Adoukonou says:

> The *Tò* (the kingdom) is a consensus between the Axovi (King-Princes) and the Anato (the plebs) which was stable enough to confront the outside world for two and a half centuries...[133]

The fear of the danger coming from the coast and the near anarchy it caused inland was enough to cement the polity, with a traumatised people surrendering to the king the legitimate monopoly of violence, allowing any doubts to be taken care of by strong state coercion both sacral and profane. Deftly using the intimate relationship between the monarchy and the "magician therapists", chiefs of the Vodún and Fá brotherhoods, a consensus was formed around the person of the king,

---

[131] See Peel, *Encounter*, 93 for an excellent interpretation of this cult.

[132] Thomas Hobbes, *Leviathan*, Oxford: OUP, 1996 (ed. E. Gaskin), section 107, 138.

[133] Adoukonou, *Vodun sacré*, 548.

holder of all power (*acɛkpikpà*). This was the tree upon which the spider wove its web.

Polanyi's description of Danxomɛ as an "archaic economy", it could be argued, was correct and the kingdom was attempting a kind of rationalisation in the management of its meagre resources, in what was admittedly a tragic trade in its own citizens,[134] through the creation of a successful state bureaucracy. Glélé, citing Montserrat Palau Marti, argues that "sacral royalty...was one of the fundamental forms of African power".[135] He states that effectively in Danxomɛ it gave rise to a legitimate nation-state, possessing and using *gànhúnŭ*, legitimate state violence, and backed up by a Machiavellian diplomacy of considerable skill. Danxomɛ succeeded in integrating many of the peoples it conquered and, as Glélé puts it in his title, moved from being a simple Ajă tribal power to being the Fòn nation-state. That this caused moral dilemmas, it could be argued, is simply part of the heartless and amoral course of history.

It is clear that Vodún was part of the overall apparatus of the state in Danxomɛ, which extended into all corners of society and was fully in the control of the monarchy. Adoukonou notes that in establishing this relationship with Vodún, the monarchy effectively "grafted its strategy of power onto an abyssal anthropological depth", thus making religion one of the most powerful tools of state power. However, this leaves several questions. Was Vodún simply a force for social integration, as religion often is in other societies, or did it go far beyond this, creating a state ruled by the "totalitarian occult"?[136] In his description of the power of the state, Adoukonou notes that while Danxomɛ had avoided the anarchy, which certainly threatened it in the early seventeenth century and later, this was done at a price. It was essentially that of imposing "*le totalitarisme occulte*" and unleashing an unlimited and unbridled *gànhúnŭ*, attacking the liberty of both the surrounding polities and people under its own authority. Its understanding of power really remains the moral question at the heart of Danxomɛ and, as we shall see in the next chapter, it refuses to go away.

Danxomɛ was, by any standards, an extraordinary polity. Peel has pointed out that in terms of Christianity it had the reputation of being

---

[134] See Honorat Aguessy, *Le Dan-Homê*, 1970, 50, 71–91.
[135] Glélé, *Le Danxomé*, 12.
[136] Adoukonou, *Nouvelle Sortie*, 150–151.

recalcitrant to the point of being almost impenetrable.[137] Missionary efforts until 1892 were little more than sallies, and whatever structural installations there were remained on the coast. Despite its proximity to Nigeria, where there had been remarkable success, Peel puts it at the extreme end of a spectrum starting from Buganda, where evangelisation by both Anglican and Roman Catholic missionaries had met with early success. He points out that this was guided largely by a kind of "cost/benefit analysis". Reactionary Danxomɛ saw little advantage in changing the system. Sadly, in so doing, it found itself opposed to unstoppable forces. Gbɛhanzın raised his hand bravely but, in the end, in vain. Adoukonou notes perhaps with a touch of sadness:

> Such a kingdom would not tolerate either dependence or equality. As the whole of its history demonstrates, Abomey was driven by a kind of will to reduce all rival powers, as well as an opinionated resistance to all domination...[138]

Both its *gànhúnŭ* and its diplomacy ultimately failed in the face of the enormous historical force of the colonial enterprise, the inherent fragility of its own political structure and internecine rivalry amongst the princes. Danxomɛ had a particularly tragic destiny in that, eventually, under these forces, it imploded. It is almost as if its strength was in the end its weakness: its institutional rigidity and the absolute nature of the monarchy seemed to make negotiation impossible; it did not bend, it broke. Following Dodds' military campaign, carried out with the encouragement of the Churches, Danxomɛ all but disappeared. In my own reflections on Danxomɛ, I have come to see it as having *imploded*, leaving a cultural, religious and socio-political quick sand upon which it has been extremely difficult to imagine a modern state and society. It has left little but painful and contested memories, the stuff of sterile polemics and social conflict.

The religious structure of Vodún, so intimately linked to the defunct monarchy, soon atrophied. As Maupoil points out, the priests deserted by the authority of the state were reduced to a kind of charlatanism, and the people faced with a spiritual and religious void. The colonial power brought its religion, and in a sense it was embraced, though for

---

[137] J.D.Y. Peel, "Conversion and tradition in two African societies: Ijebu and Buganda", *Past and Present* 77, 1977, 113.
[138] Adoukonou, *Vodun sacré*, 548.

a long time by a relatively small proportion of the population. It could not answer all the questions, however, and it was not long before the Béninois began to seek the answers himself, mixing the idioms and coming up with something new.

CHAPTER FOUR

A HISTORY UNASSUMED

> Que de sang dans ma mémoire! Dans ma mémoire sont des lagunes. Elles
> sont couvertes de têtes de morts. Elles ne sont pas couvertes de nénuphars.
> Dans ma mémoire sont des lagunes. Sur leurs rives ne sont pas étendus
> des pagnes de femmes. Ma mémoire est entourée de sang. Ma mémoire
> a sa ceinture de cadavres!
>
> Aimé Césaire, Cahier du retour au pays natal

Césaire's *Cahier*, has remained with me since I undertook this reflection
on Danxomɛ. It seems to me that Danxomɛ-Benin has been in some
way a negative paradigm for the African state. The country reflects
many of the difficulties of the African state in coming to terms with
itself. But, perhaps above all, as I shall try to show in this chapter,
haunted by memories, it has great difficulties in coming to terms with
its history. To paraphrase Naipaul, "the past [is] a cause of pain", and
this fractured history and the lack of shared cultural values means that
the modern state has had great difficulty in gaining the political texture that would allow it to make a legitimate claim on its own people.
In the latter part of this book I shall be claiming that the Christian
Churches are involved in a critique of both the history and culture of
Danxomɛ-Benin. They are attempting, with varying degrees of success, to invent another discourse, a discourse that, to use a favourite
charismatic expression, would be a *breakthrough* leading the country
to a new collective Sɛ́ or destiny.

A visit to the old Portuguese fort or the Palais Royaux creates
strong Césairesque impressions as Chatwin eloquently shows. There
is an overwhelming *tristesse* about both places, an atmosphere that
weighs as heavily as the oppressive southern climate. These are visits
of remembrance rather than any kind of celebration, and the memories
are everywhere. These have been added to and reinforced in the years
since 1992 with the erection of various monuments commemorating
the slave trade. But the impressions of the travel writer or the cultural
tourist are of little consequence in comparison with the memory of
people 'condemned to live together', to use a somewhat ambiguous
expression not uncommon in West African political discourse. This
memory seems to be a fragile basis upon which to imagine a nation.

As in all states, it is the past and its remembrance that gives shape
to both the present and the future in both the positive and the negative sense. Grim reminders of the realities in other parts of Africa, not
always distant, certainly touch the Béninois deeply. They are aware of
the inherent fragility of their own state and society, and the sparks of
dimmed memories that can be fanned to violence by contrary socio-
political winds—and closely contested elections. The significance and
the volatility of this history should be obvious, all the more so because
it has not been assumed. A Béninois colleague is close to the point
when he notes:

> Africa has no memory and the question of a faithful African memory is
> one that causes us problems. We do not know with any real precision, in
> a manner of speaking, where we come from. Everything rests on presup-
> positions, on elements that are only [...] hypotheses and myths...des
> on-dits...[1]

M.A. Glélé had indeed already raised this problem, stating that very few
if any of even the princes of Agbɔmɛ were in any position to provide
any precise and useful historical data on the kingdom. Their descriptions
were marked by "many extrapolations and much fantasy", noting that
the old men "speak little and reveal themselves only with difficulty".[2]
This is not facilitated by internecine rivalry in the manipulation of the
narratives and a resistance to any attempt to penetrate the secrets of
the closed calabash. The result is a history that is obscure, superficial
and unassumed.

Kä Mana is equally aware of the problem, identifying "a kind of
deep illness which prevents African peoples from engaging on the path
to real solidarities, responsible fraternity and the unity which is desired
and wanted by all as a path to shared happiness". The problem is not
so much economic or political, but rather ethical and spiritual, and he
defines it as the lack of "the interior strength necessary to conceive a
common project of life which imposes itself upon us as a necessity to
be together, to live together and to act together as a united historical
entity, decided to protect its unity".[3] History is at the centre of the
problem. Kä Mana seems to assume the "united historical entity" as a
fait accompli but the fact is that, in much of Africa, it has still to be

---

[1] Interview, 14 July 2002.
[2] Glélé, *Du Pouvoir*, 19–20.
[3] Kä Mana, *Nouvelle Evangélisation*, 107.

imagined. Writing of Haiti in terms reminiscent of Naipaul, Hurbon states:

> Every occasion is seized upon to sing the inevitable refrain about "les ancêtres tutélaires". One has the impression of placing oneself in the past such is the impossibility of acceding to a real memory, which would be bottomless, full of silence and from which a creative future would be thinkable. Perhaps in the Caribbean, the drunkenness of a full identity, but still badly known and violated, makes us seem heroic to our own eyes, as a result of having been and still being victims.[4]

One of the struggles in Bénin, especially since 1990, has been to come to terms with its history, in order to see if a *renaissance* is indeed possible, and if the state is to become nation and be imagined in another way. This must include the slave trade and the historical reality of Danxomε, since, for better or for worse, the kingdom is also part of the modern state and the collective memory. In Haiti, Hurbon notes:

> the deficit of critical historical research, a great proximity with the phenomenon [of the slave trade], a fresh memory, which one might say, leave it susceptible to despotism or, more exactly which makes despotism seem like the regime most congruent with the mentality of the people.[5]

It appears to me that this is what Benin has been attempting to do, however hesitantly. Since 1990, what was once a hushed, if often heated, argument has been brought into full view and there have been serious attempts to assume the memory and to move on to a more dynamic political culture. This project crystallised around the *Ouidah 92 Festival* and the UNESCO-sponsored *Slave Route Project*.[6] Opening the festival in 1993, President Nicéphore Soglo declared:

> No point is served by dissimulating our own responsibilities in the disasters that have struck the continent and continue to strike us. Our complicity in the slave trade is well established, our divisions absurd.

Following the impetus created by the various events in 1992 surrounding the five-hundredth anniversary of Columbus' discovery of America, including Ouidah 92, Barthélémy Adoukonou also reflects on Africa, and most particularly Danxomε-Benin in the light of its painful history. Adoukonou refers particularly to the "anthropological fragility" that he

---

[4] Hurbon, *Sociologie*, 100.
[5] Ibid., 268.
[6] UNESCO, "The Slave Route" Project (Resolution 27 C/3.13) 1993). See also "From Chains to Bonds: the Slave Trade Revisited", UNESCO Publishing, 1998.

sees at work "in the global political crisis that Africa is going through, and which is only the actualisation of a fragility which allowed us to send our own brothers into the transatlantic slave trade". Reconciliation with the European Other must proceed from a reconciliation with "*le Même devenu l'Autre noir américain*" and, as he emphasised in an early conversation, with the Béninois Other.[7] He goes further, however, to examine "the project of rationality at work in African cultures" themselves, the logic of which was interrupted by the transatlantic slave trade or by colonisation, "but which was the result of an endogenous choice, an internal process of selection and the oppression of possibilities".[8] He identifies three problems here which he sees as symptomatic of the overall situation. We shall come across these again in our study of the Churches: the infamous *nivellement par le bas*,[9] which sees any initiative for progress in Africa subverted by the society itself, by whatever means possible; the enduring attraction of "a culture of the arcane and the esoteric" and, finally, "that manipulation by fear which one observes in many African cultures". This anthropological fragility and the lack of technological progress that ensues from it represent "the locus of the African crisis of historical consciousness".[10]

"The task of the reconstruction of Africa requires that Africans be reconciled to their own history and their own culture."[11] The lack of historical consciousness means that Africa remains mired in its past and fails to rise above it. For Adoukonou, the theologian, the task of the Church is to help Africa to look at its history in order "to propose, in a manner adapted to each generation, responses to the eternal questions of humankind on the meaning of life, present and future, and on our reciprocal relations". For Africa, given contemporary realities, the question is all the more important. It is a question of "interpreting the signs of the times" and developing a historical hermeneutic which will allow for "a renewed rapport with the past because it has

---

[7] Conversation with Barthélemy Adoukonou, Parakou, May 1999.

[8] Barthélemy Adoukonou, "Vers une nouvelle conscience historique", in *Expérience Africaine*, 88.

[9] This attitude is perhaps best expressed in the Béninois expression that says "It is better that everything be spoiled for both of us than that it work out well for you alone".

[10] Adoukonou, "Nouvelle conscience", 89–90.

[11] Barthelemy Adoukonou, "Ethique de l'Endurance et 'Bouffe'" in *Sillon Noir*, 13, 11, 1998.

been legitimated by the truth and which does not lose from sight any stepping stone which will allow the articulation of the real".[12] First of all, however, let us examine the debate in Benin.

The ongoing polemic on the slave trade

The difficulties posed by a skewed collective memory of the slave trade is perhaps best illustrated by what came to be known as the "Eterino episode". On 21 April 2001 *The Guardian* newspaper carried a head-line story from Benin.[13] The story was the first of many accounts, over several months, detailing the traffic in children from Cotonou and other coastal ports to neighbouring countries aboard a Nigerian registered lugger, the *MV Eterino*. The girls were destined for work as domestic servants, the boys to work on cocoa plantations. It was estimated that as many as 200,000 children were involved in West and Central Africa, bought in villages of the poorest countries of the region, for as little as $10 and sold for as much as $340 each.[14]

The story broke at a particularly embarrassing moment for the Béninois authorities, in the lead-up to the UN Conference on Rac-ism (Durban, 2001). One of the most difficult themes of the confer-ence was to be that of reparations being claimed for the evils of the transatlantic slave trade. The trade was being spoken of in terms of a 'holocaust' and a 'crime against humanity', as several countries, and even more vehemently American black activists, pressed the case for reparations.[15] The claim that the trade was continuing was obviously deeply troubling. This made the pro-reparations case all the more dif-ficult, and was pointedly remarked upon by those opposed to paying indemnities of any kind.[16]

---

[12] Ibid., 90–91.

[13] James Astill, "The terrible truth about the ship of slaves", *The Guardian*, 21 April 2001; Olenka Frenkiel, "Children of the Eterino", *The Guardian*, 4 October 2001.

[14] See CLNS, "Docking of 'Child Slave ship' in Benin Deepens Mystery", Child Labour News Service New Delphi, 4 May 2001, *http://allafrica.com.stories/printable/200105040105.htm*.

[15] See Fabienne Pompey, "Durban: les descendants d'esclaves demandent réparation", *Le Monde*, 7 September 2001; Marcel Péju, "Un holocauste noir?" *J.A./L'Intelligent*, 2122, 11 September 2001, 58–60; Edgar Couao-Zotti, "La traite des Nègres est-il un crime contre l'humanité?", *La Nation*, 2754, 7 June 2001.

[16] Chris McGreal, "Racism conference rocked by new slave-trade reports", *The Guardian*, 11 September 2001. It should be noted that not all African governments were

Whatever the tragedy of child labour, the *Eterino* incident was, in fact, far removed from the transatlantic slave trade. It was, of course, a criminal trade in children from extended families in very poor circumstance, for paltry sums, but this was very different from what had happened for over two and a half centuries. What it served to do, however, was to once again bring into focus Danxomɛ's past in the most painful way, raising the spectre of the trade and the polemic surrounding it. Writing in *The Guardian*, one journalist noted that "the *MV Eterino* sailed as freely as any of the slave ships that once plundered the region of humans for the New World".[17] Government ministers were at pains to draw distinctions, as was the UN. Another *Guardian* journalist reported the following response to an inquiry to the UNICEF office in Cotonou:

> "The next journalist that calls it a 'slave ship', I'm hanging up." The UNICEF lady is exasperated. She should be pleased that a ship with hundreds of trafficked children was lost at sea off the coast of Africa had finally prompted world attention. But the journalists keep using the 's' word, which is taboo here in West Africa, and bound to cause problems.[18]

The story, of course, soon vanished from the headlines. There had been twenty-three children on board the ship, not hundreds. They were, of course, amongst the 200,000 who were part of this tragic trade, but other stories had moved to fill the space, and the Durban Conference had failed in any case.

'The occultation of the slavery' in Benin is similar to that in other African societies. Botte remarks that an historical discussion of slavery has been difficult for two reasons. First there is the fact that, historically, its abolition was the result almost exclusively of the struggle of European abolitionists, enforced by European military power, and later the colonial powers, and in this Africans cannot be said to have been the actors.[19] Béninois historian Alphonse Quenum, who provides several explanations for the demise of the trade, attributing it to a combination of exogenous political and socio-economic circumstances in Europe

---

in favour of direct reparations, with some, most notably Senegal and Nigeria but also Benin, opting for debt cancellation as a more suitable way forward.

[17] Chris McGreal, "Aboard the slave ship of despair", *The Guardian* 16 April 2001.

[18] Olenka Frenkiel, "Lost children", *The Guardian*, 25 October 2001.

[19] Stephen Smith, "Rencontre avec Roger Botte, anthropologue et chercheur au CNRS sur la question de l'esclavage", *Le Monde*, 30 August 2001. See also Roger Botte (ed.) "L'Ombre portée de l'esclavage", *Journal des Africanistes*, 70(1), 2001.

and the Americas, but not mentioning any real resistance within Africa itself, provides an interesting illustration of this.[20]

In addition to this first reason, Botte notes that "with the establishment of the colonised/coloniser relationship an analogy between the inequalities of slavery and political subjection was established." Clearly in the struggle for decolonisation and later in third-world ideology "the vision of colonialism as a metaphor for slavery excluded any attempt to study it seriously".[21] There is a malaise or repressed guilt covering the whole subject, which means discussion is more often suppressed and, unfortunately, references to it only emerge in polemical anger, which is hardly a useful form of historical consciousness. This has remained so until a more recent past, when some distance was established from the colonial period and there was a need for African societies to examine themselves. It is hardly coincidental that much of this started in 1990, some thirty years after independence for many of the countries involved, including Benin.

Elites close to Agbɔmɛ are anxious to keep both the subject of slavery and the whole history of Danxomɛ under wraps, particularly close to home, since it is what one intellectual described as "one of those rancours, seeking to explode, not without reason, and against which the people defend themselves with much attention". There is little taste for any investigation into the past for fear of "the movement that might be unleashed".[22] Another scholar explains it somewhat differently as "essentially a problem of memory", pointing out that each time there is a debate it almost always comes back to a contentious interpretation that may have little historical basis. It is, he adds, as if history began with the transatlantic trade. There is a "resentment which leads us quickly back to the problem of the slave trade [and] this blocks the whole perspective". Thus, this single question, often based on dubious historical data, becomes the "springboard" for any discussion of Danxomɛ-Benin and without it, he points out, any debate becomes "like a tree that has its roots between heaven and earth" and gets nowhere. He concludes rather sadly:

> So we need to create a new history. [But to do so] we have to start from the oldest facts and dates and it is only the slave trade that comes back

---

[20] Quenum, *Eglises chrétiennes*, 385–398.
[21] Smith, *Rencontre*.
[22] Private correspondence with a protected source; names withheld by author.

and when we begin to reflect we see, unfortunately, that we have to attach ourselves to this. [Even I] come back to it as a springboard...We can't manage to overcome ourselves; we come back to plunge ourselves into resentment in a larval form of vengeance. Of course it's a fault; the African has to learn to overcome it. If not, I start my history today and I go on. What I mean is that when history rests on facts that are too negative one has problems in 'taking off'. It is as if one wanted a plane to take off from a runway covered in mud. It's too heavy, the plane risks coming out of the sky and being broken in bits.[23]

In fact, Goudjo points out, in Benin the unwritten memory is in many ways much more stable in the negative sense than the written word. That which is written is written "once and for all" and it can be surpassed. That which is not written, however, "is maintained in the form of a myth which is recounted from father to son and in time either it is completely forgotten, or else is not forgotten at all" and remains as an insidious sub-text within the society, "a larval form of vengeance", determining its direction almost unknown to itself, and always threatening to explode into something even more virulent.

> The force of the oral recitation is to hammer in and to remind the people, through the mediation of the griot, of principles based on atrophied and sacralised facts, the non-respect of which would signify not just personal failure, but the disappearance of the lineage, even the homeland; in a word the ancestral origin and the cultural identity are threatened with death.[24]

This resembles the 'autism' Dailey detects in Haiti, connoting "the pathology of groups so enclosed in their own circle of self-righteous victimhood...that they can't listen, can't hear, can't learn from anybody outside themselves".[25]

These sources are intellectuals but they are articulating something that is a feature of more popular debates. The fact is that the issues raised in an ill-remembered, eighteeth-century history "continue to feature in historical discussion in Danxomɛ-Benin down to the present, so that current debates reproduce to a surprising degree contemporary polemics over the slave trade".[26]

---

[23] Goudjo, Interview, 14 July 2002.
[24] Goudjo, *La liberté*, 131.
[25] Dailey, *Haiti's Betrayal*.
[26] Robin Law, "Dahomey and the Slave Trade", 243.

Danxomɛ: The contemporary debate

The discussion is, of course, wider and it is a debate about the nature of Danxomɛ itself and its influence on the modern state. Amongst the historians, as we have seen, Danxomɛ has its defenders as well as its detractors. Adoukonou, Aguessy and Glélé, although quite different in their approaches, would now be seen as leading the struggle to reha-bilitate the old kingdom, as they seek in it the endogenous values upon which the modern Benin might be built. Balandier noted early on that "precolonial history and its heroes suggest symbols and themes suscep-tible to liberation emotions".[27] A brief passage from Glélé illustrates the point. Rejecting the idea of Danxomɛ as a slave state, he sees it more as a state preoccupied with its own power, but living in almost utopian "confidence" and "popular consensus" in which "a spiritual vision of the world and its laws and religious practices were the substratum of the regime and the essential factors of its survival".[28]

> The gànhúnù and the prosperity of the kingdom were the true motive and strength of the politics of Danxomɛ, a policy carried out in communion with the ancestors and the gods, the dynasty of Huébaja and the kingdom living as in mystical communion.
> It is thus one finds Dahomean society. Princes, anato (plebs), all Danxomɛnù "thing of Danxomɛ", all belong to the same community, dependent upon the authority and power of the same king, representative of Huégbaja.[29]

Glélé has no doubt that Danxomɛ was not just a state but a nation.[30] Gezò's metaphor of the holed water jar, symbol of solidarity and national unity, has indeed been revived and is appropriately set in stone outside the *Assemblée Nationale* and in several other places, as

---

[27] Georges, Balandier, *Afrique ambiguë*, Paris: Plon, 1983 edition, 299–300.
[28] Having attended *Les Grandes Coutumes* in 1964, M.A. Glélé reported the fol-lowing: "In the course of the great feasts, the people were vibrating in unison, celebra-ting and singing all the same ancestors; the king fed everybody during this time. The festival ended with offerings to all the Vodún of the kingdom; blessing was beseeched upon the king and the kingdom that it might always expand, showing itself to be ever more powerful, invincible and prosperous" (Glélé, *Le Danxomé*, 170).
[29] Glélé, *Le Danxomê*, 165.
[30] He defines the state as a permanent territory, strong central authority, a hier-archical, disciplined and decentralised administration, a king representing supreme authority and incarnating sovereignty, fiscal organisation, a dynamic economy (Glélé, *Du Pouvoir*, 167).

a symbol for the new Benin.[31] Like many Africans, as Balandier points out, Aguessy, Glélé and Goudjo have looked back at the kingdom seeking political inspiration. Adoukonou has revisited history to find in Agongló's flirtations with Christianity the aborted emergence in Danxomɛ of an ethical religion as opposed to the apparently barbaric practices usually attributed to it. He has attempted to give us a christological hermeneutic of the Vodún, thus redeeming it from its image as a religion of pure power and manipulation.[32] Though not theological, Aguessy's approach is similar in its desire to redeem the Vodún as a form of endogenous knowledge that offers hope as a culturally appropriate philosophical basis for the future of Benin, and indeed Africa, where imported ideologies have signally failed.

The attempts to rehabilitate Danxomɛ and Vodún, however, give rise in turn to a vociferous polemic.[33] An early critic, Maximilien Quenum, writing in the colonial period, claims that the Vodúnsì lives in a "perpetual nightmare", his prayer little more than "a jeremiad, a continuous list of lamentations and tortured supplications".[34] The mildest of the critics notes quite simply that Danxomɛ could never have successfully been the cornerstone of the new state. Apart from Danxomɛ itself, which became the myth, all of the other parts of the country did not feel engaged with it, indeed utterly rejected it, while within Agbŏmɛ itself there was a state of almost constant combat between the separate branches of the royal families.[35] The divisions Danxomɛ has sought to overcome by its hegemony over the other polities were reproduced within itself and they undermined it from within. However, unlike the Inca and the Aztec, Danxomɛ has not completely disappeared, and the vestiges continue to haunt the modern state.

The controversialist Roger Gbénonvi is much more forthright. In an interview, he dismisses Adoukonou, "*fils d'Agongló*", as a "*nationaliste aboméen*", accusing him of living in a state of internal conflict between his "*christianisme universel*", his "*théologie catholique*" and his "*nationalisme aboméen*", concluding: "He has to choose. But as a

[31] Glélé interprets this as follows: "If all the children of this country came with their finger to block the holes in the jar, Danxomé would be saved" (*Naissance*, 367).
[32] Adoukonou, *Ethique*.
[33] For a parallel rehabilitation of the Vodún in Haiti, see Hurbon *Sociologie*, ch. 12.
[34] Maximilien Quenum, *Au pays des Fons. Us et coutumes au Dahomey*, Paris, 1936 (3rd edition, 1986), 66, in Pierre Pluchon, *Vaudou, sorcier et empoissoneurs*, Paris: Karthala, 1987, 56.
[35] Goudjo, *La liberté*, 128–131.

prince of Abomey he cannot betray the transition ... That is a problem that he has not resolved..."[36] He is particularly critical of his attempt to rehabilitate Agongló:

> He has tried to rehabilitate Agongló by making him the first Christian etc... If this rehabilitation had worked, if it had been historically true, that would be fine, he would be reconciled, he Adoukonou, with his two cultures "la catholique romaine et l'abominable aboméenne".[37]

He is equally dismissive of what he sees as both Aguessy's and Adoukonou's attempts to rehabilitate the Vodún in any way. Although declaring himself a sceptic in religious matters, Gbégnonvi chooses traditional Christian terminology to denounce the Vodún, "all his works and all his wiles", accusing those who wish to see it otherwise of leading the people "who were walking in darkness" back to this state and condemning them to obscurantism and under-development.[38] In two devastating articles, he launches a vitriolic attack on both the Vodún and the whole history and structure of Danxomɛ as he sees it.[39] Quite amazing in ferocity, they illustrate the problem of Danxomɛ in contemporary debate.

In the first piece entitled *La bouffe, les Vodún et Mãwu*, Gbégnonvi attacks first of all the whole concept of *dù*, or eating, which we looked at in the previous chapter. He chooses several lexical examples: "eating money", "eating shame", "eating witchcraft", "eating life", to illustrate the dominance of this concept above any other, concluding "if occidental man is a thinking being, for the Fòn man is an eater of salt, *kanlìn dù jɛ*". He concludes that the Fòn is obsessed with, and defines himself by, *la bouffe*, "which the Vodún encourage, amplify and carry to the heights of their paltry heaven. Every Vodún ceremony seeks to be a febrile place of frenetic and unbridled rapacity".[40] Ultimately Gbégnonvi's sombre vision is of a society eating itself, *Vodún, Vodúnnò* and *Vodúnsì à la bouffe*, engaged in a frenzy of individual and collective self-consuming gourmandise.

---

[36] Professor Roger Gbégnonvi, linguist, journalist, president, *Transparency International*, interview, 28 July 2002.

[37] He compares his research institute *Le Sillon Noir* to a right-wing movement bearing a similar name in France, *Sillon*, founded in the early twentieth century by the Christian Democrat Marc Sangnier. *Le Sillon* broke from the church, whose authority it challenged under Pius X (1903–1914).

[38] Roger Gbégnonvi, 'La Bouffe, les Vodún et Mawu', in *Sillon Noir* 13, 3, 1998.

[39] Ibid. and Roger Gbégnonvi, 'Le devoir de repentance et justice: le Bénin et la question de sa rédemption', *La Nation*, 2763, 20 June 2001, 2; 11.

[40] Gbégnonvi, *La Bouffe*, 3.

He carries the attack even further in a section entitled *Le Vodún et le mensonge*.[41] Here he underlines "the spiders web" woven over society by the Vodún, *la bouffe* and *nùvú*, "the little thing", a euphemism for *the lie*. This system is constructed and held together:

> in order to hold the Fòn prisoner while waiting to condemn him to death and to execute him. The Vodún are constantly demanding food, and they are constantly being given to eat, which is as much as to say that man uses the Vodún as a pretext to eat unceasingly.

He quotes to some effect the expression often used by Adoukonou: *me we no ylo do Vodúnbe no nyi Vodún*.

> Everything, no matter what and no matter who, with the exception of little spiders [can be what man can call a Vodún]. Vodún occasions for *la bouffe* are created at every turn in an unbelievable imbroglio of lies.

Here he touches on something referred to in the last chapter as the Machiavellian nature of Danxomɛnù and the Fòn liking for the diplomatic ruse. Lauded by its defenders as a sophisticated diplomacy, it is excoriated by its detractors, like Gbégnonvi, not as ruse but *nùvú*, "the little thing", a euphemism for the *lie*, as opposed to *nùgbó*, "the great thing" or *truth*. *Nùvú*, he claims, is continually used to acquire *la bouffe* and what is important to the Fòn is precisely *la bouffe* and not life, which he does not hesitate to suppress in the cause of his belly.[42] For Gbégnonvi the Vodún is inextricably linked to death and the threat to life: *Vodún ce ha hu we* (My Vodún is going to kill you).

> The Vodún is linked to death as it is linked to the lie. And it could not be otherwise in this sordid universe where la bouffe constitutes the alpha and the omega and where what one calls life leads back to the belly.

In a passage of remarkable polemical ferocity, he writes:

> Bouffe, Vodún and Nùvú are three links of the infernal chain that surrounds Fòn society, suffocates it, and has pushed it from earliest times to self-destruction in a kind of nauseous marsh, where all grace and every ray of sun is forbidden. The impasse of 'the final solution', self-managed.

He accuses the Vodún of being at the basis of an egoism that is:

---

[41] Ibid., 3–6.
[42] Glélé writes, "Le dahoméen moyen a une certaine conception machiavélique de la politique. A preuve ce proverbe courant: 'L'homme a en lui du sang et pourtant crache de la salive blanche', ce qui implique duperie, sourire et façade et même une certaine fraternité, puis le coup de Jarnac" (Glélé, *Naissance*, 76).

cultivated and practised to its final consequence implicating the death of the Other for the triumph of the self. Such a system necessarily transforms the society into a closed field of generalised suspicion and leads men and women logically to render crime banal. This is what Vodún is about.

Against this he presents Măwu who is "grandeur, mercy, patience, goodness, tenderness and sweetness",[43] living in the real world of the nùgbó, the eternal and transcendental truth. Gbégnonvi claims that despite the fact that the name of Măwu is invoked continuously, one does not find a cult to him or any exclusive followers. He explains this by the fact that

> a people dedicated to *la bouffe* can only have commerce with those Vodún specialising in the able arrangement and use of 'little things' which allows them to feed at every trough in the widest sense of the word.[44]

In his analysis of the problems of modern Benin, Gbégnonvi notes that they are not a passing phenomenon, but rather they are "structural":

> The crisis is there since the origins and, like a sinister monster with a thousand tentacles as discreet as they are effective, it smothers the social body and prevents it from developing, using the phenomenon of the sucker, and sapping the society of all its energies.[45]

He identifies the Republic of Benin precisely as the inheritor of Danxomɛ, "itself the unfortunate reject of the disintegration of Tado" and thus born of treachery, strife and division. For Gbégnonvi, it is as if Danxomɛ carries the mark of Cain (Genesis 4:15), since it is built "upon a blood crime", which cannot be excused by the fact that other kingdoms may have an equally violent past. He appears almost to mock Le Hérissé, without citing him, when he writes:

> Danxomê, "ce royaume militaire remarquablement organisé" (petit Robert 2), so impressed the coloniser that he could find nothing better to do than to spread its terrible name to the whole country... It is not sure that the name that we bear and which bears us does not decide our destiny, influence our plan of life and, from this point of view, it would be better to be called Hwècehun (my sun has risen) than Zanku (night has fallen).[46]

It is as if the name alone has decided its Sɛ and keeps it a prisoner of its tragic past.

---

[43] Gbégnonvi, "*La Bouffe*", 7.
[44] Ibid., 8.
[45] Gbégnonvi, "*Le devoir de repentance*", 2.
[46] Gbégnonvi, "*Le devoir de repentance*", 2.

While there is some reason to hope that the Republic of Benin is establishing itself as a state, "the mystique of Danxomɛ"[47] can never really be the basis of its symbolic capital. As Gbégnonvi testifies, Danxomɛ is for many a kind of nightmare calling to be exorcised. His analysis is obviously embarrassing to those who seek a more positive understanding both of Vodún and of Danxomɛ, and to the outside observer it certainly appears somewhat jaundiced. This is precisely the word used by Adoukonou in his rejection of what he sees as Gbégnonvi's "hatred of self when he lacerates his Fòn roots".[48] "*Le noir est mauvais*" was an expression one heard embarrassingly often, and again Césaire is a quiet voice in the background:

> *Les-nègres-sont-tous-les-mêmes*
> *Les-vices-tous-les-vices, c'est-moi-qui-vous-le-dis.*[49]

Whatever its polemical excesses, Gbégnonvi's analysis represents a strong current in the perception of Danxomɛ by the Béninois *Other* and "hatred of self" may very well be part of that. "Abomey abominable" was a slogan repeated to me several times, often by members of the religious and socio-political elites, north and south. Over the course of my time in Benin, it became clear to me that this was a society dominated by deeply-held fears and profound divisions, affecting what Hubron describes as *le lien social* and that these penetrated into the deepest fibres of the social tissue.[50] Gbégnonvi, referring to Hazoumé's *Pacte*, dealt with this in some detail in the course of a long interview:

> Once again I come back to "Abomey abominable". It was a kingdom founded on fear [and] "suspicion". Where does this suspicion come from? In my opinion it comes from Abomey because you could not live in that kingdom without suspecting everybody, because the king had his spies everywhere [...] Confidence did not exist. It was a kingdom of fear.[51]

Glélé seems to confirm this when he states that the temperament and mentality of the Danxomɛnù

> explains the intrigues *à la florentine* which make and unmake political life, the fertile imagination prompt in creating false reports, but however unbelievable they might be, they maintain a climate of suspicion and discord.[52]

---

[47] Glélé, *Le Danxomê*, 172.
[48] Adoukonou, "*Ethique*", 11.
[49] Césaire, *Cahier*, 35.
[50] Hurbon, *Sociologie*, 136–137.
[51] Interview, 28 June 2002.
[52] Glélé, *Naissance*, 341.

As I noted above, this fear stretches into the most intimate social spaces, including the family. This is a theme that reoccurs frequently in the Churches and it is something to which they seek to respond, or in some cases perhaps a fear upon which they build. "The king had his spies everywhere, your wife, your spouse, could be a spy," Gbégnonvi says, and this leads him on to a devastating analysis of the African family, as a space deeply divided, and penetrated by fear, suspicion and division.

> Always in the questions of sorcery, it will be a question of the family. Because the family here...is seen by us as a danger. [Gide says] "Family I hate you". One has to be careful of the family, one has to be suspicious, and I am suspicious of my family. Through the grace of God, I received an education that was a little Westernised, although I was born of Béni-nois parents, completely illiterate but who brought us up in Catholicism and this distanced us from the family...We are happy for this because the family means jealousy; there is a tyranny of the family. There is a tyranny of the group; the individual does not exist. It is the group that exists, and the first group is the family. [They say] "Here we don't do it like that" and either you step in line or you are made to disappear. They say, in your individuality you are destroying our universe. It is true what you say, but if it is true, then it is our universe that is no longer true. There can't be two truths, that of the group and that of the individual. So you, individual, go back to the flock, if not we will make you disappear. You have no chance.

Several people interviewed in the course of my fieldwork spoke of the need to put up "barriers" between the nuclear family and the African family,[53] or as another put it, with more flexibility, "to put up markers".[54] Gbégnonvi goes much further:

> I don't put up markers. Quite simply, I have no contact with them. My family, for me, is my father, whom I buried two months ago, my mother, and my sisters. That stops there...Total rupture...I greet nobody, my own parents brought me up to be suspicious of everybody and on that point they were right because it is your own cousin, whom you call *little brother* who will bring you the poison. Personally, I don't believe in *juju* and all of that, but I do believe in poison and I don't want to be poisoned.

Adoukonou may be justified in observing some elements of a painful personal history in Gbégnonvi's account, but the fact remains that his views are not unique and they could be replicated 1,000 times.

---

[53] Interview, 26 May 2002.
[54] Interview, 13 June 2002.

Danxomε is a narrative of pride and suspicion, but it is equally a narrative of pain and division. It is not unique in this, as many other African countries illustrate, often in much more violent ways, but it is a part of the Dahomean narrative and, in my view, an essential element in understanding contemporary Benin and its difficulties. Glélé, inspired perhaps by Garibaldi, stated that "the Dahomean nation does not exist and is yet to be born," insisting that "the Dahomean nation can and must be born; she will be the daughter of the state".[55] Only six years after Glélé made his claim, however, even the name had been relegated to history, most probably never to be resurrected. The country was renamed, not a little ironically, under a Marxist government, with the name of another West African kingdom, Benin. While there now seems to be much more reason to hope that the Republic of Benin is establishing itself as a state, its starting point or foundation myth can never be Danxomε. Gbégnonvi is correct when he says that Benin, for better or for worse, is the inheritor of Danxomε. It is precisely this heritage that is problematic, giving rise to the need for something new. This can be expressed in terms of a "breakthrough" to the "destiny" that will free it from its apparent fate as a state under constant threat of internal division and a slide into *la misère-désolation*.

Danxomε and the modern state

Although the heart of Danxomε had been ripped out with the defeat of Gbεhanzın, parts of the myth and the underlying philosophy of the kingdom have lived on in vestigial form and reasserted themselves especially in times of socio-political stress. Following the first steps toward modern political activity following the French Africa Conference at Brazzaville in 1944, and the UN Conference in San Francisco in 1945, a tripartite system, reflecting traditional polities, emerged in colonial Dahomey.[56] This was "a two-against-the third formula" which reflected the traditional polities and their respective alliances, and in which Agbõmε was almost always "the third".[57] In the search for power,

---

[55] Glélé, *Naissance*, 333. Giuseppe Garibaldi (1807–1882), who, following unification under the House of Savoy is reputed to have said "We have created Italy, now we must create Italians".

[56] Staniland, *"The three party system"*.

[57] Dov Ronen, *Dahomey: Between Tradition and Modernity*, London: Cornell UP, 1975, 126.

the legitimacy of royal lineage, or at least the seal of royal approval, was avidly sought after by the new elites, *les évolués*, with ties to Agbŏmɛ. Others, however, defined themselves precisely *in opposition* to Danxomɛ, seeking the legitimacy emanating from other polities traditionally hostile to Agbŏmɛ, and fearful of its desire for power. The troubled troika, Maga, Apithy and Ahomadégbé was an early manifestation of this, and in many ways paradigmatic of the tripartite Dahomey politics in the whole of the post-colonial period to the present day.[58]

Making Abomey the fiefdom of his *Union Progressiste Dahoméenne (RPD)*, Justin Tométin Ahomadégbé claimed links with the royal family of Agongló[59] through his mother. In adding Tométin (son of Agongló and brother of Gezò) to his name in order to underline his princely heritage, he "would have wished to have the unanimity of the Huégbaja around himself, identifying himself in some way with Huégbaja". Known early in his career as "the monster", Ahomadégbé attempted to develop the strong man persona, projected as possessing a sacral *acɛ*, "strong and powerful, but violent and endowed with magical powers".[60] His desire for *gànhúnŭ* was all too evident, as this extract illustrates:

> The urgent task [...], is to reinvent Dahomey [...], and create the conditions that will oblige Dahomeans to want to change, to really become Dahomeans. And to be Dahomean, [...] is to love and to passionately love this country; to be Dahomean is to recognise that the Reason of State is above all; to be Dahomean is above all to silence one's interests in the interests of the Common Good.[61]

Ahomadégbé's reasoning was clear enough and clearly owed much to the philosophy of Danxomɛ: the need to reinvent Danxomɛ, to oblige

---

[58] Justin Ahomadégbé (1972), Sourou-Migan Apithy (1964–1965), and Hubert Maga (1960–1963 and 1970–1972). They all held the presidency and at one stage between 1970–1972 were a vivid illustration of the problems of the post-colonial state.

[59] Glélé contests the legitimacy of these links. See Glélé, *Le Danxomê*, 252. However, Ahomadégbé was buried in 2002 in accordance with the custom of this family. See Affissou Anonrin, 'Les obséques de Ahomadégbé piétinent à Abomey', *Le Matinal*, 18 April 2002.

[60] Ahomadégbé was reputed for his supernatural powers. He was said to be a Bokónò as well as a bòwàtó. In 1991 he was reported to have treated presidential candidate Nicépore Soglo who had been struck down by a mysterious illness. No details of the illness were ever given but it was widely rumoured to be due to occult practices. 'See Paul Akando, "Nos secrets dans leur tombe" ', *Le Marabout*, numéro 8—mai 2002, *http://www.marabout.net/008/benin.htm*. See also Glélé, *Le Danxomê*, 252.

[61] In Olympe Bhely-Quenum, "Le Benin après la mascarade: il y a trente ans le Président Ahomadégbé s'adressait aux Dahoméens" *http://www.obhelyquenum. com/lebenin.htm*.

Dahomeans to really become Danxomɛnù, with total submission to the state and a Dahomean idea of the common good, which meant the expansion of the state and the power of its ruler. He was seeking cultural and political hegemony. Not surprisingly, this met with fierce resistance from people with a very different view of history. If one is to follow Glélé, the demystification and political demise of Ahomadégbé, "*le thaumaturge*", were assured by his ignominious scramble across the marshes of southern Benin following the 1967 coup. This was something, he said, that would never have happened to Huégbaja and the legitimate heirs to Danxomɛ, "who at all times and in all circumstances represented authority and power with dignity".[62] Ahomadégbé's *acɛ* had run out and he was a spent force.

While he could not claim princely blood, Sourou-Migan Apithy, in his name, also indicated his attachment to the royal family of Porto-Novo, the traditional enemy of Agbŏmɛ.[63] Known simply as Marcellin Apithy when he was listed with Fr Francis Aupiais as candidate for the Conseil Supérieur des Colonies in 1946, the later addition of Migan indicated his lineage, again through his mother, from a *Migán*, or prime minister, of Porto Novo,[64] thus assuring the support of this area in his contest with Ahomadégbé and Maga. Apithy's references to the tradition were more than in name only, since his power was also built on his contacts with the traditional chiefs and, through them, with the Vodúnnò who guaranteed him their support and that of the Vodúnsì.[65]

Hubert Maga could not claim any royal blood. His father was from Upper Volta and his mother a Bariba from Parakou; unusually, both Muslims converted to Christianity. He had a mission education, which gained him entry into the indigenous colonial elite and the emerging political classes. Through his mother, he laid his claim as representative of *le Nord*, adroitly uniting the loose traditional Bariba kingdom of the Borgou with the acephalous groups of the Atacora around his *Rassemblement Démocratique Dahoméen*. As in Nigeria, *le Nord* is

---

[62] Ibid.

[63] A protectorate was definitively re-established with King Toffa in 1882 as part of a protective strategy. This effectively isolated Abomey, leaving it the only pocket of resistance to French penetration.

[64] The prime minister and other ministers of the crown were always anato in both Porto Novo and Abomey, thus excluding rival princes from effective political power.

[65] Sulikowski, *Eating the flesh*, 382.

largely a construction born of modern political circumstances.[66] It is
in no way homogenous and while there are strongly Islamised groups
and the Bariba—the landholders of the Borgou—are in an early stage
of Islamisation most remained attached to the traditional religion while
only more recently tentatively considering either Islam or Christianity.
Maga, apparently favoured by the French,[67] was, however, able to rally
his forces around the theme of northern resistance to "southern domination", thus establishing the persistent *leitmotif* of Dahomey politics.
This "domination" effectively came to mean Abomean domination, since
Maga's constituents made little distinction, identifying anybody coming
from south of Save (8°N) as a Fòn and therefore to be feared.

Here one comes to what I see as the other constant theme of Dahomey
politics, that of *fear*. From the beginning of modern political activity, support for candidates was given not necessarily because of their
ethnicity, "but because of fear of domination by another ethnic group
should the other ethnic candidate win".[68] This has remained a central
theme and, indeed, it is one that takes precedence over any questions
of policy or technocratic competence. Suffice it to say, however, that
Danxomε has been able, since its foundation, to improvise on the Béninois metaphor, a jar standing very precariously in the modern world
on the three regional stones that hold it up. The tripartite arrangement
led to great instability in the first twelve years after independence,
during which time the country had eleven changes of president, with
only one lasting into a second year. In this also, the country became
paradigmatic for the problems of the African state.

Kérékou the chameleon, master of myth

By 1972 it had become clear that the Republic of Dahomey could not
continue as it had started out. This led to the coup which brought to
power Colonel Matthieu Kérékou, the man who has come to dominate

---

[66] For an excellent treatment of the emergence of 'northernism' as a political construct
in Nigeria, see J.N. Paden, *Ahmadu Bello, Sardauna of Sokoto: Values and Leadership
in Nigeria*, Zaria: Hudahuda, 1986. There was a similar process in Benin but it was
less pronounced and without the essential element of Islamic identity.

[67] Ronen, *Dahomey*, 90.

[68] Ibid., 107.

Danxomɛ-Benin politics for almost as long as any individual since the Gezò.[69] In fact, Kérékou personifies many of the ambiguities of modern Benin and how it relates to its history. A Wama, from the northern Atacora province, he is the complete outsider and the perfect political chameleon. Said to be a Catholic, he is ecumenical in the tradition of the kings, and has flirted with various endogenous and exogenous religious influences and ideologies.[70] Kérékou's power is exercised in an improvised symbolic dialect that may pose problems for the outsider but certainly brings him political success. Lɛgbà also springs to mind. In the course of his long political life, he has borrowed from, and improvised upon, several traditions, religions and ideologies, while staying true to his Weberian warrior status, apparently owing absolute fealty to none. The gods and the spiritual powers emanating from them, regardless of their provenance, have served his kingdom, and in this he finds himself in the tradition of the kings.

He came to power at the head of a government dubbed *revolutionary*, but his ascendancy appears to have owed as much to chance as to anything else in what started out as 'just another military coup', when these were far from rare.[71] He was not, by all accounts including his own later versions, a Marxist. The ideological colouring of the regime came only in 1974 as a result of political expediency, and the need to compromise with harder elements in what came to be known as the "Albanian faction" who were tempted by a "*Marxisme tropical*".[72]

---

[69] Kérékou has been in power since 1972, with an interruption of six years following the 1991 election. He was re-elected in 1996 and 2001. At the time of writing, there is some debate over the holding of the 2006 presidential election, with the government appearing to hestitate and with the Assemblée Nationale and civil society actors strongly defending the constitution. Michée Boko, "Le président de la République accusé de bloquer le processus électoral", *Inter Press Service* (Johannesburg), 11 Janvier 2006, http://fr.allafrica.com/stories/200601120526.html.

[70] There is still some debate about his religious affiliation. Reputed to be a Catholic, he has also been said to be associated with the Foursquare Full Gospel church, and evangelical pastors are said to be part of his entourage. Youssouof Avocegamou, "Kérékou otage des pasteurs" *La Tribune de la Capitale* 140, 16 July 2002. Kérékou's dealings with the Vodún are vague. However, the relationship of his entourage with the Vodúnnò was widely commented upon. See Sulinowski, *Eating the flesh*, 379; C. Strandsbjerg, "*Kérékou*".

[71] The coup followed the condemnation of an officer by a civilian court. Kérékou accepted to lead the coup only if the military would stay in power. See Dov Ronen, *Ethnicity Ideology, and the Military in the People's Republic of Benin*, Boston, MA: African-Americn Issues Center, 1984, 11–16.

[72] Jean Luc Aplogan, "Bénin: Une démocratie apaisée", *Le Monde Diplomatique*, novembre, 1997, 1.

The regime went through ideologically '*hard*' and '*soft*' periods until the early 1980s, when Kérékou finally distanced himself from the *idéologues purs et durs*, settled for a *socialisme à la béninoise*, and emerged as the sole survivor and, in a manner of speaking, the absolute monarch.[73] The discourse of the PRPB regime to the end ranged between a brooding, sullen muteness, laden with implicit threat, and a vacuous but sometimes violent rhetoric.[74] Kérékou's political persona, like that of Ahomadégbé, though perhaps more subtle, was that of the powerful man. He survived the revolutionary period, which many Béninois qualify as "infernal",[75] through a combination of totalitarian military *gànhúnǔ*, personal *acê* and an adroit playing of the whole of the Danxomɛ symbolic register.

The post-PRPB Kérékou, following his defeat in the 1991 presidential election and a five-year ritual *traversée du désert*, during which he maintained an absolute political silence, has changed dramatically. It can be argued that his rehabilitation had already started at the CNFVN in 1990. In a remarkable piece of political theatre, at a crucial point in the CNFVN, he metaphorically donned sackcloth and sat in the political ashes of the defunct PRPB to ask forgiveness from the nation for its failures and abuses. Turning to the Archbishop of Cotonou, President of the CNFVN, he appealed to his sacerdotal sensibilities, pleading: "My lord, you would not hesitate to hear my confession...", and, in a remarkable admission of guilt, went on, in tears, to declare, "We are ashamed of ourselves..." This was a discomfiting position for a warrior king, but even here he was consistent with Danxomɛ.

In what appeared like a scene from a medieval play, he needed the expiation of the high priest, but instead of *Daxo*, the priest of the royal cult of Agasú who dispensed ritual purification to the kings, he called upon the priest of Mǎwu in the person of the Archbishop of Cotonou. This was more than a ritual *mea culpa*. It was a remarkable

---

[73] The period 1974–1979 was an ideologically 'hard' period which saw many changes. There was also a religious witchhunt attacking Vodún as a form of feudalism. From 1978 there was a distancing of the '*purs et durs*' from the regime, an opening to the churches, ideological revisionism, a general demobilisation of the masses, and more personal freedom. See Daniel Mellier, "Marxisme et mission—Bénin", *SEDOS Bulletin*", 18 Rome, 1982, 352–357.

[74] Bruce Chatwin recalls a five-hour Castro-like harangue while he was detained during an apparent abortive coup. See Bruce Chatwin, "A Coup", *Granta*, 10: 1984, 71–90.

[75] Aplogan, *Bénin*.

demonstration of his ability to call on the whole range of the Béninois symbolic register, to add to it if necessary, and to use it to his advantage. It was not a request for cheap grace or even a functional political calculation. In terms of the Béninois popular imagination, Kérékou, in using the word "shame", had pleaded *svólv*, a common expression expressing regret and a plea for patience or indulgence. He put himself in the position of the most abject penitent in front of the most righteous judge, not just the Archbishop but the people of Benin. Since the conference was broadcast on national radio and followed with great interest, he had gone beyond his immediate audience to the nation. At the time, and compared with Eyadema's threatening presence in his private residence in Lomé, Mobutu's sulking at Gbadolite and Sassou N'Guesso's haughty *"J'assume"*,[76] it was an astounding example of humility and not without considerable risk. It was a confessional gesture as well as high political theatre which, when followed by his self-imposed five-year silence,[77] redeemed his *acê* where it might have compromised it, as well as securing him immunity from prosecution. Culturally as well as theologically it was impossible to refuse forgiveness on these terms, and, combined with his exemplary behaviour in the following years of political penance, it was the first step in his political rehabilitation and the creation of the born-again Christian Kérékou.

Since the CNFVN there have been more improvisations on the religious theme in the register of Evangelical Christianity. A 1990 report by Reinhard Bonnke's evangelical organisation, Christ for all Nations (CfaN), on its first campaign in Benin—described as "one of the toughest ever" in what it considered to be a land of darkness—reported Kérékou to be "an unbelieving communist". A 1999 report from the same group, however, reports the conversion of the nation as "multitudes storm the Kingdom of God". "The national attitude has changed" and even more significantly "the same President is now a born-again

---

[76] Patrick Quantin points out the failure of the conciliatory aspect of the National Conference in the Republic of Congo. Sassou N'Guesso's declaration to the floor of the conference in the face of serious accusations, *"J'assume"*, was interpreted as a sign of arrogance, lacking any spirit of repentence. Quantin, personal communication.

[77] In a rare interview he gave, which I recall from this time, Kérékou was asked what he was going to do when he left power. He replied, with a wit for which he is known, "I thought I would either become a journalist, which would allow me to say anything at all, or a monk, which would allow me to say nothing".

believer" as he "welcomes Reinhard Bonnke".[78] In a remarkable play on the different symbolic registers referring back to Danxomε, but also to the CNFVN, as well as appealing to evangelical sensibilities, the French public relations guru Thierry Saussez had repackaged "Kérékou III" as *"le caméléon repenti"*.[79] This conversion appears to have been so successful in the 2001 presidential election that an evangelical group distributed tee-shirts bearing the slogan *"Avec Kérékou pour gagner le Bénin au Christ."*[80] The metamorphosis was complete, the chameleon had indeed changed his skin from demon to born-again Christian, walked the path of conversion, made the 'breakthrough' and was ready to seize his 'moment of destiny'. If he could do it, did it not offer hope to the whole nation?

"In the name of God and the spirits of the ancestors":
the inculturation of the constitution

While the early years of the PRPB regime were marked by a rejection of all that represented Danxomε, including both the name of the country and its flag, Kérékou was quick to rehabilitate and instrumentalise the elements of the tradition that would serve his purpose. First amongst these was the chameleon, which has become his totem. This reptile, which represents Lisà, had been the symbol of Akábá (1685–1708) and was apparently recommended to Kérékou by the traditional king of Aladà. Akábá used the motto: *Dεdε kákáákábáá aganma no liyá hùn* (Slowly but surely, the chameleon reaches the top of the banyan tree). Kérékou adopted the totem but improvised on the motto declaring: *Atín mó nó wέn d'áganma' lo mε* (The branch will not break in the arms of the chameleon). This is an interesting use of words. It is certainly less bellicose than those of Gezò, Glεlέ or Gbεhanzιn, which we saw in the previous chapter. In his use of the totem and the motto, Kérékou

---

[78] *http://www.pastornet.net.au/renewal/journal14/14e%20Global%20Reports.htm.*, 15 February 2003.

[79] Cotonou: Thierry Saussez "faiseur d'image" de Kérékou? *La Lettre du Continent*, 330, 03 June 1999, *http://www.africanintelligence/fr./detail/versionimpr.../p_detail_BRE.asp?/ DOC_1_DD=5603.*

[80] There are several similarities between this case study and Gifford's observations on Zambia. Cf Paul Gifford, "Chiluba's Christian Nation: Christianity as a Factor in Zambian Politics 1991–1996", *Journal of Contemporary Religion*, 1998, 13, 363–381.

is presented as the guarantor of peace and national cohesion. However, there is also the implicit threat that the branch *would break* should the chameleon fall. This threat of a post-Kérékou *déluge* has been a major, sometimes almost the only, theme of his political discourse, particularly in election campaigns. In this he has placed his person as the linchpin of national stability. He is, in his person, the symbol of unity, without which Benin would revert to the state of unbridled anarchy that followed for five days after the death of a king, and, as he often states, is the case in other African countries.

It must be added that Kérékou is not alone or altogether without justification in this strategy. On 29 March 1996, the Constitutional Court published a communiqué denouncing "*les manœuvres*" and the threats of the defeated outgoing candidate Nicéphore Soglo who had repeatedly spoken of the "imminent threat of civil war that would follow his defeat".[81] Some days earlier, the FM station Radio Carrefour had been officially reprimanded by the *Haute Autorité de l'Audiovisuel et de la Communication* for reports relating to "an appeal of a regionalist and tribalist character" in favour of Soglo".[82] A similar complaint was made against Radio Planète.[83] In one of these broadcasts, I was informed, Amazon war songs from Agbɔmɛ were played in what was considered an overt threat of Dahomean *revanchisme*, showing that they had lost little of their emotive power. At the same time Soglo had also been presenting himself as a guarantor of peace, stability and cohesion, with the additional benefit of the technocratic competence needed to lead Benin to socio-economic modernity.

In adopting the totem of an earlier king, Kérékou rooted himself, however superficially, in southern mythology. Banégas notes that the reptile "condenses a whole symbolism of temporal and mystical power made up of wiliness, wisdom and invulnerability"[84] and this indeed is how Kérékou has managed to project himself. Perhaps the best illustration of the understanding of political power in Benin as embedded in the traditions of Danxomɛ can be found in a speech given by the President of the Constitutional Court, Elisabeth K. Pognon,

[81] See Albert Bourghi "La réalité du nouveau constitutionnalisme africain", Association Française des Constitutionalistes, Association Française de Science Politique, *http://www.univ-reims.fr/Labos/CERI/la_realite_du_nouveau_constitutionnalisme_africain.htm*.
[82] Décision 017/HAAC, 20 March 2001.
[83] Décision 011/HAAC, 15 May 2001.
[84] Richard Banégas, *La démocratie à pas de caméléon*, Paris: Karthala, 463.

on the day of Kérékou's inauguration to a second democratic term in April 2001. This was published in the national daily *La Nation* under the title "*Le serment: un contrat entre Kérékou, Dieu, les mânes des ancêtres et la nation*".[85] Even the order of the words in the headline is significant. Kérékou may not be divine but by placing him first in the triad, supported by Mǎwu and the *Kúyito-to* or spirits of the ancestors, his rule becomes sacral in nature. In the speech, Pognon describes Kérékou's position as president in a way that brings to mind the Fòn expression, used in Chapter 2, underlying the role of the Vodún and the ancestors.

She underlines the importance of the *Xó*, the given word, stating that "the oath of this day…appears as a contract as a *spiritual contract between God, the spirits of the ancestors and you*". This is the plane upon which the contract is situated and it is essentially sacral. Bringing the contract onto another plane and into a more democratic era, but still in quasi-religious terms that would be recognised in Danxomε, he is described as "the incarnation of national unity, the guarantor of territorial integrity, respect of the constitution and international agreements", in effect the *incarnation* and guarantor of the *Tò*. He is to be president of the Benin-tò that has replaced the Danxomε-tò. She adds:

> It must also be understood as an historical contract between the Nation and you, and finally a juridical agreement between you and the Béninois people, the only holder of sovereignty. Only in the silence of your conscience will you respond to the accomplishment of your moral duty.

Some of this could obviously be used for the swearing in of most presidents, anywhere in the world. However, embedding it in the local tradition, she has repeated a version of the triad seen as holding Danxomε, and by extension the *gbέ*, together: Mǎwu, Kúyito-tò, and the ruler. It is certainly significant that in 1996, when Kérékou omitted the references to "*les mânes des ancêtres*", he was obliged to return to the Constitutional Court the following day to take the oath a second time. The ancestors were not to be ignored and his legitimacy depended upon it.

What is omitted, of course, is the Vodún-tò who are replaced by the Christianised Mǎwu, and this is equally significant. This brings us on to another question in the relations between tradition and modernity in modern Benin, that of the role of the Vodún.

---

[85] Elisabeth K. Pognon "Le serment: un contrat entre Kérékou, Dieu, les mânes des ancêtres et la nation", *La Nation*, 2714, 7 April 2001, 7.

Opening the calabash: Vodún and democracy

There has been a consistent movement in Benin since 1990 seeking the rehabilitation of the culture and history of Danxomɛ. In emphasising its cultural roots, Benin wanted to reconcile itself with its history, while at the same time reaching out to the Dahomean diaspora in the Americas, in an attempt to build alliances and forge links which will give it a place in the world. It was also interested in promoting a cultural tourism. Part of this was an appeal to the Vodún Diaspora. Vodún was rehabilitated as a religion, and given its own national holiday. But what was presented as a cultural event quickly came to be seen as much more.

The president at that time, Soglo, a former IMF functionary, had a reputation for technocratic competence. Distant, with a touch of royal *hauteur* and little in terms of communications skills, he soon came to be perceived as a true son of Agbõmɛ in the most negative sense. Comparisons with Ahomadégbé led his detractors to suspect a thirst for *gànhúnǔ*. Perhaps even more problematic than Soglo himself was the presence of his wife. Excoriated by his opponents (as well as by many of his political allies)[86] and held in little affection by the public, Rosine Vieira-Soglo, a highly qualified jurist, came from Ouidah. This renewal of an historic alliance between the Portuguese families of the old slave port and Agbõmɛ was already suspect. In addition to this, Mme Vieira-Soglo, whose brother, Désiré Vieira, was the Minister of Defence,[87] was said to have strongly anti-clerical views, and was seen as being behind the attempt to rehabilitate Vodún, perhaps in an attempt to diminish the influence of the Catholic Church, following the CNFVN. The end result was to create the impression of Abomean *revanchisme*, with the defence forces as well as the forces of the occult firmly under command of the new regime. It is almost impossible to verify the facts behind these suspicions. But *facts*, at least in this sense, are not really what this book is about. It is more about impressions and the part they play in the popular memory.

---

[86] Following Soglo's defeat in 2001, the party Renouveau du Bénin (RB) split between those who followed his wife, Rosine, by then president of the party, and another faction under Nathaniel Bah.

[87] Several members of Soglo's family were the core of his entourage: his brother Saturnin was Ambassador to Germany, his son Leady an influential presidential councillor, his nephew Christophe, son of a former President Soglo (Christophe Soglo, 1909–1983) was head of personal security.

The Churches were amongst the first to react in this debate. While the Catholic Church may have had some willingness for "dialogue" with Africa's traditional religions, the Evangelical and Pentecostal Churches felt no such inclination. Theologians such as Adoukonou, in line with Catholic thinking since the Second Vatican Council, albeit with great "prudence" and "respect for the values of African traditional religion",[88] have tried to see them as a "*preparation* for the Gospel, because they contain precious *semina Verbi* which can lead a great number of people 'to be open to the fullness of Revelation in Jesus Christ through the proclamation of the Gospel'".[89] Students of religion will have their own reservations about such an approach. For Evangelicals and Pentecostals, however, the case was much clearer. In a debate which finds echoes in Haiti, the rehabilitation of Vodún for all Evangelicals and Pente-costals meant the return of the *forces of darkness* and was, as such, an abomination and anathema.[90] This certainly played a part in Soglo's defeat in the 1996 presidential election. Although almost impossible to prove, there is anecdotal evidence that some pastors, privately at least, and some not so privately, gave voting instructions to their fol-lowers, and that quarters with strong evangelical communities voted for Kérékou who had, as we have seen, been repackaged as a born-again Christian. Pastor Sam Igboka of Faith Tabernacle was quite forthright in stating the Church's opposition to Soglo because of his perceived dalliance with Vodún. "We prayed him out," he said of his defeat in the 1996 election, explaining that the Church felt itself threatened by his apparent alliance with Vodún and his rehabilitation of the cult.[91] This was not untypical.

> Our pastor said "this fellow is getting it wrong" and he quoted the saying where Jesus says that he will build his Church and the gates of hell will not rise up against it. It was on this basis that the team prayed. We said, "Oh Lord, if someone wants to close your Church, you yourself have said that you would build your Church, therefore no man can close it. Act on your word and protect the interests of your Church.[92]

The Evangelicals and Pentecostals were not alone in their apprehen-sion. Abbé Pamphile Fanou, a Catholic priest active in the ministry of

---

[88] *Ecclesia in Africa*, 137.
[89] Ibid., 67. See also 7, 49, 67, 68, 137.
[90] See Hurbon, *Sociologie*, 203–254, also de Surgy, *Le phénomène*, 432–435.
[91] Interview, 25 June 2002.
[92] Interview, 3 June 2002.

healing and exorcism, told me that "the devil told an exorcist in France that his seat was in Benin [...] For a time this was diminishing but with the arrival of President Soglo, who wished to rehabilitate the culture of the country, it was revived and is gaining ground again".[93] The trope of Benin as the world centre of Vodún, defined as evil and Satanic, is a recurring theme, particularly in the Charismatic Churches but also in the CCRM. It is denounced by some academics[94] and others seeking a more sympathetic approach to traditional religions, but it is, in my view, an indication of the profound fissures in the society itself.

The reservations about the rehabilitation of Vodún in the political sphere were expressed not just on the popular level. Adoukonou, who has tried to rehabilitate both Danxomɛ and Vodún as cultural and religious expressions, did not feel that it has its place in a modern, democratic and religiously pluralistic Benin. He challenged the thinking underlying the debate surrounding Vodún.[95] Like many Catholic intellectuals, he sees the efforts to rehabilitate Vodún as an instrumentalisation for political purposes. He claims that a certain political elite seeks to "revive the Vodún world in order to make of it what many consider to be an electoral clientele".[96] In doing so, it ignores the complexity of the whole Vodún system, which is not in any case appropriate in a modern society which demands rationality, openness and transparency, an open calabash rather than closed one, with priority being given to the human person, the individual. "Our [traditional] society knew how to contain anarchy but without avoiding the occult totalitarianism of those who render the Tradition stronger than the individual."[97] Whatever his feelings about Danxomɛ's glorious past and the purely transcendent and ethical aspects of Vodún, Adoukonou's Catholic personalism makes it impossible for him to accept the rehabilitation of the political discourse of Danxomɛ and an instrumentalisation of the cult. He rejects the esoteric and the arcane, fearing the creation of a new occult totalitarianism in the hands of the few *à la Haïtienne*.

---

[93] Interview, 17 June 2002.
[94] De Surgy decries these attitudes as "unchristian". See de Surgy, *Le Phénomène*, 432–440.
[95] Adoukonou, *Nouvelle Sortie*, 147–185; also Adoukonou, *Vodun*, Sillon Noir, 1993. See also Mgr R. Sastre, 1989, "Evangile et Forces Occultes: Quelle conscience chrétienne face à la conquête du pouvoir", *CB*, 539, 2; 11.
[96] Adoukonou, *Vodun, Démocratie*, 2.
[97] Adoukonou, *Nouvelle Sortie*, 151.

Traditional society seemed to find it legitimate that all other persons be limited in their religious liberty by royal and ancestral tradition. In a state of law, one must at one and the same time avoid anarchy and totalitarianism. The ancient city, let us repeat it, avoided anarchy, but it limited with a tacit arbitrariness the wonderful expansion of liberty from the *Tò* (the city) to the *Xò* (the house) through the *Xwé* (the lineage compound). The *Tò* in legitimising an expansionist war, seeks to impose its law on all the other *Tò* and to identify itself with the *Gbɛ́* (the world, existence). The question of whether or not it is possible to legitimate violence at this level appears to receive a negative response.[98]

It would appear that Gbégnonvi might have some justification when he points to Adoukonou's position in relation to Danxomɛ. His relations with the kingdom, its history and its religion appear at times ambiguous, as he tries to separate what he feels are the essential and non-essential threads. In the polemic surrounding this debate, Haiti is often evoked as an example of where Benin *does not* want to go politically. While it is acknowledged that the Vodṹn played a positive role in the resistance to the "process of cultural amnesia brought about by the slave trade"[99] and in maintaining the identity of African slaves on the island, there is also the feeling that Haiti has come to represent everything that can happen when the Vodṹn takes over. So the relationship with the Dahomean diaspora is nuanced, as the following extract from an interview illustrates:

> What I know is that some Americans come here to take strength from occult ceremonies…It is horrible…Haitians when they say their sources are here…they are occult things…Vodṹn ceremonies etc. …They have themselves bewitched…they make pacts with the demon. That only encourages others…because they finance it and this encourages others to try the demon again, to develop the efforts of the demon in the country…and that creates a kind of fear.[100]

Goudjo says much the same thing

> I often ask myself why Haiti doesn't take off [in the socio-political and economic sense] but it's because these are our people. They live in the crassest misery, enclosed in their Vodṹn…And they come to tell us that we must plunge back in this [...] I have noted this vision of things which is too spiritualist, which blinds us and prevents us from discovering the social dynamism of the faith which should lead us to action.[101]

---

[98] Ibid.
[99] Hurbon, *Sociologie*, 245.
[100] Interview, 17 June 2002.
[101] Interview, 14 July 2002.

For its critics and even many intellectuals who seek to understand it, rehabilitating Danxomɛ and establishing links with its diaspora may be quite laudable in itself, but Danxomɛ does not represent modernity and they have serious doubts about where this rehabilitation is meant to lead. While a genuine understanding of culture and history is important, the desire is to look at these, to assume them, be enriched by them and then to move on.

The presidential elections of 1996 and 2001: a brief illustrative analysis

The divisions in Danxomɛ-Benin do indeed bring to mind the scriptural passage:

> Every kingdom divided against itself will be ruined, and every city or household divided against itself will not stand. (Mt 12, 25)

The kingdom itself was deeply divided and the modern state has been built, and continues to build, upon this division. The two-against-one logic detected by Ronen continues to dominate Benin politics, and the society itself remains extremely fissiparous along the primordial fault lines. This was well illustrated in both the 1996 and 2001 presidential elections. The most striking of these fault lines is the apparent inability of the country to renew its political leadership and, intimately linked to this, its failure to break away from the logic of primordial alliances that has dominated policy since the foundation of the state.[102] The four leading candidates, following the first round of both elections, were all veterans of Benin politics, *fils du terroir* candidates from their respective fiefdoms: Houngbedji from Porto Novo, Amoussou from the Mono, Soglo from Agbɔmɛ and Kérékou from *le grand Nord*. In the end, of course, it came down to a head-to-head between Agbɔmɛ, in the person of Soglo, and the rest grouped behind Kérékou.[103] One local

---

[102] See Cedric Mayrargue, "Les élites béninoises au temps de Renouveau démocratique: Entre continuité et transformation", in J. Daloz (ed.) *Le (non-)renouvellement des élites en Afrique subsaharienne*, Bordeaux: CEAN, 1999, 33–56; *Pan African News Agency*, "La fibre régionaliste a dominé le scrutin de dimanche", Cotonou, 08 March 2001.

[103] For reasons of political strategy, Houngbedji, who threw his weight behind Kérékou in the second round of the 1996 election, changed allegiance in 2001 and supported Soglo in the second round.

commentator spoke of an "alternation without alternatives", while the popular imagination came up with a Béninois political neologism in the term "*ninisme*" meaning "*ni Kérékou, ni Soglo*".[104] Whatever its attraction in campaign terms, the slogan clearly did not do the trick since these were precisely the candidates who emerged for the second round. In the 2001 election Kérékou gained a sizeable 45% to 27% lead, leaving Houngbedji and Amoussou as kingmakers at best in the unchanging logic of Danxomε-Benin politics.[105]

The vote was, of course, strongly regional, with Kérékou taking over 80% in the north. As the table illustrates, however, the incumbent was also the only candidate to make any inroads in the fiefs of his opponents in the first round, actually winning in Amoussou's home territory, the Mono. Soglo on the other hand, while having a landslide in his own area, made little impression in any of the other areas. This was a repeat of the pattern in 1996.

Table 1: First-round voting pattern in the four fiefs[106]

	Donga	Atlantique	Ouémé	Mono
M. Kérékou	80.46%	18.79%	27.04%	49.88%
N. Soglo	3.76%	70.90%	4.60%	14.21%
A. Houngbedji	1.20%	3.5%	64.05%	4.04%
B. Amoussou	0.62%	2.55%	1.63%	26.87%

This pattern was largely repeated throughout the country. In itself, this could be seen as a positive result, and it certainly enhances Kérékou's image as a national leader. One has to ask, however, to what extent it is at least as much a rejection of Danxomε as it is an endorsement of Kérékou. Despite Houngbedji's instructions to vote Soglo in the second round, it is far from clear that his supporters followed. In a significant note, it is reported that the *barons* of his party reminded Houngbedji

[104] Candidate Lionel Agbo is credited with inventing the term, saying that Kérékou and Soglo have engendered a bipolarisation of national politics and a bicephalism which is preventing development See *Pan African News Agency*, "Bio-express du candidat Lionel Agbo", Dakar, 20 February 2001.
[105] The four top candidates took 93.75%, with little sign of future leaders emerging amongst the remaining twelve.
[106] This is based on an early partial sample on 5 March 2001 by the CENA. The samples were as follows: Donga 25.06%; Atlantique 4.94%; Ouémé 6.6%; Mono 8.78%.

that the alliance between King Toffa I of Porto-Novo and the kings of
Agbɔmɛ was never successful and that this modern version was equally
unlikely to succeed.[107] It is hard to imagine that they were not aware
of the words of the new king *Ago-li-Agbo* of Danxomɛ, following the
destitution of Gbɛhanzɪn in 1894: "*Ago-li-Agbo, Allada Klën afo, ma
dja i o, Français ouë gni mon*" ("Take care Danxomɛ, Aladà trembled
but did not fall thanks to the French").[108] The French may no longer
play the same role, although Soglo has often expressed his antipathy
towards them,[109] but Porto-Novo, the successor to Aladà, and Danxomɛ
are clearly not reconciled and this is a factor in national life. Kérékou
finished a very respectable second in the Ouémé with 27% of the
vote in the first round, repeating his 1996 performance. Amoussou,
encouraged by the promise of a free run in 2006, had little choice but
to follow his Ajă countrymen, and throw his support behind Kérékou
in the second round. Again, one is inclined to see historical antipathies
at play, in the area that was overrun by Danxomɛ in the seventeenth
century and from where such a very large proportion of the slaves for
the transatlantic trade were taken.

The fundamental reason for Soglo's defeat in 1996 was his "inca-
pacity to build alliances on a national level". His political base "was
progressively reduced to his town of origin and that of his wife, if not
to his immediate family circle".[110] Emmanuel V. Adjovi offers another
reason: popular discontent with a "managerial philosophy" and an
over-reliance on Soglo's acknowledged technocratic skills. Kérékou,
on the other hand, had been "touched by grace (the resurrection of the
chameleon) and knew how to make the necessary alliances with the old
enemies".[111] Both of these observations are accurate but incomplete.
Both ignore the force of history that mired Soglo and was the obstacle
he signally failed to recognise and overcome. Kérékou had indeed a
tremendous capacity to build national alliances, playing one against
the other on all the registers, and as such may claim to have united a

---

[107] *Pan African News Agency*, "Tractations pour les alliances au second tour", Dakar
22 February 2001.

[108] Le Hérissé, *L'Ancien Royaume*, 22.

[109] Soglo's apparent American sympathies certainly did little to help him in France,
which favoured Kérékou in the 2001 election.

[110] Thomas Bierschenk and J.P. Olivier de Sardan, *Les pouvoirs au villages: le Bénin
rural entre démocratisation et décentralisation*, Paris: Karthala, 1998, 56.

[111] Emmanuel V. Adjovi, *Une Election Libre en Afrique: La présidentielle du Bénin
(1996)*, Paris: Karthala, 1998, 174.

real Benin *Tò*, to have achieved the renaissance which Soglo's party aspired to, and to *incarnate le Bénin nouveau* albeit with all its difficulties, ambiguities and contradictions.

With the CNFVN and the advent of a more democratic electoral consultation, it is clear that Benin has made considerable gains. The government, including Kérékou, has legitimacy in the eyes of the people, much of the violence has been removed from political life, there is personal freedom, an energetic, if sometimes irresponsible, press, and the country enjoys a real stability. Decentralisation of government, seen as "an integral part of the process of democratisation launched in 1990" may defuse some of the primordial tensions, as well as creating more localised democracy, although this has run into considerable difficulty.[112] Benin has in some ways managed to replace its neighbour Togo in Western favour, projecting itself as a haven of peace, stability and democracy, a model to be emulated. It looks on its western neighbour with perhaps a little *schadenfreude*, while reaping some small democratic dividends in the form of inward investment and aid that might otherwise have gone to Togo. The underlying social fabric, the *lien social*, however, remains fragile, and this fragility reaches in to the smallest units of society. The country is struggling to invent itself, or reinvent itself, in a way that allows it to engage with modernity. My thesis is that its struggles with its history remain its biggest challenge, as several African intellectuals have pointed out in this chapter. This struggle with its memory, in a way that fits psychoanalytical theory, means that it has not (cannot?) freed itself from it, and remains dominated by it. My impression was of a society at times turning in circles. The failure to renew its elites is really only symptomatic of its failure to renew its ideas, as even a cursory look at what passed for election manifestos and programmes for government in 2001 shows. The people one meets, and most understandably young people, appear as people looking out on a world that is quickly changing but from which they seem excluded. Mayrargue is correct to speak of a creeping "anomie and unease" in the society he encountered.[113] Like several of the people

---

[112] "Etat de la décentralisation au Bénin", Programme de Développement Municipal, Cotonou, 2000, 7. *http://www.pdm-net.org/french/cdr/decentralisation/benin/etat_benin. PDF.*

[113] Cedric Mayrargue, "The Expansion of Pentecostalism in Benin: Individual Rationales and Transitional Dynamics", in A. Corten and R. Marshall (eds), *Between Babel and Pentecost: Transnational Pentecostalism in Africa and Latin America*, Bloomington: IUP, 2001, 278.

encountered in the course of this chapter, young people too feel mired, in need of change and a breakthrough.

This is the socio-political terrain upon which religions of all kinds operate in Benin. Cotonou wakes before dawn to the cries of muezzin imploring Allah "the great and the merciful" and it goes to sleep (or doesn't) to the sound of Christian Churches praying and singing late into the night.[114] What Kä Mana describes as "the exuberance of the religious" in Benin is very striking. There is an enormous religious market offering what is craved: salvation, refuge, healing, deliverance, protection, solutions, breakthroughs, success release, prosperity, miracles, victory, and even glory. Here one encounters what Kä Mana colourfully describes as "the respectable", "the delirious", "the venerable", "illusion merchants", "true seekers of God", "counterfeiters of the sacred", "the deep breath of the spirit" as well as the occasional "terrorist of the invisible".[115]

But how effective is all this? Where does it lead? Is there what this same theologian describes as "a coherent project" out of which the "images of the world might constitute a force, a breath, a dynamic of pregnant symbols and vital representations capable of mobilising the energies [needed in Benin] to invent a new future?" To what extent and in what way, he asks, "can the Christian utopia as a horizon of existence be credible in the debates of society and in what way could the new evangelisation be presented as another way of being and of living for human societies"?[116]

The second part of this book will be an attempt to look at some of these questions. It will be an examination of the theory and praxis, the different discourses of the Churches and their place in socio-political change in the lives of the many people they touch.

---

[114] In March 2002 a presidential decree dealing with 'sound pollution' placed restrictions on the nocturnal activities of the churches. One of the churches I was visiting was stoned by people of the neighbourhood upset at the noise.

[115] Kä Mana, *La Nouvelle*, 23–24.

[116] Ibid., 20–21.

For the Vodún to exist it must be welcomed. It is man who creates the sacred.

Gɛlɛdé *is a masked cult, originally common in the Ouémé valley on the Nigerian border. Although the masquerades are performed entirely by men, women run the society which is responsible for the cult. Its purpose is a kind of spiritual policing as it seeks to combat supernatural evil influences. These misfortunes are believed to be brought about through the power of female witches the cult is called upon to assuage.*

Statue of Gbéhanzin, King of Dahomey (reigned 1189–1904, defeated y the French in 1892) at the entrance to Abomey. In inscription reads "*I will never sing any treaty which might alienate the independence of the land of my ancestor*s." In popular derision by the opponents of Dahomey his gesture is interpreted as "*Halt progress.*"

IMAGES FROM THE SLAVE TRADE

Images from a painful history. "*The task of the reconstruction of Africa requires that Africans be reconciled to their own history and their own culture.*" (B. Adoukonou)

SANCTUARIES AT SAINT MICHAEL'S PARISH, COTONOU

The main sanctuary: The casts in cement and painted locally represent the
Sacred Heart of Jesus a,d (r-l) in the back ground St. Rita, the Infant of Prague,
St. Anthony of Padua, and St Joseph. There is a statue of the Virgin Mary to
the right of this group out of picture.

A sign to the left reads: "*St. Michel, noble chief of the celestial armies, the people of your parish welcome you. Thank you. St. Michel, archangel, with your sword defend us.*" St Michel is also a major figure in the Celestial Church of Christ angelology. State of St. Michael, patron saint of the parish of St. Michel.

AN ICONOGRAPHY OF SUFFERING
AT SACRÉ CŒUR PARISH, COTONOU

A strong popular kenotic iconography has developed in Catholic parishes in
Cotonou with vivid illustrations of the suffering Christ. This is in sharp contrast
to charismatic churches where suffering is rarely mentioned, or only as an evil
to be vanquished.

CHAPTER FIVE

CIVILISATION, PACIFICATION, DEMISE: THE CHURCHES AND THE KINGDOM OF DANXOMƐ

A brief historical overview of Christianity in Danxomɛ-Benin

It takes no more than a cursory examination of the history of the Christian missionary movement to see that the response to the Great Commission (Mt. 28, 19) has always been intimately linked to more worldly developments. It has sought to respond to "the signs of the times" (Mt. 16, 3). In less theological language, the Church, from the time of the first Pauline missionary impulse, has followed closely upon, and to some extent, inspired socio-political developments, particularly within Europe. This is particularly clear at three high points in the history of mission in Western Christianity: the monastic missionary movement from the seventh to the ninth centuries, leading eventually to the foundation of what became known as Christendom; the spread of Catholicism in Latin America from the end of the fifteenth century and, later, Protestantism in North America; and colonial expansion and the "scramble for Africa" beginning in the mid nineteenth century, leading to the missionary movement which eventually implanted Christianity in sub-Saharan Africa. It can be argued that the nineteenth-century missionary movement in West Africa was inspired largely by evangelical Protestants, committed to abolition, and that Catholics followed only as the scramble became apparent and the fear of Protestant domination rose. Certainly the element of competition was never lacking.[1] The issue was, as we shall see presently, also linked to the emerging colonial situation in the region.

It has been argued that the more recent expansion of charismatic Christianity, from the 1980s on, particularly in parts of the developing world, is a similar response to a world in mutation, with Churches,

---

[1] See Pierre Trichet, "The abiding commitment of de Brésillac to Dahomey", in *Society of the African Missions, Bulletin*, 111, 2001, 41–43.

as Gifford suggests, "assuming an increasing significance in the creation of a modern pluralistic African society".[2] They are spaces within which new visions are offered and a new discourse imparted, whether or not they can contribute to realising them. Through the enormous changes, from sixteenth-century European discovery and expansion, through industrialisation, colonisation and globalisation in an inexorable movement, Christianity, in one form or another, seems to have been a constant presence, despite its retreat to a more private space in the continent where it first emerged so publicly.

There had been a Spanish and Portuguese influence on the Guinea Coast from the latter part of the fifteenth century, and a short-lived Christian missionary presence in Danxomε from the seventeenth century. However, the first more enduring presence came following the visit of the remarkable West African pioneer, Thomas Birch Freeman, of the Wesleyan Methodist Missionary Society (WMMS), at the end of 1842 and the first months of 1843.[3] This was followed by a strong Catholic presence from 1860, with the establishment of the Apostolic Vicariate under Fr Francis Borghero, leading to the foundation of the modern Catholic Church in what was to become Dahomey-Benin. Both of these efforts, which in the short term failed, were important, as they were the first encounters between Danxomε and Christianity for which we have detailed accounts. These will be examined in some detail later.

As was the case elsewhere in Africa, however, the Christian myth was not left in the sole possession of the colonial masters, and independency soon emerged. Hastings argues that this phenomenon is "in a sense endemic to Anglo-Saxon Protestantism once it ceased to be a State Church", while less likely to occur in Catholicism.[4] It is hardly surprising, then, that the first manifestations of independency in Dahomey occurred in the Methodist Church at Porto-Novo with the separation of the Bodawa and Eledja Churches in 1901 and 1937 respectively. These were Churches in the Ethiopian tradition. Significantly, Porto-Novo, on the border with Nigeria, also saw the birth of the *Eglise du Christianisme Celeste* (CCC) in 1947, a Church

---

[2] Gifford, *African Christianity*, 20.
[3] For CMS visits from Abeokuta, see E.G. Parrinder, *The Story of Ketu*, Ibadan: IUP, 1956.
[4] Adrian Hastings, *The Church in Africa 1450–1950*, Oxford: Clarendon 1994, 498, 528.

in the later Aladura tradition. This contagion alarmed the French
authorities, who feared a "proliferation—and in the case of Benin a
contamination coming from neighbouring Nigeria".[5] Today the CCC,
"the last great African prophetic movement",[6] is the second largest
Church in Benin.[7]

Benin's Assemblies of God and Sudan Interior Mission (SIM) were
established in 1946 and 1947 at Natitingou and Kandi respectively.
Following a 1949 zoning agreement with these Churches, the Methodist Church withdrew to its traditional strongholds along the eastern
border amongst the people of Yoruba origin, where the majority of
Benin's Methodists still live.

The next major, though more diffuse, religious movement occurred
in the period following the CNFVN in 1990, when a general liberalisation of public space led to the rise of an array of Churches, mostly
of the charismatic type. Here also, however, it is clear that many were
the result of Nigerian religious effervescence in the 1980s, under the
influence of Archbishop Benson Idahosa. A recent, somewhat controversial, study found that there were some 430 Churches in Benin.[8]
These range from tiny straw-covered structures bringing together a few
community members in remote villages, through a spectrum of older
evangelical, and more recent Pentecostal and Charismatic Churches
of Anglo-Saxon origin, to African Initiated Churches (AICs), two
small Orthodox Churches of somewhat uncertain origin, to the main
historical Churches, Catholic and Methodist.

This is a wide spectrum of Christianity in a small country. What was
of interest to me in the sample I studied, however, were the common
elements in the discourse in all of them, from the nineteenth century
down to the present day, in relation to the historical Danxomε and
its continuing influence on state and society in modern Benin. I shall
attempt to show that the Churches have from the earliest days played

---

[5] See J.C. Barbier, E. Dorier-Apprill, C. Mayrargue, *Formes contemporaines du
christianisme en Afrique Noire*, Bordeaux: Cean, 1998, 16.

[6] Ibid., 12.

[7] The CCC claims it had "30 million members in Nigeria during the lifetime of
pastor Oschoffa" and 500,000 members in Benin. In Benin presently 150–200,000
seems a more plausible figure (see ARCEB, *Leve-toi et Va*, Cotonou, 2000).

[8] ARCEB, *Leve-toi*. The methodology and statistics of this study were strongly
contested (Raymond Bernard Goudjo, "La Face cachée de l'ONU: Question Sociales
et familiales actuelles", *CB*, 774, 13 July 2001) J.C. Barbier confirmed the objectivity of this study.

a crucial role in determining, not always positively, the way Béninois have come to understand their history and their culture. At the same time, they have been the not always willing vector of modernity, and promoters of social change they did not control.[9] They offer a *break with the past* and various bright new horizons, mirages or otherwise; the possibility, as some of them put it, of a *breakthrough* into a much desired modernity. Whatever the arguments about helping people to come to terms with structural adjustment, or any of the many other *global* problems that beset Benin and Africa—and these are present—at the centre of this discourse lies the *local*. They are also, and, in my view perhaps above all, an attempt to come to terms with history, a bridge between the past and the future: the image of Danxomɛ as a "kingdom of darkness", the "home of the Vodún" and the slave trade and the new Benin that people aspire to. Despite the historical changes there is continuity in the discourse. The Churches continue to find their space in the anthropological fragility, which we looked at in the previous chapter. They are themselves spaces in what is perceived as a difficult, even hostile, world, where people seek to establish social bonds and the social cohesion which appear to be lacking in a state striving for modernity. Danxomɛ then, as Benin now, as I shall show, was seen as a country in need of redemption from the demons that assail it, and, in my view, the demons are from within, the demons of its own history.

Evangelical philanthropy and nineteenth-century Methodist missiology

Thomas Birch Freeman (1809–1890) is an important figure in the wider West African context. The son of an English mother and an African freed slave and, from 1837, a pioneer of missions to Asante, Danxomɛ and Abeokuta, he emerges in his own writings as a tolerant and mild-mannered man.[10] He was patient, courteous and an acute observer of all kinds of details, thus his journals provide us with lively,

---

[9] See Bayart, *Religion et modernité*.
[10] See F. Deaville Walker, *Thomas Birch Freeman, the Son of an African*, London, SCM, 1929, 165. See also Wright, *Introduction*, xxx and N. Allen Birthwistle, *Methodist Missions*, in Rupert Davies, A. Raymond George, Gordon Rupp (eds), *A History of Methodism in Great Britain* (Vol. 3), London: Epworth Press, 1983, 59.

contemporaneous, descriptions of the three most important polities
in the area at that time. Agbɔmɛ, he noted, is "quite or nearly equal
to Kumasi in size and with a similar population, though there is no
comparison between Abeokuta and Kumasi, the latter being so far
superior."[11] Freeman was of West Indian origin and his project was
greatly facilitated by a natural sympathy for Africa and its peoples
which allowed him to develop cordial relationships at every level up
to the kings he met.

Before looking in any detail at Freeman, it is necessary to situate
him in the Methodist missionary movement in Great Britain in the
first half of the nineteenth century. This movement was marked by a
growing social conscience. It was acutely aware of "the enormities of
the slave trade"[12] and strongly committed to its abolition. However,
it also expressed the strongest reservations with regard to the emerging colonial enterprise, which it perceived as a behemoth advancing
inexorably and destructively on socially fragile societies. Although
the attitude to colonialism changed over time, it would always remain
ticklish, ranging from distrust on both sides to co-operation and a
certain mutual, utilitarian, instrumentalisation.[13]

An important figure in the movement was John Beecham.[14] Beecham was an eminent Methodist missionary and mission administrator,
called to provide evidence and information on missions to a House of
Commons Committee in 1837. He was particularly important for his
reflections on the relationship of mission to the colonial project and
an early advocate of the concept of the "civilising mission", which
was the basis of his missiology. In more practical terms, he promoted
the development of the 'native ministry' seeking to work first of all
with black West Indians, inspired by Coke,[15] and later with Africans
to develop as quickly as possible a sustainable local Church. There
is evidence of his correspondence with Freeman. Though Beecham's
area of particular interest was Asia and Oceania, he also wrote a

---

[11] Freeman, *Journal* (1843) 381, 395.
[12] Walker, *Freeman*, 16.
[13] See Andrew Porter, "Religion and Empire", in A. Porter (ed.), *The Oxford History
of the British Empire: the Nineteenth Century*, Oxford: OUP, 1999, 222.
[14] John Beecham, WMMS general secretary (1831–1855), President in 1850.
[15] Thomas Coke (1747–1814) clergyman, first bishop of the Methodist Church,
close associate of John Wesley, and founder of its early missions. In 1784 he was
named by Wesley as superintendent of the new missions to North America. See
Birthwistle, *Methodist Missions*, 1–7.

substantial ethnography of the Akan based largely on Freeman's mission reports, which despite its defects, Curtin notes, "did portray one African society as a working whole".[16]

In Beecham's radical Methodist view, the colonial project was "based on wrong principles or radical defects in the system". Founded upon a "principle of unrighteousness", it was "a flagrant violation of the rules of essential and immutable justice...aggravated by our pretence to superior illumination".[17] The "most radical defect" of the system, however, was "the want of a comprehensive and adequate provision of religious instruction".[18] In Beecham's view, religious instruction would allow peoples he considered "barbarous" to be "enlightened and elevated", thus putting them in a better position to confront the modernity which was being imposed upon them. Beecham's analysis of the societies he encounters is certainly reminiscent of Hobbes as he writes:

> They have to acquire *a taste for social order*, and need to be instructed as to the benefits of it...to respect, from principle, the rights of others and to seek redress when their own rights are violated, from the opera-tion of laws, and *not by resorting to violence* and arms.[19]

Though he did not use Hobbes' words, Beecham's idea for the mis-sion was to replace what he saw as a more or less permanent "war of every man against every man" in societies, where life was necessarily "nasty, brutish and short" with a "*a well-regulated society*"[20] through the establishment of an equally Hobbesian "covenant of every one to every one".[21] This in turn would allow the "natives" to be "brought into peaceful and decorous intercourse with white strangers", once they had "submit[ted] to *the restrictions necessary* for the maintenance of such intercourse".[22] This "peaceful and decorous intercourse" would be the basis of the new colonial contract, to the benefit of all, and Christianity was to be its source and guarantor.

---

[16] Beecham, *Ashantee and the Gold Coast*, London 1841. Philip D. Curtin, *The Atlantic slave trade*, London: The University of Wisconsin Press, 1969, 335.

[17] John Beecham, *Colonization: being remarks on colonization in general, with an examination of the proposals of the association which has been formed for colonizing New Zealand*, London: Mason, 1838, 3–4.

[18] Ibid., 12.

[19] Ibid., 13, emphasis mine.

[20] Beecham, *Colonization*, 13.

[21] Hobbes, *Leviathan*, ch. 21, section 111.

[22] Beecham, *Colonization*, 13.

Beecham perceived these societies as "degraded and demoralised" because of their history, and felt that "without the Gospel, barbarous nations cannot be raised from their degraded condition and be brought harmoniously to blend with other well-ordered communities...".[23] For Beecham it was clear that:

> the Gospel humanises the heathen whom it christianises. The Gospel contains the germs of true civilisation; and wherever it takes effect, those germs expand, and a beautiful exhibition of civilised life is the certain result.

In Victorian times, it is hardly surprising to find that clothes are seen as an outward sign of this. More significantly, however, Beecham envisages a nascent 'Protestant ethic' for these emerging nations. The Gospel, he claims, makes people sedentary through a desire to remain attached to a Church community, and thus they are "no longer dependent on the chase; and industrious habits are consequently formed". The thirst for the Word leads to the desire for education in order to read it. From this follows the "moral virtues—another stage in the civilising process—truth, honesty, fidelity, chastity", and thus the disappearance of polygamy, "a fruitful source of evil amongst savage people". This will, he feels, encourage "the maintenance of the marriage vow [and] the virtues which constitute, to so great an extent, the bond of civilised life". At the same time, he sees the inevitable promotion of women in stable Christian marriage as well as the respect of ageing parents, protecting them from elimination for the survival of the tribe, and children, protecting them from infanticide, both of which were so shocking for the missionaries.[24]

True civilisation, he concludes, follows Christianity "as a necessary and natural consequence", and he emphasises that "the soothing influence of religious teaching is especially needed, to calm the excitement which the war has occasioned amongst the Kaffers".[25] Replying specifically to a question from the House of Commons Committee as to whether "it would be advisable to begin with civilisation in order to produce Christianity, or with Christianity in order to produce civilisation", Coates replies: "Most distinctly with Christianity in order to [assure] the civilisation of a savage people, in any proper

---

[23] Ibid., 15.
[24] Beecham, *Colonization*, 17.
[25] Ibid., 20.

sense of the term civilisation."[26] This language is, of course, of its day, but it is clear that it was a radical social discourse for its time and his idea of the Christian mission was essentially that of radical social change. Beecham's intention was also to palliate "the pernicious tendency of...colonial policy", since the neglect of Christian teaching as part of this policy "has increased [the colonised peoples'] depravity and wretchedness".[27] Underlying all of this, however, there is also a theme that was not uncommon at the time, that of guilt, which led him to see "a debt of justice"[28] to the colonised, and to believe that "the importation of Christianity and civilisation would have been some kind of compensation for the original wrong done to the natives..." Beecham was not a lone voice. The Anglican evangelical Robert Needham Cust, writing at the end of a career which spanned much of this period, offers many of the same arguments, specifically in relation to Africa.[29]

Beecham's ambition is no less than to set "the full tide of British philanthropy" to work in order to "compensate Africa for the wrongs that have been inflicted on her, by raising her to a place among the Christian and civilised nations of the earth". Like many Christians after him, he is seeking a *kairos*, the "set time" "to favour" "the godlike work of Africa's regeneration".[30] Africans are also part of the "redeeming plan" and have "as deep an interest in the agonies of Gethsemane, and in the sufferings endured on Calvary, as any other portion of the human family".[31] Africa too, and specifically West Africa, is the object of the Great Commission "and included within the range of its divine philanthropy".[32] The *WMN* editorial introducing the first part of Freeman's *Ashantee Journal* may well

[26] D. Coates, Esq., Rev. John Beecham, and Rev. William Ellis, *Christianity the means of civilization: shown in the evidence given before a committee of the House of Commons, on aborigines,/by secretaries of the Church Missionary Society, the Wesleyan Missionary Society, and London Missionary Society. To which is added selections from the evidence of other witnesses bearing on the same subject.* London: Mason, 1837, 99.
[27] Ibid., 21.
[28] Ibid., *Christianity*, 94.
[29] Robert Needham Cust (1821–1909), Orientalist, Honorary Secretary to the Royal Asiatic Society, but also author of *An Encyclopaedic Sketch of Modern Languages of Africa.* See Robert Needham Cust, *Africa rediviva*, London: Stock 1891.
[30] Beecham, *The Claims*, 7.
[31] Ibid., 4.
[32] Ibid., 5, 8–9.

have been written by Beecham and certainly reflects his thought, emphasising "the necessity which exists there for the exertions of evangelical philanthropy...".[33]

This idea of an African *kairos* or 'time of favour' is a recurring theme of missiology, whether Catholic or Protestant, down to the present day. In a modern parallel, the Catholic document *Ecclesia in Africa* sees in recent developments "a true *kairos* moment in Africa". This, it claims, is an *historic moment of grace* as "[the continent] today is experiencing what we can call a *sign of the times*, an *acceptable time, a day of salvation*. It seems that the 'hour of Africa' has come, a favourable time...."[34]

The Protestant theologian Kä Mana, referring to the Catholic document, declares:

> The hour has come for us to reimagine Africa and to profoundly reorient Christianity on our soil [...] in order to bring forth great utopias for this continent...so that this mission and the energy of this project will transform in depth the persons and the institutions, that they might become the ferment of a new African society and the humus of a new will to be.[35]

"Man seems the only growth that dwindles here!" T.B. Freeman and the Methodist Mission to Danxomε

The WMMS effort in West Africa was based on Sierra Leone, where work had started in 1806, and which the Society saw as a bridgehead into West Africa. Central to this were the newly liberated, returning and recently Christianised slaves, many of them Yoruba victims of Danxomεan predation. The first mission to Nigeria emerged from this movement, rather than from any requests from within, as "several liberated Africans from Sierra Leone having proceeded to their fatherland (Badagry)...[requested] the presence of a missionary".[36] The usefulness of the missions and their power connections were, however, quickly understood by the local elites,[37] not least in their

---

[33] *WMN*, 1840, 197.
[34] *Ecclesia in Africa*, 6.
[35] Kä Mana, *La Nouvelle*, 30.
[36] Report, Cape Coast Circuit, 1843, WMMS, Box 259, Fiche 35.
[37] See Peel, *Encounter*, ch. 5.

battles with Danxomε. In a significant document, the King of Lagos writes:

> As your people, who have been trained up by you at Sierra Leone, and who are now at Abeokuta, are a kind condoling and sympathising people, they visit me frequently; and from some of them, who are capable of giving me the best and true information, I have enquired more particularly of the English nation, and their manners. Having, therefore, a good deal of knowledge about the general characters and dealing of the English people; their universal benevolence, which is seen more plainly in the liberated Africans returning from Sierra Leone, and other facts, and their readiness to help anyone in distress,—by these and other proofs of the dealings of the English nation, I am emboldened to apply to you, Sirs, that you would be pleased to take my case and application to your serious consideration; and if, having done this you find that you can at all, by any possible means, do anything for me as a help, I would be at a loss how to thank you.

He then goes on to make two specific requests, the first suggesting that if he were to have the mission's "friendship and favour and protection" he would come to live with them at Badagry. The second request is that the English would intervene "by all means, and by means of the English men-of-war, [to] stop the slave-dealers coming to Lagos to buy human beings".[38]

The earliest Methodist missionary effort in Danxomε was a direct consequence of the mission to Badagry, and the need to protect its fledgling Christian community from predation.[39] Freeman's intention in going to Danxomε was to explain to the king "the real object and intentions" of the mission at Badagry, rather than to start a mission addressed to Danxomε itself. Seeking to reassure the authorities, whose extensive system of espionage kept them well informed,[40] he emphasised that his objectives "were of a strictly religious and not of a political nature". In his first encounter with Danxomε, when meeting

---

[38] Letter from Akatoge, King of Lagos, Abeokuta, 8 September 1845, *WMN*, 1846, 131–132. The letter was apparently dictated to Rev. S. Annear. Annear adds a note, perhaps with possible criticism in mind, emphasising that it is "an exact copy, without the slightest alteration".

[39] This remains a recurring theme until 1881, when a last report says the Dahomean army is "[clamouring] to be permitted to invade to Abeokuta", John Milum 'Dahomey as it is', *WMN*, 1881, 237.

[40] Freeman notes the presence of "some messengers, who came down from the King of Dahomi" in Badagry, who said they were glad to see him "but I doubt their sincerity", Thomas B. Freeman, 'Journal of the Rev. T.B. Freeman, on a visit from Cape-Coast Castle to Badagry, Yariba, and Dahomi', *WMN*, 1843, 369–400.

the Chief at Xwedá, he explains the mission he is undertaking, in
terms that Beecham would recognise as his own:

> I dwelt at length on the anxiety of the British Government, and a
> great portion the British public, to confer real benefits on the natives
> of Africa, by the introduction of civilisation; and asked him whether
> he did not consider such sentiments honourable and good on the part
> of England, and worthy of the attention of those they were intended
> to benefit. He said in answer to this, that my palaver was good, and
> that I could go up and see the King of Dahomi.[41]

This brief extract provides us with a very precise resume of Freeman's
approach to mission, which was in turn evangelical, philanthropic and
diplomatic. He was by all accounts a genuinely pious man, motivated
by a Christian zeal[42] marked by the emotion of his Methodist tradition
and "feelings of the most intense character".[43] Not a little romantic,
he is often moved by "the ever-verdant scenery",[44] with its promise of
light, life and abundance. At the same time, however, he is appalled
by the contrasting misery of a people trapped in "exceeding darkness and superstitious condition [...] to whose minds light seemed
to be almost inaccessible".[45] His biographer tells us "[the beauty of
the countryside] appeared to be so entirely out of harmony with the
warlike spirit of the people" and that "ever and anon he was sad-
dened by the abounding heathenism".[46] In a remarkable paragraph
describing Kumasi, Freeman writes:

> It is very handsome. These are thy glorious works, Parent of good,
> Almighty. But alas, how painful is the reflection, "Man seems the only
> growth that dwindles here!" What dark lines on these fair colours are
> the habitations of cruelty, superstition, and death! In vain do the pretty
> jessamine (*jasminium gracile*) and other odoriferous flowers, perfume
> the air, while man murders his brother, and taints the atmosphere with
> the noxious effluvia arising from the putrefying carcass of the mangled
> victim of his superstition and cruelty. Oh thou Almighty Being! Hasten
> the day when even sanguinary Ashantee shall be civilised....[47]

---

[41] Ibid., 373.
[42] See Birthwistle, *Methodist Mission*, 56–61.
[43] Freeman, *Journal*, 1843, 380.
[44] Ibid., 394.
[45] Letter, Cape Coast, 12 August 1854; *WMN*, 1854, 176.
[46] Walker, *Freeman*, 167–168.
[47] Thomas B. Freeman, "The Ashantee Journal: Journal of the Rev. Thomas B.
Freeman, on a visit from Cape-Coast to Ashantee in interior Western Africa", *WMN*,
1840, 212.

Freeman, understandably dismayed by some of what he sees, feels a certain empathy with those he undoubtedly considered to be his African brothers. However lost and misguided by custom and tradition they might be, he is slow to condemn them. He attempts, rather, to rationalise and understand the horrors he sees, comparing them quite understandably to Tyburn, where, he writes, "crowds of civilised and nominally Christian folk had watched men being hanged, drawn and quartered".[48] Despite his efforts, however, both Asante, and to an even greater degree Danxomɛ,[49] emerge from his texts as despotic kingdoms of misery and death, crying out for the light of the Gospel. "The tales of horror, wretchedness and cruelty...wrought in [his] mind the deepest commiseration." He writes:

Are thou the God of Jews alone,
And not the God of Gentiles too?
To Gentiles make the goodness known;
Thy judgements to the nations show;
Awake them by the Gospel call:
Light of the world, illumine all!"

Inspired by the prophet Ezekiel and in a style of discourse that is still common in many Charismatic Churches, he prays:

They are as the dry bones in the valley.
But, O Thou Fountain of Life!
Thou Spirit of eternal truth!
Breathe upon these slain,
that they may live.[50]

Danxomɛ's obduracy led to a serious deterioration in its overall situation in the decade following Freeman's first visit. He remarks in his correspondence that, following the failure of the 1851 campaign against Abeokuta and with the constant naval pressure on the slave trade, the economic situation in Danxomɛ worsened considerably,

---

[48] In Walker, *Freeman*, 177.
[49] Freeman presents Kumasi as "an immense slaughterhouse", *Journal*, 1840, 215. However, according to his biographer, he found Abomey to be "a veritable Golgotha", "the skulls and human sacrifice are overwhelming. [...] Even in Kumasi Freeman had seen nothing so terrible" Walker, *Freeman*, 173–175.
[50] Freeman, *Journal*, 1840, 201–202. See Ezekiel 37: 5–6. The text was the basis for a sermon entitled "Collective Power in the Valley" by Pastor Yemi Adafarasin at CAFM, 12 May 2002, with the pastor reminding the congregation that "anyone who is tired of this chapter is tired of God".

noting "all around the quiet stagnation of despotism".[51] This may
indeed explain the need for the state to symbolically reassert itself, and
when freeman visited Danxomε with Wharton in 1854, the town was
in preparation for the Great Annual Custom. Freeman, and certainly
Wharton, were quite shocked at the "moral desolation and ruin" they
witnessed, feeling that they were "indeed in regions of darkness on
the confines of the shadow of death".[52]

Freeman had fully accepted the missiological discourse of the
'civilising mission' and he was attempting quite consciously to intro-
duce a kind of modernity to West Africa. In his encounters with the
authorities, he extolled the benefits of European education, science,[53]
and industry, though this was treated with some scepticism by his
royal interlocutors and their entourages, who had little difficulty
understanding the socio-political ramifications for their own position of this discourse. Freeman notes: "Bad children, [they thought],
would get educated and do much mischief…for the African despot
has evidently an instinctive dread of education…"[54]

Danxomε was essentially a conservative monarchy, established on
gànhúnŭ, and in terms of politics this kind of modernity and social
change could only be a threat to its stability. The best traditions
of Dahomean diplomacy, however, would not allow a brutal (and
impolitic) rejection of modernisation, but sought to turn it to its
benefit. This Vodún too could be domesticated. From his first visit
Gezò, perhaps wary of the diplomatic advantages accruing to the
enemy Abeokuta from the presence of the European missionaries, asks
Freeman to "do something for Whydah".[55] At the same time he is
careful to keep the mission at the peripheries of power. Gezò insists
that it should remain effectively quarantined[56] at Xwedá. The town
had already been ceded to European influence, ruled by the Yóvógan,

---

[51] Freeman letter, 12 August 1854; *WMN*, 1854, 175–176.
[52] Ibid.
[53] Freeman, *Journal*, 1842, 181, 187, 190. He is excited to see a comet and comments: "The people seemed very much excited at this (*to them*) strange appearance;
and I amused myself for several minutes in attempting to explain to them its nature
and its revolutions." Freeman, *Journal*, 1843, 391.
[54] Freeman, *Letter*, 12 August 1854.
[55] Freeman, *Journal*, 1843, 394.
[56] Fisher describes the integration of new religious influences in African society
as a process moving from *quarantine*, through *mixing* and eventually to *reform* of
the society. See Humphrey Fisher, "Conversion reconsidered: some historical aspects
of religious conversion in black Africa", *Africa*, vol. 43, no. 4, 1973, 31.

the Viceroy and Minister for European Affairs, whose task it was to keep intruders at bay, prevent them from crossing the marshes and prying into Abomey.

Freeman realises that he is, to some extent, a pawn in the King's game. He notes that

> the experience of some years ago has taught [him] that, in general, whenever [the king] consents to [education], he does so not from any good feeling towards it, separately considered, but from some combination of political motives, self-interest etc. connecting itself with intercourse or desired intercourse with Europeans.

He would, however, play Gezò at his own game, astutely adding that: "These self-interested motives are generally our strong-holds (humanly speaking) on such characters at first, until time has been allowed for greater light to pervade, and purer motives to spring up in the mind."[57]

Ever a loyal Englishman, Freeman was convinced of the benevolent intent of England in executing the civilising mission.[58] This was expressed in Queen Victoria's philanthropic intentions towards Africa, and her government's desire for good relations with Danxomε. He hastens to assure Gezò that "the Queen of England had been recently turning her attentions very much towards Africa, and several times the question had been asked, 'What can be done for the good of Africa?'"[59] In fact, from the first twenty-one-gun salute received in the name of the Queen (and nine in his own honour), Freeman never really freed himself of his image as a diplomat, or seemed inclined to. For several years he quite knowingly became the favourite intermediary between the Royal Courts of Britain (or at least the Castle at Cape-Coast) and Danxomε, serving, in a manner of speaking, quite adeptly three masters at once: God, Britain and Danxomε.

Despite his diplomatic skills, there is a certain naiveté about Freeman. It is easy to imagine that, coming from a modest background

---

[57] Freeman, *Letter*, 12 August 1854.

[58] Governor Winniet "soon discovered how valuable as asset Freeman was to the cause of civilisation and good government." In 1846, Freeman advised Winniet in discussions with Gezò. The king requests "friendship" with England "but refuses a treaty for fear of his own army, set on attacking Abeokuta" Walker, *Freeman*, 165. Following a disagreement over his mission methods and perhaps over-ambitious projects in 1857, Freeman left the ministry and went to work for the colonial administration. He returned to the ministry after his retirement.

[59] Freeman, *Journal*, 1843, 394.

and finding himself thrust unexpectedly into affairs of state, he quite
enjoyed his role. There is every indication in the journals that, despite
a certain reticence about such displays on the Sabbath,[60] he revelled,
though always modestly and with great manners, in his quasi-diplomatic status and the ceremonial that often accompanied it. Following
his visits to all three kingdoms, he recounts in colourful detail his
official receptions as an emissary of Her Majesty's Government.[61]
This was a role he never refuted and one the authorities, British and
African, seemed happy to accord him. For Freeman, as well as for
the traumatised liberated slaves, England, which had delivered them,
was to be the guarantor of their freedom, and Christianity, whether
through its own spiritual powers or its place as the religion of England, was to be the religion of the new dispensation.[62]

Freeman, like all the early missionaries, was preoccupied by the
"violence and savagery" he witnessed and "gloried in describing
them".[63] He provides several macabre descriptions and, significantly,
one of only two plates in his 1844 edited account is also an image
of "human sacrifice". When they were published, his journals became
a missionary *cause célèbre*, and they, like other letters and reports
coming from the mission fields, were widely used in the *Wesleyan
Missionary Notices* to promote the appeals for funds and support for
the 'civilising mission'. For obvious reasons, the editors tended to
emphasise to an even greater extent what was seen as the barbarity
of West Africa in general, and Danxomɛ in particular.

Ellingworth suggests that from 1853 until his resignation from the
ministry in 1857, Freeman's relations with Gezò grew closer, with
the king seeking diplomatic contact, while he "redoubled his efforts
to begin missionary work".[64] In 1853 Rev. Joseph Dawson, a "native
assistant", reports his attempts to open a school at Xwedá.[65] Freeman
is very hopeful and writes to Beecham that "Admiral Bruce evidently

---

[60] Ibid.

[61] See, for instance, his perfect description of Gezò's heraldic standard, Freeman,
Journal, 1843, 30.

[62] Peel notes the relationship between "the mission and the powers" was largely
determined by a "political calculus" in "a search for ongoing allies in the ongoing
regional power struggle, and... a desire for 'cultural enhancement' *Encounter*, 123–124.
Dahomey was an important actor in this.

[63] Wright, *Introduction*, xxxv.

[64] Ellingworth, *Religion and Politics*, 216. Freeman's resignation appears to have
been at least partly due to a financial contoversy allied to other difficulties.

[65] Report, Cape Coast Circuit 1854, WMMS, Box 261, Fiche 47.

contemplates with great satisfaction our opening up a missionary communication […], and I think, myself, that our doing so […] will be of great political importance as it regards the feelings of the King of Dahomi".[66] By this stage the evangelical and diplomatic missions had become inextricably entwined.

Dawson, however, is not Freeman and his mission makes little progress. In 1855, he complains to Freeman that "the King and his people, by retarding the progress of our Mission at Xwedá and not having yet enabled us to get up a good school there, *are seriously opposing their own worldly interests*". Ellingworth comments that here "the fusion of religious and secular motives was complete: and the latter were dominant".[67] The Cape Coast Circuit Minutes for 1857 report meagre results for "a year's toil and heavy expenditure". But all is not hopeless and, with "faith and patience", they will "eventually throw by God's blessing a flood of heavenly light into the dark kingdom of Danxomɛ still overshadowed with the dragon wings".[68] By this stage, however, Freeman had left the ministry, and while the king remained friendly to the mission, he had effectively quarantined it at Xwedá.

The hapless Dawson eventually left Xwedá, in some odium, to be replaced in 1857 by another "native assistant", Peter Bernasko. Bernasko appears to have assumed something of the role of diplomatic intermediary, though certainly lacking Freeman's allure and prestige.[69] Ellingworth writes that "until work at Whydah came to an end in 1867 […], and even afterwards, Bernasko continued to regard himself as the official guide of British visitors to Abomey, and as an essential intermediary between them and the king". He certainly escorted Burton to Agbɔmɛ. He was identified with the whites and, at one point held hostage at Xwedá.[70] As the new pastor took up his position as a resident in Xwedá, the *WMN* invited readers to "pray both for the preservation of Mr Bernasko's life, that 'he may be delivered from unreasonable and wicked men'" and for success of

---

[66] Letter, 01 June 1853, in Ellingworth, 216.

[67] Ibid., 217.

[68] WMMS, Box 262, Fiche 50.

[69] Ellingworth, *Religion and Politics*, 219.

[70] Wharton letter, *WMN*, 25 November 1860, 214–216. A report in the *WMN* states that Bernasko "must consider himself in custody as a hostage for the good behaviour of the British people" *WMN*, 1862, 99.

his mission "to advance the interests of truth and humanity".[71] This
was not to be.

Like Dawson, Bernasko did not have Freeman's status or style.
Ellingworth suggests that the failure of the mission to Xwedá "must
be largely attributed to a succession of unworthy ministers".[72] While
the personal foibles doubtless played their part, Ellingworth's judge-
ment is a little harsh. In what must have been a crushing moment,
Bernasko confides to the visiting Rev. William West that "the king is
earnestly desirous of seeing 'a real Englishman', to have a general talk
with him".[73] The material difficulties of Bernasko's situation, his lowly
status, and the eventual disintegration of his ministry, reflect perhaps
the realities of "the native pastorate".[74] For our purpose, however, it
also illustrates the extent to which the mission was dependent upon
prestige and a visible relationship with the powers in the region. The
references of both Burton and Skertchly to Bernasko made it clear
that he had very little status. Freeman was clearly something of an
exception, not easily emulated by badly-educated freed slaves, thrown
into the ministry with little more than their evangelical fervour to
sustain them. It seems quite possible that Bernasko, more or less
abandoned, with only infrequent visits from Accra, did slide into
decline. In any case by 1870, Danxomε vanishes almost completely
from the *WMN*, apart from occasional references in articles dealing
with Badagary, Abeokuta or Porto-Novo.[75] It is certainly significant
that it was also at this time that the Catholic mission also withdrew
to Porto-Novo, as Danxomε crumbled.

Light and darkness

Let us hope that the excess of superstition and cruelty manifested by
the King of Dahomey in the recent Customs, and the threatenings he
has uttered against the partially Christian city of Abeokuta, which have
drawn upon him a rebuke and warning from HMG, are tokens that the

---

[71] *WMN*, 1860, 158–159.
[72] Ellingworth, *Religion and Politics*, 219.
[73] Rev. William West, letter, Cape Coast, 13 September 1862, *WMN*, 1862, 183.
[74] There are several parallels here as both Crowther and Freeman, certainly more
important figures than Bernasko, ran into difficulties in their Ecclesiastical careers.
[75] By this time the Methodist mission had become centred at Porto Novo, and
was part of the Lagos Circuit.

days of evil in that region are numbered. Light and darkness are now in conflict: revealed truth and soul-destroying error have met, and the struggle is for life.[76]

There is ample evidence to suggest that the frustration of the mission to Danxomε mounted from the time of Freeman's last visit. Bouche describes the country as "protected by nature in an enclave", leading to an exaggeration of its real size and importance.[77] It seems probable that, under increasing diplomatic pressure, Danxomε, closing in upon itself, entered a strongly rejectionist period, which was to last until its demise in 1892. The *WMN* took on an increasingly bellicose tone in its reports. One of the main critics was Wharton, who accompanied Freeman in 1854. In a letter to the *WMN*, he describes the kingdom as "this sink of iniquity", expressing his desire to "give a death-blow to its existence".[78] By 1860 the *WMN* was suggesting that:

> Surely prayer should be made without ceasing, that God would arise and have mercy on Africa [...] for her dark places are filled with habitations of cruelty to the bodies and lives of men, while their souls are under bondage to the devil, whose works they do...[79]

By this time, in the missionaries' eyes, there was no darker place than Danxomε. The frustration at the failure in Danxomε was exacerbated by continuing threats to the missions at Badagry and Abeokuta, enclaves of Christian light and hope in the midst of the apocalyptic desolation wrought by the Danxomε hordes. The kingdom came to be excoriated by the missionaries and it was at this period that there emerged in the missionary discourse what was essentially a Manichaean view of Danxomε as a kingdom of evil and darkness. In the words of the *WMN* editorial, "light and darkness [were] now in conflict...and the struggle is for life".[80] As we shall see, this is a view of the country that has persisted down to the present day in the CCC, many of the evangelical and Charismatic Churches, and in parts of the charismatic wing of the Catholic Church.

In the years following Freeman's retirement from missionary activity, the reports were increasingly alarming. The *WMN* began to

---

[76] *WMN*, 1861, 43.
[77] Pierre Bouche, *La Côte des Esclaves et le Dahomey*, Paris: Plon, 1885, 359.
[78] Letter, *WMN*, 1854, 173.
[79] *WMN*, 1860, 84.
[80] *WMN*, 1861, 43.

publish material which it saw as "supplying authentic information as to the crimes and miseries of Heathenism",[81] leading eventually to an impassioned plea which was to become a recurring theme of missionary discourse, Protestant and Catholic, British and French, in the years leading up to the demise of Danxomε:

> Would to God this might meet the eyes of some of those philanthropic Englishmen who have some feeling for Africa! Or for some man of eloquence and influence to point out to the people of England the comparative uselessness of their expensive squadron out here, and the enormous benefits that must result to this country, and ultimately to England herself, morally and materially, if she would extend her establishments on this Coast! Take away two-thirds of your squadron, and spend one-half its cost in creating stations on shore, and greatly strengthening your old stations.—"More forts, more Magistrates, more British Courts of Justice, more Missionaries. More! More! More!"

The extension of "her establishments" was, of course, the start of the colonial period, and this discourse was the basis for the collusion between the missionaries and the colonial powers that was to follow.

In an allegorical style still popular in Charismatic Churches and AICs, Danxomε came to be depicted in the *WMN* in biblical terms. Gezò and his successor Glɛlɛ́ are presented as a kind of African Nebuchadnezzar (2 Kings 24–25), leading the assaults on the Christian enclaves of Badagry and Abeokuta. Speaking in terms one would expect to hear in a Charismatic Church today, a report to the annual meeting of the Wesleyan Missionary Society held at Exeter Hall on 4 May 1874 reports that Abeokuta had been attacked by Danxomε:

> The defenders of the town were ranged in two camps, the Christians and the heathens, and the Mohamedans... Instead of the usual services camp meetings were held, and united prayer ascended from the Christian camp that God would deliver them as of old. Strange to say the Dahomean army were suddenly attacked by smallpox; hundreds of the army died of the plague, and the Egbas arose one morning to find the invaders camp deserted. This circumstance has impressed greatly the heathen mind, for they believe the deliverance was in answer to the prayers of the Christians... It is thus that upon a district over which the dark shadow of war has travelled rays of light and hope have been permitted to shine.[82]

---

[81] Whart on, letter in *WMN*, 1860, 80, 158–159.
[82] "Report to the annual meeting, Exeter Hall, 04 May 1874", *WMN*, 1874, 137.

By this stage, however, the Methodists had withdrawn from Danxomɛ, taking up a new mission in Porto-Novo, which the *WMN* correspondence testifies also had considerable difficulties.

Catholicism, commerce and conquest

While the Protestant missionaries were certainly the pioneers of the nineteenth-century missionary movement on the Guinea Coast, the Catholic Church was quick to rise to what it saw as a challenge. The historical records show that as early as 1845 plans were afoot for a mission in Danxomɛ.[83] This was at the instigation of the proprietor of the French trading counter at Xwedá, Victor Régis of Marseille, who had been trading on the coast since 1841. Régis' counter was the bridgehead upon which both the Church and France entered Danxomɛ. Writing 100 years later, Régis' grandson Jean-François Régis claims:

> Our ancestors knew how to join the noblest occupation to commercial ideas. From the first years that they set foot in these countries, they wished to attract missionaries whom they knew, by their civilising influence, would create a climate favourable to the growth of French power.[84]

Again, however, there was more than an element of diplomacy in this development. "The fact that the house of Régis maintained a monopoly was due to the fact that Gezò distrusted the English."[85] Forbes, whom we encountered briefly in the first chapter, a little peeved, conceded:

> Every time that relations between Dahomeans and English began to deteriorate the King always showed more favour to the French. It was this constant opposition of interests which explains the favour shown by the Dahomeans to the French in general and Régis in particular.[86]

---

[83] See Trichet, *The Abiding*, 18–38.

[84] Jean-François Régis, *Les Régis au Dahomey. Un centenaire familial*, Marseille: Sémaphore, 1941, in Trichet, *The Abiding*, 19.

[85] Bernard Schnapper, *La politique et le commerce français dans le Golfe de Guinée de 1838 à 1871*, Paris: Mouton, 1961, 173, in Trichet, *The Abiding*, 17.

[86] In Schnapper, *La politique*, 174.

Gezò was certainly the most adept of the kings and not averse to
a little geo-political bartering to strengthen his position in his own
ongoing battles with his eastern neighbours.

Régis' 'Christian philanthropy' and his dedication to the cause of
'civilisation' were not entirely without self-interest. He was particularly
interested in the schools the mission would provide, teaching children
reading, writing and simple arithmetic, the administrative fundamentals
of trade. His primary interest was in acquiring reasonably-qualified
African staff at little cost to himself. Trichet notes that religion is
not even mentioned on the proposed curriculum for the schools.[87]
Being seen by the religious he approached as a '*très bon chrétien*'
certainly helped his cause. However, it took another fifteen years to
actually start the mission, an administrative *lenteur* that annoyed the
practical Régis who admitted that "it is difficult to get men of the
world to understand the laws of spiritual jurisdiction".[88]

The trader had good relations with the French naval forces on the
Guinea coast and in 1851 convinced Commander Bouët-Wuillaumez,
who had negotiated "*un petit traité*" with Gezò, "to slip in a little
article favourable to the missionaries who would come to instruct his
subjects".[89] While the treaty did not explicitly favour any denomi-
nation, though it did say they should be French, Régis was quite
determined, noting, "we are Catholics and our greatest desire is to
see a Catholic mission established". Catholic *and French*, he might
have added, since his intentions were quite clear:

> The king is well disposed to the French. He would be happy if we
> established schools near our counter, and perhaps also in the interior,
> and to the capital, to teach the French language to the young Negroes.
> It seems to us that this is the way the missionaries should introduce
> themselves to Dahomey.[90]

---

[87] Trichet, *The Abiding*, 43.
[88] Letter of De Marion Brésillac to Cardinal Barnabo, Prefect of Propaganda
Fide, 03 March 1857.
[89] "*D'insinuer un petit article*". The legality of this "little treaty" of a mere ten
articles was later contested. Trichet states that Régis had certainly "instigated it"
and "even a rapid reading showed whom it was 'who gained from the crime'",
The Abiding, 44.
[90] Letter to the *PF*, 04 January 1856, Art. 10: Le roi prend l'engagement de
donner toute sa protection aux missionnaires français qui viendront s'établir dans
ses états, de leur laisser l'entière liberté de leur culte et de favoriser leurs efforts
pour l'instruction de ses sujets.

In 1855 Régis encountered the man who was eventually to help him realise his plans. Melchior de Marion Brésillac had been Catholic bishop of Combatoire (India) until his resignation that year, on issues relating to Church policy on the caste question.[91] He was therefore a man in search of a mission, and specifically "in the countries of Africa that have remained the most inaccessible to evangelical workers and which are the most abandoned".[92] His meeting with Régis convinced him that Danxomε was exactly what he was seeking. In the same letter, he affirms that he has asked to go to Danxomε "one of the most barbarous [kingdoms] in West Africa". It is also clear that de Brésillac thought the country to be much bigger than it actually was. He saw it as the opening to a vast hinterland with immense possibilities for evangelisation. The reality was much more modest, as Bouche later pointed out.[93] Régis indicated that the conditions were favourable, and that there was already a Protestant presence seeking influence, leading de Brésillac to state his case in terms sectarian competition. "[The] moment of Providence has come", he concludes, "to try to go to plant the standard cross in the interior of Dahomey".

Perhaps not surprisingly, de Brésillac's understanding of Danxomε was largely similar to that of the Methodists, and there were in his thinking many parallels with that of Beecham. From his time in India he had been a strong advocate of the formation of native clergy,[94] and of *la mission civilisatrice*, albeit with a strong French accent. In a detailed sermon given to justify his *œuvre* he gives us an insight into both his missiology and his perceptions of Danxomε. The "light of salvation will soon rise on these peoples…who [due to world events] seem more disposed than they were previously to receive…the benefits of Christian civilisation". Here, he claims, France is known "in her glory" and Danxomε "is ready to open her doors, which up to now had been closed to all kinds of civilisation." He insists on the barbarity of the kingdom and the slave trade, which has diminished through the efforts of France and Great Britain, "but the most awful despotism still holds sway".[95] Like Beecham, he

---

[91] See Patrick Gantly and Ellen Thorpe, *La voix qui t'appelle*, Rome: SMA, 1992, 207–244.
[92] Letter to the *PF*, 19 February 1856.
[93] Bouche, *La Côte*, 353.
[94] See Gantly and Thorpe, *La voix*, 97–124.
[95] *Sermon*, c. 1856.

believed that Christianity, "which gave birth elsewhere to wonders", would give birth in Danxomɛ to a developed Christian civilisation. In his sermons to raise support for his project, his discourse was not unlike that of the *WMN*. The Society was founded "[for] the most barbarous people",[96] of which Dahomey was a prime example.[97] Following the same logic as Beecham, the Danxomɛnù were perceived as bloodthirsty and degraded, since a political system based on their erroneous religion had led them far from the truth to a state in which, without religious truth in Christ, they would eventually end up as "nothing more than and agglomeration of men no better than a pack of savage beasts".[98]

He is not unaware of the geo-political context within which his mission is situated, noting that the kingdom seemed at that time to be "struck with admiration for France, and better disposed than before to letting the light of the holy Gospel penetrate…"[99] He goes so far as to draft a rather obsequious letter to the Emperor Napoleon III, requesting imperial patronage for his new venture, adding that he and his confreres would bring "with the Gospel the precious witness, always present to [their] spirit, of the grandeur of France and its Sovereign".[100]

In de Brésillac's plan, Napoleon would replace Victoria as the benefactor of the *mission civilisatrice*, and the SMA would take the place of the Methodists in executing it. Under "the little treaty" of 1843, the question of financial support from the French government for the missionaries had been discussed.[101] The link with power was quite similar if not quite identical to that of the Methodists. It depended largely on the *sympathie* of the coastal commanders, and the mutual esteem between the missionaries and the naval men who saw each other as *vrais patriotes* on a mission for Christianity, civilisation and *la France*.[102] It is interesting to note that the mission to Danxomɛ was initially turned down precisely because it felt the

---

[96] Letter to Barnabo, 20 July 1856.

[97] *Sermon*, c. 1857.

[98] De Brésillac, 'Aux demoiselles d'une pension', draft, c. 1857.

[99] Letter to the *PF*, 06 April 1856.

[100] De Brésillac, 'Note pour être remise à Sa Majesté l'Empereur', Paris, January 1857.

[101] See Paul Brasseur, "Missions catholiques et administration française sur la côte d'Afrique de 1815 à 1970", in P. Coulon and P. Brasseur (eds), *Libermann, 1802–1852. Une pensée et une mystique missionnaire*, Paris, Le Cerf, 1988, 849–882.

[102] In a letter to the Minister of the Marine, the SMA Superior General Augustin Planque writes: "I dare to hope that our officers will sometimes visit our missionaries…

security of the missionaries was not being assured "by a Catholic power".[103] This did not remain the case for long as the scramble gathered momentum. In a later letter to the Minister for the Marine, Augustin Planque illustrates the nature of the relationship, reminding him of "all the good done by French missionaries in infidel lands, which, at the same time, serve the glory of France and the extension of her influence".[104]

The idea of Danxomɛ became a driving force behind the Société des Missions Africaines, which de Brésillac founded at the request of the *Propaganda Fide*, the central mission office of the Catholic Church, in 1856. This was all the more so after his premature death,[105] when his successor Planque wrote:

> The idea of Dahomey was the point of departure for our Society and five days before dying he bequeathed to me his final thought to obtain Dahomey as the centre of our apostolic work.[106]

De Brésillac had met the man who eventually went to Danxomɛ, the Italian Francis Borghero, and was impressed by him.[107] It is clear from the correspondence that he thought him the kind of solid man needed for a difficult task.[108] Following de Brésillac's death, all the obstacles to the mission to Danxomɛ were quickly removed. Planque dismisses the health and security concerns, with what is either a touch of black humour, extraordinary callousness, or almost fanatical zeal, reasoning that:

We have no doubt that the relations of the Imperial navy with Dahomey [have aided the missionaries] [The missionaries will try to see that France] is loved and esteemed. These mutual relations seem to me advantageous to the cause of religion and that of France." (Letter, 13 September 1861). However, the relationship was often fraught and in another letter Planque declares: "Let those brave Frenchmen not fool themselves when they think that our mission is a French *œuvre nationale*." (Letter, 20 December 1863, in Marie-Claude Echallier, *L'audace et la foi d'un apôtre: Augustin Planque (1826–1907)*, Paris: Karthala, 1995, 257, 261).

[103] Letter from Cardinal Barnabo to de Brésillac, 27 April 1857.

[104] Letter 18 May 1863, in Echallier, *L'andace*, 259.

[105] De Brésillac left the SMA in the hands of Fr Augustin Planque, while he left for Sierra Leone, the area they had been assigned and had accepted despite their preference for Dahomey. De Brésillac died in Freetown on 25 June 1859, having arrived there on 14 May that year.

[106] Planque letter in Trichet, *The Abiding*, 76.

[107] Borghero, *Journal*, 58.

[108] De Brésillac, letter to Planque, 15 June 1859.

to die is to die and the blood of martyrs would be of more value to the mission and to religion than that of fever; at least blood shed as martyrs would give us a crown and a star in heaven, and we would see realised that word which is always true in the Church of God: *Sanguis martyrum, semen christianorum.*[109]

Danxomɛ was made an Apostolic Vicariate on 16 August 1860, and Borghero was appointed as the first Vicar Apostolic. He landed in Xwedá on 18 April 1861. Like Freeman, he was quarantined for almost eight months, under the *Yóvógan*, and his first visit to Abomey only took place from 25 November 1861 to 24 January 1862. This was almost certainly due to the change of regime following Gezò's death, though also perhaps a test for the new visitor.

Balard has presented Borghero's visit to Abomey as being the encounter of two totally-opposed and mutually incomprehensible cultures, and the beginning of an ongoing misunderstanding between Vodún and Christianity.[110] Borghero may not have had Freeman's diplomatic status but he certainly set out to make an impression on Glɛlɛ́. In what seems like petty arrogance, Borghero insists on a strict protocol for his visit by imposing five conditions: (1) He will not be forced by the king to do anything that is against his religious convictions; (2) in all places where he will formally pass, and within the royal palace, all idols will be removed or covered; (3) he will attend no ceremony at which anybody might be killed and nobody is to be killed in his honour; (4) in the formal ceremonies he will make no gesture of honour or distinction to the wives of the king; (5) out of respect for the sacred vestments which he insisted upon wearing, he would accept no alcoholic drink. Having had these conditions accepted, Borghero organised a procession of some twenty people, dressed in liturgical vestments:

> [They] had never seen a cortege such as ours. The idea of a priest of the whites represented for them all that the dreamy imagination of these savages could have invented: thus they were all the more impressed by this spectacle.[111]

Like Freeman, Borghero is impressed by the pomp of state, and, to his obvious satisfaction, he is received with an eighty-gun salute. However,

---

[109] Planque to Barnabo in Trichet, *The Abiding*, 70.
[110] Balard, *Mission*, 18.
[111] Borghero, *Journal*, 64–66.

it is clear from the journal that he lacked any diplomatic skills and that his discussions with the royal authorities in Abomey were far from satisfactory. He requested permission to set up his mission and the King assured him of his positive attitude to this, as well as his friendly intentions towards France. There is an obvious breakdown, however, when Borghero broaches the subject of the slave trade and the customs, at which point Glɛlɛ dismisses him out of hand, saying that if he had not been white he would have been imprisoned. The overriding impression remaining from Borghero's failed trip was of Danxomɛ as a region of dreadful darkness, as indicated in his journal for the night of 26–27 December:

> The human sacrifices continue every day. At night one hears the cadenced cries of this infernal music; all of this is part of the ceremony. It is forbidden for anybody to go out at night. Only the fetish priests and priestesses can go into the streets. What one hears of these lugubrious chants surpasses the imagination. I have heard some pieces sung which were completely infernal but more measured and well followed. This makes me think that they obtained these compositions from some European masters because contrary to their own music, these were regular and with some harmony, a thing unknown in this country.[112]

Like many missionaries, Catholic and Protestant, Borghero firmly believed that Africans were 'the sons of Ham', still under the biblical curse (Genesis 9:25). Writing in the *Annales de la Propagation de la Foi* in 1864, he says: "the rigours of God...allow this anathema to weigh upon this unfortunate people, even 1,900 years after sacrifice of reparation of Calvary".[113] It is obvious from Burton's writing that he and Borghero got on quite well. He describes the missionaries as "intelligent, amiable and devoted men, in whose society time sped pleasantly and profitably",[114] and they collaborated on making a map which was eventually used to illustrate Burton's book. Borghero makes several deferential references to Burton in his journal from March to May 1864, referring to him mistakenly as Edward Burton, "*le consul anglais*", "*un célèbre voyageur*", "*un voyageur très capable*" with whom he "*conferred*"[115] concerning possible approaches to Danxomɛ.

---

[112] Ibid., 85.
[113] Borghero, *Journal*, 420.
[114] Burton, *Mission*, 63.
[115] Borghero, *Journal*, 148, 189, 152.

Burton, however, observed the missionary's tendency "to look upon things *en noir*".[116] Their sentiments about Danxomɛ are in many ways quite similar. It is my feeling that the men themselves, despite their very different perspectives, were also quite similar. Burton, as we have seen, abandoned Danxomɛ as a hopeless case and, shortly afterward, so did Borghero. Roussé-Grosseau concludes:

> Borghero's sun was a black sun, a killer sun; the land of Danxomɛ
> is an uncertain land, a marsh into which one sinks. Everything comes
> together to give an impression of illness, of prison with, on the one
> side, men who, using the terrain, build a wall, and, on the other, the
> sea which locks in rather than opens out.[117]

For Borghero, as for Burton, Danxomɛ was a difficult, hostile country. He had great difficulty in fitting in and, again like Burton, felt that nothing could be done there, eventually leaving "bitter, discouraged and demoralised".[118] In fact, like the Methodist mission, the Catholic mission in Xwedá was forced to close in 1870, moving, like the Methodists, to the sanctuary of Porto-Novo, and only restarting in Agoué in 1874. Peel's positioning of Danxomɛ on the extreme end of a scale of resistance to Christianity is illustrated by the fact that no mission ever moved beyond coastal quarantine to penetrate the kingdom.

The problems of Borghero are not altogether difficult to understand, and it appears to me that Balard was somewhat harsh with the Italian missionary. The image of the 'white man's grave' had some justification. The terrain was undoubtedly difficult and many missionaries died at a very young age, as the cemetery in Agoué, the first mission, testifies.[119] This kind of 'culture shock' was not unusual amongst missionaries. In the final analysis, they were the relatively young sons and daughters of European farmers and artisans, who in addition to the ravages of debilitating and demoralising illness, were also most often psychologically and intellectually ill-equipped to understand

---

[116] Burton, *Mission*, 63.
[117] Roussé-Grosseau, *Mission*, 178.
[118] Ibid., 179.
[119] Gantly and Thorpe note that in the first six years ten SMA missionaries died in Dahomey (*La Voix*, 345). The average age of the fourteen religious sisters buried in this cemetery between 1884–1923 is thirty two and a half years; the figure is similar at Porto-Novo (*125 Ans NDA au Bénin*: Cotonou: NDA, 2000, 34).

or interpret the realities and practices they encountered in Africa.[120] Roussé Grosseau notes that their level of formation was weak and did little to help them understand the new world they were to encounter except in the most negative terms. They were pious and zealous but rigid and with strong ultramontane tendencies.[121] Those who went to Africa, to use an expression of Bishop Shanahan, were required above all, perhaps, to be "fat, fit and hard-working".[122] Casualties were inevitable, and Borghero went back to his native Italy obviously broken by his Dahomean experience. The experience and reports of Borghero, in all their darkness, however, played an important part in the construction of the image of Danxomε, especially in the missionary press in France. Thus we find the following piece in *L'Echo des Missions Africaines*:

> It is said that the Africans are the descendants of poor Ham, cursed by Noah…I shall leave to *savants* the task of deciding this question. But the fact that for so long the Negroes remain *the most backward of all the human races* is in fact an indication that *a curse weighs upon them*.[123]

Articles such as that confirmed and even magnified the earlier reports and amongst the Catholic missionaries there were some, such as P. Irénée Laffitte, whose attitudes were negative to the point of seeing absolutely nothing of human value in Dahomey.[124] At the same time there was amongst the Catholic missionaries a more scholarly approach represented by Bouche and Baudin.[125] By this time social Darwinism had become fashionable, particularly in Great Britain.[126]

---

[120] See Salvaing, *Les missionnaires*, 89–97, and Roussé-Grosseau, *Mission*, 93–101 for a useful commentary on the social origins of the missionaries and their training.

[121] Roussé-Grosseau, *Mission*, 99–100.

[122] Desmond Forristal, *The Second Burial of Bishop Shanahan*, Dublin: Veritas, 1987, 169.

[123] *L'Echo des Missions Africaines* 1902, 3, in Roussé-Grosseau, *Mission*, 182.

[124] In an interesting analysis, Salvaing compares the attitude of the missionaries of all denominations to West Africa, from the most pessimistic, through the paternalistic, to a more intelligent and generous understanding. See Salvaing, *Les missionnaires*, 228.

[125] See Pierre Baudin, *Fétichisme et Féticheurs*, 1884, SMA 1D010.

[126] By this time Darwin's *Origin of Species* was accepted in most scientific circles and increasingly in liberal Anglican circles. See Salvaing, *Les missionnaires*, 239–242 comparing the attitudes of Protestants and Catholics to the racial theories. Skertchly's *Dahomey* is an illustration of this, and significantly the title was later borrowed by Rev. John Milum of the Lagos Circuit (*WMN*, 1881, 211–215, 235–237, 253–258).

It was condemned by Bouche as "*une science de toute imagination et d'invention*", a "system of anthropologists which deformed the image of the black man"[127] in order to justify shameful calumnies on the black race.[128] Bouche equally rejected the sons of Ham theory espoused by many of his SMA confreres.[129] This did not mean, however, that he saw much that was positive in Danxomɛ itself. For Bouche, Danxomɛ was the victim of a long and painful history, "a people worthy of pity on whom for too long has weighed the yoke of slavery and disdain". Like Freeman, he sees in the Danxomɛnù "the man and brother". But he is "a fallen brother, degraded by ignorance, and the corruption of paganism; an unfortunate brother, long oppressed, to whom we must at least extend the hand of pity and compassion which misfortune deserves".[130]

Bouche is very conscious of what he sees as the despotism of the monarchy and its effect on the Danxomɛnù's character.[131] Driven by fear, the Danxomɛnù "is constantly on guard against abuses of power, and the treachery of those who surround [him]". This response to a totalitarian regime encourages a "salutary prudence", which is, however, brought to an extreme whereby he becomes "suspicious, secretive and separates himself in some way from the rest of society".[132] Is it not possible to see in this observation an early manifestation of the kind of problem with the social bonds that we have already raised? For Bouche, the Danxomɛnù is a captive within his own society, lacking the liberty necessary for human development, rather than the capacity for it as the race theorists would have it. Like most of the Catholic missionaries at the time, he believes the principal culprit within Danxomɛ was the religious system, Vodún, or "*le fétichisme*" as they called it. Even the king was a victim. In thrall the "fetish-priests" "king, chiefs, ministers are dragged along by the priests of fetishism who reign over all, and whose orders are allowed without discussion".[133]

---

[127] Bouche, *La Côte*, 14.

[128] Bouche, *La Côte*, 253.

[129] Ibid., 17.

[130] Ibid., viii.

[131] Bouche clearly has a particular affection for the Nagot whom he describes as "*plus sociable que le Dahoméen et le Mina.*" The Mina are described as "*rusés*" whereas the Danxomɛnù "*est d'un servilisme abject, cache ses rancunes qui ne s'éteignent jamais, il fait le mal avec cynisme*" (Ibid., 20).

[132] Ibid., 25.

[133] Ibid., 169. Bouche, citing Borghero, accuses the religious authorities of having

In Bouche's view, Danxomɛ has been the victim of a tragic history, which has unleashed upon it a politico-religious absolutism where even families "are without the strength to protect their children against the abuse of power by the chiefs, the king, and the fetish-priests".

> The king dominates the people, the *ballés* and the chiefs: rich and poor, master and slave, submit to the yoke, except the fetish-priests. The only counter-weight to his absolute power is the fetish-priests and their prescriptions, with the sanction of poison.[134]

He identifies the Yoruba *Ogboni* and other secret societies as "a kind of occult Masonic society", affiliated to civil and religious power and who dominate the state as an obstacle to all outside influence, "and at the same time to the freedom of action of the supreme power". Even God has been displaced by the totalitarian process in which "everything is arbitrary and at the whim of the powerful". He emphasises that this is particularly the case in Danxomɛ, for which, it must be said, he has less empirical evidence. The system, he asserts, is a vicious circle of tyranny, held in place by the capriciousness of the beneficiaries, particularly the priests through the use of the occult and poison.

> Thus despots succeed despots, until the time when Christianity will come to enlighten the intelligence, purify the sentiments, redress and fortify the will. Only then will chiefs, kings, ministers of religion devote themselves to the noble mission that God has assigned them, to serve those who are submitted to them.[135]

In Bouche's view the people are simply victims of the system under which they live, a system which over years of a sad history has gone woefully wrong and become absolutist, turning its people into victims of its own predation. Although he sought earnestly to understand what he saw, he also contributed to the overall picture of Danxomɛ which made its destruction almost inevitable, and this leads us to the final missionary character in this period, Père Alexandre Dorgère.

---

assassinated Gezò because he refused to satisfy their demands for further sacrifices. There is no evidence to support this.

[134] Ibid., 170.
[135] Ibid., 171–172.

From "la mission civilisatrice" to "la mission pacificatrice"

By the time Dorgère enters, the Danxomε narrative is into its final chapter. The missionary can be said to epitomise the extremely complex relationship between the Catholic mission, the French colonial force and a doomed Danxomε. This is perhaps most clearly illustrated on the frontispiece of a hagiographic memoir of Dorgère, written by Vice-Amiral de Cuverville, where the missionary is shown seated, wearing his cassock, a mission cross, the medal of the *Légion d'Honneur* and with his chair placed on a panther skin.[136] From the evidence he emerges as one of those larger-than-life characters who people mission history, becoming involved in various adventures, including being held hostage by the king of Danxomε, and never shrinking from a little publicity. At the same time, the archives suggest, he became a symbol for the mission in Danxomε as a *mission pacifica-trice*, benefitting from de Cuverville's treatment, a later memoir by his SMA confrere Réné Guilcher and a series of missionary articles that appeared in *La Croix Nantaise*.[137]

Dorgère, like many of his SMA confreres, was *Vendéen*, from an area of France where being French and being Catholic were almost synonymous. Ultramontane, patriotic and right-wing, probably with royalist sympathies, Guilcher tells us he returned "triumphant" from his mission to Glεlέ *"un héraut portant son propre fanion aux couleurs françaises, marqué d'un Sacré-Cœur"*.[138] He would not have come to prominence, however, had it not been for de Cuverville, commander of the French naval force on the Guinea Coast. Breton, Catholic and patriotic, one feels the two men were kindred spirits, sharing 'une certaine idée de la France' and her role in the world. Like Freeman, Dorgère was to become an unofficial ambassador to Danxomε and,

---

[136] Amiral de Cuverville, *Le Père Dorgère au Dahomey*, Auxerre: Imprimérie Chambon, 1900.

[137] Planque had also lost patience: *"Détruisez ce repaire de pirates [et] l'escla-vage ne sera plus alimenté à l'est et à l'ouest [...] C'est une honte pour la France de laisser ruiner par le Dahomey, Porto-Novo qui s'est mis sous la protection du pavillon français"* (Report to the Minister of the Colonies, 28 April 1889).

[138] René-François Guilcher, *L'activité pacificatrice d'un missionnaire*, conférence du 13 March 1942, SMA 3J41. The use of the banner was usually accompanied by the ultramontane, royalist chant "Sauvez Rome et la France au nom du Sacré-Cœur". From 1871 a good number of Catholics, priests and bishops desired a restoration of the monarchy and SMA members letters reflect this (see Roussé-Grosseau, *Mission*, 96–99).

in common with his Methodist predecessor, he showed considerable skill and revelled in his probably unexpected quasi-diplomatic role. According to de Cuverville:

> Dahomey became for him a *patrie*, or better a battlefield where God had confided to him the name of France, the interests of the Church, the rights of the poor and miserable exploited by an infernal despotism…[139]

Dorgère was a typical Catholic of his time and, not unlike Freeman, anchored in sentiments which, in general, left no doubt about the link between the two causes: that of God and that of *la patrie*.

As we can see from de Cuverville's statement above, Bouche's analysis of Danxomɛ had continued to hold sway. It was "*un despotisme infernal*", apparently resistant to all change and a major obstacle to be dealt with in the scramble leading up to the Berlin Conference (1885). By 1882 Porto-Novo had become a French Protectorate, partly as a defence against the predation of Danxomɛ. Treaties governing the port of Cotonou had been negotiated in 1868 and 1878, but Danxomɛ had subverted them. Negotiations between Glɛlɛ and Admiral Rayal, concerning French rights at Cotonou and Porto-Novo's vassalage to Danxomɛ, had failed in 1889. This led to French retaliation with the bombing of Xwedá, an act considered treacherous by the new king, Gbɛhanzin, who in turn retaliated, kidnapping Dorgère and several other French citizens at Xwedá. De Cuverville had received instructions from Paris to bring about a treaty with Glɛlɛ "by all possible means". Knowing Dorgère had been to Abomey and met the king, de Cuverville had appointed him in charge of ambulance services at Cotonou. His reason was that, in the event of a conflict, he would "have this religious near to hand". The commander's preference was for a "decisive" expedition against Danxomɛ and he considered any negotiation to be no more than a temporary measure. Paris, however, was less bellicose and so de Cuverville called on Dorgère, telling him that it would be to his great honour that "*l'incident du Dahomey*" could be resolved "*par voie transactionnelle*".[140] In a letter to Dorgère, he assures him that he has the full consent of the appropriate ecclesiastical authorities. He is counting on the priest's knowledge of the country and its customs. However, even more importantly, he

---

[139] De Cuverville, *Dorgère*, 1.
[140] Ibid., 4.

will also go accompanied not just by the flag of France of which he
will be the bearer "but also by the priestly garment always respected
in this country, where the bloody customs have their origins in a
perverted religious sense".[141]

While Dorgère's hagiographers' have presented his mission as one
of pacification, de Cuverville's understanding was somewhat different. The missionary was being sent to present "France's views in
clear and precise terms" but, in effect, not to bring about peace. De
Cuverville adds: "Before opening hostilities, I wish to exclude any
misunderstanding, and this is the objective I assign to your efforts
and to your devotion".

The Admiral claims that he had obtained from Paris "*pleine liberté
d'action*" for Dorgère. In reality, however, his terms of reference were
in fact very restricted:

> He was not charged with negotiating peace but with making France's
> intention clear to Gbɛhanzın, and obtaining from him powers for a
> delegation which would meet representatives of the Admiral at Ouidah;
> and to obtain from the king, as a guarantee of sincerity, the liberation of
> any French *protégés* who might still be in the prisons of Abomey.[142]

This was clearly quite different from anything Freeman had ever been
asked to do and one suspects that Dorgère may have been somewhat
overawed by *Monsieur l'Amiral*, who was after all, one imagines,
"*un très bon chrétien*". In any case, Dorgère is to reclaim Cotonou
(without compensation) under the terms of the treaties and to demand
the safety of Porto-Novo. The "honour of France is committed" and
it is Dorgère's task to make this clear. De Cuverville concludes his
letter somewhat unctuously, assuring him that whatever happens, the
interests of his *œuvre* will have been served.[143] Dorgère would never
have doubted it since, in his eyes, the interests of France and the
interests of the Church were in complete convergence. No doubt he
hoped that Danxomɛ would also come to see where *its* interests lay.

In a letter to Gbɛhanzın, de Cuverville entrusts the missionary's
safety to him. He emphasises Dorgère's attachment to the people of
the kingdom but also, again, "the sacral character in which he is
covered and the symbol of which he is the bearer". Dorgère chose a

---

[141] Ibid., 5–6.
[142] Ibid., 27.
[143] Ibid., 4–6.

Dahomean idiom, insisting to the king, "It is useless to traffic with my head, given that, according to a local expression, I have given it to the king of France". Neither did he hesitate to add more than a hint of menace, stating that "the day [his head] falls, many fathers, mothers and children will shed tears for the whole of their lives".[144]

It is difficult to know to what extent this is a kind of bravura after the fact, since Dorgère certainly was lionised and enjoyed his status, but it is in any case an indication of how his role came to be perceived. His embassy to Abomey is narrated in the most triumphal terms. In a telegram to Paris, de Cuverville reports:

> Père Dorgère received with princely honours. One 100 cannon rounds; 10,000 rifle rounds; parades of chiefs and warriors; the Father's firm, simple and loyal attitude seems to have deeply impressed the king who covered him with attention and flattery.[145]

Like Freeman, these "honneurs princiers" and the military salute must surely have flattered him. While Freeman and others saw a certain nobility in Gezò, if only in his physical stature, Dorgère's impression of Gbɛhanzın, if one is to believe Guilcher's account, was less than positive, describing him as a "*roitelet...prétentieux [et] vaniteux*".[146] Royal diplomacy, however, still remained formidable and, in a telegram to Paris, de Cuverville reports:

> Black diplomacy, able, tried to get apparently inoffensive concessions for Kotonu, which I refused outright, because if they preserve the self-esteem of the king, they would place France in the posture of the vanquished vis-à-vis Dahomey.[147]

France, of course, was not vanquished and Dorgère's return to Xwedá, bearing the French flag for the first time, seven days ahead of schedule, is equally triumphal. It can be said that, in symbolic terms at least, this represents the high point in the collaboration between the Church and the French state in Danxomɛ. There is, however, evidence that Dorgère's role here was the subject of some controversy. In a debate at the Assemblée Nationale on the ratification of the treaty, the government was accused of having prevented de Cuverville from seeking a "*solution définitive*". Dorgère is accused

---

[144] Ibid., 8.
[145] De Cuverville, *Dorgère*, 11.
[146] Guilcher, *R.P Alexandre Dorgère*, 14.
[147] De Cuverville, *Dorgère*, 13–14.

of having played upon the Admiral's religious convictions "*pour se faire valoir et donner une importance à l'Eglise*".[148] This confirms my own impression from reading later mission journals and histories that despite Gambetta's later admonition that "*L'anticléricalisme n'est pas un article d'exportation*" the relationship between the Church and the colonial authorities was very dependent on the individuals involved on both sides.

In the negotiations that followed his intervention, Dorgère was to take a more modest role, reduced to "arbitration" but remaining effectively "outside the debates...and particularly the hostilities that may follow".[149] De Cuverville provides some evidence that Dorgère through his "*intervention bienveillante*" did have a somewhat conciliatory effect on the negotiations, leading the Admiral to accept a compromise he might have otherwise refused.[150] In any case, the Admiral concluded, "the robe of a religious had produced in Danxomɛ an effect that would not have been obtained by a war expedition".[151]

De Cuverville provides a final irresistible detail to conclude this narrative. Following the apparently successful final negotiations with Gbɛhanzɪn's delegation, they requested Dorgère to sing a *Te Deum*, while the Admiral adds a little stiffly: "*Je me suis associé à cette manifestation par un salut de vingt-et-un coups de canon...*"[152] Leaving the Guinea Coast, he sent a telegram thanking the SMA for their assistance, concluding: "nos religieux ont montré une fois de plus qu'ils ne séparent jamais l'amour de Dieu et l'amour de la patrie, qu'ils en soient rémerciés". As de Cuverville initially predicted, the peace was not to last. Dorgère, providentially or otherwise, was absent from Danxomɛ when it finally fell in 1892.

The demise of Danxomɛ must be set in the context of the sub-region. In Chapter 2, I noted that "Danxomɛ did not bend, it broke". It is clear that in the enormous changes that took place during the second part of the nineteenth century, Danxomɛ was the big loser. It is tempting to recall Bouche's observation on the "social nature"

---

[148] Guilcher, *R.P. Alexandre Dorgère*, 36. De Cuverville was obliged to submit Dorgère's name to the Assemblée Nationale twice before he was granted the medal of the *Légion d'honneur*.

[149] De Cuverville, *Dorgère*, 33.

[150] Ibid., 36.

[151] Charles Simond, *Les Français en Afrique*, 158, cited in Alladaye, *Les Missionnaires*.

[152] Ibid., 17.

of the Nagot and extrapolate from this the reasons for Yorubaland's success, "the making of the Yoruba". The demise of Danxomɛ in contrast is a story of failure in socio-political change. Yorubaland went forward to meet the world, while Danxomɛ remained closed behind the marshes, turning itself into "the enemy", keeping the world at a distance, and ultimately imploding.

The early missionaries clearly played an important role in both cases, a role that has all the ambivalence of the relationship between the colonial powers and the missionaries, as Porter noted. Could it have been different? The question is extremely complex and it is impossible to second-guess history. The missions were clearly part of the tide of history, on occasion helping to create it, while, at other times, being carried along on it. When the tide of history went out on Danxomɛ, the Catholic Church was the one on the spot and it continued to play an important role as an important interlocutor of both the colonial and post-colonial state down to the present day, a role we shall examine in the next chapter.

CHAPTER SIX

CATHOLICISM, THE ELITES AND THE CREATION OF
BÉNINOIS NATIONALISM

> Both history and experience teach that when once the rulers of a people
> have been converted to Christianity, the common people follow closely
> in the footsteps of their leaders. (Pius XI, *Rerum Ecclesiae*, 1926)

The defeat of Gbɛhanzın by Dodds in 1892 effectively brought the
Kingdom of Danxomɛ to an end. Colonial Dahomey was quickly
negotiated and sketched on to the maps over the following seventeen
years to give the country the shape it has today. Porto-Novo had been
a full protectorate since 1882. Danxomɛ had effectively vanished
ten years later, although the French maintained the facade for a few
years with the appointment of Agoli-Agbo I (1894–1900). The 1898
Niger Convention, established following Lugard's 1894–1895 Niger
expedition, and 'a little treaty' established with the French at Kandi
effectively divided the important northern Borgou emirate between
Britain and France. There had been agreements with Germany in
1885 and 1899 covering the western border with Togoland, and a
final flourish in 1909 sketched in the northern frontier with Niger
and Haute Volta, roughly along the Niger and Pendjari Rivers. The
cartographic task was relatively easy, using two more or less straight
lines from the coast to about 9°N and a few more following some
rough topographical features to map out the expansive Guinea savannah regions of the north. Ethnic groupings did not feature in any of
this, and, in almost every case, they straddle the borders.

If the cartography was fairly straightforward, there remained a much
more difficult political task. The simple truth was that the Dahomey
on the new map of Africa was not Danxomɛ, it was much more.
The problem, given the myths and complex histories, not to speak
of the subjective memory of the peoples involved, was, to paraphrase
Benedict Anderson's term, how to "imagine" the political community
that might be Dahomey. The challenge was to breathe life into the
nascent state and create what was essentially a new identity for its
people who would be Dahomeans without being Danxomɛnù. This

process has proved to be much more difficult. Gbenonvi notes that the notion of the nation is essentially an imported one and that, even today, the Béninois lives more within the idea of the *tò*, concluding that "from this point of view, the nation remains to be created".[1] An essential part of this process, as we have seen, was to drop the notion of 'Dahomeans' altogether. Danxomε could never be the cornerstone; it was in fact quite the opposite, the Achilles heel of any political development. From the outset, the Catholic Church was to play an important role. It was present even before the colonial state, giving it a certain right based on a kind of enduring tenure. It is not impossible, however, to imagine that the Church, and certainly many of the missionaries, would have been quite happy had it found its place in the traditional polity rather than the nascent colony. The Church might indeed have been quite happy with a monarchy that it could have fashioned in the image of "*la fille aînée*" it increasingly felt it had lost.[2] The Sacré Cœur would replace the royal totems on the national flag, and they would have a *Dahomey chrétien avec un roi chrétien*.[3] Failing this, as we have seen in the previous chapter, the Catholic Church played an important role in the establishment of colonial Dahomey, and the Churches, now very much in the plural, continue to play various roles in the imagining of Benin down to the present day. The final chapters of this work will be an examination of this role.

Uprooting and replanting: the Church, the rehabilitation of African cultural values and the formation of a new elite

Adoukonou is understandably struck by an anecdote recounted by Mgr Steinmetz,[4] recalling the reception following the consecration of the new cathedral at Xwedá in 1909. Balard, using historical data, develops the anecdote further, turning it into what she rightly claims

[1] Interview, 28 June 2002.
[2] Writing of Rwanda, Linden makes precisely this point: "The spiritual Gold Rush in which they [the missionaries] staked the first claims had as its dreams the Golden Age of Church history. In the dream [King] Musinga appeared in the role or Charlemagne" (Linden, *The Church*, 59).
[3] See Paul Poupard, *France, fille aînée de l'Eglise*, Paris: Régnier, 1995, 16–19.
[4] Hazoumé, *50 ans*, 14.

could be a metaphor illustrating "the political cultural and religious history of Dahomey"[5] in the period following the conquest.

Perhaps in recognition of Dorgère's role in the "pacification", the French administration had provisionally put at the disposal of the Church both the Place Djêgbé[6] and Agoli, the residence of the Yovógán. Noting that "in this place was hidden the sufferings endured in February 1890 by Fr Dorgère and six other Europeans", Steinmetz found these locations very suited to the needs of the mission.[7] Balard correctly points out the symbolic value of this premeditated dispossession. The Christian compound was, in effect, to be erected on the ruins of a royal residence, a sacred space designed "to manifest the titular power of Abomey".[8] She points out that the imposing cathedral, which stands directly in front of the Dangbé-drê and the Dangbé-xwɛ, can be said to be even more "insolently" situated.[9] To complete this picture of ostentatious triumphalism, Adoukonou recounts how, at the reception following the consecration of the cathedral, Steinmetz raised his glass in a toast, pointing to both the cathedral and the Dangbé-xwɛ with the remark "*ceci détruira cela*". It would seem that two powers had certainly faced up for battle.

While shocking in its arrogance, the remark is, of course, consistent with what had been the missionary attitude since about 1850. The "civilising mission" became "a mission of pacification", and while the Church would say it had not participated directly in the destruction of Danxomɛ, it had most certainly considered it to be an obstacle to "civilisation" and sang a *Te Deum* to mark the French victory.[10] Steinmetz recounts with fervour "the triumphal entry of General Dodds to Xwedá", where he was welcomed as a "saviour" by a "the local population, which was now assured of walking in the way of French civilisation moulded out of Christianity".[11]

---

[5] Balard, *Mission*, 299–301.
[6] The public square where the population of Ouidah assembled to hear the messages of the King.
[7] Hazoumé, *50 ans*, 14.
[8] Balard, *Mission*, 300.
[9] *Dangbé-drê* is the sacred forest for of the royal python *pytho regius*, a divinity of the *Xwedá* since its transfer there from Saxé in 1727. *Dangbé-xwɛ* is the principal temple of the cult (Segurola and Rassinoux, *Dictionnaire*, 121).
[10] Steinmetz gives many examples of people who celebrated the fall of Danxomɛ which, he claims, they excoriated for its brutality and rapacity. See Hazoumé, *50 ans*, 21–44.
[11] Ibid., 12.

For Steinmetz the mission was essentially a *mission civilisatrice* that could only be advanced by the demise of the monarchy. However, it had the added dimension of being *"une œuvre apostolique et française"*.[12] The missionary clergy were never anything other than totally committed to the colonial enterprise, despite occasionally feeling what Steinmetz describes as the "winds of anticlericalism" and *"Combisme"*.[13] A century on, the post-revolutionary French Church was learning to live with whatever regime might be in power, trimming its sails and tacking to suit contrary political winds, an exercise that would serve it well later in Dahomey-Benin. Steinmetz notes, somewhat naively one suspects, that "the colonisers and the European functionaries maintained cordial relations with the mission and recognised in us, the first artisans of the Christian civilisation that was being implanted in this country".[14] Whatever they thought about current government policy, they never doubted *la grandeur de la France* and her mission in the world, and their part in it. The problems of France could be left in France and Clemenceau's *mot* would be observed. Whatever thoughts the later indigenous clergy might have had on the matter were kept strictly to themselves as they were instructed to give "an example of the obedience due to the civil authorities" and were absolutely forbidden to take part in any "internecine squabbles or public contestation".[15]

Steinmetz was, in fact, the type of the ideal missionary bishop in Africa. He was physically robust, intelligent if not an intellectual, resourceful, dynamic and, despite the example stated above, with a genuine interest in and feeling for the world in which he lived for sixty years.[16] He is widely acknowledged as the architect of Catholicism

[12] François Steinmetz, *Une œuvre apostolique et française*, SMA 1C047.
[13] Hazoumé, *50 ans*, 72–73. Emile Combes (Premier 1902–1905) approved anticlerical legislation, especially in education, leading to a break between France and the Holy See. *La loi de 1905* is considered to be the cornerstone of modern, French secularism.
[14] Hazoumé, *50 ans*, 72–73.
[15] *Statuts du clergé africain formé à St Gall*, 1951, 40, SMA 1G044.
[16] Several sources spoke with deep admiration for Steinmetz's successor Mgr Louis Parisot, who played a major role in the formation of the local clergy, and led the Church with apparent serenity up to independence in 1960 (interview with Bernardin Card. Gantin, Former Archbishop of Cotonou, former Dean of the Sacred College, Rome, 5 April 2001). See also Paul-Henry Dupuis, *La Bonne Nouvelle est Annoncée aux pauvres: Mgr Louis Parisot (1885–1960), Premier Archeveque de Cotonou, Père du Bénin Chrétien*, Cotonou, 1985, SMA 1C72.

in Benin, where a main street in Cotonou still bears his name.[17] He had a reasonable grasp of Fongbè, publishing an early catechism. He trekked widely, developing good relations and coming to be known as Daága, "the tall father". Although he continued to see the traditional religion as an obstacle to be overcome, he appears to have developed a more respectful understanding of the Vodún through his relationship with the Vodúnnù Aginlo.

A builder in the more literal sense, and in a strong missionary tradition, he was also adept at raising funds for his projects, the building of the cathedral at Xwedá, several chapels, schools and starting agricultural development.[18] He was also a diplomat, adroitly handling relations with the authorities during the difficult period in the early part of the twentieth century and getting his work done as he wished.[19] He quickly set about realising de Brésillac's ideal of the formation of a local clergy. Despite setbacks, work began on the Seminary at Xwedá in 1911 and the first Dahomean priest, Fr Thomas Moulero Djogbenou, was ordained in 1928.[20]

While Steinmetz sketched in broad outline, another striking figure added substance to the presence of the Church in Dahomey, Fr Francis Aupiais. Aupiais was in Dahomey from 1903 until 1926, continuing to work in France for what he came to see as the Dahomean cause until his death in 1946.[21] His missiology was in the tradition of "the civilising mission" as part of the colonial project. He writes:

> Everywhere the missionaries have gone to plant the cross, one has not only seen them in their sacristies, but they were present on all the building sites where the edifice of civilisation was being built...[22]

---

[17] It is certainly significant to note that three of the main arteries in Cotonou bear the names of prominent Catholic churchmen, Jean Paul II, Monseigneur Isidor de Souza, and Steinmetz.

[18] See Alladaye, *Les Missionnaires*, 128–132.

[19] Anticlericalism was tempered in the colonies by the 1919 Treaty of St Germain en Laye which "called upon the government to favour the religious and cultural activities of missions..." (Alladaye, *Les Missionnaires*, 244.)

[20] There were five Dahomean priests by the time Steinmetz retired in 1934, forty-seven at independence and 379 in 2002.

[21] Alladaye is much more critical of Aupiais, accusing him of forming "culturally alienated, defenders of the colonial order, of whom Paul Hazoumé is the prototype" (*Les Missionnaires*, 330).

[22] Francis Aupiais, *Les missionnaires au service de la colonisation*, Semaine Coloniale de Clermont-Ferrand, ndg, 3, SMA 3H21.

Aupiais made remarkable contributions in two areas, which contributed greatly to situating the Catholic Church in the socio-political space that, it can be argued, it has held in Dahomey-Benin ever since: the rehabilitation of African culture and the education of an early colonial local elite.[23] In this he was consistent with the Catholic missiology of the time. Writing in 1926, Pius XI emphasised the importance of Catholic elites for the development of the Church and society.[24] Developing this theme, Mgr Mulla writes:

> Bishops and indigenous priests incontestably form the elite of elites [...] in the pagan or Muslim masses. Christians, by the simple fact that they are Christians, constitute the elite in whatever country they are found.[25]

This had certainly been the approach of Aupiais who wrote:

> The missionaries understood that it was necessary in order to form elites, to bring forward these men, their neophytes, who had already become by virtue of their baptism the yeast in these same masses...the missionary alone is capable of doing something durable.... because he remains for a long time in the country. He can interpret the country for the authorities, because he has the knowledge of it.[26]

Ali Mazrui notes that "missionary education in the majority of African countries helped provide the first wave of modern African nationalists".[27] Bediako has remarked that:

> the expansion of the intellectual horizons of Africans, eased by Christianity, enhanced a new African self-understanding and self-appreciation beyond the immediate traditional circles of kinship and lineage, and so paved the way for the modern expressions of African nationalism which finally challenged and overturned Western rule.[28]

In the south of Dahomey at least, little enough encouragement was needed for the children of traditional elites, exiled from power on

---

[23] Francis Aupiais, *Les Elites noires*, conférences, ndg, SMA 3H17; *Elites indigènes, milieux fétichistes*, conférence aux semaines sociales de Marseille, 1931, SMA 3H18.

[24] Pius XI, *Rerum Ecclesiae*, Rome 1926, 31.

[25] Mgr Mulla, *Le problème social aux colonies*, conférence aux semaines sociales de Marseille, 1931, in Alladaye, *Les Missionnaires*, 174.

[26] Aupiais, *Les missionnaires*, 4.

[27] Mazrui, *Political Values*, 168.

[28] Kwame Bediako, *Christianity in Africa: The Renewal of a Non-Western Religion*, Edinburgh: Orbis, 1995, 234.

their own terms, as well as others with socio-political aspirations, to understand that the road to power and success passed necessarily through the schoolyard. In this way one might eventually move from "interpret [ing] for the authorities" to *being* an authority in the new colonial dispensation.[29] Education was the new Vodún, the source of power, as the kings already suspected, and it was avidly pursued once its value was understood.

The colonial capacity in education, in a period that saw two world wars, was unable to fill the growing need, thus muting somewhat the newly-found sacred principle of *laïcité* in schools. The Church also had a certain right of tenure, having established some of its schools before the new state itself had been established. Under Steinmetz, and with Aupiais as director, it established an important schools programme. This continued right up to independence with Fr Jacques Bertho proving to be a dynamic director of schools and an able negotiator with the civil authorities through to the 1950s.[30] By the school year of 1954–1955, there were 28,492 pupils in Catholic schools with 24,683 in the public sector. By the time of independence, the Church was involved in every area of education. In fact the school-going population in Dahomey was "well above the A.O.F. [L'Afrique occidentale française] average".[31] This contributed elsewhere to the reputation of the colony as the *quartier latin de l'Afrique*, coupled somewhat ironically with the darker Dahomean reputation of being *"forts dans la chose-là"* or *"assis sur des batteries"*, popular euphemisms for occult powers. This involvement in education, despite very slow development in evangelisation, was to determine the position of the Catholic Church in both colonial and post-colonial Dahomey. This was particularly the case in later PRPB Benin when its links with the politico-administrative elite were to be of great importance for its own preservation.[32] Steinmetz had initiated the formation of the future civil elite, but also the formation of the future clergy, two influential social bodies in a country that still

---

[29] This was not the case in the northern Borgou kingdom, where elite families were very reticent, often sending the children of Gando slaves in their place.

[30] Jacques Bertho, *Les Ecoles catholiques*, 1956, SMA 1C004/8.

[31] "Statistiques," A.O.F Magazine, 15 August 1956, 237 in Alladaye, *Les Missionnaires*, 269.

[32] See Richard Banégas, *La démocratie "à pas de caméléon": transition et consolidation démocratique au Bénin* (Thèse), IEPP, 1998, 175–176.

has a literacy rate of only 37%.[33] These elites are not unconnected, as even a cursory look through the handbook of the Catholic clergy today will reveal. The names here are often those one finds on the books written by Béninois intellectuals, as well as those important figures in the politico-administrative elite since 1960. There is, indeed, what Bayart has described as a "reciprocal assimilation of elites",[34] and while this was stretched somewhat in the PRPB period, it has always been there and remains, with the commonality of aspirations and interests that this implies.

Education was not Aupiais' only contribution. Rejecting the pseudo-scriptural theories of both his SMA confreres and the racial theorists of the time, he studied Dahomean culture in general and came to admire its conservative values, which he saw as under threat from the unbridled modernity which accompanied colonisation. He is acutely aware of what he sees as the clash between "two apparently irreconcilable" world-views, community on the one hand and the individualism that inevitably accompanies modernity on the other.[35] The theme of anthropological fragility, however, also emerges here. Aupiais is critical of the vanished kingdom, which he accuses of a "universal levelling into subordination" of its population, which, in his view, accounted for the destruction of any spirit of initiative in the population, social divisions and the under-development of the country.

> Suspicion on the part of the king, jealousy on the part of the subjects, the suppression of all individuality in the conglomerate of the tribe, this is what explains the fact that these populations remain in straw huts, the grinding stone and the dugout canoe.[36]

It is certainly significant to note here that the infamous *nivellement par le bas*, is explained by Adoukonou as "the result of an endogenous choice, an internal process of selection and the oppression of possibilities",[37] which in his view is the cause of the country's developmental problems. The Protestant theologian Kä Mana refers to

---

[33] See http://www.cia.gov/cia/publications/factbook/geos/bn.html#People.

[34] Jean-François Bayart, "Les Eglises chrétiennes et la politique du ventre: le partage du gâteau ecclésial", *Politique Africaine*, 35, 68–76, 1989.

[35] Francis Aupiais, *Les Noirs, leurs aspirations et leur avenir*, Paris: Comité National d'Etudes Sociales et politiques, 1927, 13–23; SMA: 3H16.

[36] Aupiais, *Les Noirs*, 22.

[37] Adoukonou, *Nouvelle conscience*, 88.

"a kind of communitarian dictatorship which destroys the strength of the individual in function of the group". He says "it was this culture which we brag about, and present as *our culture*, that was actually defeated", and calls for a greater emphasis on the individual "as a source of creativity...for a new African culture which must be thought out as a balance between the individual and the community".[38]

Alladaye, as I have noted, is critical of Aupiais' contribution. He interpets his collaboration with the colonial scholar/administrators Hardy and Delafosse, and later with Levy-Bruhl and others, in more or less Orientalist terms.[39] He considers it to be essentially a scheme, as Said expresses it, "to divide, deploy, schematise, tabulate, index, and record everything in sight".[40] Things are put in the family *senegalensis, guineensis, sudanensis* or even *dahomeensis* rather than *orientalis*, but with essentially the same aim of describing and defining Africa—and even the soul of the African—on their own terms, unveiling the mysteries, particularly perhaps of the religion, making it accessible and comprehensible on their own terms, the better to impose the colonial project.[41] Anderson has described a largely similar process as essential to the imagining of the colonial state.[42] In Aupiais' defence, however, one must note that he opposed what Saïd has described as the "incomplete and mal-assimilated science"[43] that went into the racial theory of the time. Aupiais took this defence to academic circles, such as the Comité National d'Etudes Sociales et Politiques, where he saw it as part of his mission to debunk racial theory by presenting Dahomey and its people in their humanity and with their legitimate aspirations for the future.

---

[38] Kä Mana, Interview, 13 June 2002.

[39] Aupiais certainly supported the idea of a "scientific" study of Africa: "La liturgie de leur religions, les préceptes de leur morale, les canons de leurs droits civil, les règles de l'étiquette et de l'hospitalité, les noms, les caractéristiques etc...Mais il faut qu'ils soient étudiés par des personnes compétentes plutôt que par des jeunes soldats plus ou moins ignorants" (Aupiais, *Les Noirs*, 5).

[40] Edward Said, *Orientalism*, London: Penguin, 2003, 86.

[41] See Maurice Delafosse, *L'âme nègre*, Paris: Payot, 1922. Compare with Aupiais' *L'âme primitive*, Intervention à la Société française de Philosophie, Sorbonne, 1 June 1929, SMA 3H19. Also Francis Aupiais, *Mise en valeur par le Christianisme des aspirations religieuses des Noirs (pierres d'attente)*, 1943, conférence, SMA 3H1; Georges Hardy, *Histoire sociale de la colonisation*, Paris: Larose, 1953.

[42] See B. Anderson, *Imagined communities*, ch. 6.

[43] Said, *Orientalism*, 232.

Aupiais' defence of African cultural values, underscored by his role in the advancement of an aspiring Catholic elite, was vital in establishing this essential relationship. They helped to give credibility to the Church in an atmosphere of growing anti-colonialism, particularly amongst intellectuals and the future political elites, in the period leading up to independence, thus legitimising its status in public debate.[44] Balard's analysis is very useful when she notes the "convergent political interests at the end of the war between the *évolués* and the missionaries: for the former in establishing new political rights and for the latter in countering eventual *laïc* influence and in assuring their future in the country".[45] To a certain extent, at least, the former owed their new status to the latter and the outline of an 'old boy' network was in place, which its creators must have felt boded well for the future.

There is indeed ample evidence of the Church's determination to play a role in influencing the ideological direction of what it must by then have known would be the independent republic of Dahomey. In the post-war period, one finds in the Catholic press, essentially *La Croix au Dahomey*, regular articles reflecting the socio-political worries of the Church at that time, concerning workers, the power of unions, the right to strike, social issues and, not surprisingly, communism.[46] These were of course issues for the whole of the Catholic Church during the Cold War, and in Dahomey they were seen as mortal dangers to be averted as independence became inevitable. Its relationship with the emerging elite was to be its lifeline, its guarantee of a place in the nascent state, and everyone's interests would be served by developing these ties.

Young and impressionable Dahomean students, it was felt, were mixing in radical circles in Paris, which, while the capital of France, was also a hotbed of liberal thinking. It was becoming urgent for

---

[44] See Robert Sastre and Robert Dosseh, "Propagande et vérité", in *Des Prêtres Noirs s'interrogent*, Paris: CERF/Présence Africaine, 1956, 146–147.

[45] Balard, *Mission*, 293–294.

[46] See for instance, Anon, "L'Eglise et les ouvriers" *La Croix au Dahomey*, 7, 8, 1951, 3–6; Robert Sastre, "La grève, pourquoi faire?", in *La Croix au Dahomey*, 3, 1957, 8–11; Paul Falcon, "Revendiquer chrétiennement", *La Croix au Dahomey*, 16, 1948, 4–7; "Divorce et polygamie", *La Croix au Dahomey*, 16, 1948 12–15; George Yèche, "Pour ou contre le Christ", in *La Croix au Dahomey*, 8, 1947, 6–11; Anon, "Encore le Communisme", *La Croix au Dahomey*, 4, 1948, 4–6; Anon, "Les Catholiques peuvent-ils être Communistes?" in *La Croix au Dahomey*, 4, 1949, 9–10.

them to be educated at home. Hazoumé, the leader of the Catholic
elite, felt some of these dangerous doctrines were already taking root
at home and posing a danger to the Dahomean 'soul'. By now a
sage as well as being a *Lauréat de l'Académie Française*, he warns
against alcohol and pornography, but also against the "sophisms of
the century", atheistic materialism and misguided profane science[47]
which he sees becoming "the religion of the future".[48] For Hazoumé,
the answer would be a Catholic college, which would give a "teaching
of quality...with a religious basis".[49] At the opening of the college,
he set out its objectives in words that his *"père spirituel"* Aupiais,
whose name had been given to the new foundation, would have
taken as his own:

> Dahomean families have the assurance that their sons will acquire right
> here the western humanism, the Christian humanism that will serve as
> a ferment to African traditionalism, to animist traditionalism, and will
> cause it to evolve harmoniously. This is the guarantee for our families
> that Dahomean youth will pursue their studies at home will be less
> exposed to corruption and uprooting than those who been expatriated
> in search of western science....
>   For balance, for a harmonious evolution of this country, one must
> neither prevent the intellectual development of Africans, nor create in
> them a disdain for manual work, because Africa, in order to progress,
> for its material and moral development needs technicians as much as
> it needs intellectuals.
>   Excellencies, my dear Fathers, Dahomey has the certitude that at the
> desks of your college her sons will acquire not simply the culture neces-
> sary for their advance to higher studies, but also, from your example,
> the taste for work, the desire for perfection, and the love of good.
>   Yes, while their minds are filled with science, they will enrich their
> hearts with noble sentiments, without which science, however broad
> and deep it may be, is in vain.[50]

Not only was the future elite to be formed, but so were the future
wives of this *petite bourgeoisie* in the many *écoles d'enseignement*

---

[47] Pope Pius XII in the encyclical *Humani Generis* (Of the Human Race), 1950,
written at this time attempted to reconcile Christian faith with evolutionary theory.
[48] Paul Hazoumé, "Dahoméen, prends garde de ton âme", *La Croix au Dahomey*,
5, 9, 10, 1950, 1–4; 6–8.
[49] This had been planned since 1925 when the Pope had given a sum of 100,000
francs. The government gave a subsidy after the war. It opened with a few students
in 1949, *College Notre Dame des Apôtres* for girls had opened in 1946. See Paul
Hazoumé, "Collège Catholique", *La Croix au Dahomey*, 5, 10, 1950.
[50] Hazoumé, "Collège Catholique".

ménager or vocational schools, where they could learn what were considered the essential domestic science that would allow them to become "*épouses modèles*". It was noted at the time that the young *évolués* expected this from their future spouses.[51]

With the primary schools, the vocational schools and the foundation of the secondary colleges in Cotonou, Alladaye notes in somewhat negative terms that "no sector of education escaped the Catholic missionaries by the end of the colonial era".[52] The same author is dismissive of this group of "cultural aliens", devoted, as he sees it, to the spread of an alien civilisation, "collaborators and allies of colonialism" rather than "the best representatives of the culture and the deepest aspirations of the populations they have come from".[53] Whatever Alladaye's opinion of these people, it is certainly clear that the Catholic education system had played a major role in forming the new elite. This continues to be the case, as illustrated by the fact that out of twenty-one members of Kérékou's 2001 ministerial cabinet, nineteen were Christians (seventeen men and two women) and only two are Muslims. This clearly does not reflect the demographics of the country, but certainly does reflect the history of Catholic influence on education and the public services, although this is not the only factor in this equation. These were formed mostly by the schools, but one also finds amongst them former seminarians who had abandoned their aspirations to the priesthood and opted for another life, but were still equipped with the education, including philosophy, they had received. While it is certainly true that many of them maintained relatively close links to the Church and continued both to support it and to turn to it in times of socio-political turbulence, it is equally true that, as had happened elsewhere, others carried with them the anger produced in authoritarian and doctrinaire institutions and, in time, turned their anger on the institution itself.[54] This happened particularly during the revolutionary period when a discourse of perverted theology, as well as political opportunism, was not rare. Former students of Catholic schools and Catholic youth movements brought with them both a

---

[51] Letter to Mlle du Rostu, NDA Archives, in Alladaye, *Les Missionnaires*, 264.
[52] Ibid., 268.
[53] Ibid., 173.
[54] Mgr Nestor Assogba, interview, 21 June 2002. Roger Gbenonvi studied theology but is now critical of the Catholic Church. His polemics in *La Nation*, lead him into debates with Catholic clergy in its pages; interview, 28 June 2002.

discourse and a sense of cellular organisation and mass animation that could be, and was, put to use in the cause of the revolution. In the period 1987–1990, the *dérives* of this elite were bitterly noted by Church authorities. The bishops frequently remarked, albeit in more informal settings, that "those who are ruining the country are not the Sourou's and Abdoulaye's of Benin, but the Pierres, the Pauls, the Jean-Maries who have received a Christian education".[55] This perceived betrayal of their values by a Christian elite is a recurring theme and it is certainly true that the Catholic-educated elite featured across the political spectrum during the whole of the revolutionary period and in the transition which brought this to a close.[56]

The Church as 'podestà'

Aupiais' election to the Constituent Assembly in 1946, and his replacement by Jacques Bertho following his sudden death just after the election, sealed this alliance between a certain conservative elite and the Church. Politically, the 1946 election was very significant, as it can be argued that it marked the beginning of the fissures and tripartite division that have been a feature of Dahomey-Benin politics ever since.[57] These are already visible in this brief extract from a letter from Hazoumé to Aupiais:

> The Dahomean elite wants to test your love for them... they ask you to consent to this sacrifice... This is what it means: a delegation of my compatriots came to request me to intervene with you in order that you accept to become a candidate in the forthcoming elections to the Conseil Supérieur des Colonies. *The choice of the Dahomean elite has fallen on you because it no longer wants those delegates who fool us.*

Augustin Azanzo pleads with him:

---

[55] See Mgr I. de Souza, "Je ne vois pas suffisamment de désintéressement et d'amour du pays", *Le Courrier*, 128, Paris, 1991, 21–22. More positively, the CEB reminds the church of "the impressive number of political leaders who bear Christian names" with the implication that this imposes ethical demands; CEB, *Au Service du relèvement de notre pays*, Lokossa, February 1990 in Goudjo, *Discours social*, 113.

[56] See Banégas, *La démocratie* (Thèse), 175–176.

[57] See Staniland, *The three party system*. Also Dov Ronen, "Preliminary notes on the concept of regionalism in Dahomey", *Etudes Dahoméennes*, 12, 1968, 11–14.

You know what awaits us. There Father, the task is beautiful and noble—it requires someone of your talent and dedication. Take the wheel of the African ship and start this rescue mission in the gulf of Benin.[58]

Aupiais stood with Sourou-Migan Apithy, marking the beginning of the Apithy's political career, on what was definitely a Porto-Novian ticket given his ties to the royal family of Porto-Novo. In doing so, he was covering over the fissures that were putting strain on the social tissue of the emerging state, standing in a political vacuum created amongst the vying Dahomean elite, which was based at least partly on historical questions and the fear of a resurgent Danxomε. In fact, he played some of the role of the Italian *podestà*, "summoned from outside the group, not for the purpose of creating a new social order, but to provide a detached social arbitrator, especially for cases where the adversaries are of the same social status".[59]

In order to play this role, the Church must also know when to withdraw to its own space and the pastoral and development activities that give it its legitimacy. From there it can issue regular reminders of its presence in the form of pastoral letters which are often a form of social commentary, if not quite analysis. This was notably the case at the time of independence, which the Church welcomed in a pastoral letter "with sincere and profound joy" as a sign of "political maturity", rejoicing and with confidence "in the will of the young states to take their rightful place in the concert of nations". It rejoiced particularly because it was attained "without violence and without the painful rupture with those that Providence in various forms, human, sentimental, economic and political, had tied to our temporal and even our spiritual destiny".[60] The Church's own role in education, and unity of vision amongst the country's elite, no doubt had some part to play in this peaceful transition, which had also been facilitated by Dahomey's "*Oui*" in the 1958 referendum.[61] There was not to be rupture and the letter calls for continued "constructive collaboration, free from bias and reciprocal sensitivity and preserved

---

[58] Balard, *Mission*, 289–290.
[59] Weber, *Sociology*, 49.
[60] CEB, 1960; "Au Clergé et aux fidèles de tout le Dahomey", *La Quinzaine Religieuse de Cotonou*, vol. 1, 9 August, 2.
[61] The Catholic Church in Dahomey was by this time led by Archbishop Bernardin Gantin, appointed Auxiliary bishop of Cotonou in 1957, at the age of thirty-five, and succeeding Mgr Parisot as Archbishop in 1960.

from false nationalism..." with missionaries and with the former colonial power.[62] This was perhaps a rebuke to the more nationalistic Robert Sastre and certainly expresses a desire not to offend either the French clergy, still a majority in the Dahomean Church, or European benefactors, who continued to support it financially.

At the same time, there is to be a complete break with direct clerical involvement in politics, and clergy are invited to remain in "the serene heights to which [their] vocation has elevated [them]" and to seek above all the spiritual well-being of the people. The role of the clergy is to be a ministry of peace and reconciliation. Pleading that this position does not mean "indifference or silence in the face of injustice, nor complicity in error or lies", the Archbishop establishes as an "absolute rule of behaviour, the strict abstention from all participation in the political struggle" by the clergy of the whole of Dahomey.[63] This task is handed over to lay Catholics who are encouraged to take an active role in public life "in order to transform the mores of social life and bring to it a sense of public service and the common good".[64]

Hastings observed that "the coming of independence to most of black Africa brought a far slighter shift in Church-State relations than might have been anticipated".[65] The Béninois historian P. Mêtinhouë appears to confirm this when he remarks that the period after independence was one of "almost perfect understanding" between the Catholic Church and the State,[66] while M.A. Glélé concluded: "The Catholic Church represents an incontestable political force in Dahomey... [and] apart from the army, the clergy constitutes the only organised body, capable and very influential".[67] Gantin, also a son of Danxomε, had effectively steered through the turbulence of the transition and confirmed the Catholic Church's role as an established, and now

---

[62] CEB, *Au Clergé*, 2.

[63] Mgr B. Gantin, "Face aux élections", *La Quinzaine Religieuse de Cotonou*, vol. 1, 15, 1960, 10–11.

[64] Mgr B. Gantin, *100 Ans de Foi*, 3 February 1961, in Raymond B. Goudjo (ed.), *Discours Social des Evêques du Bénin de 1960 à 2000*, Cotonou: Flamboyant, 2000, 29.

[65] Adrian Hastings, *A History of African Christianity 1950–1975*, Cambridge: CUP, 1979, 147.

[66] P.G. Mêtinhoüe, "Monseigneur Christophe Adimou, un évêque au service de la vérité et du dialogue sous un régime marxiste-léniniste", *Eglise de Cotonou*, vol. 33, 7, 1993, 66.

[67] Glélé, *Naissance*, 45.

indigenous—or at least *indigenised*—actor in the post-colonial state. The Church preserved its own traditional interests: the chapels, schools, dispensaries and other charitable works under its control. It alleviated the social burden to some extent and there was little reason for the state, with the burgeoning demands of its political clientele and severe budgetary restraints, as well as severe political strains, to interfere and further stretch its own very limited capacity. Everything appeared to be on a very steady course.

1972–1989—The years of rupture

Nothing, of course, can prepare for revolution and the period following the 1972 coup—following twelve years of political mayhem which saw the *quartier latin de l'Afrique* become *l'enfant malade de l'Afrique*, the model for all the ills of the post-colonial state—was one of considerable difficulty. Strains were beginning to show in the intervention of Archbishop Gantin in 1970, taking the regime of Colonel de Souza to task for summary executions. The real rupture, however, was to come in 1974, with founding of the PRPB and the adoption of a Marxist-Leninist ideology. While it is probably overstating the case to say that the Church during this period "moved to the catacombs",[68] it is certainly true that it was a period of *tracasseries*, "vexations and uncertainty".[69]

For the Churches, the most difficult period was from 1974 until the visit of Pope John Paul II in 1982, which the regime attempted to instrumentalise. In 1974 the regime, in the first flush of ideological fervour and benefitting from favourable economic conditions, pursued its harder ideological options, including the incorporation of the cherished Catholic schools into the detested pedagogy of the *Ecole Nouvelle*.[70] The regime also expelled a number of vocal missionaries deemed *anti-revolutionary*. Fr Alphonse Quenum, Director of College

---

[68] I. Pinon, "El papel decisivo de dos obispos", *Mundo Negro*, July–August 1993, 49.

[69] J.-R. de Benoist, "Les clercs et la démocratie", *Afrique Contemporaine*, 4e trimestre, 1992, 182.

[70] CEB, "Nos suggestions et propositions pour l'élaboration d'une idéologie dahoméenne", *Eglise de Cotonou*, vol. 15, 4, 1974, 105–111; Alphonse Quenum, "Le programme national d'édification de l'Ecole Nouvelle", *Eglise de Cotonou*, vol. 15, 2, 1974, 31–41. The system was abandoned after the CNFVN.

Aupiais, an intellectual and social critic, was given a death sentence, later commuted, following his alleged implication in a coup attempt. In an atmosphere of ongoing tension, several other clerics, including Bishop Sastre, were harrassed or detained, while all were impeded in their movements for a time.[71]

It could be said that during this period the Catholic Church was, for the first time, in rupture with the state in which it felt it had established and merited its place. Leon Brathier, editor of *La Nation*, notes, however, that "the Church always knew how to take position vis-à-vis the regime, in order not to be completely out of phase with it".[72] It had, it seems, learned lessons from the history of the *'église mère'*, in surviving the slings and arrows of outrageous political fortune and riding the turbulent tides of history. Its attitude was essentially non-confrontational and its profile discreet, even cryptic at times.[73] In a figurative sense at least, it could be said that it took to the *maquis*. Excluded from education, tentative in its relationship with the political elites, although it did maintain reliable contacts within the politico-administrative structure, it moved into areas it had previously neglected, developing its relationship with subalterns. Influenced by agencies such as INADES in Abidjan[74] and funded by external agencies which perceived it as a persecuted 'Church in need', led by bishops such as the socially committed de Souza, the articulate Sastre, and the more discreet but effective Assogba, the Church expanded its involvement in both the *quartiers populaires* of Cotonou and the larger towns, as well as in the rural hinterland. This took on a practical form through projects in rural development, health and hygiene, water supply, women's issues, and perhaps a certain rather timid consciousness-raising on a local level, as it increasingly

---

[71] CEB, "Lettre au Président de la République Populaire", *Eglise de Cotonou*, 15, 1 April 1975, 10–13 (following death sentence for treason passed on seven people including Fr Alphonse Quenum).

[72] Interview, 13 August 2002.

[73] Some of the people I interviewed felt that it was too discreet during this period. Alphonse Quenum is said to have been deeply disappointed at his treatment by the Church authorities during his ten years in prison. He apparently refused a pardon unless his colleagues were also pardoned. I did not discuss this with Fr Quenum when we met in Rome in April 2001.

[74] Institut African pour le Développement Economique et Social (INADES), founded by the Jesuits, specialising in research and social action in urban areas (literacy, health and economic activities).

attracted urban and rural subalterns keen to contest dominant elites in more local arenas. It became a local as well as a national actor.

All overt political discussion by pastoral agents was, however, strongly discouraged in order to allow the Church to maintain its position '*discrètement et efficacement sur le terrain*'. Mgr Assogba remarks that "after the revolutionary tempest" the state had to acknowledge the institutional solidity of the Church, noting that this was in part due to its discretion during the revolutionary period. He says that during the revolution "*le grand congolais*"[75] was watching them, but they said: "No, we are in our own field of action. We are apostles; we are not partisans of this or that. We try to work with the people as a people, in the name of our faith".[76] Heavily influenced by official Church thinking of the time, which we shall look at a little further on, the emphasis was on *development* rather than *liberation*, which was in any case a spent discourse following fifteen years of PRPB propaganda. It came to be perceived as *an organisation* with *resources* that could deliver in a state which had neither and was delivering nothing.

By 1984, however, the Church was slowly beginning to grasp the political nettle with the publication of Penoukou's very moderate political theology, calling on it to take a political position in society.[77] In the following years, Sastre began to write increasingly on socio-political and development issues. He became particularly prolific from 1987, contributing several articles on social, political and development themes to *La Croix du Benin*. By 1985, when the PRPB went into terminal decline, the Church was beginning to present the profile of an alternative and, apparently, more successful society. At the same time, it can be argued, it was playing an important role in holding the strained social fibre together, by occupying at least some of the spaces abandoned by an increasingly atrophied and dysfunctional state. The regime itself seemed to acknowledge this by granting tax exemptions on vehicles imported for use in all Church projects, a privilege rescinded by the later democratic regime. This wider presence certainly accounts, in part at least, for its dramatic expansion in the

---

[75] A euphemism for the state security apparatus.

[76] Interview, 21 June 2002.

[77] See Efoe-Julien Penoukou, *Eglises d'Afrique, proposition pour l'avenir*, Paris: Karthala, 1984.

north during this period. It is certainly significant to note that in the period 1980–2001 the Catholic Church almost doubled the number of its parishes in Benin, with half of these being established in the terminal years of the PRPB, 1980–1990.[78]

While there was wide social involvement, there was also another form of activity within a purely voluntary and strictly religious or devotional structure, which affected urban areas more particularly. These were the catechism classes, Bible groups, prayer groups, choirs, the CCRM and various fraternities and movements. Essentially, because of their devotional nature, these spaces eluded the grasp of the state and assimilation into party or state structures. They thus provided spaces which were outside state control for a population seeking relief and refuge from *un état défaillant* that was also potentially *un état violent*. At the same time they provided social structures in a society that was in serious difficulty and they certainly contributed to maintaining a certain social order in what had become a situation of extreme crisis. We shall look at these in more detail in the next chapter.

By the time the first signs of economic and social strain appeared, with student strikes in 1985 and the eventual economic collapse in 1987, the Catholic Church had regained a strong public profile. It represented institutional continuity in a way that had not been seen since the colonial period, as well as offering secure spaces in an increasingly insecure state. Having discreetly maintained its relationship with important members of the politico-administrative elite, it was in a position to play a role in the debate that was about to take place.

Writing from a Protestant missionary perspective, Goldschmidt suggests that "the refusal of the Catholic Church to compromise in any way and at any time with the Marxist regime"[79] was an important factor in the role it eventually took at the CNFVN. While the Church certainly maintained a distance from the Marxist-Leninist regime, neither is there any evidence that the regime tried to woo it, as had been the case for instance in both neighbouring Togo and in Zaire. Quite the opposite, it had 'robbed' its treasured schools

[78] Based on statistics in CEB, *Annuaire de l'Eglise Catholique au Bénin*, Cotonou, 2002.
[79] In A. Agbononci, "Bénin: l'avancée d'un pays parmi les moins avancés vers la démocratie", *Perspectives Missionnaires*, 22, 1991, 32.

and generally made life difficult through *des petites tracasseries* in a climate of growing uncertainty.

As Cedric Mayrargue correctly points out, the Church "follows events, but does not in any way anticipate them"[80] and certainly does not precipitate them. The Church adopted survival tactics and waited for the situation to implode, which it inevitably did, leaving a dangerous political vacuum in need of serious management if the ever-dreaded chaos was to be avoided. The army was a discredited force and so not an option, unless this was to come in the form of very junior officers. The lessons of Rawlings' Ghana and Sankara's Burkina Faso had been learned by the PRPB: junior officers are dangerous when they make a move and the Church was a safer option. I would contend that when the time came, the early period of Church intervention on the political scene in Dahomey was the model for its policy, and most particularly Archbishop de Souza's appointment[81] as president of the CNFVN in 1990 and later of the *Haut Conseil de République* (HCR). As I noted in a previous analysis:

> His understanding of his role was that of a neutral arbitrator or facilitator, with a certain moral authority. He played the role of a "gatherer", bringing the sides together and acting as "a kind of 'thermostat'", a regulator which would allow the conference to function in good conditions.[82] It is almost the classic profile of the *podesta*.[83]

Boillot has argued, in my view correctly, that the visibility of the Church on the early 1990s political landscape indicated not so much its political commitment, or the relevance of its discourse, but, rather, the political vacuum created by the absence of consensual political actors.[84] I would add that this absence of consensus, and indeed the absence of a coherent political discourse and meaningful political choices, other than those based on regionalism, is created largely by the historical and cultural factors which led to the social fractures

---

[80] Cedric Mayrargue, *Religions et changement politique au Bénin*, Mémoire de DEA "Etudes Africaines", CEAN, Bordeaux, 1994, 31.

[81] Mgr I. de Souza, "Eglises Africaines au sein de l'Eglise Universelle dans un monde en mutation" (Conférence), *Revue de l'Institut Catholique de l'Afrique de l'Ouest*, 5–6 Abidjan, 1993, 69, 72.

[82] Mgr I. de Souza, "l'Eglise arbitre", interview in *Croissance: Le Monde en Développement*, 336, Paris 1991, 21.

[83] Claffey, *The churches*, 36.

[84] Françoise Boillot, "L'Eglise catholique face aux processus de changement politique du début des années quatre-vingt-dix", *Année Africaine*, 1992–1993, 142.

we examined earlier. These remain a central factor in post-CNFVN
Benin's difficulties in coming to terms with its history, moving on
to renew its political elites and developing a modern and dynamic
political culture. This was unfortunately demonstrated in both the 1996
and 2001 presidential elections, which I dealt with in some detail
in Chapter 3. The competitive cut and thrust of modern politics, its
abrasive rhetoric, which in Benin so quickly turns accusatory with
the finger pointing at Abomey, and the necessary possibility of political alternation, in a society where the fundamental understanding of
power is as sacral and therefore unchanging, may tax the tissue of
this fragile society beyond its limits of tolerance. Ultimately, it may
threaten it with the chaos it has for so long been trying to avoid, and
which it sees threatening many other parts of the continent. Peace
and cohesion become the permanent *leitmotif*, the recurring trope of
political debate, used in a threatening sense to maintain the status quo.
At times it appears to dominate the whole of the political debate. It
is also the dominant theme of the discourse of the Catholic Church
in Benin, and one that at times may lead it to neglect other urgent
socio-political issues.

Central to my thesis is the argument that this fragility allows the
space for other more robust institutions in civil society to assert
themselves, and indeed may require it, particularly in situations of
social crisis. This is obviously all the more so when the institution
concerned is using a discourse designed to assuage and palliate
threatening tensions. In African political history, this situation is not
unique to either Catholicism or to Dahomey-Benin: it is witnessed,
for instance, in the place of the Islamic religious hierarchy in the
negotiation and maintenance of the *contrat social Sénégalais*.[85] With
traditional institutions lacking the discourse, the techniques or, as in
the case of Danxomɛ, the credibility to question developments, the
Church, with a history in Dahomey-Benin that pre-dates the modern
state, has found itself squarely—if at times somewhat reluctantly—at
the centre of socio-political developments, the most public of which
historically was the CNFVN. Kérékou, as we have seen, was indeed

---

[85] See D. Cruise-O'Brien and M. Diouf, "La réussite du contrat social sénégalais"
in D. Cruise-O'Brien and M.-C. Diop, *La Construction de l'Etat au Sénégal*, Paris:
Karthala, 2002, 9–15. The authors note that in more recent years the chiefs of the
Muslim brotherhoods have succeeded in turning themselves into social arbiters in
times of tension.

happy to benefit from its ministrations in his political penance and
the purification of his power, which had been so badly tarnished by
the excesses and eventual bankruptcy of the PRPB period, when the
Marxist monarch was left without his clothes. So too, however, was
a population which was facing the chaos and the unbridled violence
that would almost inevitably follow the demise of the king. Whatever
Bolliot's opinions on the relevance of its discourse in terms of pure
political content, the important thing was that the Church *actually had
one*. In fact, as we shall see, in Benin it has two. The first, coming
from outside, draws heavily on the social doctrine of the Church
and was backed up at this time by the figure of John Paul II. The
other, which is in a sense more 'inculturated', comes from within
the local Church, and addresses precisely the question of social cohesion and 'peace'.[86] In addition to its sacral power and its discourse,
its considerable capacity, both nationally and internationally in the
field of health and social development,[87] and an ability to deliver on
the ground, give it material as well as symbolic capital. This adds
considerably to its profile and credibility in public eyes, even if the
sharing out of this *gâteau ecclésial* brings with it the disadvantages
of managing considerable resources—though perhaps not as considerable as is popularly believed—and creating greater expectations than
it could reasonably be expected to deliver.

---

[86] See Jacob M. Agossou, *Christianisme africain: Une fraternité au delà de
l'ethnie*, Paris: Karthala, 1987. Again there are similarities with the discourse in
Senegal where Islamic "fraternity" is seen as superseding other considerations
(D. Cruise-O'Brien, personal communication).

[87] See Dorothé Aïdasso, *Les Œuvres sociales de l'Eglise Catholique dans le
Diocèse de Cotonou: 1958–1996*, Mémoire de Maîtrise, UNB, 2000.
The Catholic Church in Benin receives substantial financial aid for development
from international Catholic donor organisations. However, in interviews with both Fr
Jean-Joachim Adjovi, Coordinator (SCDIH), Cotonou (July 2002) and Fr Stéphane
Raux (BIBAD) in Parakou (June 2002) the question of clientelism and rent-seekers
was evoked several times. Fr Adjovi was particularly critical of the problems caused
by overseas development aid to the point of saying that ultimately it did more harm
than good and that the Benin Church should be self-financing in this regard. A case
concerning a credit union managed by Fr Adjovi received coverage in the national
press (See Joël Toffoun, "Solliciter l'arbitrage de Mgr Nestor Assogba", *La Nation*,
11 June 2001). Fr Raux was more technocratic in his approach, but was also critical
of what he saw as a poor understanding of development. For a critical study of this
problem, see Jean-François Bayart, "Les Eglises chrétiennes et la politique du ventre:
le partage du gâteau ecclésial", *Politique Africaine*, 35, 1989, 68–76.

Catholic social doctrine and its application in Dahomey-Benin

There has been an increased emphasis on the development of an overtly political theology in most of the historical Churches in Europe since the Second World War.[88] Huntington notes that the "repositioning of the Church from a bulwark of the status quo, usually authoritarian, to a force for change, usually democratic, was a major political phenomenon of the 1960s".[89] This was brought a step further in the early 1970s through the development of liberation theology in Latin America, with its Marxist analytical bias, and its emphasis on cellular organisation in the *communidades de base* for analysis and action for social change, revolutionary if necessary in the more extreme cases.[90] There were local variants of this in Africa, most notably in the work of Jean-Marc Ela,[91] though to what extent they were ever widespread is debatable. This was theology on the fringes in what some sociologists and political scientists tend to see in purely functional terms as an attempt by theologians to find a socially-relevant discourse. Little trace of this theology, however, is to be found in Benin. It was in any case unlikely to have much of an audience after seventeen years of *marxisme à la béninoise*, while elsewhere it was also becoming clear that the Marxist tide of history was quickly ebbing and would soon run out. Perhaps more significant, however, was the reason advanced

---

[88] The French Catholic social thinker Emmanuel Mounier (1905–1950), dealing in the pre-war period with "military problems, colonialism, syndicalism, strikes, and fascism" (Lucien Guissard, *Emmanuel Mounier*, Torino: Borla [Italian Edition], 1964, 58), is credited with inspiring the Catholic left following the war. His *personalist* philosophy continues to influence Catholic social doctrine. In the 1960s, the German Protestant theologian Jurgen Moltmann (1926–) began to develop his "theology of hope", "political theology," "theology of revolution".

[89] Samuel Huntington, "Religion and the Third Wave", in S.P. Ramet and D.W. Treadgold (eds), *Render unto Caesar: the religious sphere in world politics*, Washington: AUP, 1995, 73.

[90] "[Liberation] theology uses Marxism purely as an *instrument*....[It] freely borrows from Marxism certain 'methodological pointers' that have proved fruitful in understanding the world of the oppressed such as: the importance of economic factors; attention to the class struggle; the mystifying power of ideologies, including religions (Leonardo Boff and Clodovis Boff, *Introducing Liberation Theology*, London: Burns and Oates, 1997, 28).

[91] See, for instance, Jean-Marc Ela, *L'Afrique des Villages*, Paris: Karthala, 1982; *From Charity to Liberation*, London: Catholic Institute for International Relations, 1984; *My faith as an African*, New York: Orbis, 1988; *Afrique: l'irruption des pauvres: société contre ingérence, pouvoir et argent*, Paris: L'Harmattan, 1994.

by one Béninois theologian, who comments: "Liberation theology will never work here, we do not have enough anger against our former coloniser. Our hatred is in fact turned against ourselves".[92] Only one of the Catholic movements I encountered in my fieldwork had anything of a liberation discourse and it appeared to be very marginal.[93] It is certainly significant to note that, along with Adoukonou's approach to the Vodún, the only other theology emerging from within Benin addresses the question of Christianity and ethnicity, the creation of fraternité[94] rather than that of liberation, and certainly not revolution with its implications of violence and class struggle.

The institutional Church, however, has also developed an important socio-political discourse and there has been increasing emphasis since the Second Vatican Council on what has become known as the "social doctrine" of the Church, which, it can be argued, has filtered down to some extent in the local Churches.[95] Other agencies at different levels in the Church are also involved in this kind of work through local Church bodies. Many of the latter would be more outspoken in their interventions and some still retain a certain sympathy for liberation theology. The social doctrine was developed and heavily emphasised during the long papacy of John Paul II, adapted for different situations,[96] and preached in a total of twelve extended visits

---

[92] Interview, 30 June 2001.

[93] This was *Association des Amis de Jean Sulivan*, whose director Albert Gandonou professes to be a Christian Marxist and has spent time in prison under both the Kérékou and later Soglo regimes for his political activities. Jean Sulivan (1913–1980) was a French priest and writer with sympathies for the worker-priest movement and other aspects of social Catholicism in the spirit of Emmanuel Mounier.

[94] See Agossou, *Christianisme*.

[95] The role of the Pontifical Council for Justice and Peace is defined as follows: it collects information and research on justice and peace, about human development and violations of human rights; it ponders all this, and, when appropriate, shares its conclusions with the groupings of bishops. It cultivates relationships with Catholic international organisations and other institutions, even ones outside the Catholic Church, which sincerely strive to achieve peace and justice in the world. (art. 143, § 2). See, for example, Bernard Mununo (ed.), *The Challenge of Justice and Peace: The Response of the Church in Africa Today*, Symposium of the Pontifical Council for Justice and Peace Harare, 29 July–1 August 1996, Rome: Libreria Editrice Vaticana, 1988.

[96] John Paul II addressed apostolic exhortations to different geographical areas of the world: *Ecclesia in Africa* (1995), *Ecclesia in Asia* (1999), *Ecclesia in America* (1999), *Ecclesia in Oceania* (2001), *Ecclesia in Europa* (2003). All of these contain a central chapter on the social doctrine as well as a brief analysis of what are seen as the major socio-political issues facing the area in question. Much of the information

to thirty-eight countries in Africa[97] in the period 1980–1999, including two to Benin in 1982 and 1993. Not surprisingly, it was markedly different from liberation theology.

By the 1980s the liberation theme, which marked the post-Vatican II period and was a response to *Populorum Progressio*,[98] whose developmentalist discourse was seen as encouraging dependency, came increasingly under scrutiny for its Marxist methodological bias. During the early years of a decidedly anti-Marxist pope, it was officially rejected as a tool of analysis.[99] Writing in 1988, the Pope stated:

> Recently, in the period following the publication of the encyclical *Populorum Progressio*, a new way of confronting the problems of poverty and underdevelopment has spread in some areas of the world, especially in Latin America. This approach makes liberation the fundamental category and the first principle of action. The positive values, as well as the deviations and risks of deviation, which are damaging to the faith and are connected with this form of theological reflection and method, have been appropriately pointed out by the Church's Magisterium.
>
> It is fitting to add that the aspiration to freedom from all forms of slavery affecting the individual and society is something noble and legitimate. This in fact is the purpose of development, or rather liberation and development, taking into account the intimate connection between the two.[100]

John Paul II developed a discourse of his own, based on earlier Catholic teaching. This was built essentially on a theme of conservative moral values and a critique of atheistic communism, Western secularism, and an amoral neo-liberalism.[101] *Development* was reasserted as a central concept and, in a style emphasising continuity that is quite typical of all papal documents, *Populorum Progressio* was strongly reaffirmed.[102] As the above quotation indicates, *liberation* as

---

and analysis for such documents comes from the Pontifical Council for Justice and Peace, Rome, which "is at the service of the Holy Father and also collaborates with other departments of the Roman Curia" (interview, Rome, 9 April 2001).

[97] All in sub-Saharan Africa, except Morocco, Tunisia, Egypt.

[98] Paul VI, *Populorum Progressio*, Vatican, 1967.

[99] Joseph Cardinal Ratzinger, *Instruction on Certain Aspects of the "Theology of Liberation"*, Congregatio pro Doctrina Fidei Rome, August, 1984.

[100] John Paul II, *Sollicitudo Rei Socialis*, Vatican, 1987, 46.

[101] See Clifford Longley, "Structures of Sin and the Free Market", in Paul Vallely (ed.), *The New Politics: Catholic Social Teaching for the Twenty-First Century*, London: SCM, 97–113, for a treatment of this theme in the social doctrine.

[102] Notably in *Solcitude Rei Socialis*, published to mark the anniversary of the earlier document. The word *liberation* occurs only nine times, most often to be either

a concept was officially spurned, to be replaced by the concept of *solidarity*, with its echoes from the shipyards of Gdansk.[103] Backed by a pope with a strong media image, this message was preached over the length of his papacy.

Paul Vallely has suggested that the social doctrine may be the basis of a "new politics". He argues that

> Catholic notions about the nature of human dignity, the common good, subsidiarity and structural sin may well constitute the compass which our post-modern society needs as it sets out on its journey into the next millennium.[104]

Whatever one thinks of the social doctrine, it is clear that the Church does have a well developed, closely reasoned, essentially conservative, multi-layered political argument to make that has been built up over a long history. The American conservative political commentator George Weigel adds:

> Roman Catholicism is, first and foremost, a religious community that makes certain truth claims about the human person, human community, human history, and human destiny, all understood in their relationship to God. To proclaim those truths, and to witness to them in worship and through service of the community, is the Church's reason for existence.[105]

Clearly, because of its history, Catholicism has never really operated from the wings, unless confined to this space by other forces. It has been described as a Constantinian Church in its assertion of its rights in public space, "seeking the mediation of *political society* in order to ensure its pastoral presence in *civil society*",[106] and once

---

refuted or reinterpeted. *Solidarity* occurs twenty-eight times, definied as "a firm and persevering determination to commit oneself to the common good; that is to say to the good of all and of each individual, because we are all really responsible for all" (*Solicitudo Rei Socialis*, 38).

[103] In what appears like a direct snub to contextualised theologies, in *Ecclesia in America* (1999), the term "liberation" occurs only once, whereas "solidarity" occurs thirty-seven times.

[104] Paul Vallely, "Towards a New Politics: Catholic Social doctrine in a Pluralist Society", in Vallely *The New Politics*, 160.

[105] Weigel, *Roman Catholicism*, 22.

[106] Pablo Richard, *Death of Christendom, Birth of the Church: Historical Analysis and Theological Interpretation of the Church in Latin America*, New York: Orbis, 1987, 133, in René Padilla, "The future of Christianity in Latin America: Missiological Perspectives and Challenges", in *International Bulletin of Missionary Research*, 23 (3), 1999, 108.

out of the catacombs it has certainly been loath to be confined to the sacristies.[107] Weigel notes that:

> In the first thirty years of the post-World War II period, the Holy See's vigorous re-entry into international public life took place in classic 'high politics' terms: bilateral negotiations and agreements with sovereign states, and participation in international organisations, amplified by the occasional moral exhortation, usually couched in rather abstract terms.[108]

This is still the case, to some extent, as the Church has wide diplomatic representation throughout the world, through Nunciatures,[109] and this certainly plays an important role in determining Church-State relations. In effect, however, the nuncio wears two birettas. He is charged with maintaining relations with the civil authorities in the name of the Vatican, as we have just seen. He is also meant to keep a watchful eye on the theology and the pastoral practices of the local Church, sharpening the socio-political discourse where he feels the local ecclesiastical authorities are being overly reticent and reining them in when he feels they are becoming too involved in the political arena.

In the past thirty years, during the pontificates of Paul VI and John Paul II, the Catholic Church has moved out of the diplomatic corridors and become more visible on the popular world stage. John Paul II, seen as highly political in the wake of the fall of the Eastern bloc,[110] travelled widely with a message that was often considered political.[111] Huntington suggests that these visits came to play "a pivotal role" in the "third wave" and the struggle of the local Churches against authoritarian regimes, noting that: "John Paul II seemed to have a way of showing up in full pontifical majesty at critical points in democratisation processes".[112]

---

[107] Mgr I. de Souza, "Pas question de se réfugier dans la sacristie", *Actualité Religieuse dans le Monde*, 15 September 1990, 35–37.

[108] Weigel, *Roman Catholicism*, 32.

[109] The number of nunciatures, Vatican embassies, increased dramatically during the reign of Paul VI, rising from sixty-one in 1963 to 109 in 1978 to 172 in 2004.

[110] Huntington and other commentators such as Bob Woodward rank him with Ronald Reagan and Margaret Thatcher in terms of his influence. See Huntington, *The Clash*, 282, 292.

[111] Patrick Claffey, "Pageants and TVignettes: The Theatre of Papal Visits in Africa", unpublished paper for "*Theatre Politics in Asia and Africa: Subversion, Collusion, or Control*", symposium at School of Oriental and Africa Studies, University of London, 18–19 January 2002.

[112] Huntington, *Religion*, 77.

The text of the visits was built up from the conservative moral doctrine that is a strong central element, and often the most criticised element,[113] to the more overtly-political teaching and calls for justice, peace, respect for human rights, subsidiarity in governance and solidarity in socio-economic relations. At the same time, direct involvement by clergy in politics is strongly condemned.[114] The distant intellectual inspiration of the modern political teaching is to be found in the *personalist* philosophy and the political theology of thinkers such as the French left-wing Catholic thinker Emmanuel Mounier, moulded like John Paul II by the trauma of the war, an abhorrence of totalitarian ideologies and the post-war conditions facing Europe.[115] The doctrinal inspiration is to be found in the social doctrine of the Catholic Church, particularly as developed since the Second Vatican Council. The document *Gaudium et Spes: On the Church in the Modern World* (1965) remains central, as does *Populorum Progressio* (1967),[116] reiterated in John Paul II's own letter *Sollicitudo Rei Socialis* (1987).[117] The themes are essentially those of the dignity of the human person, justice, peace, social solidarity and the common good, in societies where subsidiarity is respected. With regard to Africa, these have been further refined over the years and over the papal visits into the document addressed specifically to the continent which attempts to address some of the economic and socio-political problems: *Ecclesia in Africa* (1995). There is therefore, whatever one thinks of it, a reasoned and consistent discourse of radical/conservative social analysis and political content addressed to Africa, as well as calling on the conscience of the developed world.

---

[113] See Greg Noakes, "Cairo Population Conference Still Controversial", *Washington Report on Middle-East Affairs*, 1995, 67, 100–101.

[114] During the 1982 visit to Nicaragua, he appeared to publicly chastise Ernesto Cardenal, priest, poet and liberation theologian who had accepted the role of Minister of Culture in the first Sandinista government. Cardenal's *Psalms of Struggle and Liberation* (New York: Herder, 1971) is typical of a liberation reading of scripture.

[115] See Emmanuel Mounier, *Écrits sur le personalisme*, Paris: Seuil, 1961, 65–80. This section of the book was written before the death of John Paul II. For the moment, Benedict XVI has not published any important documents, although he was clearly involved in the formulation of the important magisterial documents of his predecessor. However, he refers more often to the revolutionary events of 1968 as having been influential on his thinking.

[116] See Julian Filochowski, "Looking out to the World's Poor: The Teaching of Paul VI", in Vallely, *The New Politics*, 61–83 for a treatment of this historically important document.

[117] For a concise treatment of the social doctrine as developed by John Paul II, see Ian Linden, "People before Profit", and in Vallely, *The New Politics*, 84–96.

A brief analysis of the socio-political chapters of *Ecclesia in Africa* is revealing. This is concentrated in a small section of Chapter II giving an outline, rather than an analysis, of the socio-economic political problems confronting the continent:

> In Africa, the need to apply the Gospel to concrete life is felt strongly. How could one proclaim Christ on that immense Continent while forgetting that it is one of the world's poorest regions? How could one fail to take into account the anguished history of a land where many nations are still in the grip of famine, war, racial and tribal tensions, political instability and the violation of human rights? This is all a challenge to evangelisation.... [And] issues in Africa such as increasing poverty, urbanisation, the international debt, the arms trade, the problem of refugees and displaced persons, demographic concerns and threats to the family, the liberation of women, the spread of AIDS, the survival of the practice of slavery in some places, ethnocentricity and tribal opposition figure among the fundamental challenges addressed by the Synod.[118]

This is further developed in Chapter VI of *Ecclesia in Africa*, entitled "Building the Kingdom of God: Kingdom of Justice and Peace". This analyses the problems further, asserting the Church's right and duty as witness and an actor for development, becoming "the voice of the voiceless"[119] and encouraging Catholics to join with others in seeking the solutions. There is an analysis and listing of the most pressing social problems.[120]

The address to the state in Africa comes in sections 110–113, which emphasise the *Good administration of public affairs, Building the nation, The rule of law, Administering the common patrimony.* In two remaining sections, 114 and 120, the document looks to a wider audience in a discussion on *The international dimension* and the specific question of *The burden of the international debt*, respectively. Papal documents are unlikely to use Bayartian *politics of the belly* vocabulary or IMF *good governance* terminology. However, the critique is essentially the same, where moral admonitions are linked to socio-economic and political analysis in something of a civics lesson or political pep talk to ruling elites, even calling them to *holiness*.[121]

---

[118] John Paul II, *Ecclesia in Africa*, Rome, Libreria Editrice Vaticana, 1995, 51.
[119] Ibid., 106.
[120] Ibid., 108–109.
[121] Ibid., 111.

Casanova points out that the social doctrine is expressed in three clearly-defined instances. It seeks "to protect not only [the Church's] own freedom of religion but all modern freedoms and rights, and the very right of a democratic civil society to exist against an absolutist, authoritarian state". At the same time, it has as its task "to question and contest absolute lawful autonomy of the secular spheres and their claims to be organised in accordance with principles of functional differentiation without regard to extraneous ethical or moral consider-ations", for example the arms race, nuclear arms, world debt. In addi-tion, it seeks "to protect the traditional life-world from administrative or juridical state penetration, and in the process opens up issues of norm and will formation to the public and collective self-reflection of modern discursive ethics", for example Moral Majority and the Catholic stand on abortion.[122]

Casanova adds that "in the first instance religion would serve in the very constitution of liberal political and social order", while in the second and third instances it "would serve to show, question, and contest the very 'limits' of the liberal political and social order". The Church engages the "institutions of rule in order that they would more clearly define themselves and the state in ethical terms with due regard to *solidarity* and *subsidiarity*",[123] fundamental principles of the social doctrine. While it is clear that the second and third instances are central elements, the first has been widely used in Africa, some-times to the irritation of regimes, to challenge authoritarian states to come to a different relationship with their subjects. This discourse in turn has been instrumentalised by civil society leaders, and aspiring political actors, to encourage a greater democratisation.[124] It has been seen as a useful discourse in times of tension, with the authority of a certain history, and the weight of a conservative institution.

These then are the major themes—challenges perhaps but not open contestation—that constituted the socio-political text of all the papal visits and all the other texts addressed to Africa from 1980, and that developed in different ways as the situation required, but were essentially quite consistent and intellectually coherent. What in the end, however, did all of this amount to? There have certainly been

---

[122] Casanova, *Public Religions*, 57–58.
[123] Filochowski, *Looking out*, 61.
[124] This was the case in Nigeria during a papal visit towards the end of the Abacha regime in 1998. See Claffey, *Pageants*, 15.

some very painful disappointments, as in Rwanda and Burundi. The
theologian Kä Mana cites the tragedy of Rwanda as symptomatic of
the failure of Christianity to take any real hold on the imagination of
the continent, which, in his view, underlines even more the importance
of the appropriation of a Christianity with the social doctrine as an
important element.[125]

The political scientists hold a more sceptical view. More vulgar positivists see it simply as an opiate, adding to the problems, perhaps, more
than contributing to a solution or simply jumping on the bandwagon
for purposes of proselytism.[126] Certainly, there is little to indicate direct
contestation of any of the more dubious regimes it deals with, more
than perhaps some chiding and a little discreet diplomacy. However,
it appears to me that direct contestation is hardly the purpose. The
social doctrine is predicated on a particular socio-political discourse
based on the following elements: the dignity of the human person,
the primacy of truth, the idea of the common good and the call to
justice for all, which implies subsidiarity in the system of government and social solidarity both within states and in the international
order.[127] This, rather than *democracy* as such, forms the basis of the
discourse. In the view of John Paul II, the social doctrine "is not a
'third way'" that places itself somewhere "between liberal capitalism
and Marxist collectivism" or any other kind of socio-political theory.
He refuses to call it an ideology, saying that it is

> the accurate formulation of the results of a careful reflection on the
> complex realities of human existence, in society and in the international
> order, in the light of faith and of the Church's tradition [...] its aim is
> thus to guide Christian behaviour.[128]

The stated implication is that a state that is true and can lay a claim
to the loyalty of its people will be based upon and tested against
these principles. Of course, this alone may be a form of contestation.
It is unlikely that the field tested would be anything other than the
moral one, and it is certainly one where questions need to be asked
in the light of the dysfunctionality of so many African states. Neither

---

[125] See Kä Mana, *La nouvelle évangélisation*, 82–109.
[126] See Mayrargue, *Religions et changement politique.*
[127] See William A. Barbieri, "The Expansion of the Common Good in Catholic
Thought", in *The Review of Politics*, 63, 3, 2001, 723–754.
[128] *Solicitudo Rei Socialis*, 41.

ideological nor liberal technocratic solutions seem to have advanced things very much, and seem unlikely to do so unless the state can be imagined in another way, which includes a sound ethical basis. In the specific case of Benin, the Catholic sociologist Adè insists that "insofar as there is no ethical basis to politics in Benin, democracy will always be precarious, always threatened"[129] and the state itself will remain fragile.

The social doctrine has become the discourse of the hierarchical Catholic Church in Benin in its relations with state and society, and particularly the political elite. Following the CNFVN, the Church sees itself as having a responsibility for the democratic process it was involved in creating, and which appears to me to have become the basis of a *nouveau contrat social béninois*. It has, therefore, taken an increased interest in the socio-political formation of lay people as civil society actors and potential political elites who, in a tradition going back to Aupiais, it is hoped will take the process in the right direction. While confessional political parties of any kind are not permitted under Article 5 of the Constitution, the Church encourages the participation of Catholics in all the political parties in a spirit of disinterested public service.[130] An early documents states:

> The Christian who loves his country and who is really capable of serving must be able to find a place in the political, economic and social structures of the Nation, in order to really play his/her role of salt, yeast and light.[131]

This again is in conformity with Church teaching on the subject, which frowns on clerical participation in political activity, seeing it as the domain of the laity.[132] This is essentially a discourse directed at elites, perhaps in the hope that a leader of genuine stature with a roughly Christian-democratic conservative vision, a de Gaulle, or an Adenauer, would emerge. In the course of an interview Kä Mana observed:

> We need people who incarnate this possibility of development, of going further. There is a deficit of incarnation in our projects. In fact our politicians play below the state in their personal interests, instead of

---

[129] Adè, *Les fidèles*, 70.
[130] CEB, *Au Service*.
[131] CEB, *Béninoises et béninois*, 6.
[132] John Paul II, *Christifideles laici*, Vatican, 1988, 23.

saying that we are at a stage of consciousness that unites us...We need men who incarnate [a vision], a de Gaulle...Nyerere did it...Mandela also.[133]

Fr Raymond B. Goudjo, a priest of the Archdiocese of Cotonou, has studied the social doctrine and is now director of the *Institut des Artisans de Justice et de Paix* (IAJP) in Cotonou. The IAJP seeks to be a centre for the socio-political formation of the laity, civil society actors and future elites of a democratic Benin. The IAJP publishes significant amounts of material in this field, most of it written by Fr Goudjo himself (see Bibliography). The institute springs directly from the Church's understanding of its role in the CNFVN, which it sees as having led the country from the crises it has suffered since independence, several *coups d'état* and the Marxist revolution.[134] This has resulted in its perception of itself as having a special responsibility for the *nouveau contrat social béninois*, which it feels the conference represented, and its interest in promoting what it sees as the legacy of that period. This is well illustrated in a 1992 text of the CEB:

> Benin had the privilege of inaugurating in sub-Saharan African, the smooth passage toward a state of law. We thank God who heard our prayers. This adds to our responsibility on the international scene. Our advance is irreversible and must lead us to success, we must succeed whatever it costs, first of all for the good of our people, and then for the example that this can give to others.[135]

While democracy may not have paid the dividend that was expected,[136] the CNFVN, and the Church's role in it, represents a historical point beyond which the country does not want to return. It is at least a rejection of the totalitarianism and the state violence that marked the first thirty years of independence, culminating in the PRPB regime, and it offers some hope for the future. The CEB seems to have

---

[133] Interview, 13 June 2002. An almost identical theme emerged in an interview with R.B. Goudjo, who spoke of the need for a charismatic leader, someone who could be "almost a myth".

[134] While the Catholic Church certainly played an important role in the period leading up to the CNFVN, the other churches also contributed, particularly *The Porto Novo Declaration*. See CIEPB, Ethique chrétienne et politique dans le Bénin d'aujourd'hui: Colloque des 12–13 February 1990, Déclaration", Porto-Novo, in *Perspectives Missionnaires*, 22, 1990, 44–50.

[135] CEB, *Exigences de la démocratie* (Pastoral Letter) Abomey, 14 February 1992, 130.

[136] Mgr I. de Souza, L'Afrique est déçue par la démocratie (Interview), *Jeune Afrique*, 1836, 13–19 March 1996, 30.

assumed the role of periodically reminding "the sons and daughters of Benin", "all Christians and all people of goodwill", of this pact in pastoral letters. It invites the faithful to keep the memory of "the good things God has bestowed on Benin" in "leading the country on the road to democracy in serenity and peace".[137] This was a new beginning, a kind of new covenant, and certainly a new *contrat social*. The letters constantly emphasise the historical difficulties, the social stagnation of the country, the nightmare of the PRPB period, the gains made since 1990, the need to "exorcise the demons of violence" and tribalism and the need to safeguard peace and national unity.[138]

While it would be a mistake to speak of any kind of Catholic nationalism in Benin, there certainly has emerged within Catholicism a kind of Béninois nationalism.[139] This is expressed in the idea that, despite the sufferings of the past, this is a country blessed by God, called to a new destiny at the CNFVN, and with a divine vocation to be a light to others. It is almost as if the country, with its painful past, had been reborn to a new destiny at the CNFVN. As we shall see in the final chapter, this discourse of a "rebirth" or "breakthrough" for a "Nation chosen and set apart by God" (Leviticus 20: 26) is one that marks all the Churches in Benin. In quite nationalistic terms, the CEB emphasises that "there are not two Benins: our Benin is one from North to South, from East to West".[140] In a recent, privately-circulated document from the retired Cardinal Gantin, on the prestige of the national flag, he concludes with an exhortation almost in the tone of an anthem:

> *Children of Benin, let us stand up.* Not alone to sing, but even more, that on the horizon, by the grace of God and thanks to our own efforts, a New Dawn will arise, brighter and more prophetic than ever, on our dear country.[141]

---

[137] CEB, "Aux chrétiens et aux hommes de bonne volonté Cotonou" (Pastoral Letter) 24 January 1996, in Goudjo *Discours*, 151–155.

[138] CEB, *Pour un nouvel essor de notre pays*, Cotonou, 24 January 1996, in Goudjo, *Discours*, 141–148; CEB, *Pour préserver*, 159.

[139] See Penoukou, *Eglises d'Afrique*, particularly three chapters: *Foi et Culture, Foi et politique*, and *Foi et développement* (46–106).

[140] CEB, *Pour préserver*, 161.

[141] Bernardin Card. Gantin, *Le Prestige du Drapeau National*, Cotonou, 7 February 2003 (privately published and circulated manuscript received from author).

The IAJP's largely Christian-democratic orientation would seem to be confirmed by the support it receives from the *Konrad Adenauer Stiftung*,[142] which has been actively involved in democratic political development in Benin since 1990, as well as its contacts with the German Catholic business world. Dr Tardy Ostry, director of the KAS, says: "Our aim is to strengthen the social doctrine of the Church", and in this to contribute to the consolidation of democratic institutions within the state.[143] The IAJP discourse is essentially that of the social doctrine. It is somewhat abstract, conservative and appears to me to be little adapted to the political realities of the country, although it does touch on questions such as ethnic identity.[144] Essentially, however, it repeats with little variation what it sees as classical Thomist positions and the social doctrine as enunciated by John Paul II. It is difficult to know to what extent it contributes to the imagining of the state in contemporary Benin. I posed the problem to Fr Goudjo in the course of an interview. He acknowledges the problem but says that it is one of finding an appropriate discourse that will express a political philosophy for Africa today. He has chosen that of classical Thomism because, he says, when African intellectuals meet they need a schema of debate "because [they] don't have a philosophical springboard...that is thought out and co-ordinated". In fact, he points out, all of them are using exogenous discourses, whether developmentalist, Marxist/dependency or neo-liberal, and in this *IAJP* is no different.

> We can take a few of our local sayings but this is not a discourse, and in order to establish a discourse one must find another logic. We haven't been formed in an African logic—even those who pass for Africanists. I often think one should try to find the philosophical basis of their discourse, on what conceptual basis are they basing their argument? There is not an African thinker who has the logical coherence upon which we could found our philosophical springboard. My springboard is founded upon the Catholic faith, that is all I have done. Catholicism and Thomism for the very simple reason that I admire Thomas

---

[142] Founded in 1956, "The Foundation offers political education, conducts scientific fact-finding research for political projects, grants scholarships to gifted individuals, researches the history of Christian Democracy, and supports and encourages European unification, international understanding, and development-policy co-operation". See http://www1.kas.de/stiftung/englisch/intro.html.

[143] Interview, 11 June 2002.

[144] Raymond B. Goudjo (ed.), *Identités ethniques et intégrité nationale*, Cotonou: Flamboyant, 1998.

Aquinas...his capacity and the strength of his synthesis...because of these titanic ideas he has succeeded in establishing.

I'm doing what I can...If I write a lot, it is because of that, it is because we find ourselves in a *no man's land*... So we have to accept the entry into our politics of external elements which are completely strange to us but which at the same time impose upon us a conversion in the way we look at things...[145]

This is, in his view, an attempt to imagine a state that is completely different from the historical polity, a modern Benin based on a new ethic. The ethical values expressed in the social doctrine are those that he considers to have contributed to the construction of other success-ful polities in the Christian Democratic tradition.[146] These states are based on the dignity of the human person, the primacy of truth, the common good, and justice for all, in a state that is respectful of the subsidiary entities that compose it, allowing them room to develop in a spirit of solidarity with others and the wider world. This certainly contests more totalitarian models of sacral power which have been historically dominant.[147] It is difficult, however, to see how this is making any real inroads in the cut and thrust of everyday politics in Benin. Amongst the Catholic intellectuals I encountered, includ-ing clergy, several were overtly critical of the IAJP and Goudjo's work, in what appeared to me at times to be an internecine *bagarre* amongst elites, and perhaps the need for the laity to reassert a certain independence in relation to a very strong institution which it may perceive as trying to set the agenda and dictate the pace. One source suggested that Goudjo and other Béninois Catholic intellectuals were being inhibited in their research and discourse by an ultramontane hierarchy, whose most celebrated member, Bernardin Cardinal Gantin, was until quite recently a prominent member of the Roman Curia. This discourse can indeed sometimes sound like little more than mimicry. It appears to void all contemporary local social analysis, and in a kind of theological extraversion—to improvise on Bayart's

---

[145] Interview, 14 July 2002.

[146] See Giuliano Amato, Jean-Luc Dehaene et Valéry Giscard d'Estaing, "L'Europe demain: la fausse querelle des 'petits' et des 'grands'", *Le Monde*, 13 November 2003, 18–19. This long piece in *Le Monde* attempts to show how these values have been fundamental to the construction of European politics and how they have been incorporated into the proposed European constitution.

[147] Bediako emphasises the importance of Christianity in "desacralisation of author-ity and power" in the African context. See *Christianity*, 243–251.

term—it echoes papal texts and seeks safety in the shelter of an imposing international institution and overseas benefactors it might be hesitant to offend in a more independent analysis.[148]

The model here often seems to be Germany, where several Béninois Catholic intellectuals, including Goudjo, Adoukonou and Gbégnonvi have done their studies and maintain strong contacts. It is almost as if Germany has replaced France as the paradigm for a rational *ordnung* and *modernismus* that can be aspired to, free from the bitterly-remembered colonial chauvinism where all that was best and all that was civilised was to be found "*chez nous en France*". It is significant to note here what seems like a parallel distinction made by a Charismatic Church member, who distinguishes between "*l'évangile anglophone et l'évangile francophone*", noting that the former preaches success and prosperity, while the latter emphasises the virtue of poverty.[149] He notes that *l'évangile francophone* was brought by the colonial power, and there appears to be an implied critique of both Catholicism and France in this former Catholic opting for a Charismatic Church that looks to America as a model for *l'évangile anglophone*. Not by coincidence, German Catholic aid organisations, which are highly organised and very well funded in comparison with their French counterparts, are also major contributors to both the social and pastoral projects, which give the Catholic Church its considerable capacity in these areas. The discourse appears abstract and, as Goudjo himself acknowledges, lacks contact with the social realities in the popular *quartiers* of Cotonou and the bush villages of Benin. On the other hand, it is a ready-made and convenient theological hybrid and is used as a certain form of socio-political commentary.

An examination of the working document for the Synod in the Archdiocese of Parakou shows a full chapter entitled *L'Homme Debout: Justice Paix et Développement* which is essentially a reprise of these themes developed and applied on a more local level.[150] So it can be argued that there is a 'filter-down' effect to some extent, and

---

[148] See Gifford, *African Christianity*, 308–325 for a more general treatment of this concept of "extraversion" which "is most obvious in the case of the Catholic Church" (308).

[149] Interview, 13 June 2002.

[150] *A l'Ecoute de l'Esprit*, Synode Diocésain, Document de travail, Parakou 1999, 21–38.

certainly the perception of a Church that has a language that allows it to approach the State when and if this is necessary. One has the sense, however, that what people, including those in the other religious confessions, seek in the Catholic Church is not primarily a discourse, but rather institutional substance at times when the state and society itself are threatened by their own fragility. While its discourse may not penetrate very deeply and is quickly abandoned when the political dust settles, it is one that can serve a purpose in situations of tension, as was certainly the case in the terminal PRPB period. At times such as these, a conservative yet critical discourse, borrowed from a distant institution and backed up by international contacts, can indeed serve the purpose of aspiring elites. It can, indeed, be read as a critique of the status quo and a motor for change, or perhaps more accurately, access to power since real change appears to be slow in coming. It becomes almost opposition by proxy while at the same protecting from much feared violence and chaos that appear as a constant subtext and threat. This leads us on to the more local and perhaps more inculturated pastoral discourse of the Church. It is in this area that it appears to address itself to the fragility that we have looked at.

"Dieu aime le Bénin":
A new nationalism in an inculturated pastoral discourse

While the Catholic Church certainly adopts much of the social doctrine in its ongoing dialogue with state and society, it also has a more local discourse, which has become a strong feature since the PRPB period, and which we have touched upon to some extent above. This is based around three central ideas: that Benin is somehow threatened by a great evil or chaos from within itself that menaces it at all times; that despite this God loves Benin; and that, as if to avoid the evil, there is continuing emphasis on national unity and the need to safeguard it. It is my contention that this is the CEB's response to the perceived anthropological fragility, the weakness of the social bonds which, as we have seen, are such a strong feature of this society.

The CEB identifies the historical lesions that continue to trouble Béninois society, "those that we have inherited from our ancestral tradition, those which have been transmitted to us by the civilisation into which we have entered by our own will or by force".[151] In the same document it goes on to identify what it describes as *le mal commun*:[152]

> *La débrouillardise*,[153] juggling, favouritism, nepotism, privilege, sharp tricks, jealousy which often has recourse to occult forces... In politics, the lack of transparency, regionalism, ideological intolerance, a partisan spirit, the servile imitation of foreign models in order to stay in power, and, with the same intention, recourse to more or less admissible practices.[154]

On a more popular and somewhat moralistic level, it states that "the root of our situation... resides in the fact that we do not really love our country and that we do not love one another".[155] Despite the changes of recent years, the CEB claims that this mentality, which engenders a paralysing fear, "a logic of mental inertia" is blocking all development and "is responsible for [...] endemic social immobility".[156] It notes that "while the country has not seen fire and blood in the streets, events invite us to exorcise the demon of violence division and war".[157] The demon can indeed be either the state, or the absence of the state, depending on the prevailing conditions. De Surgy, writing on the ECC, suggests that it is the "rivalry between the power of culture and the powers of chaos which have been transposed, without any problem, in afro-Christianity, under the form of the opposition between God and Satan".[158] While the bishops' analysis is certainly couched in apparently more rational language than is habitual in CCC theology, they also subscribe to a form

---

[151] CEB, *Au Service*, 113.

[152] Note that there is a certain ambiguity in this French expression, which could be translated as either *the common ill* or the *common evil*.

[153] A popular West African expression which expresses the idea of managing to get by in life with little ruses, its moral ambiguity well expressed in the popular song *Débrouiller n'est pas voler*.

[154] CEB, *Au Service*, 117. See also See Mgr R. Sastre, "Evangile et Forces Occultes: Quelle conscience chrétienne face à la conquête du pouvoir", *CB*, 539, 1989, 2; 11.

[155] CEB, "Convertissez-vous et le Bénin vivra", Lokossa, 1989 in Goudjo, *Discours*, 107.

[156] CEB, *Pour un nouvel essor*, 143.

[157] CEB, *Pour préserver*, 159.

[158] De Surgy, *L'Eglise*, 49.

of Afro-Christianity. The demonic metaphor, or indeed Lɛgbà, the Vodún of uncertainty, is never far from hand to explain the sense of impending chaos and anomie which, it seems to me, many Béninois of all denominations live with.

Significantly for this book, this same document identifies what I have tried to present as a major obstacle in the development of the state in Benin: its failure to come to terms with its history. In a very brief section referring to the instrumentalisation of ethnic tensions for political ends, which may well reflect the influence of Adoukonou, they emphasise the need to "heal [the Béninois] memory". This also reflects the thinking of Agossou, who encourages "a fraternity that rises above the tribe". The CEB notes the "dishonest use of history", pleading that ethnic groups should not "be closed in the errors and faults committed by the ancestors for centuries".[159] The CEB itself is reticent in confronting the question head on and, as is usual in these documents, it does not point the finger. However, it is clear to me and to anybody with a knowledge of the history of Dahomey-Benin, what the real issue is, and it is the unresolved question of Danxomɛ, the tensions of which are felt within the CEB itself. An illustration of this is the fact that in recent years there have been tensions over the appointment of bishops to the northern dioceses. Contestation of these appointments ran along ethnic lines and accusations of southern domination of the Catholic hierarchy and the resources of the Catholic Church, in Bayart's term, "*le partage du gâteau ecclésial*".[160]

Both the public and the more private discourse of the Catholic leaders is marked by an almost apocalyptic sense of threat and the idea that the social cohesion of the country is fragile and menaced by malevolent forces. However, this is countered by another discourse based on the popular expressions "*Dieu fera*",[161] or "*Dieu est là*". These expressions are to be found in the languages of Benin and other West African languages. Sanneh notes that they express a popular theology that affirms "that God exists as an invisible force; but he also exists as an efficacious power, the one who makes promises and keeps them, and may indeed be approached to fulfil human

---

[159] CEB, *Pour préserver*, 162.
[160] Bayart, *Les Eglises chrétiennes et la politique du ventre*.
[161] CEB, *Convertissez-vous*, 5.

needs".[162] The popular pidgin expression: "*God dey like he no dey, but he dey kang-kpë*" is an excellent illustration of this theology. It reaffirms the existence of a God that is invisible, transcendent but ultimately powerful and efficacious. In the 1989 document, *Convertissez-vous et le Bénin Vivra*, written in a time of deep crisis, the CEB asks: "How many amongst us exclaim so often that 'God is great! God loves us and loves our country! Otherwise we would have known the worst!'" In the past this kind of social tension, the CEB argues, would have led to "bloody confrontations and useless deaths". This has not been the case, however, "because the hand of God has been upon us and protects us. His spirit guides our steps so that we will not strike the stone of self-destruction and reciprocal destruction." Using this starting point, the document attempts to develop a spirit of "hope" based on "acts of piety, sacrifices, fasting... As if we are responding to the prophet Jonas, who is once again proclaiming to our hearts the message of God at Nineveh.... 'In forty days Nineveh will be destroyed...'" (Jonah 3: 4–9).[163]

During the terminal PRPB period, at the height of the political crisis, the parishes and Christian communities were asked to pray in the belief that "God is there" and that "God loves Benin" and would protect it from all evil. It can be argued that this contributed to maintaining a certain serenity and cohesion in the face of events, especially in the large parishes of the south, and particularly in Cotonou, which was the centre of much of the social tension. This has become, however, a recurring theme of CEB discourse, which continues to stress that although there has been a marked improvement in the situation since 1990, the threat is ever present and must be guarded against. In 1992 the CEB was echoing the tones of Agossou's *théologie de la fraternité*:

> You are called upon to fraternise. Consequently, be and remain defenders of all that can unite the Béninois. Do everything to extinguish the redoubtable fires of tribalism and the spirit of the clan. From north to south, from east to west, Benin is one people, one Nation, which we must save. Remember: *Every kingdom divided against itself will be ruined, and every city or household divided against itself will not stand* (Mt 12: 25). Let us seek, therefore, national unity in good times and bad. Let

---

[162] Lamin Sanneh, *West African Christianity: the Religious Impact*, London, 1984, 240.
[163] CEB, *Convertissez-vous*, 6.

us build it with all our strength. Let us remember that every attitude of suspicion or indifference to our people, whether economic, political or social, is a resignation from our Christian commitments.[164]

Since that time there have been several other pastoral letters drawing attention to the threats and reiterating the need for national unity. Clearly, the demons have not been completely exorcised and history comes back to haunt. In this, rather than in the repetition of the social doctrine, the CEB appears to be much closer to the popular discourse which we shall examine in the final chapter of this book. There is undoubtedly the influence of the theologians we have mentioned and, of course, their experience as Béninois themselves, engaged in the same struggle as the faithful with the still-to-be placated demons of history.

The Catholic Church in Benin remains as a strong presence and from this study, it should be clear that its presence is quite complex. Leon Brathier says:

> It is an influence that is difficult to tie down. One knows that it is there, one cannot bypass it…There are many evangelical communities but only one Catholic community. One could say that it is the only community that has resisted all winds. It has always known what position to take in order not to be completely out of phase with the regime. They say it is the Church of Rome but it is really a very political Church because it knows when to move and when not to move, and this is true in many areas.[165]

This has certainly been and remains the case in Benin. The Catholic Church has, as we have seen, effectively inserted itself into a state and society where it plays an important role. It has taken its place centre stage, as the historical situation required. It has been a political actor, a *podestà*, while it has also been instrumentalised, albeit knowingly and with an eye to its own position. However, once the desired change has occurred, it quickly leaves the stage, as was evidenced in the period following the CNFVN, when it quickly returned to the wings, while keeping a watchful eye on socio-political developments.[166]

[164] CEB, *Exigences*, 137–138.
[165] Interview, 13 August 2002.
[166] See "Bénin: l'évêque de Cotonou reprend son activité pastorale, chef de l'Etat pour une période de transition", *APIC*, 99, 9 April 1991, 4; and "Nous nous posons des questions sur la démission de Mgr. Isidor de Souza du Haut Conseil de la République", *CB*, 21 May 1993, 1,7.

I have little doubt that should a crisis on the scale of the 1989–1990 period occur again, the Catholic Church would be called upon to play the role it appears to have played since at least 1946. However, I would like to feel that, despite all the weaknesses of democracies in developing countries, the CNFVN has genuinely provided a new beginning for Benin. Benin's democracy is no doubt as Banégas has wistfully described it *"une démocratie à pas de caméléon"*. But it has helped to establish political markers for the state, particularly in relation to human rights, individual liberties and the control of state violence. This is aptly expressed in the following, from an *ancien combattant*:

> All ways are now open, everyone can do what he likes, but one has to know how to choose... In facing the state, we need to know how to group ourselves. Contrary to what happened under Kérékou [in his PRPB period], the state can kill one, two, or three people, but not thirty.[167]

The CNFVN was a renunciation of totalitarianism and at least the opening of a more participative democracy. Banégas is particularly positive and optimistic in his evaluation, noting that this represents a qualitative change "in the relationship between governors and governed which bears witness... to an important evolution in the foundations of *'gouvernamentalité'*".[168] At the same time, it has opened some economic possibilities for external contacts and development, although with this have come the problems of an extraverted economy, which has put the whole edifice under some strain, particularly following the devaluation of the CFA franc. Although decentralisation, which emanated from the CNFVN, has run into some obstacles, it also seems to offer possibilities for greater subsidiarity and participation in government by local actors. There is the hope that it may contribute to the stabilisation of the state and the perception of it as a polity that is habitable and secure for its citizens.[169] When the Béninois looks around him, to the east or to the west, this may not seem like such a poor option and, in any case and always one hopes, *"Dieu fera"*.

---

[167] In Bierschenk and Olivier de Sardan, *Les pouvoirs*, 235.
[168] Banégas, *La démocratie*, 480.
[169] Hubert O. Akponikpe, "Mieux comprendre la décentralisation", *La Nation*, 2 August 2002, 6.

The Catholic Church clearly stakes its claim to at least some of the credit for this development. It retains a strong presence in society, and certainly remains a formidable interlocutor for the state, which in a sense, it challenges to exist, if only to control it and to claim the space that is properly its own. This is perhaps well illustrated in recent times by a controversy surrounding the licensing of the Catholic radio station *Ave Maria*, which is in fact the only station to have almost national coverage on medium wave. Despite a liberalisation of the media, up to my last visit to Benin in 2002, the state had resisted granting the radio station a licence for four areas of the country (Ketou, Lokossa, Nattitingou and Kandi), as well as for a Catholic TV station, without providing any explanation. Interestingly, Goudjo speculates that "perhaps the sovereignty of the state is threatened because it does not have the possibility to spread national radio...and no state would want to be supplanted by a private radio".[170] Léon Brathier concurs largely with this view, noting that the Church is *"une force terrible"* in a state of limited capacity.[171] There is certainly validity in these arguments, given the importance of the media as a social space.

Not quite the same, but in a similar logic, was the controversy surrounding a ministerial decree imposed on religious groups in May 2002, limiting the hours in the night beyond which they could continue their sometimes quite noisy services.[172] This drew the following quite extraordinary response from the pastor of one of the Charismatic Churches:

> I believe this nation is coming to a time of revival. It is in for a blessing. That's why the devil wants to kill the noise and stop the revival. I believe the blessing of God is about to hit this house like never before...
>
> New Satanic decrees are designed to kill the worship of God. In Sweden you can no longer preach against homosexuality from the pulpit and in Europe they have a law against beating your children. This is against God's law. Fathers, train your children, spare the rod and spoil the child.

[170] Interview, 14 July 2002.
[171] Interview, 13 August 2002.
[172] A copy of this document circulated by the municipal authorities was shown to me by Pastor Sam Igboka, Freedom Tabernacle, Akpakpa 24 May 2002, with the comment "they only complain when it is 'religious noise'".

Are you going to obey God or Satanic decrees that contradict God's law? Otherwise you will never get what God wants for you. Shadrach, Meshach and Abed-Nego refused to bow to Nebuchadnezzer's decree. (See Daniel 3: 16–30)

Nebuchadnezzar, I cannot obey you even though you are the president. You are mighty, you are powerful. I fear you but I fear God more. You are a king and a lord, but I fear the king of kings and the lord of lords more. You are powerful, but the one I serve is most powerful. You are a mortal man, I will fear the One Eternal. Rather, fear what will happen your soul in eternity than what will happen to you now. I will not compromise my principle, my ethic; God will take you all the way!

You are in control down here but God is in control up there. If my God is in control, then everything you are threatening me with and doing to me, God has allowed it. My redeemer is able to deliver me from the problem. God can only fight for you when you stand firm in what you believe. If you compromise there will be more problems for yourself. You are delaying your own blessing.[173]

This is certainly a contestation of space within the state and one that in the end demands a response from the state if it is to control space within its own borders. It is, in fact, part of a process of secularisation, which, somewhat paradoxically, the Churches could be said to be drawing on themselves as they force the state to assert its authority, including its authority over the Churches. In this society, the state will certainly not seek an overt confrontation with religious bodies that may well serve other purposes, as we have seen, and certainly have an inherent strength. As we have seen in Kérékou's case in Chapter 3, he is more likely to play the Reformation prince, setting the religious groups off against one another, while reaffirming his own Christian legitimacy, perhaps with a view to tempering to some extent the strength of the Catholic Church. The state is, in any case, obliged to move to claim what authority it can in order to affirm its own existence and its relevance to the lives of its people.

The Catholic Church moves in much more subtle ways. Even amongst the other religious groups, it remains the 'big player', the body to which they turn in times of crisis.[174] In a way that is certainly

[173] Pastor Michael Adeyemi Adefarasin, CAFM Service, 26 June 2002.
[174] An administrator at SIM speaks of this Evangelical group benefitting from the interventions of Mgr De Souza on the question of visas for missionaries and other administrative questions during the tense PRPB period. Interview, Parakou, 18 July 2001.

consistent with Béninois logic, it is seen as having a certain *droit d'aînesse* in historical terms, as well as useful external references and institutional strength in times of trial.[175] I think one can conclude that because of the coherent, if conservative, nature of its discourse, both hierarchical and popular, its institutional substance, as well as the kind of nationalist discourse it has developed, which confers a religious legitimacy on the Benin, it will remain an important interlocutor for the state and continue to play a role in society.

---

[175] A senior member of the CCC refers to the Catholic Church as "*notre mère*" (interview, 20 July 2002). Pastor Michel Alakpo refers to its "structural strength" (interview, 28 June 2001).

CHAPTER SEVEN

MY ROCK, MY SHIELD, MY STRONGHOLD AND
MY REFUGE

> My God is my rock, in whom I take refuge, my shield and the horn of
> my salvation. He is my stronghold, my refuge and my saviour—from
> violent men you save me. (2 Samuel 22: 2–4)

The form of Christianity we looked at in the previous chapter is
essentially a religion of the elite: much of it is imported, reformu-
lated and to some extent adapted, to be enunciated by a hierarchical
Church, often in somewhat abstract terms, and addressed primarily
to the class in Benin society that, historically, it has sought to create,
educate and influence. It is backed up by the institutional substance
and considerable capacity of the Catholic Church, which, with all the
external connections that contribute to its considerable socio-political
weight, has established itself as a significant local actor. It is discreet,
conservative and always has an eye on its own survival *sur le terrain*. In real terms, this means that it usually intervenes only when
it sees its own interests being threatened or when what it regards as
essential moral precepts are being neglected in the formulation of
legislation. Its influence reached something of an apotheosis in the
period 1989–1993 when its participation in the CNFVN brought it
into a more active role. Since then, however, its has retired again to
purely pastoral and development activities with the occasional homily addressed to the political elite or to the country at large, which
serves as a reminder that it is still there.

As has been the case elsewhere in Africa, however, there has also
been a movement '*par le bas*', the development of popular, indigenous
forms of Christianity, as well as the importation of other forms, most
notably charismatic, which have had remarkable success over the past
two decades. These have sought to adapt the Christian myth, most
strikingly in the CCC, but also in more recent developments across
the denominations, with the development of theologies and ministries
that can be seen as an attempt to respond to the more immediate needs
of this fragile society.

The emergence of a Christianisme béninois

Benin appears to be moulding a Christianity of its own across the different denominations. While the missionaries may have felt the constraints of Cartesian rationalism in their approach to their ministry, eschewing visions, healing and miracles '*outre ceux de la science*', Béninois Christians feel no such constraints in the development of homiletics, rites and rituals, far beyond the limits of what is foreseen by a more orthodox version of *inculturation*.[1] These are used to confront a world that continues to be perceived as fundamentally fragile, unstable and threatening. This is a world where Lɛgbà is never far away, as this brief prayer by a member of the *Eglise Africaine Apostolique* illustrates:

> May those who have had their eyes burst by Lɛgbà recover their sight in the name of Jesus. May they find the road to his kingdom.
> May all the forces of Vodún be exterminated in Benin.[2]

As well as this adaptation of the Christian myth, there is the development of new forms of Church organisation. These tend to be less hierarchical, more participatory and more community-based, though they are clearly still dominated by the *big men* of God. These attract large numbers of adherents as they seek to offer new spaces and new communities or quasi-communities in a society, which, as we have seen, has great difficulty in attaining the social cohesion necessary for state construction. In terms of political science, this may be the Church as 'exit option' but, in the terms of the adherents, it is the Church in more biblical terms as *rock, shield, stronghold* and *refuge*. It is from within these spaces of relative security, these quasi-communities, that *le petit béninois chrétien*—the urban trader, artisan, apprentice, housewife and their aspiring but often frustrated children—look at state and society and struggle to find a utopian vision discourse that

---

[1] Inculturation is a recurring theme in Catholic theological discourse, particularly in Africa, though many theologians now prefer the term *interculturation*. Defined as "the process by which catechesis *takes flesh* in the various cultures". *Ecclesia in Africa* notes that: "Inculturation includes two dimensions: on the one hand, the intimate transformation of authentic cultural values through their integration in Christianity and, on the other, the insertion of Christianity in the various human cultures" (*Ecclesia in Africa*, 59).

[2] In de Surgy, *Syncrétisme*, 54.

will lead to change and reconstruction, in Kä Mana's terms or, in more charismatic terms, the breakthrough to a new destiny.

My original intention in approaching this book was to examine the Churches across a denominational spectrum in the belief that while the Catholic Church and the other mainline Churches functioned at one level in relation to state and society—that of the elite—the others were performing perhaps a different function at a more popular level. While this approach had certain validity in looking at elites, where, as we have seen in the previous chapter, the Catholic Church is an important actor, it soon broke down as I moved into the sphere of popular religiosity. In my encounters with Christians of all denominations, including Catholics, I discovered many common features, fundamental preoccupations and forms of religious expression across the spectrum that blur the well-defined colours of the denominational prism. It is part of what Karla Poewe describes as "a global popular religiosity which is transcultural, eclectic and fluid".[3] Transcultural but also trans-denominational, since amongst the Churches themselves I discovered a lot of borrowing and improvisation, as they look both to each other and to traditional religions in an attempt to come up with new forms more suited to meeting the realities of living in Benin today and of a rapidly—expanding religious market.

The Catholic Charismatic Renewal Movement (CCRM), a significant strand in popular Catholicism, for example, has developed a discourse that has much in common with other forms of popular Christianity.[4] This is to be seen in its exuberance, but also its strong emphasis on healing, deliverance, exorcism, and even hints of seed and prosperity theologies.[5] It is also seen in its organisation, which strongly emphasises participation and lay leadership, while at the same time attaching much

---

[3] See Karla Poewe, "On the Metonymic Structure of Religious Experiences: The Example of Charismatic Christianity", *Cultural Dynamics*, 1989, vol. II, no. 4, 361–380.

[4] There may be as many as 20,000 CCRM members (de Surgy, *Le choix* 43).

[5] Jean Pliya (1927–), writer, former Rector of National University, government minister and civil servant, founder and Berger National of the CCRM in Benin. *Donner comme un enfant de roi* (Paris: F.X. de Guibert, 1993) is certainly a version of *seed theology*. Pliya is the author of several short works on health problems and is the proprietor of a large pharmacy, specialising in homeopathic medicines, which has its premises in a multi-storeyed building belonging to the Catholic Archdiocese of Cotonou. The large parish of St Michel in central Cotonou organises weekly masses specifically addressed to businessmen which appears to be an attempt to respond to Businessmen's Fellowships.

importance to charismatic leaders. This is the case, for example, of the somewhat enigmatic Jean Pliya, *le Berger National*. His personal peregrinations over the years, through politics and civil administration, from the esoteric to charismatic religion, with a specialisation in homeopathic medicine, are probably no more than a fair reflection of the search of many in his flock. Although there are significant differences between the CCRM and charismatic movements of Protestant origin, one can speak of a strong and influential charismatic current, leading some observers to speak of a Pentecostalisation of popular Béninois Catholicism

At the same time, the CCRM and other movements, while apparently rejecting indigenous religious expression, look to it in improvising their language. A good example of this is to be found in the monthly processions of the Blessed Sacrament organised by the CCRM. Bringing together three very rich strands—Catholic para-liturgical ritual, Pentecostal fervour, with a clear reference to the traditional processions associated with the Vodún—they produce something quite different. This was undoubtedly the most striking expression of popular religiosity I observed during my fieldwork. In St Michel Parish, the biggest in Cotonou, for instance, the tabernacle, unusual for a Catholic church, is placed several steps above the main altar, giving the distinct impression of a small hill, requiring the vested priest to ascend in order to bring the Blessed Sacrament back in procession. The resonances here were both scriptural[6] and to an indigenous religious tradition.[7] A member of the CCRM notes that when there is a procession there are many cases of healing:

> There are healings …immediately…And people recover a sense of peace in their hearts. Because the fact of seeing with their own eyes the symbol of the body and blood of Christ gives perhaps the conviction that Jesus is there, that it is really him and that he can heal them [...] We would say people are seeking healing and there are very few who understand that Jesus is not only someone who distributes healing.[8]

---

[6] "So Abraham called that place The Lord Will Provide. And to this day it is said, 'On the mountain of the Lord it will be provided.'" (Genesis 22: 14).

[7] The CCC also attaches great importance to natural sites (see de Surgy, *Le Christianisme Céleste*, 136). Sites such as the seashore, rivers and hills are important and can be incorporated, as has always been the case in Christianity (see Jean-Claude Barbier, *Les collines enchantées de Tchetti (Centre Bénin)*, unpublished ms, CBRST, 1999).

[8] Interview, 9 September 2002.

De Surgy notes that "the adoration of the Blessed Sacrament, taken out and then brought back to the tabernacle, and in the meantime often carried in procession, presents a direct similitude to a fetish cult".[9] The Gɛlɛdɛ́ and Zàngbèto cults certainly spring to mind when one follows this procession, which was received by the faithful with enormous enthusiasm. This was expressed by joyful singing in local languages, dancing and ululating, as the women lay their clothes on the ground before the coped priest as he processed, monstrance held high, to the four cardinal points of the church and back to the altar for the Benediction. It appeared to me that this ritual had brought together several elements from different traditions in a particularly successful expression of popular religiosity. It is then, as de Surgy concludes, "not surprising that these processions are particularly appreciated in charismatic groups" and they certainly seem to fit in with a pattern of reciprocal assimilation between elements of Catholicism and of Vodún, wherever both are found together.[10]

The CCC is not, of course, unaware of both the Vodún and the Catholic traditions. It borrows from both, as witnessed in its basic cosmogony, particularly the role of the angels,[11] the choice and layout of its sacred spaces, its use of offerings of fruits and other food, and the liturgical use of vestments, incense, candles, water, oil, the crucifix and other cultic objects in its liturgies.[12] At the same time, there is evidence of increased use of some of these elements in the newer African Charismatic Churches. De Surgy observes that these "manage to reconcile in an original way the apparently incompatible characteristics of prophetic Churches, Protestant or Evangelical Churches (mostly Pentecostal), and the Catholic and Orthodox Churches".[13]

One Methodist theologian, who had, somewhat reluctantly, become

---

[9] Albert de Surgy, *La Recherche de miracles dans les Eglises chrétiennes, en République du Bénin*, unpublished ms, CBRST, ndg, 10.

[10] See, for instance, Donald J. Cosentino (ed.), *Sacred Arts of Haitian Vodou*, Los Angeles: UCLA Fowler Museum of Cultural History, 1995. There are also striking illustrations of this from Brazil at the Museum at Ouidah.

[11] See de Surgy, *L'Eglise*, 55.

[12] While CCC members can find biblical references justifying these elements, the use of the crucifix in the CCC, as well as other elements, has been interpreted as a rejection of the Methodism of Porto-Novo whose symbolic vocabulary may have had less appeal than that of pre-Vatican Council Catholicism. The scented oil of St Michael, for instance, is on sale outside all the large Catholic parishes and is also increasingly used in charismatic churches.

[13] De Surgy, *Syncrétisme chrétien*, 10.

involved in a deliverance ministry, says that the people perceive the pastor as a Bokonù. They come to him as to a Bokonù, he says, with "serious problems" hoping to "find satisfaction". He admits rather prosaically but honestly that it is this perception that has obliged him to "do these gymnastics" and develop a ministry for which he admits he does not feel any great calling or charism. However, it responds to a pastoral need, while at the same time fending off competition from Churches which present themselves as having a particular ministry in this area. [14]

All of this serves to illustrate the amount of borrowing, improvisation and reinvention that is a feature of Benin Christianity, and the examples could be multiplied. I feel that it is justified to speak of a *Christianisme béninois* which lies as a sub-stratum across the denominations, constructed to meet local needs, and which is, in my view, a reflection of the society that has produced it. It is this popular, trans-denominational *Christianisme béninois* that I shall examine in this final chapter.

Christ Roi, Christ Victoire

One of the features of early Evangelical and Pentecostal Christianity was its reticence with regard to the things of "the world", as well as a strong emphasis on the Pauline imperative of obedience to the existing authorities. Romans 13: 1–7 is cited as underpinning this notion of authority:[15] "Everyone is to obey the governing authority, because there is no authority except from God and whatsoever authorities exist have been appointed by God". This has undoubtedly contributed to the perception of this kind of Christianity as being submissive and often even in collusion with the most dubious regimes which it appears to believe should remain in place until God decides otherwise. In the earlier part of this study, I noted the apparent proximity of evangelical leaders to the power elites in Benin and Kérékou's apparent identification with this brand of Christianity since his conversion.

Speaking of the early American fundamentalists, Bruce comments:

---

[14] Interview, 11 July 2001.
[15] The text was used by P.W. Botha to describe what he saw as the interaction between religion and politics (Ranger, *Religious Movements*, 20).

> If life was due to become ever less pleasant until the righteous were
> lifted out of the world at what was called 'the rapture', there was little
> point in engaging constructively with the world: better to remain pure and
> clean by remaining aloof. The operating principle was separatism.[16]

To a certain extent, this attitude still prevails and evangelical Christians
protest a certain kind of apoliticism with God as the final arbiter. De
Surgy refers to "the disgust of Pentecostals for the political".[17] An
elder of CAFM states it is important for the Church to participate in
decisions concerning the direction of the nation. However, he warns
that any kind of direct political involvement runs the risk of leading
it to "compromise",[18] as well as distracting the Church from its main
objective, the salvation of souls.

   This, however, is full of ambiguity. Poewe notes that Charismatic
Christianity "is particularly lively... in those areas that are under pressure to change, are questioning their major traditions, are experiencing
cultural and linguistic ambivalence, and/or are subject to considerable
human transience".[19] This, of course, could be a description of large
parts of sub-Saharan Africa, and is certainly the case for Benin. In the
Pentecostal mind, there can be no neat republican separation between
Church and state, the religious and the political, since, as I was often
assured, God is Lord and Master of all "*et si le président est toujours
là, c'est que Dieu le veut ainsi*". Contemporary Evangelicals in the
United States, for instance, have a strong domestic moral agenda and
have little doubt about whose side God is on in international affairs
and the creation of a 'new world order'. André Corten, writing about
Brazil, notes the apparent "indifference" of Pentecostals to politics.
However, the same author points out that this does not necessarily
mean that they are irrelevant to the political process, since their very
indifference means that political actors find them very difficult to either
control or understand.[20] In societies where totalitarianism is a strong
feature of politics this clearly poses problems. Churches can become
'spaces of insubmission' or 'exit options',[21] which elude the control
of the political elite, and within which people find refuge from the

---

[16] Steve Bruce, *Fundamentalism*, Cambridge: Polity Press, 2000, 67.
[17] De Surgy, *Le choix*, 50.
[18] Interview, 13 June 2002.
[19] Poewe, *Metonymic Structure*, 366.
[20] André Corten, "Transnational Religious Needs in Latin America", in Corten
and R. Marshall-Fratani, *From Babel*, 119.
[21] See Banégas, *La Démocratie* (thèse), 173.

totalitarian or dysfunctional state, as happened to some extent in Benin in the terminal PRPB period. Corten notes that:

> The new religious needs that characterise the remarkable expansion of Pentecostalism are constructed. However, they do not directly depend on the heterogeneous elements in circulation. They are needs which respond to extremely diverse situations and yet are endowed with a certain characteristic coherence. To borrow a Durkheimian problematic, they are the product of a collective consciousness. Within Pentecostalism, three new religious needs can be identified: a strong externalised emotion; a pursuit of the sacred through the representation of frightening powers; and fantasies of dramatic transformation.[22]

For anybody who has studied these Churches it is clear that the emotional remains an essential feature. Corten suggests that "Pentecostalism is emotional insurrection; it is a reaction of society upon itself" and this is the thinking that underlies my interpretation of large sections of what I have described as *le Christianisme béninois*. The second trait, that of the representation of the devil and other evil forces, is equally important, since "while the elite identify the sacred with purity and beauty, contact with the sacred within popular circles is less sanitised. Hence conversion is associated with deliverance—liberation—from evil forces". Marshall suggests that this kind of discourse is in fact a critique of corrupt state powers which, in a veiled way, are dismissed as being amongst the "powers and principalities" of Satan himself, from which one must be delivered.[23] This, of course will be part of the third trait, the "fantasies of dramatic transformation" that will be the salvation of the individual and of society. Komolafe more recently suggested that from the 1980s neo-charismatics in Nigeria "set to work by attempting to refigure the moral order. They spoke a 'new political language' that empowered the people to develop strategies for overcoming the oppression they felt from bad government".[24]

It can thus be argued that the Pentecostal Churches are in themselves a commentary on the failure of the state and politics in the developing

---

[22] Corten, *Transnational Religious Need*, 110–111, 119.

[23] Marshall, *Power*, 213–241. This is not a uniquely Christian phenomenon. The Muslim elect in Senegal did not hesitate to demonise the state for its own ends. See "Supping with the Devil: the Mouride Brotherhood and the Senegalese State, 1967–88", in Donal Cruise O'Brien, *Symbolic Confrontations: Muslims Imagining the State in Africa*, London: C. Hurst, 2003, 32–48.

[24] Komolafe, *Changing Face*, 223.

world. Writing of the Caribbean, Hurbon notes that the "social boy-cott" expressed by Pentecostalism "applies pressure to the 'political syntax' and appears as 'a force for transformation'".[25] Commenting on the terminal apartheid period in South Africa, the Marxist histo-rian, Charles van Onselen, noted that "the emergence of charismatic Christianity had everything to do with that society being involved in a low intensity civil war". He argues that "the one thing that stands between this society and utter barbarism [is] the working and middle class African Christian woman who is involved in some form of char-ismatic Christianity".[26] The CCRM during the PRPB period in Benin could be said to have been something of a proto-protest movement. A favourite slogan during their meetings, "*Christ Roi, Christ Victoire*", has been explained to me as a protest from within a space of "insubmis-sion" and a warning to a totalitarian state that all was not in order and that a day of reckoning would eventually come. The message here was couched in more or less biblical terms but it was quite clear and can be compared with that of the CAFM pastor referred to in the previous chapter, addressing the state:

> You are a king and a lord, but I fear the king of kings and the lord of lords more. You are powerful, but the one I serve is most powerful. You are a mortal man; I will fear the One Eternal. Rather, fear what will happen to your soul in eternity than what will happen to you now. I will not compromise my principle, my ethic; God will take you all the way![27]

So, whatever the protestations of apoliticism, Charismatic Christian-ity cannot be said to be without an import for questions of political and social change. It has become a protean movement, subject to local pressures. As a result the socio-political aspect will be variable, but it is nonetheless real, if only because it provides a corner into which one can go and sulk—surely the ultimate 'social boycott', and a sensible option in the face of regimes that crave unreserved public approval.

This leads us to look at several areas where I have found common elements across the denominations and which I feel illustrate my basic

---

[25] Laënnec Hurbon, "Pentecostalism and Transnationalism in the Caribbean" in Corten and Marshall-Fratani, *From Babel*, 136.

[26] Poewe, *Metonymic Structure*, 366.

[27] Pastor Michael Adeyemi Adefarasin, CAFM Service, 26 June 2002.

thesis that the success of this form of Christianity is largely due to the fragile nature of the society within which it seeks to take root. It is both a commentary upon the society within which it finds itself and the expression of a desire for change and transformation—a new Sé, a new destiny. I shall therefore examine the perception of Benin society in the Churches, their understanding of the Church as a sacred and secure space within this fragile society, allowing for the creation of new communities or quasi-communities, the development of adapted theologies, rites and rituals that seek to respond to the needs of their adherents.

The perception of Dahomey-Benin society in the Churches

Although the leadership of all the Churches has changed in the years since independence and is now almost entirely African, if not always Béninois, the perception of Danxomε-Benin at this level often bears a striking resemblance to that of the early travellers and missionaries. The negative stereotype remains largely intact and can be illustrated by countless anecdotal examples from my fieldwork, as well as from interviews with pastors I encountered who make it a regular theme of their prayers "for the nation". This is also the representation of Benin one finds in much evangelical mission literature and on the Internet. This brief passage, a "prayer alert", from the website of the American evangelical International Fellowship of Intercessors is not untypical:

> Benin is the original source of the dark voodoo religion. This blood-soaked land has a history replete with slavery and human sacrifice, and it is difficult to think of any single nation that has had so strong a negative spiritual impact. A long time exporter of spirit worship, idolatrous fetishism and voodoo, Benin is a country languishing in primitive and fearful spiritual bondage; lives held captive to the elemental spirits of the air are everywhere in evidence in this poverty-stricken nation.[28]

This "nation", like Israel in the Old Testament, is to be led away from its dark past in order that it might be saved and led to the new destiny God promises for the elect. Let us look at just a few contemporary examples from across the religious spectrum.

---

[28] *http://www.ifa-usapray.org/IFI_Benin.htm*, 11 October 2003.

During the 'message' at an Assemblies of God Sunday service, the pastor takes the example of Israel who has abandoned God "to adore the Vodún", adding that this "merited the anger of God". In modern Benin, he says, these realities persist and he prays for the disappearance of "the fetish and python convents".[29] A CAFM member says that "in the coastal region in general [the former kingdom], we are in a country where most Christians have had attachments to the Vodún, where they have done many things and even contracted alliances with the devil which are preventing them from evolving". Therefore "God reveals to the pastors" that they must preach deliverance "in order to lead the country out of this situation".[30] As in the CCC, which we shall look at presently, the discourse of these Churches is marked by a very distinctive reading of scripture. The preferred texts depict apocalyptic war scenes, battles they would claim continue today between the same forces of good in "the zones of war".[31] In a typical sermon based on 2 Corinthians 10: 3–4,[32] charismatic bishop James Saah, possibly inspired by the day, 4 July, drew direct parallels between Pharaoh (Exodus 5–13), the Taliban and the daily battle of Béninois Christians with the devil. He encouraged his listeners to remain armed for battle with the Evil One and insisted on rupture with "all that does not emanate from God or has not been reabsorbed into Him".[33]

This theme of diabolical alliances, as well as that of the Manichaean combat between good and evil in Dahomey-Benin, is a recurring one across all the Churches. This is really the representation of a fragile society, socially, politically and economically static,[34] balanced between "culture" and "chaos", as de Surgy notes,[35] with the inevitable anomie this creates especially in the poorer sections of the population. It is my conclusion that it is symptomatic of the weakness of meaningful social bonds; it is a direct result of anthropological fragility and the incohesion of the social tissue.

---

[29] Assemblies of God, Jericho, Cotonou, 28 April 2002.
[30] Interview, 3 June 2002.
[31] James Saah, *The Zones of War*, CAFM, Cotonou, 4 July 2002.
[32] "For though we live in the world, we do not wage war as the world does. The weapons we fight with are not the weapons of the world. On the contrary, they have divine power to demolish strongholds."
[33] See de Surgy, *Le phénomène pentecôtiste*, 119–120.
[34] Mayrargue *Les élites*, 33–56.
[35] De Surgy, *L'Eglise*, 49.
[35] Ibid., 47.

Mainstream Catholicism has developed a desire for "a serene and prudent dialogue"[36] with traditional African religions. However, it is not difficult to see in the 'serenity' and the 'prudence' a certain reticence, and elements in the CCRM have become increasingly radical in their condemnation of the traditional religion. Christians in this movement, as in other charismatic groups, feel the tension between parts of a suffocating tradition and a desire for modernity. This is partly, no doubt, in response to the more uncompromising discourse of the Charismatic Churches. It is also due, however, to a shared ambivalence about the tradition and a tendency to portray it as inherently evil. Thus, we find a senior member of the CCRM arguing vehemently that "the demon is a reality in this country where we know the Vodún". As we saw in the previous chapter, even the Catholic bishops refer repeatedly and somewhat ambiguously to the threat they feel hangs over the country. People, this CCRM member argues, are involved "in practices that are clearly against the will of God" and, in terms one finds in most AICs and Charismatic Churches, he claims they are bound "in pacts with the divinities". Others are simply victims of the "malice of evil people" who seek "to destroy their lives", but this too is symptomatic of the society they live in, where life is perceived as always under threat.[37]

In an interesting analysis, the 1999 Synod of the Catholic Archdiocese of Parakou identified *fear* as one of the main factors responsible for social stagnation in the villages of the diocese, describing it as "a logic of mental inertia" blocking all development. It continues:

> There is fear of drawing upon oneself those who are jealous and who in the end could physically eliminate anyone showing some enterprise; this encourages the acceptance of the status quo and leads to stagnation: everybody is afraid of everybody else and nothing moves. This fear is responsible for our endemic social immobility.[38]

This is a quite perceptive social analysis drawn up by Catholics of the Archdiocese and the same document contains several rational recommendations for confronting the problem. However, rationality

---

[36] *Ecclesia in Africa*, 67; see also sections 7 and 47. The phrase itself makes it clear that there remains a deep ambivalence in the Church's attitude to African religions.

[37] Interview, 10 May 2002.

[38] *A l'Ecoute de l'Esprit*, Synode Diocésain, Document de travail, Parakou, 1999, 25–26.

is not always the course taken. In the past ten years there has been a dramatic development of the rite of exorcism in the Catholic Church, particularly in the south, based on the same perception of Béninois society as being intimately tied up with the Vodún, atrophied by fear and in thrall to evil. One of the four official exorcists for the Archdiocese of Cotonou insisted that "the devil has his See in Benin", explaining that "the ancestors were already involved in these affairs". He identifies the period of Nicephore Soglo's presidency (1991–1996) as the time when there was a recrudescence of the Vodún.[39] He also cites the case of Haiti as that of a country that has ceded completely to what he sees as the evils of the Vodún, a totalitarianism of the occult, and that has been destroyed by it.[40]

Such an attitude is decried by many intellectuals, particularly European scholars[41] but it is none the less real on the ground. Across the Christian spectrum on the popular level, there is great ambivalence and even confusion in relation to the history and traditions of Danxomε. For those involved, this is not a politically-correct, ivory-tower debate among sociologists of religion but the articulation of real tensions within the society. While there is a genuine attempt, at least amongst intellectuals, to understand the Vodún, attitudes at the grassroots level remain marked by ambivalence and, often, fear.

In Poewe's view, "charismatic Christianity is a religion of the imagination". Deconstruction, she claims, is its main attraction since "it offers a reconstructive [or potentially reconstructive] breakthrough… It is a religion of change". In seeking change, however, it eschews rational philosophy, theology and politics in favour of "sensation, emotion, intuition, intellect and, most importantly imagination".[42] I found a striking illustration of this point in the CCC, a Church that eschews theology and rational articulation and functions almost entirely on the level of visions, dreams and powerful imagination. Here the battle with tradition and the Vodún has been imagined quite dramatically as a confrontation between the celestial armies under their commander Michael the

---

[39] Interview, 17 June 2002.

[40] This kind of opposition of both the Catholic Church and evangelical churches to the Vodún is also a feature of Haiti. See Hurbon, *Sociologie*, 204–206.

[41] De Surgy attacks, somewhat immoderately, churches who criticise the Vodún comparing them to the crusades and those who sought to "impose Christianity by terror and the sword", refuting any criticism of the traditional religion. See de Surgy, *Le phénomène pentecôtiste*, 439–440.

[42] Poewe, *Metonymic Structure*, 365.

Archangel, the Protector of the Church, the Angel of Victory,[43] and Satan, commander of the underworld. It is often expressed in hybrid sci-fi imagery, reminiscent of both *Star Wars* and *The Lord of the Rings*. As de Surgy notes, in the CCC "the combat against the devil who *'prowls around like a roaring lion looking for someone to devour'* (1 Peter, 5: 8) is incessant". To be a Christian means "taking sides in the camp of God in order to be associated with the celestial armies against Satan".[44] Military metaphors abound since life is a struggle where "everything is explained in terms of a combat between the angels and the forces of evil...[and] everything is played out in an apocalyptic scenario".[45] It is modernised by mixed metaphors from *Star Wars*, which have both God and his "Commander-in-Chief" Michael attacking their enemies with "celestial missiles and lasers" and "striking at the heart of their defences".[46] De Surgy quotes a typically apocalyptic prayer:

> Come and do your work so that we can see your strength...
> Annihilate our enemies... Come to subdue whoever seeks to do evil to your child.
> We ask you to bring down your army in our midst to combat all those around us, all spirits visible and invisible.[47]

In the kind of adaptation and assimilation that is so common in Béninois Christianity, there are also parallels with Haiti. We find that the cult of Michael the Archangel has also become very developed amongst Catholics, not only in the parish bearing his name but also in novenas dedicated to the saint[48] beseeching "protection" and "liberation". The following prayer by Pope Leo XIII, is a good example:

> Saint Michael, Archangel, defend us in the battle, be our help against the malice of the demon. We humbly ask that God may exercise upon him his empire, And you, prince of the celestial militia, push back to hell, thorough your divine virtue, Satan and the other evil spirits who roam throughout the world seeking the loss of souls.[49]

---

[43] Michel Guéry, *Christianisme Céleste: Notes de travail*, unpublished ms, SMA, Cotonou, 1973, 40.

[44] De Surgy, *L'Eglise*, 47–48.

[45] Guéry, *Christianisme Céleste*, 135.

[46] Interview, 9 August 2001.

[47] De Surgy, *L'Eglise*, 50.

[48] A ritual novena of prayer and devout action takes nine days. The rituals described in the pamphlets include not just prayers but also ritual objects such as the oil of Michael the Archangel, incense and candles, as well as recommended gestures during both the sleeping and the waking hours.

[49] 'Supplique à Saint Michel' in *Neuvaine et prières à St Michel et aux neufs*

While it is almost unthinkable that one would still hear this prayer
in most other parts of Catholicism, it clearly has meaning here. The
similarities with de Surgy's CCC text are not difficult to see and
they occur repeatedly both in prayers and in conversations with the
members, whose whole world appears to be imagined in terms of
combat.

In a similar Catholic cult to *Notre Dame des Victoires*[50] we find the
following prayer:

> Holy Mother of God, we have recourse to your protection:
> Do not disdain the prayers we offer in the midst of the afflictions that
>   weigh down upon us:
> Ah glorious and ever blessed Virgin; deem us worthy of delivery from
>   all the dangers that threaten us…

Concluding with the Latin doxology:

> Sub tuum praesidium confugimus, sancta Dei Genitrix;
> Nostras deprecationes ne despicias in necessitatibus, sed a periculis
>   cunctis libera nos semper, virgo gloriosa et benedicta.[51]

In a society which sees itself as the scene of an ongoing battle the
logic is the same whether appealing to St Michael or to Our Lady
of Victories: the search for protection from mortal peril and victory
in the combat between light and darkness.

Deeper fissures: "the enemy within"

What is perhaps surprising is the apparent depth of the social fissures
in a society where much is made of the idea of family solidarity. As
I showed in Chapter 3, these fissures reach into the most intimate
social spaces, most notably the family. This theme reoccurs frequently
in the Churches and it is something to which they seek to respond,

---

chœurs des Anges, 19, pamphlet, no publication details given, purchased outside
Paroisse Sacré Cœur, Cotonou. Many of these pamphlets, sold along with other
religious objects such as oil also dedicated to St Michael, by market women are
of very obscure provenance and are tolerated rather than promoted by the Catholic
Church.

[50] The Virgin Mary is noticeably absent from all CCC texts and I have never
heard her mentioned in the course of any service.

[51] 'Prière Mariale', in *Neuvaine à Notre Dame des Victoires*, Paris: Stand de la
Presse de la Basilique, 23.

or, in some cases perhaps, a fear upon which they build. A couple in CAFM note the need to build "barriers" or at least put down "markers" between their Christian nuclear family and the extended African family,[52] which is perceived as threatening their existence. The family, under strain since the beginning of the colonial period,[53] has thus become the locus of much tension and the focal point of much attention in many of the charismatic movements and ministries alongside the mainline Churches. This is witnessed for instance in the number of seminars dedicated to this subject across the Churches.[54] A CAFM seminar led by Rev. Dr Abraham Chigbundu of Voice of Freedom Ministries, Benin City, Nigeria, on the theme *Destined for Glory,* is a striking example. The opening message is worth a more detailed analysis, as it appears to me to touch upon many of the elements, albeit in a somewhat caricatural fashion, that I found in Béninois Christianity.

The message was based on the scripture text Mark 11: 1–11, the entry of Jesus into Jerusalem. In a style typical of the genre, it consisted of a remarkable and highly theatrical interpretation of the text. This is apparently a standard sermon, and it was followed with enthusiasm by an audience awaiting the inevitable dénouement.[55] The focus of the sermon is on the first seven verses, the dialogue between the disciples and the owners of the tethered colt, and the emphasis is entirely on the situation of the tethered colt. Jesus needs the colt for his triumphal entry to the Holy City, the animal is thus called to share his glorious *destiny*, but he is *tied*: "You are *Destined for Glory*…BUT…BUT…BUT… You are tied…You are tied… You are tied. You are destined for glory but you are tied".

---

[52] Interviews, Cotonou, 13 June 2002.

[53] Aupiais, for example, was very aware of the pressures on social structures and looked in some detail at the question of polygamy, seeing its value as a social institution. See Francis Aupiais, Les noirs de l'Afrique et l'Evangile, *La Documentation Catholique*, 432, 16 June 1929, 1477.

[54] The Catholic Church runs an important Institut de la Famille dedicated to the promotion of the Catholic social teaching on family matters (interview, *Institut Pontifical Jean Paul II* pour l'Afrique Francophone, Cotonou, 16 August 2002). CAFM runs regular seminars on the family dealing with family issues and specially conflict within families. See Joseph and Caroline Quinan, *Les Epreuves et les Conflits dans le Foyer*, CAFM, Cotonou, 7 June 2002.

[55] My colleague Jane E. Clifford reports a similar interpretation from a church in Ghana.

In a note on charismatic homiletics, Poewe speaks of the importance of the traditional Pentecostal concept of "the smiting word". This is "a specific word for an individual" which contains "a simple, single, and usually conflict resolving message". Being smitten, she asserts, leaves the person with the impression that "the whole sermon was specifically addressed to him or her" and that this is a word or sign upon which his/her world may be deconstructed and immediately reconstructed in a more positive way.[56] Gifford interprets it somewhat differently, noting that what is happening in the Charismatic interpretation of scripture is an attempt to cope with the prevailing social conditions.[57] There is certainly something of both of these techniques to be found here. Rev. Chigbundu emphasises the fact that he is addressing one person in the congregation tonight, one person who is *destined for glory* but who is also *tied*. He projects himself into the person's mind with the smiting title for the sermon *Destined for Glory*:

> I feel the presence of God here tonight. He knows about me, he knows where I have been tied. [*Assent from the congregation.*] He has sent his servant to loose me; my time of glory has come.

Then he reasserts his own place in the scene that is to unfold:

> I just pray that you will catch this revelation tonight.

His own role is one of a prophet among the "men of God" who make up West African Pentecostalism. He clearly comes as a spiritual "big man", possessing spiritual *acε* which he is willing to share or give access to—but at a price.[58] He is here to lead the congregation, or a chosen member, to his/her Sε, the promised *destiny*, which is *glory*. It is not difficult to see the parallels to the role of the Bokonù.

Rev. Chigbundu is also strong in his support of the local "man of God" as the conduit through which all kinds of blessings will pass.[59] He suggests quite overtly that this is a question of "being connected".

---

[56] Poewe, *Metonymic Structure*, 370.

[57] See Gifford, *Ghana's New Christianity*, 71–82 for an examination of the use of the Bible in Charismatic Christianity.

[58] He raised donations of 10,000 cfa (about €15) from 100 members of the congregation that night.

[59] There was evidence during my research at CAFM during the summer of 2002 that there was a lot of tension within the church which was putting the pastor under pressure.

The Church, he suggests, is part of a kind of ecclesiastical rhizome, stretching to Nigeria and beyond, ultimately to the USA, where the pastors are certainly proud to proclaim their own connections.

> It is through our connection that I am connected to you [...] What I mean is that I am here because of my connection with him. Am I communicating? [*Yes, we hear you.*] If you had written to me to ask me to come I would not have come but because I know this "man of God" I have come. [*Applause for the local pastor.*] The more you value your pastor, the more he will connect you and bring blessings to you, like today.

Having established these parameters, he moves to the chosen text, explaining how and why both the colt and members of the congregation are tied:

> The Master told them to go and bring the horse. The horse is tied [...] They say "the master has told us to come and bring the horse", the horse must be freed for his destiny, because this horse is *destined for glory*. He can move a little within the limits of the rope but he is tied. He cannot break free; he cannot go further than the rope. He cannot do what the free horses are doing; he cannot reach his *destiny*.

This is then applied to the life of the person he has been called to address on this night:

> You are also tied. You have a car, a little car. You have a job, a little job. You have money, a little money. *But that is not your destiny*. You have come to the city. Now you are at the junction of two roads [...] Your business was going well but now it has slowed down. It is not like it was, because *you have been tied*.

That is, of course, the *situation*[60] of many of those in the audience, which is made up largely of people in the 25–50 age group, urban, junior office workers, civil servants and traders, more or less equally divided between men and women. These are certainly people who feel themselves to be caught in a *situation* of socio-political and economic stagnation, and to be victims of what Daloz describes as

---

[60] This often-used term has its origins in the school of positive thinking of Norman Vincent Peale, which contributed to the development of *faith gospel* in the USA. See S. Brouwer, P. Gifford, S.D. Rose, *Exporting the American Gospel: Global Christian Fundamentalism*, New York: Routledge, 1996. See also Paul Gifford, "The Complex Provenance of some elements of African Pentecostal Theology", in Corten and Fratani-Marshall, *From Babel*, 62–79.

"*le (non-)renouvellement des élites*".[61] In this *situation* and in this social group, one of the choices is flight:

> It is not enough to be born-again. You must go on further to your destiny. You need to be *relocated* to where *you ought to be* [...] *to where your abundance is waiting for you.*

Not, however, if one is *tied*. He takes two people from the audience and a microphone cord and attaches himself to demonstrate his limited movement, playing well with pauses and timing, adding darkly:

> There are people assigned to this horse... Their assignment is that nobody should loose this horse...Are you understanding me? [...] [*We hear you, sir.*] But it does not matter who is watching you because you will be freed, *in Jesus mighty name.* [*Alleluias.*] Your cry has reached heaven...Your time of release has come...from *mamywata*...from witches and wizards... Your time of release has come, in Jesus' mighty name. [*Alleluias.*] Those assigned against you will lose their job tonight. [*Applause.*]

This reference to the loss of a job is very ambiguous since it can certainly be interpreted as a vengeful curse, rather than the simple fact of losing the job of tethering the colt. There is definitely a suggestion of the spiritual power that is to be gained here. As the horse is freed and goes up to Jerusalem, he develops an intriguing narrative. Here Jesus is sidelined as he goes on to further emphasise the colt in the role of a *big man* returning to his native village, reflecting, no doubt, the social aspirations of many in the congregation who have come to the city to seek their fortune:

> Is this the horse from that village, now decorated...? They are spreading their clothes and palms on the streets shouting "Hosanna", before him, behind him and beside him. Who walks on the clothes they have spread out? It is not Jesus?... No it is the horse. [*Cheers.*] Hosanna they are shouting.
> You are a miracle about to happen, you are packaged, you are about to explode. [*Wild applause here.*]

---

[61] J.-P. Daloz (ed.), *Le (non-) renouvellement des élites en Afrique subsaharienne*, Bordeaux: CEAN, 1999.

But if he is to be a true Bokonù, he must identify the source of the problem, what he described in a subsequent session of this weeklong seminar as "the enemy within". He continues somewhat ominously, inviting the expected response:

> But my question now is "who tied the horse? [*Silence.*]... The horse did not tie itself... The horse did not tie itself [*Yes sir, we hear you.*] No it did not tie itself, but who tied it? The devil? Satan? Enemies in the world?...No, it was not the devil. No, it was not Satan. No, it was not his enemies in the world. *IT WAS THE OWNERS OF THE HORSE WHO TIED THE HORSE.* [*Voice faltering with emphasis.*] Are you understanding me?... [*We are hearing you, sir. Applause for a very obvious resonance.*]

The final dénouement, as one might imagine, is significant as it moves to the "enemy within" the family itself:

> And now I ask you. What is holding you in the house? Is it the devil? No. Is it Satan? No. Is it your enemies in the world? No. It is the enemies within the house and they are the most difficult to get out. [*Here the French translators use some obviously colourful idiomatic expressions in Fongbè that attract applause and laughter.*] It is the members of the household that are tying you. You can't marry well because they have not married well. You cannot advance because they have not advanced. You cannot have money because they do not have money... *It is time to say No!* [*There is wild applause and shouting here as he hammers the point.*] Your wife, your children, your success, your promotion, your visa, are waiting for you at the gate. This is the place of your *coronation.*
>
> Let God expose those enemies in your house: father, mother, brother, sister, uncles, aunts...those who say they are your friend. May they be exposed. Lord, expose all those who are trying to kill me. Expose them. Let me go.
>
> I know you are saying I have described *your situation...*

From the congregation I profiled above, it is seems very likely that he has indeed described their *situation*. This is a very dramatic presentation of the case but the *situation* is not uncommon. "*Nous sommes une génération maudite,*" a Catholic secondary-school student, unwittingly echoing Fanon,[62] tells me, citing AIDS, chronic unemployment, a future without hope or promise if he does not manage to flee to Europe or the USA. The distance between him and the world he

---

[62] Franz Fanon, *Les Damnés de la Terre*, Ed. François Maspéro, Paris 1961.

aspires to, and increasingly peeps at for 400 cfa an hour in internet cafés, seems to grow daily. The tension between the global and the local, tradition and modernity, is almost unbearable.[63] He is, he says, "blocked" in his progress at school and in his other "*projets de vie*". Not surprisingly, the enemy is "within", since he believes his father's first wife has put a curse on him.

> I go to sleep and I dream that cattle are chasing me, or a lion or... anything, any animal, they are chasing after me at night. So any of those things that present themselves to a human being are making allusions to witchcraft. As well as this, at school I feel fine... But in the examinations I don't succeed. This does not depend on my will, since I am doing everything that could be said to be my duty in order to succeed... The curse wants to block everything, everything that might come to me as happiness... I don't understand this but we are born here in Africa, and in all of this we are obliged to follow the tradition as has been done since the time of our ancestors, because we were born into a tradition of fear.[64]

In the absence of a ministry of protection and deliverance in the Catholic Church in his local area, the secondary-school student has started attending prayers with a charismatic pastor who had recently set up a Church in the area and promised him deliverance:

> I kept going to him for the prayer sessions... This was for some time before the examinations... So now that I have succeeded at the BEPC (Intermediate level examinations). I have understood that perhaps I was somewhat delivered and that the road is open to me.

This could be dismissed as the fear and frustration of an adolescent but a senior bank official appears to confirm his view when I ask him what he is seeking in CAFM:

> First of all spiritual protection for ourselves and our children and then the possibility of developing ourselves as a man and an individual in the society in which we live. You will not be unaware of the fact that we live in a country where there is a development of malefic power...You know that Benin is the cradle of Vodún, that witchcraft still exists in Benin. The advantage of this Church is that it knows how to give spiritual protection and to show that in Jesus Christ we have been saved for the future.[65]

---

[63] Online shopping sites are amongst the most frequently visited.
[64] Interview, 9 September 2002.
[65] Interview, 26 May 2002.

Albert de Surgy reports an almost identical response but the conclusion is more radical:

> Africans start their life with a malediction since when we are born in our families we find customs and traditions. These customs and traditions are maledictions that Satan has introduced into our families. We must cut the ties with our ancestors. Alleluia... The fetishes and idols we possess are maledictions that are blocking our path, that block all progress... You who are Christian ...if you continue to conform to the customs and the traditions, to eat the meat of the Devil, cease doing it this very evening. Some among you are not true Christians. You are still Béninois. Me, I may have been born Zairois, but I crush my culture, my traditions, to save my brothers and sisters. This is what we must do. Amen.[66]

Taken together, this evidence is very significant, with several common themes which, in my view, reveal a society in considerable difficulty. In the most negative sense, they represent a rejection of family and culture that can only result in extreme alienation and certainly poses problems for the construction of a modern state and society. They can be replicated in other interviews many times over across the whole spectrum of Benin Christianity and the sermons and seminars addressing these issues are the most common. It is essentially a search for *Alǎfià* or *Gbédudu*, as I explained them in Chapter 2, but it is a search that is often frustrated by the weight of society and tradition. This may then require, as Rev. Chigbundu would have it, *relocation*. The visa to the USA or elsewhere[67] is a constant in the promises of the pastors, the prayer requests of the faithful, and in the testimonies of those to whom it has been granted. It is essentially a flight from the apparent suffocation of traditional society, as well as the stress and frustration of living in a socio-economic miasma caught halfway between tradition and modernity. It is the search for a rational, bureaucratic modernity, a land of opportunity if not quite a biblical land of "milk and honey"[68] where individuality is the key to success rather than the target of the jealous.

---

[66] De Surgy, *Le choix*, 48. One of the books on sale at family seminars was Ofoegbu Timothy Godwin, *Skeleton of the Ancestors: Heal Your Family Tree*, Lagos: Flame Books, 1999.

[67] Germany rather than France often appears to be the second-choice destination, especially for the less qualified.

[68] "So I have come down to rescue them from the hand of the Egyptians and to bring them up out of that land into a good and spacious land, a land flowing with milk and honey..." (Exodus 3: 8).

Adè provides a tenable social-anthropological explanation of this phenomenon, and this is the theory that underlies my own interpretation of much of this *Christianisme béninois*. He ascribes Dahomey-Benin's notorious political instability, notably in the period 1960–1972 as well as its inability to move out of a miltaro-Marxist dictatorship for seventeen years to the "fragility of interpersonal relations resulting from an erroneous rapport with the world".[69] Hurbon, referring to Haiti, elucidates this line when he writes of a society

> where there is a continuous *chevauchement* of the private and the public, a constant confusion between the two spheres, a consequence of which is the fact that the individual ends up by losing all the symbolic references which would help him to orient himself in his relations with the other and the world.[70]

While this world-view may be slowly changing in Benin, it is still, in my view, largely intact, as several of the cases I reported indicate, and proving an obstacle to the kind of development to which the country genuinely aspires. Ideally this development is the *Aláfíà* or *Gbédudu*, which, as we have already seen in Chapter 2, is the optimal scenario envisaged for the country by 2025 and described by President Kérékou in the following terms:

> To make Benin a haven of peace, of democracy of consensus, a country of prosperity, social well being, and cultural influence...to build the country, vanquish poverty and conquer modernity... rise to the challenge of the future...take in hand and assure the fullness of its national destiny.[71]

The social tissue, however, is in Adè's view characterised by "a hypertrophy" in the development of interpersonal relations to the detriment of a more positive effort for social transformation. This, he asserts, has led to a closing in upon a familial collectivism, which, in a nascent modernity, leaves the subject with "a kind of hybrid personality drawn between collectivism and individualism", victim, in Hurbon's terms, of the "constant confusion between the two spheres". When there is an attempt to assert modern individualism "the subject experiences

---

[69] Adè, *Les fidèles*, 67.
[70] Hurbon, *Sociologie*, 236–7.
[71] Matthieu Kérékou "Vaincre la pauvreté et conquérir la modernité", speech on forty-second anniversary of national independence, *La Nation*, 3042, 2 August 2002, 7.

a kind of insecurity which pushes them to a flight from the clan and from the fatherland in order to find security in an international system invented and organised by the West where they will function with competence".[72] One can imagine the consequences for national development. Goudjo sadly confirms this impression:

> People of work and quality abroad, the Béninois become extraordinary dilettantes when it comes to investing at home. Worse, it is rare to find any who wishes to invest at home, since they are discouraged by so many family, social and political problems. They are demoralised and obliged to move abroad, they go away.[73]

The transnational advantages of Charismatic Churches have often been emphasised and come into play here, offering an "access to the universal".[74] However, it is not so much that the Churches themselves have much to offer in terms of concrete opportunities, apart perhaps from the occasional scholarship to a Bible college. What they do offer is the promise of the ever-popular Psalm 23,[75] or, to use the terminology of Rev. Chigbundu, a "connection" that may lead to "a relocation to where you ought to be...To where your abundance is waiting for you". They speak of success and how it can be grasped; they speak of signs and miracles, of destinies and glory on offer that are the stuff of dreams. Even the names of many of the Churches contain the promise: *Cathedral of Miracles, Winners' Chapel, Action Faith, Solution Chapel, Victory Chapel, Freedom Tabernacle*. This, however, raises questions in terms of real change. It is part of the anthropological fragility referred to in the previous chapter, and of the difficulty the country has in establishing the common bonds necessary for the building of a modern, prosperous and inclusive state. From its history, or perhaps lack of a reflected and understood history, Benin remains a society symbolically divided against itself and seeking solace and solutions in both the esoteric and new forms of Christianity. Goudjo is biting in his analysis when he speaks of minimising the crucial problems resulting from "the incohesion of the

---

[72] Adè, *Les fidèles*, 67.
[73] Goudjo, *La liberté*, 136.
[74] Mayrargue, *The Expansion*, 289.
[75] "The Lord is my shepherd, I shall not be in want. He makes me lie down in green pastures, he leads me beside quiet waters, he restores my soul...Even though I walk through the valley of the shadow of death, I will fear no evil" (Psalm 23: 1–3, 4).

social tissue" through "religious oracles", seeing in this attitude an "anachronism" and an "aberration". The return to the tradition and to religious esotericism, he states in terms reminiscent of Marxist "false consciousness", is little more than indifference to the multiple ambiguities of both Benin's history and of modernity. It is, he claims, the "choice of a closing in on the self" which is effectively a final resignation in the face of reality.[76] From a rational point of view, it is certainly difficult to disagree with him. While my critique of the Catholic social teaching was that it tended to maintain an ivory-tower distance from social reality, charismatic preachers appear to be building castles in the air while failing to engage with the struggles of the people on the ground. Making promises of *miracles* and *breakthroughs* that defy all logic while failing to engage in any concrete way with state and society. The hard reality in Benin is that *Miracles, Winners, Solutions, Victory* and ultimately *Freedom* cannot be plucked from the sky and require more commitment both in terms of good governance on a local level and solidarity on the international level. In the end, ephemeral or illusory as they may seem, hope and promise count in Lɛgbà's world, where the alternative might be chaos. We are a long way from lasting solutions here and in many cases the most that can be asked for is enough hope to get by. In the words of the classic spiritual from the African Diaspora:

> Oh, by and by, by and by,
> I'm going to lay down my heavy load.
> I know my robe's going to fit me well,
> I tried it on at the gates of hell.
> Oh, hell is deep and a dark despair,
> Oh, stop, poor sinner, and don't go there!
> Oh, by and by, by and I'm going to lay down my heavy load.[77]

The search for new spaces and new communities

And he said, Draw not nigh hither: put off thy shoes from off thy feet, for the place whereon thou standest is holy ground. (Exodus 3: 5)

---

[76] Goudjo, *La liberté*, 158.
[77] Negro spiritual, text as in Michael Tippet, *A Child of Our Time*, London: Schott, 1944.

The whole point of charismatic Christianity seems to be *change*, or at least the desire for a breakthrough to something new and better. Relocation in the broader geographical sense, however, is not always a realistic option. There is therefore the necessity for new spaces closer to home. In Chapter II, I pointed out the density of religious spaces that mark the Benin landscape. This example was based on the CCC alone but it is replicated by many of the Churches, if not quite with the same intensity. This involves the creation of new communities, which we shall look at later. However, it also involves the creation of spaces that are *sacred* and, perhaps above all, *secure* for those who take refuge in them.

This is particularly striking in the case of the CCC where the whole of the parish compound is seen as intensely sacred and a space of security from the impending chaos of a threatening world (See Appendix 12b). It is, in Eliade's terms, "a strong significant space [in] the formless expanse surrounding it",[78] a *rock*, a *stronghold* and a *refuge* in biblical terms. It is not difficult to understand the significance of this discovery for this thesis, which has been essentially about the struggle to discover meaning and security in the apparently 'formless expanse' of a fragile world inhabited by strong and often unpredictable forces. In the CCC this has been strongly expressed in the construction of the compound, across the threshold of which "no evil spirit can penetrate".[79] The compound is considered sacred and must be entered with bare feet, but it has within it a range of even more intensely sacred spaces.

The *Zungbómè* or *prayer garden* is a feature common to several prophetic Churches I have visited both in Benin and in Nigeria. This is a small rectangular area of the compound, covered in very clean sand and set aside for more intense spiritual activity by the faithful, both individually and collectively, at the Friday "prayer of sanctification". It represents the forest[80] and the stream or well of miraculous

---

[78] Mircea Eliade, *The Sacred and the Profane*, London: Harcourt Brace, 1959, 20.

[79] Interview, 26 April 2002.

[80] *Zungbómè*, the great bush or great forest (Rassinoux, *Dictionnaire*, 2000: 161). Each *Zungbómè* has a tree, in my experience always a kola, *Cola nitida* or *Cola-verrat* rather than *Cola monocotylédone*, or *Garcinia kola* which is used in ritual. My sources said the prophet did not specify the species, only that it provide shade, but in all the cases I verified, including Porto Novo, it turned out to be *Kola nitada*. De Surgy, however, explains that this area has several different sources, not just the forest but also the desert, the seashore and the Garden of Gethsemani. See de Surgy, *L'Eglise*, 104–105. Jane E. Clifford reports on the importance of Achimota

water known as *Mignonsi*[81] at Porto Novo, which was the locus of the Prophet Oschoffa's own founding vision. Here the faithful of the CCC go, often sleeping overnight on the bare ground, to commune with God and to receive the gift of the Holy Spirit.[82] The references to a more traditional worldview are quite obvious. The forest was the place of initiation to Fá, even if the CCC members reject such associations, preferring to use the more scriptural analogy of Eden or Gethsemani. De Surgy affirms that the forest is the stage

> upon which the primary confrontation between the divine powers and the inferior or diabolical powers which oppose them takes place. It is thus an appropriate location for a contact of initiation with the forces of evil, with their incorporation and reinforcement in the spirit of all.[83]

In the CCC, however, the *Zungbómé* becomes the special space where the faithful seek communion with the Holy Spirit and the angels of the celestial army in the struggle to combat the evil forces that surround them.

The *Agbŏglŏ* (literally, "The place of security for a time") is perhaps more interesting since it represents a space where the faithful can regain their orientation in a world that is threatened by chaos. The CCC gives a biblical origin for this concept, which comes from the prophet Oschoffa, in the flight into Egypt (Mt. 2: 13–23) seen as a search for security in a time danger. De Surgy notes that the term is also used in Vodún but that these CCC spaces bear little resemblance to the Vodún *Agbŏglŏ*.[84] This is a place for the reconstruction of the world for those who come to seek refuge within it. Those who feel threatened by the malevolent forces take refuge here for specified periods of seven, fourteen, or twenty-one days[85] in order to refound their threatened world.

Forest near Accra for several African churches including Solid Rock International (personal communication).

[81] Said to "cure all kinds of illness even HIV/AIDS, which is only the anger of God, see Dt. 28: 60–61" (Christophe Akodjetin, *Pasteur Oschoffa, sa vie et son œuvre*, CCC Pamphlet Cotonou, (ndg), 52).

[82] Saulnier, quoting Paul Hazoumé, notes that the time of sleep is also a time of initiation when the *aziza* or spirits of the forest plunge the hunter into deep sleep in order to reveal to him their secrets, allowing him to participate in their invisible nature before sending them back to their families (Saulnier, *Le Meutre,* 77, cit. Hazoume, *Le pacte,* 13).

[83] De Surgy, *L'Eglise,* 105.

[84] Ibid., 106.

[85] In the course of my fieldwork I followed the case of one young boy, showing symptoms of cerebral malaria, who remained at the *Agbŏglŏ* for fourteen days. The

It became clear that this understanding of sacred space has been appropriated in the compounds of the two Catholic parishes I studied in some detail (See Appendix 10a, 10b). In the case of Sacré Cœur, it is certainly significant that there has been a change from missionary to Béninois personnel in recent years. This has led to a very different emphasis in the pastoral direction as well as the whole understanding of the space itself in a large urban parish. I have little doubt that the planting of trees, as well as the addition of a Blessed Sacrament Adoration Chapel, where people often slept on the floor overnight, and the addition of a *Golgotha*,[86] under which those thought to be possessed were prayed for, were a more or less direct replication of the CCC concept of sacred space, which in itself is a reference to an older tradition.

The ideas of the cross and redemptive suffering, represented in the *Golgotha*, are almost entirely absent from the new charismatic Christianity. Suffering is not seen as a road to redemption but an evil to be conquered. One member of CAFM defines this kind of suffering Christianity as Francophone and Catholic, as opposed to his own which he sees as American and Protestant with a strong emphasis on health, wealth and success. He notes: "If you see an individual you can know whether he is prosperous or whether he is miserable", explaining that the prosperous "radiate" prosperity. There is more than a little of the "big man" here.[87] He dismisses the Beatitudes (Matthew 5: 1–12)—which many Christians, and even Nietzsche in a perverse way,[88] would feel to be at the heart of the gospel—as little more than an obscure passage which he finds difficult to understand.[89] Pierre Legendre, however, reflecting on the addition of the *Golgotha* sees a relation to a similar kind of iconography that emerged in France during the 100 Years War, when there was a great emphasis on the physical dimension of the suffering of Christ. Adè refers to the slave trade as "the expression of a

treatment included several visits by the visionaries, ritual offerings of bananas and other foods, as well as the use of modern drugs paid for by the CCC.

[86] This scene of the Crucifixion and Pietà first appeared when Abbé Dagnon was parish priest of Saint Michelin the 1980s, and it has become a feature of many parishes in recent years and is widely requested in others (interview, 5 July 2001).

[87] He developed this theme of the quest for personal *acè* in a sermon (Isidore Godonou, *Prince sur le Monde*, CAFM, Cotonou, 7 April 2002).

[88] "Better songs would they have to sing, for me to believe in their Saviour: more like saved ones would his disciples have to appear unto me!" (Friedrich Nietzsche, *Thus Spake Zarathustra, XXVI, The Priests*.)

[89] Interview, 23 June 2002.

historical experience of the Cross". He notes that the development of a
"piety more attentive to the Cross... is above all the preference of *les
petites gens*" and reflects the socio-economic situation of crisis within
which they find themselves. This "spiritual intuition", he suggests, is
worthy of serious consideration, since he feels that it may constitute
a way out of a more closed pietism. "It gives way to a contemplation
of that which gives meaning to the crucifying experience of daily life
(*au vécu crucifiant*) and gives reasons to hope". This popular intuition
can find theological expression that can articulate and create "a trans-
formative energy" and potential for Béninois society.[90] It is interesting
to note that *A Prayer for the Country*, composed by the CEB, includes
the following lines:

> Deign to throw an affectionate and compassionate look on your sons
> and daughters of Benin. Confident in your great mercy and in your
> power, we come to you, weighed down by the weight of suffering
> and misery. We wish to tell you again and again of our hope and our
> faith. We are decided, under your inspiration, to bring ourselves back
> together again to build the country you have given us.[91]

This is nothing if not, as Kä Mana might put it, a *"prière pour un
temps de crise"*.[92] It is not difficult to imagine that all of Africa may
feel itself to be going through an interminable war, which may well
last thirty or even 100 years, and it is hardly surprising that this kind
of devotion should emerge in such a time of profound crisis.

While this is not true to the same extent of all the Churches, it is
clear that many of them have become significant spaces for their members. In many cases perhaps, this is simply to while away some time
or establish a useful contact for a *petit job*, but in others cases they act
as spiritual *strongholds* and *refuges* from a difficult world. Here their
troubles are closely identified with the suffering of Christ, but there is
the hope for a resurrection to *new life*. It is certainly significant that
this parish, where a particular cult of *Golgotha* as well as a healing and
deliverance ministry has developed, draws people from other Catholic
parishes for some of its services, most notably those of healing and
deliverance, which we shall look at presently.

---

[90] Adè, *Les fidèles*, 55–61.
[91] CEB, *Pour préserver*, 165.
[92] Kä Mana, *Théologie africaine*.

While the understanding of space may vary, what is consistent is the search for a new community or quasi-community within which to function. Peel has noted: "The historic importance of Islam and Christianity was that they asked searching questions of existing definitions of community and proposed significant extensions to it".[93] In more recent times Gifford noted that Pentecostal Churches in Liberia "effectively provided an alternative community".[94] Poewe suggests that "making identities, cultures and languages ambivalent is precisely what this form of Christianity is all about". She observes that

> it extends and cultivates ambiguity precisely because it is based on Spirit theology or a 'language of no-place and no-one'. But while it makes uncertain and deconstructs all that is 'of the whole,' it makes certain and reconstructs under one truth all that is 'of God's kingdom'.[95]

From the evidence above, it becomes clear that traditional social structures pose problems for modern Béninois and there is a search for something new, which is perhaps more voluntary and less constraining but will nonetheless provide the support that is needed. While in some cases the solution is flight to a new society, this is not always possible and there is the need for something nearer home. This need became even more acute in the PRPB period when traditional social structures were reviled as "retrograde", and others, including the family, had been penetrated to a great degree by a totalitarian regime. It was not uncommon, for example, to hear of cases of political denunciation by family members and this was encouraged by the regime.

It is certainly significant that it was during this period that CCC parishes began to experience development. This was when this Church, which had hitherto been considered, and considered itself to be, "a Church of the less well off",[96] began to attract members from among the intellectual and socio-administrative elites.[97] By 1980 the Church had become a target of serious political repression and was finally banned.[98] The CCC seeks to be, as we have seen, a Church of secure spaces. It is equally a Church of small communities, with the many parishes

---

[93] Peel, *Encounter*, 87.
[94] Gifford, *Christianity and Politics*.
[95] Poewe, *Metonymic Structure*, 366.
[96] Interview, 19 April 2002.
[97] Interview with Paul Gonçalves, World Secretary of the CCC, Superior Evangelist, former Inspector General of Finance, Cotonou, 28 July 2002.
[98] See de Surgy, *L'Eglise*, 25–31 for an account of this.

having only a few dozen members and even the largest having only about 200. These communities were obviously of great importance to those fleeing the pressures of an increasingly hostile world, the Vodún and the evil spirits, but also an increasingly intrusive totalitarian state that was seeking to eat them.[99]

The Catholic Church was quite different in its structure, especially in the cities and larger towns. It was also during this period, however, that there was a change in its organisation in Benin, which was also certainly due to the pressure of an increasingly invasive state. Catholic youth movements with the simple *voir, juger, agir* methodology of social analysis[100] had been banned by the regime. Almost immediately, however, new groups emerged, the most notable being the Pentecostal sounding *Feu Nouveau* movement founded at Sacré Cœur parish by Sister Monique Matton, with the assistance of P. Michel Dujarrier in 1974.[101] The movement is essentially a prayer group but it sought "to deepen the faith of young people" by having them apply the gospel texts of each Sunday to daily life through the use of a simple questionnaire. The following years saw the founding of a series of similar groups which were, in my experience, a remarkable feature of the Catholic Church in Benin. Significantly, rather than being known as *mouvements*, which might imply a certain *activisme militant* in the socio-political sense, these became known as *communautés* or *fraternités*, which it could be said had more of a monastic resonance, thus making them less suspect as a political threat.[102] As is often the case

---

[99] Banégas notes "par son action et ses structures, l'Eglise tente de se poser en recours face à la prétention totalisante du pouvoir révolutionnaire qui prétend agir et contrôler l'ensemble de la société. Ainsi peut s'interpréter, en 1982, la création de Communautés Chrétiennes de Quartier à Ouidah qui font pendant aux cellules de bases et autres Comités locaux de défense de la révolution" (Banégas, *La démocratie*, 173).

[100] These were Jeunesse Ouvrière Chrétienne (JOC), and the Jeunesse Estudiantine Chrétienne (JEC), founded by Fr Joseph Cardijn in Belgium in 1925 and in France in 1929, where it was strongly influenced by the social Catholicism of Emmanuel Mounier. It was already present in Africa from 1932 in the Belgian Congo.

[101] Sr Matton later worked in Latin America and Burkina Faso before returning to Benin. Apparently she was quite critical of the methodologies of groups influenced by liberation theology for being over-involved with social analysis and less interested in the purely spiritual.

[102] Adè notes both the slippage of the Catholic Action movements and the "fever" of pious devotions which characterised this period when, he says, Christians were "everywhere except where they could inform political and social action through their faith" (Adè, *Les fidèles*, 54).

with charismatic groups, they looked for their inspiration to the primitive Christianity of the second chapter of the *Acts of the Apostles*,[103] as well as the later monastic tradition, being described as communities "of prayer and sharing" (Acts 2: 42–44). There was a strong emphasis on prayer, the study of scripture, catechesis, personal reflection and solidarity in times of difficulty rather than any kind of overt social analysis. One of the leaders of the period points out that "these new movements, which were purely spiritual, allowed for the continuation of reflection within the Church, and prevented their assimilation into the PRPB",[104] although they were kept under scrutiny by internal security. It is problematic to harass people who appear to be simply praying, reading the Bible or taking religious instruction. For their members in Marxist Benin, the *communautés* and *fraternités* appear to have been essentially places of spiritual refreshment, renewal and solidarity, and in that sense they were analogous to the *Agbŏglŏ*, if not quite the same. They were also consistent with the Catholic Church's historical relationship with social elites. These groups brought together the same students who in the past would have gone to Catholic schools. Many of them eventually emerged to be part of the post-PRPB political and administrative elite, thus maintaining the privileged ties of the Catholic Church with this group.

The *Sillon Noir*, in the analysis of two of its members, provides an interesting picture of that period and of the whole Dahomey-Benin crisis.[105] They observe that it had extended well beyond the domain of the socio-economic or the political institutions to the more fundamental question of values and identity, all of which, quoting Isaiah, they claim had been "everted and inverted by those holding power" in the PRPB and the administration.

> Woe to those who call evil good
> and good evil,
> who put darkness for light

---

[103] This was confirmed by M. Dujarrier, an influential member of these early groups, who continues to develop a theology based on this thinking (interview, 20 April 2004).

[104] Interview, 5 July 2001. It is notable that in neighbouring Togo, both JEC and JOC had been, to some extent, assimilated into the ruling RPT, becoming cells of its youth movement.

[105] Etienne Soglo and Cyprien Tindo, "Les Chrétiens Comme Force Vive de la Nation au rendez-vous politique du Premier Trimestre 1990", in B. Adoukonou (ed.), *Expérience Africaine*, 41–49.

and light for darkness,
who put bitter for sweet
and sweet for bitter.
Woe to those who are wise in their own eyes
and clever in their own sight. (Isaiah 5: 20–21.)

The Béninois were seeking change but, as they explain, without knowing "*terminus a quo*" or "*terminus ad quem*", the points of departure and the points of arrival of any such change. The Béninois, they infer, has no grasp of history, seeing the past in "paradisical" or "mythical" terms as he moves further away from it, with the present situation depicted, rightly or wrongly, as an apocalyptic hell. He longs for "*Yovo hwenu*" (the time of the Europeans), "*Maga hwenu*" (the time of Maga) or "*Apithy hwenu*", predicting rather prophetically in 1990 that he would eventually long for "*Kérékou hwenu*", but there is a failure to engage constructively with the present.[106] One is reminded of V.S. Naipaul's biting reference to the Congo "where even after the slave-trading Arabs and the Belgians, the past is yearned for as '*le bon vieux temps de nos ancêtres*'".[107]

In his 2004 Reith Lectures, Wole Soyinka emphasises the importance of *dignity* and the role of communities, including religious communities, in providing this.[108] Those who came to the *communautés* and *fraternités* were seeking holiness rather than contestation, shelter and refuge from an increasingly dysfunctional and violent state, which did not know either where it was coming from or whither it was going. Poewe suggests, however, that holiness can be equated with a certain dignity, something which, if we accept Adè's analysis as well as anecdotal evidence from the period, was certainly in short supply during the most ideologically hard years of the PRPB, and continues to be in an Africa continually threatened by uncertainty and even chaos. It is hardly surprising that some chose to take refuge in these quasi-monastic groups since, as Durkheim points out, this form of life "artificially organises a milieu that is apart from, outside of, and closed to the natural milieu where ordinary men live a secular life, and [...] tends to be its antagonist".[109] A brief look at the names of these groups gives us an idea of the philosophy behind them. The *Communauté Fraternelle*

---

[106] Soglo and Tindo, *Les Chrétiens*, 42.
[107] Naipaul, *India*, 43.
[108] Wole Soyinka, *The Quest for Dignity*, Reith Lecture 4.
[109] Durkheim, *Elementary Forms*, 37.

Emmanuel,[110] for adults, was founded, again at Sacré Cœur, by Michel Dujarrier, in 1976. These groups, however, are often less than democratic in their structures and show fissiparous tendencies as they split into smaller, more specialised communities. The Communauté Novíéyò (The Brother is Good) for functionaries and workers soon emerged from the *Communauté Emmanuel*, as did *Communauté Fífáton* (*Fífá* is literally, coolness, humidity, freshness, sweetness, peace, blessing). *The Communauté Hwenusu* (It was Time) brought together functionaries and private-sector workers with an emphasis on Christian responsibility in the professional sphere. The CCRM came into existence in 1977, under the leadership of Jean Pliya, himself a member of the intellectual socio-administrative elite. While this is seen as a mass movement, and certainly organises impressive mass meetings, it is also subdivided into "life-groups", local fraternities and communities.

In general, these movements were perceived as refuges, helping Christians to "get through" or "hold up"[111] in trying times and in a hostile world. In the words of a former member they were "an attempt to create a coherent spirituality"[112] in a world that was increasingly incoherent. They were small in size and modelled on a "domestic family unit". In my view, however, parallels can also be drawn with the *Gbɛ* or local, voluntary, peer-group associations or clubs. Writing of these groups in Yorubaland, where they are known as *egbe*, Peel notes that they are "models of community to the extent that they emphasise commonality of condition"[113] with a certain egalitarianism. At the same time, they represent autonomous spaces free from the constraints and demands imposed by the lineage. The *fraternités*, though not as gender specific as the *gbɛ* is, correspond to this model insofar as they bring together peers, youth and adults in their respective groups, who share the same condition. At the same time, they seek to attenuate ethnic tensions in the creation of a "*fraternité au-delà de l'ethnie*".[114] While eschewing the methodology of the JEC, Legendre confirms that there was "a recognition that society had to be remade on new bases, those of the gospel and the fraternity which flows from this".[115] This can be

---

[110] To be distinguished from a neo-conservative Catholic movement in Europe.
[111] Interview, 20 April 2001.
[112] Interview, 7 July 2001.
[113] Peel, *Encounter*, 58.
[114] This is an important theme of the Benin school of theology (Agossou, *Christianisme*).
[115] Interview, 5 July 2001.

seen as an attempt to create a new identity through the deconstruction of the world outside and the reconstruction of a world within, where the members become a *brother* or *sister* and all is made new.

These groups continue to play an important role in the pastoral activities of the Catholic Church in Benin. Perhaps traumatised by events in Rwanda and the Church's failures there, in recent years these have been widened. There has been an increasing emphasis on the *communautés ecclésiales de base*, parish cell groups in the *quartiers* which, while retaining the spiritual dimension of the *fraternités* and *communautés*, seek to open and broaden them. Here there is the incorporation of something of the old JEC methodology, with more involvement in the practical social problems of their members, while at the same time responding to what the Catholic Church sees as "the multiplicity of sects".[116] The aim of these groups is to increase a sense of belonging in the larger parishes, where many members feel anonymous and turn to other smaller Churches that may respond better to their needs or, to put it in the somewhat pragmatic terms commonly used, "*where we find satisfaction*". The Archdiocese of Parakou, for example, largely echoes *Ecclesia in Africa* as it recommends the creation of these groups

> where the faithful know one another, come together to pray and to practise solidarity, forgiveness and seek to improve the life in the *quartier*, while being witnesses to the non-Christians around them. For this we need places of prayer in the *quarters* and villages.[117]

This can be seen as a strategy of the Catholic Church to maintain its control on the ground, and this is certainly, to some extent at least, the case. Large parishes do not work in large cities and the faithful fall away to the smaller communities. Most of the Charismatic Churches are already *communautés ecclésiales de base*, at least in their size and in their location in the *quartiers populaires*, and where they are larger they too split into smaller groups and *fellowships*, where the members can find their place and feel at home. And so, marking out the landscape, the multiplication of sacred space and the creation of new communities go on, described by the more enthusiastic as a *foisonnement chrétien* and by others as the signs of a deepening *malaise social*. In a positive interpretation, one can say that at least

---

[116] Synode Diocésain, *A l'Ecoute*, 4.
[117] Ibid., 8. See also *Ecclesia in Africa*, 89.

these communities bring people together and form some kind of bonds when the alternative could be much worse, and this is certainly what seems to be feared in Africa today. One of the recurring themes in the Church is that of peace and the dangers of civil breakdown. Many of the members of the Charismatic Churches I visited had been themselves victims of such breakdown, in Liberia, Sierra Leone, both Congos, or of more local conflicts, as in neighbouring Togo. They appear as living reminders of what could happen, and it was often heard in their testimonies as they sought new reference points and communities within which to reconstruct their lives. The Churches of all denominations pray constantly "for the nations" and "for peace". One female CAFM member expresses it thus:

> We pray for everything! We pray first of all for the nations. Every time there is a president somewhere and it is not the will of God, that God may remove him... replace him by somebody of his heart, somebody who can rule... [We pray] that the Lord would try to give every president an entourage who will speak the same language as himself... Because if they are not united, the nation will not be united... We pray for peace... So that the noises of war may be turned into noises of peace. We pray a lot for Rwanda; countries at war... in difficulty. And we also pray for this country so that the Lord will bring to completion that which he has started. So that God might seize those who are on top... To exclude certain people among them... Others have changed, but the essential thing for me is that people can have peace in the Eternal, whether they go or stay.

To some extent at least this appears to bear out Marshall's suggestion that some aspects of Pentecostal discourse can be construed as a political critique of the "powers and principalities".[118] They do contain something of a commentary and make some claims upon the state, but the above remarks were recorded in a situation of relative stability and security and by somebody who was clearly favourable to the regime in power. The slogans on two campaign tee-shirts noted in Cotonou are probably, however, a better reflection of the real political preoccupations of this level of *le Christianisme béninois*, one on a market lady "*Avec Kérékou pour gagner le Bénin au Christ*" and the other on a member of the CCC "*Pour la paix et l'unité nationale: Votons Kérékou*". The renewal of elites may well be desirable

---

[118] Marshall, *Power*, 213–241.

in political terms, but in a land where Lɛgbà still has his place, it can be a risky business, and it may be better to leave the converted chameleon on his branch.

Healing and deliverance

There is a balm in Gilead,
To make the wounded whole.

(Negro Spiritual) [119]

Benin was rated 158th on the UN Human Development Index in 2002.[120] It is a society that has its own understanding of illness, its causes and cures. Here the population is constantly threatened by HIV/AIDS and malaria, for which there is no known vaccination and, in the case of the former, little in terms of affordable treatment. In a state that has little capacity in the area of health services, and even less so in the wake of 1990s SAPs, it is hardly surprising to find that one of the most common preoccupations among all Christians is that of healing and deliverance. Eric de Rosny notes the importance of the *nganga*, or traditional healer in Cameroon,[121] the equivalent of the *Bòwàtó* in Benin, as a "regulator of social relations". Health, he adds, in the widest meaning of the term is *"well-being, order"*, in effect *Alăfià/Gbédudu*. He adds, *"present life* is such a common and primordial aspiration in Africa that those charged with controlling it have an eminent position in society". This position, he notes, has been reinforced "by the degradation of other traditional functions"[122] in the face of modernity which itself seems to be failing to bear much fruit. While Fá and the Bokonù may still have their place to some extent, they are not able to meet the burgeoning needs of a society where the social bonds are so fragile and which is at the same time involved in a process of seemingly chaotic development. De Rosny further suggests that the growth in individuality, which results pre-

---

[119] See also Jeremiah 46: 11.
[120] "Le Bénin classé 158ème". *Le Républicain*, 406, 20 July 2002.
[121] For a useful description of this holistic approach to health questions in Africa, see Eric de Rosny, *L'Afrique des Guérisons*, Paris: Karthala, 1992, 30–31. See also Eric de Rosny, *Les yeux de ma chèvre. Sur les pas des maîtres de la nuit en pays douala (Cameroun)*, Paris: Plon, 1981
[122] De Rosny, *L'Afrique*, 33.

cisely from a tenuous social 'great leap forward' to modernity, is accompanied by a multiplication in the incidence of witchcraft and spirit possession, creating demands that the tradi-practitioner can never hope to meet. "Treatments are less successful because there have never been as many witches as today", which, he notes, is the same as saying "that there were never as many individualities as today".[123] The space is clearly open for something else and it is not difficult to understand the proliferation of Churches, first of all the CCC, and later the development of Charismatic Churches, developing healing and deliverance ministries.[124] The mainline Churches, which traditionally opted for conventional medicine and ran important hospitals and health centres, have more recently become involved in the development of healing ministries and a renewed emphasis on exorcism, which we shall look at presently.

As I noted above, *le Christianisme béninois* is above all a pragmatic religion. A quick word check through my field notes is revealing. The word *problem* occurs some 450 times and the words *satisfaction* or *solution* fifty-seven times. Although a little arbitrary perhaps, these figures convey an accurate impression of the approach of the Béninois to their religion, and it is borne out by de Surgy's extensive research across the Churches on the "causes of conversion".[125] The recurring expressions are *problem*, *solution* and *satisfaction*. As noted earlier, even one of the Churches bears the name *Solution Chapel*. The narrative is almost always of a personal *problem* (a recurring illness, mental or physical, impotence, infertility, possession or other problems arising from occult practises) and the fruitless search for a *solution*, until the *satisfaction* is found in the Church in which the person is presently a member. This comes often only after several attempts in other Churches and in 'tradithérapie'. Monsieur N. of the CCC offers a good example. A former Catholic, he became a member of the CCC in 1984, following a recurrent illness. He does not say exactly what the illness was except that it was not what he describes as a "*maladie d'hôpital*" but rather "*une maladie venant de la famille*". It was in the CCC that he eventually found "*satisfaction*". He explains:

---

[123] Ibid., 37.
[124] Hurbon notes that in Haïti the proliferation of new religious movements was to some degree due to the "failure of the spirits" to meet the growing needs (*Culture et Dictature*, 143).
[125] See *L'Eglise*, 183–204; *Le Phénomène*, 209–212.

> Rather than going to the hospital and spending money uselessly for an
> illness that is not a hospital illness, we come here and they will do the
> job as it should be done and for very little cost.[126]

In terms of cost-benefit analysis, it could hardly be clearer and his
language is quite utilitarian. He speaks of *"les travaux spirituels"*
prescribed by the visionaries,[127] most often women, and carried out
"comme il faut", most often by men. The CCC has built its reputation largely on healing and deliverance. These ministries are used
both by members of the Church and also, apparently in a somewhat
clandestine manner, by members of other Churches and of the elite
who would not necessarily wish to be seen to be involved with the
CCC, despite a measure of recently acquired respectability.[128] The
CCC vision has come to push Fá and the *Bòwàtó* aside in many
areas. Or, perhaps more accurately if we accept de Rosny's view, it
has added its services to those already available to people without
the means to go elsewhere, or for whom modern *hospital treatment*
will not be effective. The result for the CCC is usually a very solid
adherence of the person and his/her family, expressed in the wearing
of the white garments, since there is always the suggestion that if
one were to move away from this place of security the evil might
strike again.

Healing is not confined to the CCC, however, and it is also a strong
feature of many Charismatic Churches. In an earlier chapter we looked
at the importance of potency and fecundity for the Béninois and these
are recurring themes across *le Christianisme béninois*. An interesting
practical example of this comes from a seminar at Freedom Tabernacle
Church.[129] This seminar was presided over by Rev. Victor Okorie, a
visiting pastor from Nigeria, described by the local pastor as a "prophet"
who runs a "miracle factory". In the course of his two-hour sermon,
Rev. Okorie announces that there is somebody in the congregation
"who cannot pregnant his wife" [sic].

---

[126] Conversation at CCC, Akpakpa, 10 May 2002.

[127] See de Surgy, *Le Christianisme Céleste*, 205–269 for a detailed description of
the ministry of the visionaries in the church.

[128] The Church appears to live under something of a cloud based on alleged
compromise with occult practices, the moral behaviour of some of its members and
hierarchy, and internal divisions often linked to financial questions.

[129] Faith Alive Christian Church, Freedom Tabernacle, Akpakpa, Cotonou, 13
May 2002: Seminar: *Turning Point 2002, Your time for change, Miracles, Healings,
Signs and Wonders*.

This is not a shameful time. His sperm count is low. Jesus specialises in treatment. If shame doesn't allow you to come now, then come tomorrow with 20,000 naira (approx. €120). You have to pay the price of shame, to admit to it. Come now for free or come secretly and pay the price of shame.

Two men appear at this point and there is applause from the congregation. He points to one and threatens to make him pay 10,000 naira because he refused to obey the Holy Ghost when he hesitated in stepping forward. He seems to single out one, telling him "Any time you want to meet your wife, witches pollute your sperm and it turns to water". But he reassures him: "You are a man...you can pregnant your wife". He tells him to meet him tomorrow with a bottle of oil that he will bless. He then calls up the wife and prays over them, laying on hands, and calling on the Holy Spirit:

> Before the end of this year a baby will cry in this family. [*Man falls down, as does woman.*] I send you and your husband to a bed with the Holy Spirit where a baby will come... This is a husband and wife. When a woman gets to the maturity of marriage, she should have children and also her husband. So whatever has power over your sperm [should be gone].

This was a remarkable scene. It illustrates the importance of fecundity, if only in the fact that these two young men faced what was at best considerable embarrassment and, what appeared to a female research colleague and myself, humiliation, in order to be cured. In fact, if we follow Adoukonou's argument, it was not a simple question of being "cured"; it was a struggle for life itself. *Hlònhlón* and *kúngbígbá* are, in fact, the real meaning and purpose of Gbέ, and the young men were willing to pay the price.

But deliverance is not something one receives once and for all. In life one is constantly threatened by all kinds of forces and so one is in constant need of protection, healing and deliverance. Madame G., a member of CAFM, provides and example.

> I was in France for many years. And when I came back my parents and especially my in-laws asked that we go to get protection... They began bringing us into the interior of the country to Cové, Agoni etc. This was their understanding of our protection [...] It was to charlatans [i.e. a Bokonù] We did almost everything.

This was a family aspiring to modernity, returning from the land of modernity (France), where both husband and wife had acquired solid

academic and professional qualifications and were now seeking rein-
sertion in Béninois society as members of the local, modern, socio-
economic elite. This was not something to be undertaken lightly, and
in traditional terms required the intervention of Fá in the search for
spiritual armour or, as it is commonly called *le blindage*, they would
need for protection. The attack soon came in the form of an illness
attacking one of the children, but also in the trauma of the mother (a
chronic asthmatic), often expressed in dreams that echo quite closely
those of the student referred to earlier in this chapter.

> at the end of every month when my husband brings home his salary,
> she has an attack. My in-laws started again, "you have to go here,
> you have to go there (to charlatans)…" We did the whole round, there
> was no solution, and this lasted for nine years… every month. It was
> often at midnight…or when my husband was going away… I don't
> know, I don't want to traumatise you… Cats walking on two legs…
> I had lizards under the pillows, all kinds of bad things that were hap-
> pening to me.

De Rosny observes that it is in this social class that traditional
solutions are no longer effective. This is precisely "because of the
distance that has been established between them and their family
and traditional milieu".[130] This collapse of the tradition creates the
need for new solutions and new solidarities in town. In this case, the
child's illness and the mother's trauma clearly had the same cause
and the Fá was not effective, since in the course of our interview it
became clear that she had little idea of what Fá actually meant. The
problem, however, remained and the search for a solution went on
as they continued to attend the Catholic Church with the occasional
nod towards an apparently powerless *Bòwàtó*.

> A pastor came from Abidjan who was working with the *Full Gospel
> Businessmen's Fellowship*. He prayed […] I saw things happening…
> these weren't like things that were happening before …We were invited
> to the *FGBF* in November 1989. I saw that he was doing things that
> weren't ordinary. So I invited him… [He] came to my house, and
> while he was there my daughter had an attack. He took my daughter,
> he prayed, he did something with blood. Since 1989 [she] hasn't had
> any further attacks.

---

[130] De Rosny, *L'Afrique*, 37.

This event led almost inevitably and understandably to adherence to this new community which has answered the problem and provided the solution.

> First of all I attached myself to this man, whom I took in the beginning to be God [...] He asked me did I pray and I said yes. I read the psalms. [...] And in that way, it was the healing of my daughter that anchored me [in the Lord].

A final narrative from the CCRM is very similar but brings together a number of the elements, notably the relationship between illness, the family, the wider social relations and the place of occult forces in society. Madame S. is a senior member in one of the parishes in Cotonou and came to CCRM during the illness of her husband, which eventually led to his death. The course followed during the illness is largely similar to that of her CAFM 'sister', and certainly not uncommon. There was recourse to Fá divination, esoteric groups, the CCC ("only for the visions"), the Church of the Cherubim and Seraphim and the Orthodox Church in Benin. Eventually, she came back to the Catholic Church of her childhood, but with the additional step of coming to CCRM, which seemed to respond to her needs. Her husband, who had also returned to the Church, died, however, and this led to the following reflection:

> This made me think. If we could have done all we did...We spent a fortune trying to heal him through occult forces. It didn't work. The Lord asks nothing from us, not a single franc and he is merciful with everybody. So I'm not going to go on living that life. Therefore I gathered up everything in the house [i.e. *gris-gris* etc.] and I burned them myself and then I went back to communion... It was from then I learned that Jesus, whom I took only as someone who could heal, is someone with whom one can live in intimacy [...] He is more than someone who can heal.

The cost-benefit analysis, which we have seen is a recurring theme, was also favourable here, while at the same time there was much need for "the intimacy" and security the CCRM provided when she was accused of being responsible for her husband's death.

> [They said] that I prepared food, that I put crushed glass in it. That I did this and that... and that I would have to die myself...They did everything... and when they buried him they did something, they put something in his hands so that he would kill me. But curiously, it was in their ranks that the heads began to fall.

The final line here is a hint at something quite different; it is the
search for effective spiritual power that will help her not only to
defend herself but ultimately to overcome her enemies. The battle had
not ended with the death of her husband, who in death had possibly
become her enemy. Now that she was alone in the world, this kind
of protective power was even more necessary. Echoing a poster in
CAFM which implores "Arise oh God, and fight all my enemies",
she says that she has not been harmed but rather "it was in their
ranks that the heads began to fall".

These narratives are very typical, whether coming from a work-
ing-class member of the CCC, a member of the more socially-mobile
CAFM, or a Catholic widow. They tell of people stranded in a society
between tradition and modernity, in a world marked by deep tensions,
grasping at straws of meaning and putative solutions. They are to be
found right across *le Christianisme béninois* and indeed in the whole
of Béninois society. They are narratives of deep suspicion with the
constant need for protection from enemies in all quarters, illustrating
the depth of the social fissures. The charismatic movements are no
doubt attempting to respond to this in some cases, but in others they
sometimes appeared to feed off it, and indeed to perpetuate and even
deepen the suspicion.

For Madame V., in Benin it all goes back to the "alliances with the
Vodún", or in the terms of Rev. Chigbundu, the feeling of "being tied"
to occult forces for whatever reason. She adds:

> It is not only in the CCRM that deliverance and healing are necessary,
> if one accepts that every African, *at least every Béninois*, has gone
> through certain stages before coming to the Catholic Church. [...] So
> prayers of healing and deliverance are necessary... before people come
> along with us they have to be disencumbered of the *Vodún*.

This leads to the final area I would like to look at in this chapter, the
development of the ministry of healing, deliverance and exorcism in the
Catholic Archdiocese of Cotonou and which works to some extent in
co-operation with the CCRM.[131] While exorcism has traditionally been

---

[131] This has not been without some reaction on the part of the hierarchy and
the authorities in Rome, somewhat suspicious following the controversial ministry
of Archbishop Milingo, formerly archbishop of Lusaka. Abbé Pamphile Fanou,
one of the official exorcists, told me that the Archbishop of Cotonou had suspended
him from this ministry for a period (interview, 10 June 2002.) I was reliably
informed that this followed an intervention by the Apostolic Nuncio. He was later
reinstated.

a reserved ministry[132] in the Catholic Church, and to my knowledge only rarely used, the Archdiocese now has four exorcists running regular services of healing, deliverance, and, where it is judged necessary, exorcism.[133] The Friday morning service at Sacré Cœur, when several other priests assist Abbé Pamphile Fanou, regularly draws as many as 2000 people.[134] There is also a highly-developed ministry dealing with individual cases of suspected possession requiring exorcism over an extended period. As I noted above, Fanou explains this phenomenon by a reference to Benin's history and the place of the Vodún in society. However, not unsurprisingly, he vehemently denies any connection, parallels or similarities between his function and that of the *Bokonù*, saying the two cannot be compared. He is equally disdainful of any reference to the CCC and is keen to emphasise his submission to the discipline of the Catholic Church, which he says is the source of legitimacy for his ministry. A superficial analysis would suggest that this official ministry was created at least partly in response to something more spontaneous that was emerging in the Catholic Church in Cotonou from the 1980s, most notably the appearance of visionaries, as well as phenomena associated with crying or bleeding statues.[135] This had much in common with aspects of the CCC and other Churches involved in healing and deliverance, and clearly worried the Catholic hierarchical authorities mindful of the Milingo case in Lusaka.[136] But it is also clear that this development follows the search for "endogenous knowledge" and solutions being pursued by Aguessy, Hountondji and others, which we looked at in Chapter II. Cartesian rationality and modern rational Christianity, however

---

[132] Only priests officially appointed to the task by the local bishops have the right to act as exorcists (see *Code of Canon Law*, 1172 §1, 2).

[133] Abbé Gilbert Dagnon is seen as having been the early advocate of this movement. See Gilbert Dagnon, *Libérer de la divination et de la sorcellerie*, Cotonou, 1999.

[134] Friday has also been developed in the CCC with special morning and evening services as well as a special devotion on the first Friday of each month. See de Surgy, *L'Eglise*, 119–123.

[135] These appear to have been closely attached to P. Gilbert Dagnon but were apparently also taken seriously by Archbishop de Souza. Among these was a young woman who claimed to have been spoken to by the Archangel Gabriel, who indicated to her a holy well at Gbédjomedi, near the Paroisse Sainte Rita in Cotonou. This well has become known as Golgotha and the water is regularly sought (and bought) for use in healing and deliverance services. It is used by the Abbé Fanou who provided some details on this phenomenon. Apparently there have been other similar cases.

[136] See Gerrie ter Haar, *Spirit of Africa: The Healing Ministry of Archbishop Milingo of Zambia*, London: Hurst, 1991.

socially committed, have failed to deal with *le mal béninois* and so
there is need for a *solution béninoise.*

A member of the CCRM explains it thus:

> I think it's a pastoral necessity in Benin. There is a lot of *méchanceté*
> among us...and when we are not happy with the other we go and ask
> occult forces to harm him/her...so I think what they are doing on Friday
> [the healing and deliverance services] are a kind of inculturation.

She notes the success of the CCC, which she accuses of syncretism
in the combat against witchcraft and curses, while admitting that she
has benefitted from their visions. At the same time, she notes that
when people fall ill with diseases that are not a *"hospital illness but
come from the witch"*, it is the CCC which is successful in treating
them. This she claims has led the Catholic Church to develop this
ministry:

> to show that in the Catholic Church also, without having the obligation
> to buy candles, and to pay colossal sums for the visions and oils and
> soaps they prepare,[137] without giving one franc one can also be *satisfied*
> from this point of view also. So I find that this is necessary, that it
> responds to a need... A great need, the need to feel protected by the
> Lord. And so since it has started one find that everybody is coming...
> Muslims... Vodúnsì... even Celestials.[138]

In the words of one pastor, the search appears to be for "an unction
that functions", at the best possible price, wherever it is to be found. It
is, however, perhaps more appropriate to take the terms of the classic
Negro spiritual and see it as a search for the balm of Gilead, to heal a
society still suffering from the wounds of its painful history and allow
it to move into a much longed-for modernity. The question of healing
and deliverance has become central all across the Christian religious
spectrum in Benin. When one considers the understanding of illness
one sees that this is just as much a commentary on a fractured society
as it is on either endemic illnesses or the state of the health service.
In a recent exchange on this subject, a Nigerian student commented:
"You can improve the health services all you want, but this will not

---

[137] See de Surgy, *Le Christianisme Céleste,* 56–59 for an explanation of the use
of cultic objects in the CCC.

[138] Interview, 9 September 2002.

solve the problem. The problem is relationships amongst people".[139] The underlying question, therefore, remains the fragility of the common bonds that are supposed to tie this society together. In the face of this fragility, modernity, as de Rosny pointed out, has only exacerbated the problem. There is indeed evidence that in the words of the student quoted earlier, Béninois today, and no doubt other West Africans, see themselves as a *"génération maudite"*. In terms of state-building, this poses serious problems since it is on the basis of these common bonds that the state is to be imagined, and their fragility will inevitably be reflected in the state itself. The recourse does indeed appear to be to the irrational rather than to socio-political engagement. There is indeed a kind of flight to the security of safer space across the protective walls of which one can shout the occasional veiled protest. It can be argued that at least these Charismatic Churches, ministries and movements provide a framework that channels the frustration of this generation and may prevent it from turning to something much worse, as the cases of Liberia, Sierra Leone and Ivory Coast graphically illustrate. There are other forces at work here and Lɛgbà can all too easily unleash unbridled violence in Benin too. In the absence of any real social agenda or any institutional substance, however, it is difficult to see how this level of Christianity can address the root causes of Benin's social and political problems. It is certainly significant that in the moments of real difficulty it aligns itself behind the mainline Churches that seem more adequately equipped for the task. On the other hand, they bring together large numbers of people and organise them, however loosely. There is evidence that when the circumstances appear to warrant it, a body such as the Christian Association of Nigeria (CAN) can spring into life and become an effective voice. In Benin this was to some extent the case during the CNFVN when, for a brief period, doctrinal divisions and inter-confessional competition were set aside and all the Christian Churches lined up behind the most powerful amongst them until social and political order had been restored. This did not go unnoticed by the state, and while the Churches have sensibly withdrawn from the political field they still remain a force that can be activated in times of stress.

---

[139] Comment by a Nigerian student during a class on Pentecostalism, Milltown Institute, Dublin, March 2004.

CHAPTER EIGHT

AFTERWORD

As I pointed out in the Introduction, this book started out as a personal reflection, and it eventually broadened into something more. It was written after a career in Africa, and after thirteen particularly enjoyable, interesting and rewarding years in Benin where my thinking on Africa in general developed considerably. During that time I developed many friendships and I left with a deep respect and affection for the Béninois in their dignity but also in their struggles. I am not unaware of their foibles, as they are not unaware of mine. I am aware of the limitations of my understanding, my cultural myopia, even after all those years. *"Le Blanc est toujours le Blanc, on n'y peut rien"*, however good a 'participant observer' he or she might be. To quote the Lɔkpa proverb: "It is not because the log floated in the water for a long time that it becomes a crocodile". Cultures yield their secrets reluctantly and we are often reduced to more or less educated speculation. I hope that this book will be read with this in mind.

Perhaps because of an innate personal optimism, I have not become an Afro-pessimist, although I do sometimes wonder where Africa is actually going. In the six years it has taken to write this book, I have not abandoned my belief that religion can make a positive contribution to social and political development. This can come from the symbolic capital and the discourse of the faith groups involved, which can have the potential both for unifying and dividing societies, as history attests. It also comes through the witnessing and actions of believers, and more discreetly in the changes it affects in personal attitudes and behaviour, as Weber so impressively demonstrated. To borrow a line from the Christian scripture, I hold the hope that believers of all traditions can be "salt" and "light" (Mt. 5: 13–14) in the creation of a more just society in Benin. Apart altogether from the fact that it would pose considerable existential questions if I had abandoned this conviction, I have also met many people who are actually trying to make a difference and they are doing so on the basis of their faith and religious convictions. Religious commitment does not necessarily mean bloody martyrdom or fanaticism. People professionally or, as they would put it, vocationally involved with religion, or simple believers, who try to use religious faith—Christian or otherwise—as a starting point in their lives can and do make a difference. Corresponding to the scriptural image of "the leaven" in the dough (Mt. 13: 33), it is often discreet but it is real and it occurs at all levels of society either through people's vision for society or through their very concrete actions to bring it about. This was something I came to appreciate even more deeply during my long conversation with Kä Mana. Despite the violence done in the name of religion—rightly pointed out by its critics—there is also evidence to suggest that it can contribute to the building of a just and peaceful society. While it may not be judged politic in some quarters to acknowledge this in the political and constitutional texts, I believe that, whatever its shortcomings, the Christian Church is one of the traditions that have contributed immensely to the edification of much that is best in our European tradition. While in Africa the tangled relationship with the colonial project requires further research and clarification, as well as some objectivity from all sides, there is evidence that when Churches commit themselves to change, it can be brought about, however slowly. There is also evidence and that they have made a positive contribution. That it does not happen more often may be due to their procrastination and an apparently innate conservatism but of course it can also be due to the sheer weight of the change that is required and the desire to make it happen. Sometimes it seems that even faith may not be enough to move mountains.

In his study of the Reformation, Elton notes:

> It will not do to treat the radical reformers as though only their theology mattered; neither the spread of their ideas nor the reaction of others can possibly be understood unless the secular discontent to which they give tongue is kept in mind.[1]

It is a fundamental theoretical tenet of my thesis that religion does not exist outside social circumstances and it responds to these in different ways. Thus, it can take on forms that one may find difficult to recognise as 'religious' in the more conventional sense. The course of religious history has often been one of decay and reformation. It seems to go down blind alleys and into dead ends to the point where

---

[1] G.R. Elton, *Europe from Renaissance to Reformation*, London: Folio Society, 2001, 68.

it becomes a caricature of itself, making Faustian deals of all kinds with the powers of *the world*. In these circumstances, it is certainly difficult to see it making a contribution to the edification of a more just society. Religion, then, can be aberrant or perhaps more accurately, aberrations occur within religions. It can also be, however, that one fails to recognise the dynamic of what is going on in a religious movement. This is particularly true, I feel, for the *outsider* coming with a weight of theological, doctrinal and cultural baggage which tends to define what 'true religion' *is*. One of the benefits I feel I have reaped from this research is the revision of my own idea of that. Religion as such, I have come to understand, really just *is*, across a very wide range of human experience. Defining it as 'true' or 'false', 'good' or 'bad', 'pure' or 'impure' is a tricky business and may lead to one missing the whole point. In an earlier chapter, I referred to Kä Mana's wonderful description of the religious spectrum in Africa as being composed of "the respectable", "the delirious", "the venerable", "illusion merchants", "true seekers of God", "counterfeiters of the sacred" and "the deep breath of the spirit" as well as the occasional "terrorist of the invisible". In the course of my fieldwork I encountered many of these fascinating characters. They were not all confined to one Church or ministry, there were bits of them in all, and in some cases several of them could be found, in some measure, in one individual. My deepest interest, however, has not been with what Weber describes as the religious "*virtuosi*", the professionals or what one Béninois described as "*les techniciens de la religion*". In my work I encountered people in many Churches who made a very positive impression on me as being, in my view, 'genuinely religious', 'true seekers of God' as well as true seekers of a better world. I did, of course, also encounter several people with something of an Elmer Gantry profile.[2] These were the religious 'big men' for whom, I admit, I found it very difficult to develop any empathy, and indeed few of whom seemed inclined to enter into any kind of relationship with me other than the purely perfunctory. Again, these were spread across the denominational spectrum. But my real interest was what I came to call 'the view from the pews'. The logic underlying the success of the professionals, saints or charlatans, is that they will only exist as long as they are reflecting what their followers want to hear,

---

[2] Sinclair Lewis' novel *Elmer Gantry* (1927) was an attack on the ignorant, gross, and predatory leaders who had crept into some of the Protestant Churches in the USA.

need to hear. My interest was in hearing what the followers were saying themselves, since I felt that it was here that I would find the answers to my questions. In addition, the faithful, in contrast to some of the professionals, were more than willing to talk about their lives and their experiences. Of the several hundred pages of field notes I compiled, by far the most interesting material came from these kinds of encounters (I hesitate to call them interviews). I only regret that I have not been able to use more of it in this book. For these people religion was as real as the often sad stories of their lives.

These narratives were my way into understanding something of what is going on in Benin today. They often bear witness to the fragility of the texture of Béninois society, even in its most intimate recesses. They help us to understand why there is such difficulty in establishing the kind of *contrat social* that would allow state and society to advance. I think the Béninois scholars I have cited are correct in their analysis of this. They have a real understanding of the problems besetting their society. What is less clear is what can be done to change the situation. The choice seems to be the recourse to the invisible, leading to what Mbembé has described as "*la prolif-eration du divin*". He suggests that it is the "intellectual atrophy" of the movement for socio-political change in Africa in general that has led to the rise of various "nativist ideologies and new cosmologies articulated around religious symbolism and the rehabilitation of occult forces".[3] Several of my sources among the Churches have reflected on this phenomenon with some regret, as I have noted in earlier chapters. One bishop expressed his frustration at the phenomenon, declaring, "Let's stop seeing the devil everywhere and let's start build-ing". Of course, it is not as easy as that, and even the intellectuals are tempted into what appears to be futile speculation in the search for an elusive endogenous knowledge, which itself often appears as a further retreat into the irrational. Goudjo speaks of the need for a "philosophical springboard" in order to find a way out of this impasse, and, wherever it is to be found, it is difficult to disagree with him. There is, as I suggest in my title, the desire for a *breakthrough* but finding it is not proving easy.

---

[3] Achille Mbembé, "Esquisses d'une démocratie à l'africaine", *Le Monde Diplo-matique*, March 2000, 20. See also Achille Mbembé, "Prolifération du divin en Afrique subsaharienne", in G. Kepel (ed.), *Les politiques de Dieu*, Paris: Seuil, 1993.

More positively, however, there has been the success of the CNFVN. No doubt its light has dimmed somewhat over the sixteen years since it happened, but having lived through it like many of my Béninois friends, I still like to think that the conference was at least the beginning of a new social contract for Benin. I, like them, *want* it to succeed and there are positive signs that it is doing so. It is still rightly spoken of with a certain pride as the "example" Benin has given to the rest of Africa. One can, of course, belittle this, but in the face of the alternatives at the time and events elsewhere in the region down to the present day, it has proved remarkably durable. In recent times there have been worrying signs of political atavism but these were resisted with strong calls for change. There were rumblings of reticence from the presidential palance and attempts to meddle with the constitution in order to make Kérékou *'président à vie'*, based on the claim that "peace, liberties, national unity and above all stability" can only be assured through a revision of the constitution *"around president Matthieu Kérékou"*. These, however, were strongly resisted and a successful presidential election was held in March 2006.

The election of Yahi Boni as President will serve to enhance this reputation and win the country plaudits for steady improvement on the democracy balance sheet and on governance. Despite numerous logistical gremlins, the election was considered both nationally and internationally to have been free and fair. Perhaps even more significantly the result has not been contested by any of the losing candidates. Indeed, quite to the contrary, they have been congratulating both the victor and the Béninois people on the consolidation of democracy in the country. Losing second-round candidate Adrien Houngbedji said:

> Our country has opened a new page in its history. It is the duty of all of us to get to work in order to open the page of reinforcing our unity, deepening our democracy, and launching our development.

This magnanimity was reciprocated by the victor. The result has been duly confirmed by the electoral commission and the Constitutional Court under whose authority the new president was sworn in on 6 April 2006.

In an astute comment on this and other recent elections in Africa, notably Ghana and Senegal, D. Cruise-O'Brien comments that perhaps the losers are to be applauded at least as much as the victors since their acceptance of defeat seems to indicate an acceptance of the process in which they have participated and to give due respect to the idea of the state and its legitimacy. And there were many losers in this election, with twenty-six contenders in the first round, on 5 March. Of these, four emerged as serious players; these included two 'dinosaurs' of Benin politics—Adrien Houngbedji, the sixty-four-year-old leader of the Democratic Renewal Party, a veteran politician who twice served as President of the National Assembly and who has made three previous attempts at winning the presidency, and Bruno Amoussou, the sixty-seven-year-old leader of the Social Democratic Party, also a veteran, former President of the National Assembly with four previous attempts at the presidency—and two newcomers to the scene—the non-party, former West African Development Bank (BOAD) technocrat Yahi Boni aged fifty-four, and Lehady Soglo, of the Benin 'Renaissance' party, son of the former president Nicéphore Dieudonné Soglo, who was himself excluded from contesting the election on grounds of age.

Outgoing president Matthieu Kérékou was also excluded on grounds of age, although there were ongoing rumours over the past year that the constitution might be changed to allow him to run again. This was ruled out by the Constitutional Court. One of the newspapers was also accused of reporting irresponsibly of a threatened coup in the lead-up to the election with the objective of allowing Kérékou to remain in office. Kérékou was, in fact, another one of the losers in the election since his preferred candidate was Houngbedji. In a situation similar to that which developed around the candidacy of Allasane Ouattarra in Ivory Coast, Kérékou was said to be behind moves to prevent the candidacy of Boni on the grounds that he was living and working abroad—in this case in neighbouring Togo. Kérékou also made curmudgeonly noises in the lead-up to the election, saying that funds were not available to run it and criticising candidates who he said were attempting to buy the electorate, apparently referring to Boni. Both the political institutions and civil society actors held firm in the face of this provocation and the elections went ahead peacefully, albeit in a somewhat shambolic fashion. However, as one observer noted, in typical Kérékou fashion the chameleon has had a final moult[4] and he now seems to have accepted the result which in the end will enhance his image as '*le père de la démocratie béninoise*' and assure

---

[4] Jean Baptiste Ketchateng, "Bénin: Mathieu Kérékou: la dernière mue du 'caméléon'", *Le Quotidien Mutations*, Yaoundé, 21 March 2006.

his place in history. A skirmish lost, a bigger battle perhaps won, it
can be hoped that if Kérékou is true to his previous form, he will
now retire quietly to a retirement that is unlikely to be threatened,
leaving the institutions of the state considerably strengthened.

It appears to me that religious groups contributed to the success
of this process of political stabilisation and development. This was
done first of all in their holding communities together in a period of
severe stress when the threat of violence was very real. I think they
also contributed to the success of the CNFVN and the transition by
providing a discourse of both change and reconciliation that allowed
the country to take at least some small steps forward. Some of the
Churches at least continue to follow this evolution with a genuine
interest and concern for 'the nation' in the most positive sense, and as
such, it appears to me, contribute to the edification of 'a nation' that
is struggling to imagine itself as just that. They have indeed retired
to a more pastoral space since the CNFVN, but this does not mean
they have disengaged from the process that the conference initiated.
To maintain their influence, however, as I pointed out in Chapter 6,
there is the ongoing need for intellectual reflection to be mirrored in
practical engagement on the ground, not just in charity and development but in building the dynamic within communities that can
make them effective actors in the arena of local and national politics.
There is the need to avoid the flight into the invisible which only
increases the power of the "the delirious", "the illusion merchants",
"the counterfeiters of the sacred", and "the terrorists of the invisible"
who lurk behind any false religious dawn. The temptation is to think
in terms of 'market share' and the attempt to counter what is often
seen as 'leakage' to 'sects' by improvisation in the name of some
kind of superficial *inculturation*. This appears to me to be an error
and, in the long run, damaging.

One of the great achievements of the Reformation was to bring
religion out of the cloisters and the hands of the religious *virtuosi*
and inject it into the real lives of people, making it more 'worldly'
and ethical and thus a greater force for social change. There has been
talk of an African Reformation[5] and the hope of an African *Kairos*
but it is not yet clear that this is actually happening. Whatever the
claims of several of the authors I have mentioned earlier in this book

---

[5] Anderson, *African Reformation*.

regarding religious groups and social change, particularly in Pentecostalism, there is much evidence to suggest that what is actually
happening is often a flight from the world into a kind of religious
marronnage. What is sometimes hailed as a *"foisonnement chrétien"*
is indeed more a sign of deep social malaise, a commentary on a
society in difficulty and crying out for help.[6] Some of the religious
leaders clearly realise this but it is equally true that there is a lot of
improvisation among the pastors of all denominations that is inimical
to any kind of real development. The "false prophets", the "vultures"
preying on the poor received harsh treatment in the scriptures (Galatians
1: 10; Galatians 4: 17; 2 Timothy 3: 6; 2 Peter 2: 3; 2 Peter 2: 18;
Revelation 2: 14; Revelation 2: 20) and the history of the Church is
darkened by many examples of the abuse of religious power, again
almost always at the expense of the poor. Many of the things I saw
in the course of my research across the denominational spectrum
left me with a feeling of deep unease. I will no doubt be accused of
rationalist Eurocentrism for expressing these reservations. However,
while I acknowledge the complexity of the religious field, and the
many different levels on which it operates, I remain convinced of
the need for a faith informed by reason and I am deeply suspicious
of any flight into the esoteric, the arcane or the irrational. While
one seeks to understand what is happening, critical reason cannot be
abandoned in the face of arguments based on some kind of essentialist
argument about 'authentic African religiosity' from whatever quarter
it may come—and these will not be just African.

   In my view, the greatest challenge facing Benin is in coming to
terms with its history, making the jump from what Achille Mbémbé
has described as "the victimisation paradigm"[7] into a more positive
engagement with the world. As Smith points out, "the exploitation"
of an Africa living in a kind of *primordial solidarity* "by Western
cupidity is a caricature, even if there is abuse of confidence and
inequality in the relations of strength which place the continent in
a position of weakness".[8] Young Africans are increasingly sceptical
of what they see as a vacuous trope of ivory-tower intellectuals and

---

[6] See Patrick Claffey, "Foisonnement chrétien ou signes de malaise social?", *Spiritus*
171, 2003, 190–205.
[7] Achille Mbembé, *On the Postcolony*, Berkeley/London: University of California
Press, 2001.
[8] Smith, *Négrologie*, 58.

a corrupt political elite short of ideas. In the face of globalisation, however, Smith notes the tendency of Africa "to reinvent its difference and to close in increasingly upon itself". Goudjo has made similar observations in an earlier chapter in speaking of Benin and its need for new *springboards* from which to launch itself into modernity and come to terms with its past. Part of this process must inevitably be an acknowledgement of and reconciliation with the past, a healing of the memory, to use the expression of Adoukonou, which allows society to move on. In my time with scholars in Benin, I saw both sides of this problem. At two gatherings, one Catholic and one Protestant, I was appalled at the repetition of the victimisation thesis in a way that seemed to me hopelessly negative and to be digging the hole even deeper. I am not sure to what extent this was exacerbated by my presence as the sole European. If this were the case, it would be even more worrying, as it would illustrate the depth of the problem in entering into any kind of relationship with the Other. On the other hand, I met several scholars who privately acknowledged the depth of this problem and the urgency of dealing with it and this must be taken as a hopeful sign. If the Churches can contribute to this process, if they can tell an *Exodus* story, then they will have made an important contribution.

APPENDIX 1: THE KINGS OF DANXOMƐ[1]

Gangnihessou (c. 1600)[2]

Symbols: A bird (a *gangnihessou*), a drusm and a club.
Motto: I am the biggest bird and the most sonorous drum. One cannot prevent the bird from singing or the drum from sounding.

1. **Dako** (c. 1620) Overthrew Gangnihessou to take the throne.

Symbols: A jar of indigo and a war club.
Motto: Dako kills Konou as easily as he would break a jar of indigo.

2. **Huégbaja** (c. 1645–1685) Son of Gangnihessou. Considered to have been the real founder of the dynasty and the creator of a strong political culture. Centred the kingdom at AgbŏmƐ and built the first palace as well as starting the policy of expansion and conquest and imposing legislation and a bureaucracy.

Symbols: A fish, a fish trap, and a hoe in the form of a club.
Motto: A fish that escapes from the trap will never return.

3. **Akábá** (c. 1685–1708) Son of Huégbaja and Nan Adonon. Little known apart from a few local innovations.

Symbols: A wild boar, a sabre. Also chameleon.
Motto: When the wild boar looks to the sky his throat will be cut. Also: Slowly but surely the chameleon will climb the Banyan tree.

4. **Agajá** (1708–1732) Son of Huégbaja and Nan Adonon. Known as "the Great Warrior". Led the biggest expansion in the history of the kingdom, particularly the conquest of both Xwedá and Aladà. Established the first contact with the European traders and the monopoly

---

[1] *Sources*: Honorat Aguessy, *Du mode d'existence de l'Etat sous Guezo 1818–1825.* (Thèse), Paris, Sorbonne, 1970, Francesca Piqué; Leslie H. Rainier, *Les Bas-reliefs d'Abomey: L'Histoire racontée sur les murs*, Cotonou: Flamboyant/Paul Getty Trust, 1999; Basilio Segurola and Jean Rassinoux, *Dictionnaire Fòn-Français* Madrid: SMA, 2000; Jean Rassinoux, *Dictionnaire Français-Fòn*, Madrid: SMA, 2001.
[2] Gangnihessou's place amongst the kings is unclear since the line is generally considered to have started with Dako.

of the monarchy over the slave trade, thus imposing a certain order in the anarchy that had reigned. Apart, perhaps, from Gezò, the most influential king in the history of the dynasty.

Symbols: A European caravel
Motto: Nobody can set fire to a big tree felled with all its branches. First of all it must be cut up.

5. **Tegbesú** (1732–1774) Son of Agajá and Nan Huanjile. Held under house arrest in Oyo as a young man as part of the tribute to that kingdom. Oversaw the expansion of the port at Xwedá but was also forced to pay tribute to Oyo following defeat in 1738.

Symbols: A buffalo wearing a tunic. Also a blunderbuss and a door decorated with three heads with noses.
Motto: Nothing will make the buffalo take off his tunic. Also: All the weeds and leaves that cover the ground will not prevent the young Tegbesú from growing.

6. **Kpénglá** (1774–1789) Son of Tegbesú and Nan Cai. Reinforced the army, adding conquests of coastal towns, consolidating the royal monopoly of the slave trade.

Symbols: A bird (*akpan*). A rifle.
Motto: The *akpan* will kill other birds when annoyed. Also: A stone neither feels nor fears while cold when it is in water.

7. **Agøngló** (1789–1797) Son of Kpénglá and Nan Senume. Known as a great reformer. Opened the kingdom to Christian missionaries and apparently also to Muslims. There is some evidence that he was seeking a new theological basis for the monarchy. Also reinforced the Vodún and introduced the rite of Zomadónv as an exclusive cult of the dynasty. The first king to have a European wife.

Symbol: A pineapple.
Motto: Lighting will strike the oil palm, but never the pine, which lies, nears the ground.

♦ **Adandozan** (1797–1818).[3] Eldest son of Agøngló. The most controversial of the kings. His name has been removed from the line

[3] Adandozan's place is not fully recognised because his reign ended in disgrace, although there are now efforts to rehabilitate him.

to this day, although there is some evidence that he may be rehabilitated. There is evidence of a severe power struggle during this
period. Overthrown in a palace coup because he wanted to reduce the
power of the Vodúnnò, extend the slave trade and human sacrifices to
include princes. It seems possible that he was mentally ill or suffered
from alcoholism. Significantly he was not forced to 'eat the parrot's
eggs' but went into several years of internal exile. He survived his
successor and died only in 1861, when he was apparently buried in
accordance with royal custom.

Symbol: A large umbrella.
Motto: The king makes shade for his enemies.

8. **Gezò** (1818–1858) Son of Agøngló and Nan Agontimè. Succeeded
Adandozan following a coup. Much lauded by those who see the
kingdom in a more positive light. In his doctoral thesis *Du Monde
de l'existence de l'Etat sous Guézo (1818–1858)*, (1970), Honorat
Aguessy, stretched the reign of the hero-king by one year to 1859,
thus allowing him to attain forty-one years of reign. The figure forty-
one has arcane significance for the Fòn being the figure of perfection,
four cords of ten beads, plus one. A diplomat, he managed to unite
the kingdom following the coup. Reinforced the army and ended the
tribute to Oyo.

Symbols: The holed water jar. The buffalo.
Motto: The powerful buffalo strides across the country and nothing can
oppose him or stop him. Also: The red feathers of the Red Bishop
bird *[Euplectes hordaceus]* may look like fire but they cannot set
light to the bush.

9. **Glɛlέ** (1858–1889) Son of Gezò and Nan Zognidi. Following a
contentious succession, in the face of the remaining supporters of
Adandozan, he faced both internal and external opposition. Con-
solidated the supremacy of Danxomɛ in the region following thirty
military campaigns. Developed cultural activities as well as the Vodún
cults. Was widely reputed in Europe as one of the great African kings,
leading to the missions of Burton in 1861 and 1864. He resisted the
anti-slavery movement but eventually had to concede.

Symbols: A lion. The ritual knife of Gʋ, the Vodún of war.
Motto: The knife of Gʋ will punish the rebels.

10. **Gbɛhanzın** (1889–1894) Son of Glɛlé and Nan Zevotin. His name derives from the expression *"gbɛ hɛ́n azin ayi jló"* (The world holds the egg that the earth desires). The last king, he resisted colonisation fiercely but fell to Dodds in 1894. Exiled to Martinique in 1895. Died in Algeria in 1906.

Symbols: An egg. A shark.
Motto: I am a shark, I shall not abandon one inch of my territory.

11. **Agoli-Agbŏ I** (1894–1900) Son of Glɛlé and Nan Kannanyi. Installed by the French following the exile of Gbɛhanzın. Sought to rebuild the palaces at Abomey. However, when he refused the purely symbolic role assigned to him by the French, he was exiled and the monarchy was abolished.

Symbols: A foot hitting a stone. A sweeping brush.
Motto: Take care! The dynasty of the kings of Danxomɛ has trembled but it has not fallen. Also: The king is like a brush that sweeps away his enemies.

APPENDIX 2: THE VODÚN PANTHEON

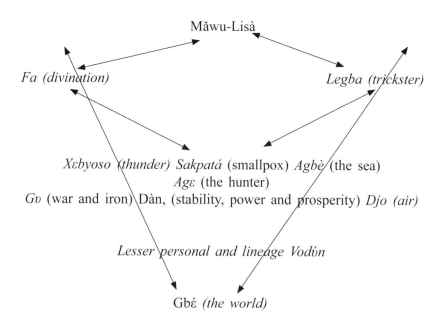

Măwu-Lisà

Fa (divination)

Legba (trickster)

Xɛbyoso (thunder) Sakpatá (smallpox) Agbè (the sea)
Agɛ (the hunter)
Gʋ (war and iron) Dàn, (stability, power and prosperity) Djo (air)

Lesser personal and lineage Vodún

Gbɛ́ (the world)

APPENDIX 3A: AN INTERPRETATION
OF THE ACTIVE RELATIONSHIP BETWEEN
THE VISIBLE AND INVISIBLE WORLDS[1]

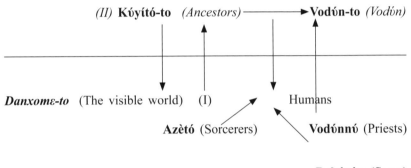

The invisible world   *(III) Absolute—The Supreme Being (MÇwu)*

(II) **Kúyító-to** *(Ancestors)* ──────►**Vodún-to** *(Vodún)*

Danxomɛ-to (The visible world)   (I)   Humans

Azètó (Sorcerers)   **Vodúnnú** (Priests)

Bokónòn (Seers)

Bòwàtó (Healers)

E nyi Vodún-to do t,e lononu Kúyito-to do te o, Danxomɛ-to ko gba a.
(If the world of the ancestors and the world of the Vodún hold together,
then Danxomɛ will hold together.)

[1] Based on Sodokin Codjo, *Les "Syncrétismes" Religieux Contemporains et la Société Béninoise (Le Cas du Christianisme Céleste)* (Thèse de doctorat de 3ème Cycle en Histoire et Civilisations), Université de Lyon, 1984.

APPENDIX 3B: NOTES ON THE MASKED CULTS

Egún

If, as the saying in Appendix 3a states, Vodún was one leg of the cult that held Dahomey together, the other was the deceased ancestors. Peel notes that these aspects of religious life "reach out"[1] to each other in interdependence and link to form a cohesive world. Thus there were, and still are, public manifestations of devotion to the ancestors as a collective group[2] in the colourful masked cult of Egún. Peel gives an elegant interpretation of this phenomenon, which is consistent with the way I have attempted to describe the religious world of the Fòn:

> The Orisha had as their first function to represent alien and obdurate forces of nature, powers that we 'out there' but prone to intrude with devastating effect on human life. Ancestors, by contrast, were continuous and consubstantial with their descendants, which guaranteed their human approachability. The one stood for realism about the conditions in which life had to be lived, the other represented hope that something could be done about its problems. The 'dream ticket' of Yoruba religion was a natural power with the qualities of a parent. To the extent that it was impossible to achieve a lasting high-level synthesis of hope and realism, what emerged was a shifting series of trade-offs: the *Orisha* were the outcome of moves to humanise alien or natural powers, while *Egungugun*…were deceased parents correspondingly enhanced.[3]

The reasoning in Danxomɛ was very similar and in this synthesis of realism and hope the Gbɛ́ was held together however tentatively.

Gɛlɛdé

Gɛlɛdé is another masked cult, originally common in the Ouémé valley on the Nigerian border. Although the masquerades are performed

---

[1] Peel, *Religious Encounter*, 93.
[2] Peel notes that in this form the ancestors were not individual but "collapsed into one another to be represented in this collective form" (ibid., 97).
[3] Ibid.

entirely by men, women run the society which is responsible for the cult. Its purpose is a kind of spiritual policing as it seeks "to combat supernatural evil influences which sow discord in villages, decimate populations through epidemics and destroy harvests through prolonged drought and the invasion of rats".[4] These misfortunes are brought about through the power of female witches the cult is called upon to assuage.

Zàngbètó

More mysterious in appearance than either the *Egún* or *Gɛlɛdɛ́*, *Zàngbètó* is represented as a mobile stack of straw, often very small, and dancing in the impressive, stylised, swirling fashion. Verger describes it as a *"chasseur de nuit"* and a kind of "policeman" or "night watchman".[5] Associated with Lɛgbà, his protector, he also demonstrates a kind of anarchical and unpredictable nature and a tendency to overstep the limits of his authority in being aggressive even to innocent bystanders.

---

[4] Verger, *Notes*, 566.
[5] Ibid., 566–567.

APPENDIX 4: ADAHOONZOU'S SPEECH, UPON HEARING WHAT HAS PASSED IN ENGLAND UPON THE SUBJECT OF THE SLAVE-TRADE[1]

I admire the reasoning of the white man; but, with all their sense, it does not appear that they have thoroughly studied the nature of the blacks, whose disposition differs as much from that of the whites, as their colour. The same Great Being formed both; and since it hath seemed convenient for him to distinguish mankind by opposite complexions, it is a fair conclusion to presume, that there may be as great a disagreement in the qualities of their minds. There is likewise a remarkable difference in the countries we inhabit. You, Englishmen, for instance, as I have been informed, are surrounded by the ocean, and, by this situation, seem intended to hold communications with the whole world, which you do by means of your ships; whilst we Dahomeans, being placed on a large continent, and…hemmed in amidst a variety of other people, of the same complexion, but speaking different languages are obliged by the sharpness of our swords, to defend ourselves from their incursions, and punish the depredations they make on us. Such conduct in them is productive of incessant war. Your countrymen, therefore, who alledge [sic] that we go to war for the purpose of supplying your ships with slaves, are grossly mistaken.

You think you can work a reformation, as you call it, in the manners of the blacks, but you ought to consider the disproportion between the magnitudes of the two countries; and then you would soon be convinced of the difficulties that must be surmounted, to change the system of such a vast country as this. We know you are a brave people, and that you might bring over a great many of the blacks to your opinions, by the points of your bayonets; but to effect this a great many must be put to death, and numerous cruelties must be committed, which we do not find to have been the practice of the whites; besides, that this would militate against the very principle which is professed by those who wish to bring about a reformation.

---

[1] From Archibald Dalzel, *The History of Dahomey—an Inland Kingdom*, London, 1793/1967, 217–221.

In the name of my ancestors and myself I aver, that no Dahomean man ever embarked in war merely for the sake of procuring
wherewithal to purchase your commodities. I, who have not long
been master of this country, have, without thinking of the market,
killed many thousands, and I shall kill many thousands more. When
policy or justice requires that men be put to death, neither silk, nor
coral, nor brandy, nor cowries, can be accepted as substitutes for
the blood that ought to be spilt for example sake. Besides, if white
men chuse [sic] to remain at home, and no longer visit this country for the same purpose that has usually brought them hither, will
black men cease to make war? I answer, by no means. And if there
be no ships for their captives, what will become of them? I answer
for you, they will be put to death. Perhaps you may ask, how will
the blacks be punished with guns and powder? I reply by another
question; had we not clubs, and bows, and arrows, before we knew
white men? Did you not see me make Custom for Weebaigah, the
third King of Dahomey? And did you not observe, on the day such
ceremony was performing, that I carried a bow in my hand, and a
quiver filled with arrows on my back? These were the emblems of
the times, when, with such weapons, that brave ancestor fought and
conquered all his neighbours. God made war for all the world; and
every kingdom, large or small, has practised it more or less, though
perhaps in a manner unlike, and upon different principles. Did Weebaigah sell slaves? No, his prisoners were all killed to a man. What
else could he have done with them? Was he to let them remain in
his country, to cut the throat of his subjects? This would have been
a wretched policy indeed, which, had it been adopted, the Dahomean
name would have long ago been extinguished, instead of becoming,
as it is at this day, the terror of the surrounding nations. What hurts
me most is, that some of your people have maliciously represented
us in books, which never die, alledging, that we sell our wives and
children for the sake of procuring a few kegs of brandy. No, we are
shamefully belied; and I hope you will contradict, from my mouth,
the scandalous stories that have been propagated; and tell posterity
that we have been abused. We do, indeed sell to the white men a part
of our prisoners, and we have a right to do so. Are not all prisoners
at the disposal of their captors? And are we to blame, if we send
delinquents to a far country? I have been told, you do the same. If
you want more slaves from us, why cannot you be ingenuous and tell
the plain truth; saying, that they slaves you have already purchased

are sufficient for the country for which you bought them, or that the artist who used to make fine things are all dead, without having taught any body to make more? But for a parcel of men with long heads, to sit down in England, and frame laws for us and pretend to dictate how we live, of whom they know nothing, never having been in a black man's country during the whole course of their lives, is to me quite extraordinary. No doubt they must have been biassed [sic] by the report of some one who has had to do with us, who, for want of a due knowledge of the treatment of slaves, found that they died on his hands, and that his money was lost; and seeing others thrive by the traffic, he, envious of their good luck, has vilified both black and white traders.

You have seen me kill many at the Customs; and you have often observed delinquents at Grigwhee, and others of my provinces, tied, and sent up to me. I kill them; but do I ever insist on being paid for them? Some heads I order to be placed at my door; others to be strewed about the market place, that people may stumble upon them when they little expect such a sight. This gives a grandeur to my Customs, far beyond the display of fine things, and gives me such a name in the bush. Besides, if I should neglect this indispensable duty, would my ancestors suffer me to live? Would they not trouble me day and night, and say, that I sent nobody to serve them, that I was only solicitous about my own name and forgetful of my ancestors? White men are not acquainted with these circumstances; but I now tell you, that you may hear, and know, and inform your countrymen, why Customs are made, and will be made, as long as black men continue to possess their own country. The few that can be spared from this necessary celebration, we sell to the white men. And happy, no doubt, are such, when they find themselves on the path for Grigwhee, to be disposed of to the Europeans. We shall still drink water, they say to themselves; *white men will not kill us; and we may even avoid punishment, by serving our new masters with fidelity.*

APPENDIX 5: FORBES' ACCOUNT OF THE CUSTOMS[1]

If I were to conclude the history of this day's Customs here, I should merely remark that there might be a policy in making appear munificence the distribution of a sum of money, that if doled out to each individually, would prove a miserable pittance, although it tended much to debase the minds of this people, if that were possible. But what follows is almost too revolting to be recorded.

As if by general consent, and evincing a slight dawning of decency, hardly to be expected from these truly barbarians, silence reigned, and when broken, the eunuchs would strike a metal instrument each was supplied with, to enforce it, sounding the knell of eleven unfortunate human beings, whose only crime known to their persecutors was that they belonged to a nation Dahomey has warred against, Attahpam.[2] Out of fourteen now brought upon the platform, we, the unworthy instruments of Providence, succeeded in saving the lives of three. Lashed as described in yesterday's journal, except that only four were in boats, the remainder in baskets, these unfortunates gagged, met the gaze of their enemies with a firmness perfectly astonishing—not a sign was breathed. One cowardly villain put his hands to the eyes of a victim, who say with his head down, to feel for moisture; finding none, he drew upon himself the ridicule of his hellish coadjutors. Ten of these human offerings to the vitiated appetite of his soldiers, and the alligator and cat, were guarded by the male soldiers, and to the right of the King; four to the left were guarded by women.

Being commanded into the presence, the King asked if we wished to be present at the sacrifice; with horror we declined, and begged to be allowed to save a few by purchasing. After a little hesitation, we were asked which we would have; I claimed the first and last of the ten, while Mr Beecroft claimed the nearest of the four, and 100 dollars being stated as the price, was gladly accepted. In all my life I never saw such coolness so near death: the most attentive ear could

[1] Extracts from T. Coates (ed.), *King Guézo of Dahomey, 1950–52: the Abolition of the Slave Trade on the West Coast of Africa*, London: The Stationery Office, 2001, 65–66.
[2] Atakpamé, now in neighbouring Togo.

not have caught the breath of a single sigh—it did not look reality, yet it soon proved fearfully so.

Retiring to our seats the King insisted on our viewing the place of sacrifice. Immediately under the Royal canopy were six or seven executioners armed with large knives, grinning horribly; the mob now armed with clubs and branches, yelled furiously, calling upon the King to "feed them—they were hungry".

Scarcely had we reached our seats, when a demoniac yelling, caused us to look back. The King was showing the immolations to his people, and now they were raised over the heads of their carriers, while the Monarch made a speech to the soldiers, telling them that these were the prisoners from Attahpam, he called their names. The Charchar[3] left at the same time with ourselves, but Ignacio and Antonio da Souza remained spectators.

The unfortunate being nearest the King, stripped of his clothes, was now placed on end on the parapet, the King giving the upper part of the boat an impetus, a descent of twelve feet stunned the victim, and before animation could return, the head was off; the body, beaten by the mob, was dragged by the heels to a pit at a little distance, and there left prey to wolves and vultures.

After the third the King retired; not so the slave merchants. When all was over, at 3pm, we were permitted to retire. At the foot of the ladder in the boats and baskets lay the bleeding heads.

It is my duty to describe; I leave exposition to the reader.

---

[3] The King's representative at the slave port of Ouidah, the viceroy of Ouidah.

APPENDIX 6: EXTRACTS FROM PAUL HAZOUME'S NOVEL DOGUCIMI

Scene portraying a father delivering his child for sacrifice
in the Customs, p. 88

To console the poor victim of a despotic custom and restore her confidence, the head of the family told her after finishing his prayers: "Stop crying, my child, don't worry about the future. The ancestors will watch over you and lead you to happiness; the banana only becomes soft when it begins to ripen. Out of this harsh separation happiness will grow."

The head of the family arrived at the Governor's residence with the young girl and said as he kissed the ground: "I am returning the ward that was entrusted to my custody so that it can be sent to the one who is Father and Mother of the People."

The separation was painful, but the relatives had to resign themselves to it, the Dahomênou was but a mere breeding animal for the royal herd. The offspring belonged neither to the male nor to the female. The Master of the World could dispose of them as he saw fit. One could hardly blame Guezo, who was simply the heir to the tradition. (88)

Scene portraying Dogucimi's resistance to the King, p. 112

"Because you want to shed innocent blood in total disregard for the wishes of your ancestors, perform your crime without trying to justify it. But I will be ashamed for you, you who consider yourself above the human race, if I ever meet you in the realm of the spirits, because unfortunately for you, I will not close the Door to the country of the dead!"

"What you are saying is true, Mahinou! All the crimes perpetrated against innocent people in this kingdom will not remain unpunished!" applauded Dogucimi, who rose above the prostrate crown at the foot of the throne. She continued, addressing the king: "You did not go to Togoudo to purify yourself, as the custom, which was scrupulously respected before you, requires one to do each year. How did you dare show yourself in an impure state at the tomb of Agonglo, and make offerings to him? Neither he nor his predecessors approve of anything that comes from hands that have been stained with the blood of their descendants…"

The crowd had been transfixed by the blasphemies of the "horse" and the audacity of Dogucimi, whose diatribes against the Master of the World upon his return from Hounjroto were still fresh in people's minds at the court.

APPENDIX 7: SOME OF THE MOST IMPORTANT NINETEENTH-CENTURY CATHOLIC ORDERS OR INSTITUTES DEDICATED TO MISSION IN AFRICA

Male Institutes

La Congrégation du Saint Esprit et du Cœur Immaculé de Marie (1846)
La Société des Missions Africaines (1856)
Instituta delle Missioni per la Nigrizia later known as the Congrégation de Fils du Sacré Cœurs de l'Afrique (Verona Fathers) (1867)
The Society of Missionaries of Africa or Pères Blancs (1868)

Female Institutes

Sœurs de l'Immaculée Conception de Castres (1850)
Religieuses de Notre Dame de Lyon (1861)
Sœurs de Notre Dame de l'Afrique (1869)
Sœurs de Notre Dame des Apôtres (1876)

APPENDIX 8: DEMOGRAPHIC STATISTICS AND SOME SOCIO-ECONOMIC INDICATORS[1]

Total population: 6,558,000 (Cotonou population 673,903 (10.6% of population). Under 18: 3,463,000; under 5: 1,145,000. Offical unemployment: 13%. Population growth rate (1990–2002): 2.9%. Percentage of population urbanised: 44%. Average annual growth rate of urban population (%): 4.9%.

Under-5 mortality rate: 156 per 1,000 (2001). Life expectancy at birth (years): 51 (2002). Life expectancy: females as a % of males: 110.

GNI per capita: (US$) 380 (2002). GDP per capita average annual growth rate (%): (1990–2002). 2% Inflation: 8%. Percentage of central government expenditure allocated: health 6%; education 31%; defence 17% (1992–2001).

Overseas Development Aid: Inflow in US$: 273 million (2001). ODA inflow as a % of recipient GNI: 11% (2001).

Debt service as a % of exports of goods and services: 6%.

Total adult literacy rate: 38% (2001). Adult literacy rate: females as a % of males: 45%.

Net primary school enrolment/attendance: 54%.

Net secondary school enrolment/attendance: 22%.

Estimated number of people living with HIV/AIDS: 120,000 (end-2001).

Note: Benin was classified 158th amongst the coutries of the world based on the above data (2002 Report of the United National Programme for Development).

[1] *Source*: Http://www.unicef.org/infobycountry/benin_statistics.html.

APPENDIX 9A: DEFINITIONS OF THE KEY ELEMENTS FROM THE CATHOLIC SOCIAL TEACHING

The Dignity of the Human Person

John XXIII wrote the basic principle of the social doctrine is that individual men and women are necessarily "the foundation, cause and end of all social institutions,..." (John XXIII, Mater et Magistra, 1961: 219) The council document *Gaudium et Spes* adds: "In the economic and social realms...the dignity and complete vocation of the human person and the welfare of society as a whole are to be respected and promoted. For man is the source, the centre, and the purpose of all economic and social life," (*Gaudium et Spes*, 63).

The Supremacy of Truth

The Supreme good and moral good meet in truth: the truth of God, the Creator and Redeemer, and the truth of man, created and redeemed by him. Only upon this truth is it possible to construct a renewed society and to solve complex and weighty problems affecting it, above all, the problem of overcoming the various forms of totalitarianism, so as to make way for the authentic freedom of the person. "Totalitarianism arises out of a denial of truth in the objective sense. If there is no transcendent truth, in obedience to which man achieves his full identity, there is no sure principle for guaranteeing just relations between people. Their self-interest as a class, group or nation would inevitably set them in opposition to one another," (John Paul II, *Veritatis Splendor*, 1993, 99).

The Common Good

By the common good is to be understood "the sum total of social conditions which allow people, either as groups or as individuals, to reach their fulfilment more fully and more easily" (*Gaudium et Spes*, 26).

"The common good concerns the life of all. It calls for prudence from each, and even more from those who exercise the office of authority. *It consists of three essential elements*: First, the common good presupposes respect for the person as such. In the name of the common good, public authorities are bound to respect the fundamental and inalienable rights of the human person. Society should permit each of its members to fulfil his vocation. In particular, the common good resides in the conditions for the exercise of natural freedoms indispensable for the development of the human vocation, such as "the right to act according to a sound norm of conscience and to safeguard... privacy, and rightful freedom also in matters of religion" (*Gaudiam et Spes*, 26).

Second, the common good requires the social well-being and development of the group itself. "Development is the epitome of all social duties. Certainly it is the proper function of authority to arbitrate, in the name of the common good, between various particular interests; but it should make accessible to each what is needed to lead a truly human life: food, clothing, health, work, education and culture, suitable information, the right to establish a family, and so on. Finally, the common good requires peace, that is the stability and security of a just order. It presupposes that authority should ensure by morally acceptable means the security of society and its members. It is the basis of the right to legitimate personal and collective defence." *Code of Canon Law*, nn, 1906–1909).

Justice for all

Justice for all is based on the joint principles of *solidarity* and *subsidiarity*. "African cultures have an acute sense of *solidarity* and community life. In Africa it is unthinkable to celebrate a feast without the participation of the whole village. Indeed, community life in African societies expresses the extended family. It is my ardent hope and prayer that Africa will always preserve this priceless cultural heritage and never succumb to the temptation to individualism, which is so alien to its best traditions." (*Ecclesia in Africa*, 1995: 43).

"God has not willed to reserve to himself all exercise of power. He entrusts to every creature the functions it is capable of performing according to the capacities of its own nature. This mode of governance ought to be followed in social life. The way God acts in governing the world, which bears witness to such great regard for human freedom, should inspire the wisdom of those who govern human communities. They should behave as ministers of divine providence. The principle of *subsidiarity* is opposed to all forms of collectivism. It sets limits for state intervention. It aims at harmonising the relationships between individuals and societies. It tends toward the establishment of true international order," (*Code of Canon Law*, nn, 1883–1885).

APPENDIX 9B: EXTRACTS FROM THE SOCIO-POLITICAL CHAPTERS OF *ECCLESIA IN AFRICA*

Ecclesial dimension of witness

106. The Synod Fathers drew attention to the ecclesial dimension of this witness and solemnly declared: "The Church must continue to play her prophetic role and be the voice of the voiceless" (208).

But to achieve this effectively, the Church, as a community of faith, must be an energetic witness to justice and peace in her structures and in the relationships among her members. The *Message of the Synod* courageously states: "The Churches in Africa are also aware that, insofar as their own internal affairs are concerned, justice is not always respected with regard to those men and women who are at their service. If the Church is to give witness to justice, she recognizes that whoever dares to speak to others about justice should also strive to be just in their eyes. It is necessary therefore to examine with care the procedures, the possessions and the life style of the Church" (209).

In what concerns the promotion of justice and especially the defence of fundamental human rights, the Church's apostolate cannot be improvised. Aware that in many African countries gross violations of human dignity and rights are being perpetrated, I ask the Episcopal Conferences to establish, where they do not yet exist, Justice and Peace Commissions at various levels. These will awaken Christian communities to their evangelical responsibilities in the defence of human rights (210).

107. If the proclamation of justice and peace is an integral part of the task of evangelization, it follows that the promotion of these values should also be a part of the pastoral programme of each Christian community. That is why I urge that all pastoral agents are to be adequately trained for this apostolate. "The formation of clergy, religious and laity, imparted in the areas of their apostolate, should lay emphasis on the social teaching of the Church. Each person, according to his state of life, should be specially trained to know his rights and duties, the meaning and service of the common good, honest management of public goods and the proper manner of

participating in political life, in order to be able to act in a credible manner in the face of social injustices" (211).

As a body organized within the community and the nation, the Church has both the right and the duty to participate fully in building a just and peaceful society with all the means at her disposal. Here we must mention the Church's apostolate in the areas of education, health care, social awareness and in other programmes of assistance. In the measure that these activities help to reduce ignorance, improve public health and promote a greater participation of all in solving the problems of society in a spirit of freedom and co-responsibility, the Church creates conditions for the progress of justice and peace.

Social and political difficulties

51. "In Africa, the need to apply the Gospel to concrete life is felt strongly. How could one proclaim Christ on that immense Continent while forgetting that it is one of the world's poorest regions? How could one fail to take into account the anguished history of a land where many nations are still in the grip of famine, war, racial and tribal tensions, political instability and the violation of human rights? This is all a challenge to evangelization" (64).

All the preparatory documents of the Synod, as well as the discussions in the Assembly, clearly showed that issues in Africa such as increasing poverty, urbanization, the international debt, the arms trade, the problem of refugees and displaced persons, demographic concerns and threats to the family, the liberation of women, the spread of AIDS, the survival of the practice of slavery in some places, ethnocentricity and tribal opposition figure among the fundamental challenges addressed by the Synod.

The salt of the earth

108. In the pluralistic societies of our day, it is especially due to the commitment of Catholics in public life that the Church can exercise a positive influence. Whether they be professionals or teachers, businessmen or civil servants, law enforcement agents or politicians, Catholics are expected to bear witness to goodness, truth, justice and love of

God in their daily life. "The task of the faithful lay person...is to be the salt of the earth and light of the world, especially in those places where only a lay person is able to render the Church present" (212).

Co-operation with other believers

109. The obligation to commit oneself to the development of peoples is not just an *individual* duty, and still less an *individualistic* one, as if it were possible to achieve this development through the isolated efforts of each person. It is a responsibility which obliges *each and every man and woman*, as well as *societies and nations*. In particular, it obliges the Catholic Church and the other Churches and Ecclesial Communities, with which Catholics are willing to cooperate in this field (213).

In this sense, just as Catholics invite their Christian brothers and sisters to share in their initiatives, so, when they accept invitations offered to them, Catholics show that they are ready to cooperate in projects undertaken by other Christians. In the promotion of integral human development Catholics can also cooperate with the believers of other religions, as in fact they are already doing in various places (214).

Good administration of public affairs

110. The Synod Fathers were unanimous in acknowledging that the greatest challenge for bringing about justice and peace in Africa consists in a good administration of public affairs in the two interrelated areas of politics and the economy. Certain problems have their roots outside the Continent and therefore are not entirely under the control of those in power or of national leaders. But the Synodal Assembly acknowledged that many of the Continent's problems are the result of a manner of governing often stained by corruption. A serious reawakening of conscience linked to a firm determination of will is necessary, in order to put into effect solutions which can no longer be put off.

Building the nation

111. On the political front, the arduous process of building national unity encounters particular problems in the Continent where most of the States are relatively young political entities. To reconcile profound differences, overcome longstanding ethnic animosities and become integrated into international life demands a high degree of competence in the art of governing. That is why the Synod prayed fervently to the Lord that there would arise in Africa *holy politicians*—both men and women—and that there would be saintly Heads of State, who profoundly love their own people and wish to serve rather than be served (215).

The rule of law

112. The foundation of good government must be established on the sound basis of laws which protect the rights and define the obligations of the citizens (216).

I must note with great sadness that many African nations still labour under authoritarian and oppressive regimes which deny their subjects personal freedom and fundamental human rights, especially the freedom of association and of political expression, as well as the right to choose their governments by free and honest elections. Such political injustices provoke tensions which often degenerate into armed conflicts and internal wars, bringing with them serious consequences such as famine, epidemics and destruction, not to mention massacres and the scandal and tragedy of refugees. That is why the Synod rightly considered that an authentic democracy, which respects pluralism, "is one of the principal routes along which the Church travels together with the people...The lay Christian, engaged in the democratic struggle according to the spirit of the Gospel, is the sign of a Church which participates in the promotion of the rule of law everywhere in Africa" (217).

Administering the common patrimony

113. The Synod also called on African governments to establish the appropriate policies needed to increase economic growth and investment in order to create new jobs (218).

This involves the commitment to pursue sound economic policies, adopting the right priorities for the exploitation and distribution
of often scarce national resources in such a way as to provide for
people's basic needs, and to ensure an honest and equitable sharing
of benefits and burdens. In particular, governments have the binding
duty to protect the *common patrimony* against all forms of waste and
embezzlement by citizens lacking public spirit or by unscrupulous
foreigners. It is also the duty of governments to undertake suitable
initiatives to improve the conditions of international commerce.

Africa's economic problems are compounded by the dishonesty
of corrupt government leaders who, in connivance with domestic or
foreign private interests, divert national resources for their own profit
and transfer public funds to private accounts in foreign banks. This
is plain theft, whatever the legal camouflage may be. I earnestly
hope that international bodies and people of integrity in Africa and
elsewhere will be able to investigate suitable legal ways of having
these embezzled funds returned. In the granting of loans, it is important to make sure of the responsibility and forthrightness of the
beneficiaries (219).

The international dimension

114. As an Assembly of Bishops of the universal Church presided
over by the Successor of Peter, the Synod furnished a providential
occasion to evaluate positively the place and role of Africa in the
universal Church and the world community. Since we live in a world
that is increasingly interdependent, the destinies and problems of
the different regions are linked together. As God's Family on earth,
the Church should be the living sign and efficacious instrument of
universal solidarity for building a world-wide community of justice
and peace. A better world will come about only if it is built on the
solid foundation of sound ethical and spiritual principles.

In the present world order, the African nations are among the most
disadvantaged. Rich countries must become clearly aware of their duty
to support the efforts of the countries struggling to rise from their
poverty and misery. In fact, it is in the interest of the rich countries
to choose the path of solidarity, for only in this way can lasting peace
and harmony for humanity be ensured. Moreover, the Church in the
developed countries cannot ignore the added responsibility arising
from the Christian commitment to justice and charity. Because all

men and women bear God's image and are called to belong to the same family redeemed by Christ's Blood, each individual should be guaranteed just access to the world's resources which God has put at the everyone's disposal (220).

It is not hard to see the many practical implications of this. In the first place it involves working for improved socio-political relations among nations, ensuring greater justice and dignity for those countries which, after gaining independence, have been members of the international community for less time. A compassionate ear must also be lent to the anguished cries of the poor nations asking for help in areas of particular importance: malnutrition, the widespread deterioration in the standard of living, the insufficiency of means for educating the young, the lack of elementary health and social services with the resulting persistence of endemic diseases, the spread of the terrible scourge of AIDS, the heavy and often unbearable burden of international debt, the horror of fratricidal wars fomented by unscrupulous arms trafficking, the shameful and pitiable spectacle of refugees and displaced persons. These are some of the areas where prompt interventions are necessary and expedient, even if in the overall situation they seem to be inadequate.

The burden of the international debt

120. The question of the indebtedness of poor nations towards rich ones is a matter of great concern for the Church, as expressed in many official documents and interventions of the Holy See (231).

Taking up the words of the Synod Fathers, I particularly feel it is my duty to urge "the Heads of State and their governments in Africa not to crush their peoples with internal and external debts" (232).

I also make a pressing appeal to "the International Monetary Fund and the World Bank and all foreign creditors to alleviate the crushing debts of the African nations" (233).

Finally, I earnestly ask "the Episcopal Conferences of the industrialized countries to present this issue consistently to their governments and to the organizations concerned" (234).

The situation of many African countries is so serious as to leave no room for attitudes of indifference and complacency.

APPENDIX 10A: OUTLINE PLAN OF THE CCC COMPOUND, AKPAKPA

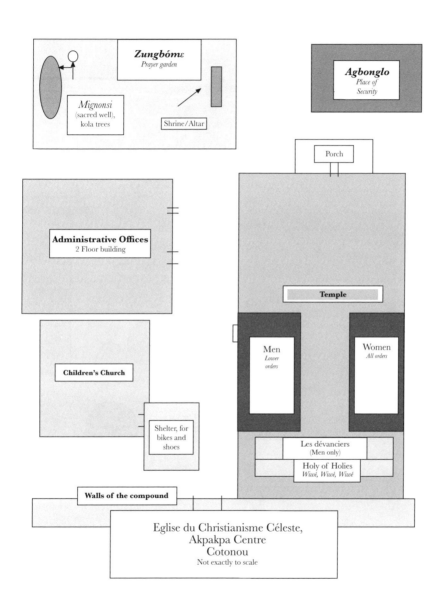

Zungbóme
Prayer garden

Mignonsi
(sacred well),
kola trees

Shrine/Altar

Agbonglo
*Place of
Security*

Porch

Administrative Offices
2 Floor building

Temple

Men
*Lower
orders*

Women
All orders

Children's Church

Shelter, for
bikes and
shoes

Les dévanciers
(Men only)

Holy of Holies
Wiwé, Wiwé, Wiwé

Walls of the compound

Eglise du Christianisme Céleste,
Akpakpa Centre
Cotonou
Not exactly to scale

APPENDIX 10B: OUTLINE OF THE COMPOUND OF PAROISSE ST. MICHEL, COTONOU

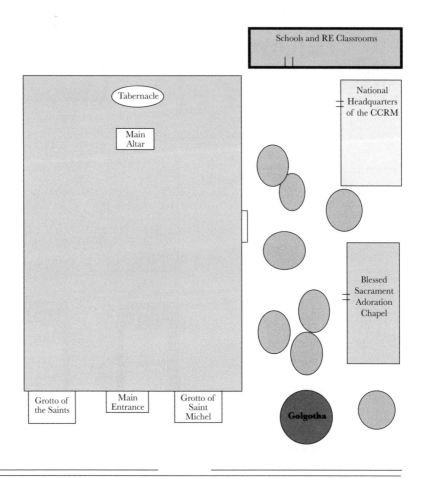

Schools and RE Classrooms

National Headquarters of the CCRM

Tabernacle

Main Altar

Blessed Sacrament Adoration Chapel

Grotto of the Saints

Main Entrance

Grotto of Saint Michel

Golgotha

Boulevard Saint Michel

Paroisse St. Michel,
Cotonou
Compound layout, not strictly to scale

SELECTED BIBLIOGRAPHY

Books and articles

Adè, Edouard (1992), "L'Eglise face à la conscience historique de la jeunesse universitaire africaine", in *Une Expérience Africaine d'Inculturation (III Politique et Développement)*, Cotonou: Q.I.C./Sillon Noir, 93–108.
—— (1992), "Les fidèles laïcs et la politique au Bénin", in *Une Expérience Africaine de l'Inculturation (III Politique et Développement)*, Q.I.C./Sillon Noir, Cotonou, 51–91, 67.
Adjovi, S. (1995), *De la dictature à la démocratie sans les armes*, Paris: Edition CP99.
Adoukonou, Barthelemy (1980), *Jalons pour une théologie africaine, essai d'une herme-neutique chrétienne du Vodoun Dahoméen*, 2 vols, Paris-Namur: Lethielleux.
—— (1993), "Vers une nouvelle conscience historique", in *Une Expérience Africaine de l'Inculturation (III Politique et Développement)*, Q.I.C./Sillon Noir, Cotonou, 111–141.
—— (1993), *Vodun, Démocratie et Pluralisme Religieux*, Cotonou: Sillon Noir.
—— (1998), "Ethique de l'Endurance et 'Bouffe'", *La Nation*, 23 January.
Agossou, Jacob M. (1977), "Pour un christianisme Africain", *Cahiers des Religions Africaines*, 11, n. 21–22, 221–238.
—— (1987), *Christianisme africain: Une fraternité au delà de l'ethnie*, Paris: Karthala.
Aguessy, Honorat (1972), *Les religions africaines comme source et valeur de civilisation*, Paris: Présence Africaine.
Akindélé, A. and Aguessy, C. (1953, reprinted Amsterdam, 1968), *Contribution à l'étude de l'histoire de l'ancien royaume de Porto-Novo*, Dakar.
Akinjogbin, I.A. (1966), "Archbald Dalzel: Slave Trader and Historian of Dahomey", *Journal of Africa History*, VII, I, 67–78.
—— (1967), *Dahomey and it neighbours 1708–1818*, Cambridge: CUP.
Anderson, A.A. (2001), *African Reformation: Africa Initiated Churches in the Twentieth Century*, Trenton, NJ: African World Press.
Anderson, Benedict (1991), *Imagined Communities*, London: Verso.
Anikpe, Euloge (2002), "Une Eglise au service de Dieu (Ministère Chrétien pour la Conquête Mondiale/MCCM)". *La Tribune de la Capitale*, no. 140, 16 July.
Argyle, W.J. (1966), *The Fon of Dahomey*, Oxford: Clarendon Press.
Atkins, John (1735/1970), *A Voyage to Guinea, Brazil and the West Indies in His Majesty's ships "The Swallow" and "Weymouth"*, London: Cass.
Balard, Martine (1998), *Mission catholique et culture vodoun: l'œuvre de Francis Aupiais (1877–1945)*, Perpignan: Presses Universitaires.
Banégas, Richard (1995), "Action collective et transition politique en Afrique: La conférence nationale du Bénin", *Cultures et Conflits*, 17, Printemps: 137–175.
Barbier, Jean-Claude (1996), *Géographie religieuse du Bénin*, unpub note Porto-Novo: CBRST.
Barbier, J.-C., Dorier-Apprill, E., Mayrargue, C., (1999), *Formes contemporaines du christianisme en Afrique Noire*, Bordeaux: Cenan (Serie: Les bibliographies).
Bayart Jean-François (1989), *L'état en Afrique: la politique du ventre*, Paris: Fayard.
—— (1989), "Les Eglises chrétiennes et la politique du ventre: le partage du gateau ecclésial", *Politique Africaine*, 35, 68–76.

Bayart, Jean-François, Mbembe, Achille and Toulabr, Comi (1992), *Le Politique par le bas en Afrique noire*, Paris: Karthala.
—— (1993), *Religion et modernité politique en Afrique noire*, Paris: Karthala.
de Benoist, J.-R. (1992), "Les clercs et la démocratie", *Afrique Contemporaine*, Numéro spécial, 4ᵉ trimestre, 178–192.
Bierschenk Thomas and Le Meur, Pierre-Yves (1997), *Trajectoires peules au Bénin*, Paris: Karthala.
Bierschenk, Thomas and Olivier de Sardan, J.P. (1998), *Les pouvoirs au villages: le Bénin rural entre démocratisation et décentralisation*, Paris: Karthala.
Biton, Marlène-Michèle (2000), *L'art des bas-reliefs d'Abomey: Bénin ex-Dahomey*, Paris: Harmattan.
Boillot, Françoise (1992), "L'Eglise catholique face aux processus de changement politique du début des années quatre-vingt-dix", *Année Africaine*, 115–142.
Bonfils, Jean (1991), *Débuts de la Mission au Dahomey à partir du XVIIᵉ siècle*, Cotonou.
Borghero, Francis (1997), *Journal de Francis Borghero premier missionnaire du Dahomey (1861–1865): Sa vie, son journal (1860–1864), la relation de 1863*, Paris: Karthala.
Bosman, William (1705/1967), *A new and accurate description of the Coast of Guinea*, London: Cass.
Boulaga, Fabien E. (1993), *Les Conférences Nationales: une affaire à suivre*, Paris: Karthala.
Bowen, Thomas. J. (1857), *Adventures and missionary labours in several countries in the interior of Africa 1849 to 1856*, Harleston.
Brasio, Antonio (1953–1988), *Monumenta missionaria africana: Africa occidental*, 16 vols, Lisboa: Agencia Geral do Ultramar, Publicacoes e Biblioteca.
Bratton, Michael (1994), "Civil Society and Political Transition in Africa", in Harbeson, J.W. et al., *Civil Society and the State in Africa*, Lynne Riener, 51–79.
Brégand, Denise (1998), *Commerce caravanier et relations sociales au Bénin*, Paris: L'Harmattan.
Brodie, Fan M. (1967), *The Devil Drives: A Life of Sir Richard Burton*, New York: Norton.
Burton, Richard (1893/1966), *A Mission to Gelele King of Dahome*, London: Rout-ledge (an abridged version of Burton's 1893 version in 2 volumes, *A mission to Gelele, King of Dahome: with notices of the so-called "Amazons", the grand customs, the yearly customs, the human sacrifices, the present state of the slave trade, and the negro's place in nature*, ed. by Isabel Burton London: Tylston and Edwards, 1893).
Casanova, José (1994), *Public religions in the modern world*, Chicago: University of Chicago Press.
Césaire, Aimé (1983), *Cahier d'un retour au pays natal*, Paris: Presence Africaine.
Chatwin, Bruce (1980), *The Viceroy of Ouidah*, London: Vintage.
Claffey, Patrick (2001), "The Place of the 'imaginaire religieux' in Social Change and Political Recomposition in Sub-Saharan Africa", *Anthropos*, 96: 200–206.
Coquery-Vidrovitch, Cathérine (1971), "De la traite des esclaves à l'exportation de l'huile de palme et des palmistes au Dahomey", in Claude Meillassoux (ed.), *The Development of Indigenous Trade and Markets in West Africa*, London: Oxford University Press for the International African Institute, 109–112.
—— (1985/rev. edn 1992), *Afrique Noire: permanences et ruptures*, Paris: L'Harmattan.
Coundouriotis, Eleni (1999), *Claiming History: Colonialism, Ethnography, and the Novel*, New York: Columbia University Press.
Cruise-O'Brien, D., Diop, M.-C. and Diouf, M. (2002), *La Construction de l'Etat au Sénégal*, Paris Karthala.

Curtin, Philip D. (1969), *The Atlantic Slave Trade*, London: The University of Wisconsin Press.

Dalzel, Archibald (1793/1967), *The History of Dahomey—an inland kingdom*, London.

de Rosny, Eric (1992), *L'Afrique des Guérisons*, Paris: Karthala.

de Souza, Germain (1972), *Conception de vie chez les Fon*, CNRS Paris.

de Surgy, Albert (2001), *Le phénomène pentecôtiste en Afrique noire: Le cas béninois* Paris: L'Harmattan.

—— (2001), *L'Eglise du christianisme céleste:Un exemple d'Eglise prophétique au Bénin*, Paris: Karthala.

Djivo, Adrien (1978), *Guézo: la rénovation du Dahomey*, Tournai, Belgium: ABC, Grandes Figures Africaines.

Duncan, John (1847/reprinted 1968), *Travels in West Africa*, 2 vols, London.

Dunglas, Edouard (1957), "Contribution à l'histoire du Moyen Dahomey", *Etudes Dahoméennes*, XIX, 90.

Dupuis, Paul-Henry (1998), *Le Temps des semeurs (1494–1901): Histoire de l'Eglise du Bénin*, Cotonou.

Ellingworth, Paul (1980), "Christianity and politics in Dahomey, 1843–1867", in *The History of Christianity in West Africa*, ed. O.U. Kalu, London: Longman: 235–250.

Ellis, Stephen and ter Haar Gerrie (1998), "Religion and politics in sub-Saharan Africa", *The Journal of Modern African Studies*, 36 (2), 175–201.

Eltis, David (1987), *Economic Growth and the Ending of the Transatlantic Slave Trade*, New York, Oxford: Oxford University Press.

Forbes, Frederick (1851/reprinted 1966), *Dahomey and the Dahomeans*, 2 vols, London.

Freeman, Thomas B. (1844/reprinted 1968), *The Journal of Various Visits to the Kingdoms of Ashanti, Aku and Dahomey*, London.

—— (1871), *Missionary Enterprise No Fiction, a Tale Founded on Facts*, London: Eliot Stock.

Frenkiel, Olenka (2001), "Children of the Etireno", *The Guardian, G2*, 4 October, 6–7.

Fugelstad, Finn (1977), "Quelques réflexions sur l'histoire et les institutions de l'ancien Royaume du Dahomey et ses voisins", *Bulletin de l'IFAN*, Série B, XXXIX, iii, 493–517.

Garcia, Luc (1988), *Le Royaume du Dahomé face à la pénétration coloniale (1875–1894)*, Paris: Karthala.

Gbegnonvi, Roger (1998), "La Bouffe, les vodun et Mawu", *La Nation* 13 January, (reprinted in *Le Sillon S'Explique* (1998), Cotonou: Les Publications du Sillon Noir, no. 13, 1–10.

Geertz, Clifford (1963/1971), *Old Societies, New States: the Quest for Modernity in Africa and Asia*, New Delhi: Amerind.

Gifford, Paul (ed.) (1992), *New Dimensions in African Christianity*, Nairobi: All African Conference of Churches.

—— (1993), *Christianity in Samuel Doe's Liberia*, CUP, Cambridge.

—— (1998), *African Christianity: Its Public Role*, London: Hurst.

Glélé, Maurice A. (1969), *La naissance d'un état noir: L'évolution politique et constitutionnel du Dahomey de la colonisation à nos jours*, Paris: LGDJ.

—— (1981), *Religion, culture et politique en Afrique noire*, Paris: Présence Africaine, 1981.

Gonçalves, Paul (1988), "Paul Gonçalves, Secrétaire Mondial du christianisme céleste, fait des révélations étonnantes", interview in *La Gazette du Golfe*, no. 16, 16 October.

Goudjo, Raymond B. N.-M. (1997), *La liberté en démocratie: L'éthique sociale et la réalité politique en Afrique*, Frankfurt/Paris: Peter Lang/Presses Universitaires Européennes.

Hair, P.E.H., Jones, Adam, and Law, Robin (1992), *Barbot on Guinea: the Writings of Jean Barbot on West Africa, 1678–1712*, London: Hakluyt Society, 1992.

Hanciles, Jehu. J. (2000), "Anatomy of an experiment: the Sierra Leone Native Pastorate", *Missiology*, XXIX (1): 63–82.

Hastings, Adrian (1979), *A History of African Christianity 1950–1975*, Cambridge: CUP.

Haugerud, Angelique (1995), *The culture of politics in Kenya*, Cambridge: CUP.

Hazoumé, Paul (1937), *Le pacte de sang au Dahomey*, Paris: Institut d'Ethnologie, 1937.

—— (1938/English translation 1990), *Dugucimi*, Washington: Three Continents Press.

Hebga, Meinrad (1976), *Emancipation d'Eglise sous tutelle. Essai sur l'ère post-missionnaire*, Paris: Presence Africaine.

Heilbrunn, John. R. (1992), "Social Origins of National Conferences in Benin and Togo", *Journal of Modern African Studies*, 31, 2, 277–299.

Herskovits, Melville, J. and Frances S. (1958), *Dahomean Narrative*, Evaston.

Herskovits, Melville, J. (1958), *The Myth of the Negro Past*, Boston: Beacon Press.

—— (1938/1967), *Dahomey: an Ancient West African Kingdom*, Evanston: Northwestern University Press.

Horton, Robin (1971), "African Conversion", *Africa*, 41: 85–108.

—— (1975), "On the Rationality of Conversion", *Africa*, 45, 219–235.

Hountondji, Paulin J. (1994), *Les savoirs endogènes: pistes pour une recherche*, Paris: Karthala, 1994.

Huannou, Adrien (1984), *La Littérature béninoise de langue française*, Paris: Karthala.

Huntington, Samuel (1995), "Religion and the Third Wave", in S.P. Ramet and D.W. Treadgold (eds), *Render unto Caesar: the Religious Sphere in World Politics*, Washington: American University Press.

Inikori, Joseph E. (1976), "Measuring the Atlantic Slave Trade: an assessment of Curtin and Anstey", *Journal of African History*, XVII, 2.

—— (ed.) (1982), *Forced Migration: the Impact of the Export Slave Trade on African Societies*, London: Hutchinson University Library.

Inikori Joseph E. and Engerman, Stanley L. (eds) (1992), *The Atlantic Slave Trade: Effects on Economies, Societies and Peoples in Africa, the Americas and Europe*, Durham, NC, London: Duke University Press.

Iroko, A. Félix (2002), "L'Historien face à la problématique de *la culture* ou *des cultures* béninoises", *La Croix*, no. 797, 26 July.

Jennings C.C. (1976), "French policy toward trading with African and Brazilian slave merchants", *Journal of African History*, 17, 4: 515–528.

John Paul II (1995), *Ecclesia in Africa*, Yaounde.

Johnson, Marion (1978), "Bulfinch Lambe and the Emperor of Pawpaw: a Footnote to Agaja and the Slave Trade", *History in Africa*, 5, 345–350.

—— (1980), "Polanyi, Peukert and the political economy of Dahomey", *Journal of African History*, 21, 395–398.

Joseph, Richard (1993), "The Christian Churches and Democracy in contemporary Africa", in J. Witte (ed.), *Christianity and Democracy in the Global Context*, Boulder: Westview, 231–247.

Kä Mana (1992), *Foi chrétienne, crise africaine et reconstruction de l'Afrique*, Nairobi: CETA.

—— (1993), *L'Afrique va-t-elle mourir?: essai d'éthique politique*, Paris: Karthala.

—— (1993), *Théologie africaine pour temps de crise: Christianisme et reconstruction de l'Afrique*, Paris: Karthala.

—— (1993), *Christ d'Afrique: enjeux éthiques de la foi africaine en Jésus-Christ*, Paris: Karthala.

Labouret, Henri and Rivet, Paul (1929), *Le Royaume d'Ardra et son évangélisation au XVII*ᵉ *siècle*, Paris: Insitut d'Ethnologie.

Laloupo, Francis (1993), "La conférence nationale du Bénin: un concept nouveau de changement de régime politique", *Année Africaine*, 1992–1993, 89–113.

Lamb, Bulfinch (1744/ reprinted 1967), "Abomey, 27 Nov 1724", in William Smith, *A New Voyage to Guinea*, London.

Law, Robin (1969), "The fall of Allada, 1724—an ideological revolution?", *Journal of the Historical Society of Nigeria*, 5 (1), 157–163.

—— (1977), "Royal monopoly and private enterprise in the Atlantic slave trade: the case of Dahomey", *Journal of African History*, 18, 4, 555–577.

—— (1977), *The Oyo Empire c. 1600–c. 1836: A West African Imperialism in the Age of the Atlantic Slave Trade*, Oxford.

—— (1983), "Trade and politics behind the Slave Coast: The lagoon traffic and the rise of Lagos, 1500–1800", Journal of African History, 24, 321–348.

—— (1985), "Human sacrifice in pre-colonial Africa", *African Affairs* 84, 3, 53–87.

—— (1986), "Islam in Dahomey: a case study of the introduction and influence of Islam in a peripheral area of West Africa", *Scottish Journal of Religious Studies* 7 (2), 95–122.

—— (1986), "Dahomey and the Slave Trade: Reflections on the historiography of the rise of Dahomey", *Journal of African History*, XXII, ii, 237–267.

—— (1987), "Ideologies of Royal Power: the dissolution and reconstruction of royal power on the slave coast", *Africa*, LVIII, iii, 321–342.

—— (1988), "History and legitimacy: aspects of the use of the past in pre-colonial Dahomey", *History in Africa*, XV, 431–456.

—— (1988), "A neglected account of the Dahomean conquest of Whydah (1727), the 'Rélation de la guerre de Juda' of Sieur Ringard of Nantes", *History in Africa*, XV, 327.

—— (1989), "'My head belongs to the king': On the political and ritual significance of decapitation in pre-colonial Dahomey", *Journal of African History*, 30, 399–415.

—— (1989), "Slave raiders and middlemen, monopolists and free-traders: The supply of slaves for the Atlatic trade in Dahomey, c. 1715–1850", *Journal of Africa History*, 30, 45–68.

—— (1989), "Between the Sea and the Lagoons: The interaction of Maritime and Inland Navigation on the Precolonial Slave Trade", *Cahiers d'Etudes Africaines*, 29, 209–237.

—— (1990), "The common people were divided: Monarchy, aristocracy and political factionalism in the kingdom of Whydah, 1671–1727", *International Journal of African Historical Studies*, 23, 201–229.

—— (ed.) (1990), *Correspondence from the Royal African Company's Chief Merchants at Cabo Corso Castle with William's Fort, Whydah, and Litle Popo factory, 1727–1728*, University of Wisconsin-Madison African Studies Program.

—— (1990), "Further Light on Bulfinch Lambe and the 'Emperor of Pawpaw': King Agaja of Dahomey's Letter to King George of England, 1726", *History of Africa*, 17, 211–215.

—— (1991), *The Slave Coast of West Africa 1550–1750: the Impact of the Atlantic Slave Trade on an African Society*, Oxford: Clarendon.

—— (1991), "Religion, trade and politics on the 'Slave Coast': Roman Catholic missions in Allada and Whydah in the seventeenth century", *Journal of Religion in Africa*, 21 (1), 42–77.

—— (ed.) (1992), *Further correspondence of the Royal African Company of England Relating to the "Slave Coast", 1681–1699: Selected documents of Mrs Rawlinson C745-747 in the Bodleian Library*, Oxford, University of Wisconsin-Madison African Studies Program.

—— (1992), *Dahomey and the End of the Atlantic Slave Trade*, Boston: African Center, Boston University.

—— (1992), "Warfare on the West African Slave Coast, 1650–1850", in R. Brian Ferguson and Neil L. Whitehead (eds), *War in the Tribal Zone: Expanding States and indigenous warfare*, Santa Fe: School of American Research Advanced Seminar Series, 103–126.

—— (1994), "On pawning and enslavement for debt in the pre-colonial Slave Coast", in Toyin Falola and Paul E. Lovejoy (eds), *Pawnship in Africa: Debt bondage in historical perspective*, 55–69, Boulder: Westview Press.

—— (1994), "'Here is no resisting the country': the realities of power in Afro-European relations on the West African Slave Coast", *Itinerario: European Journal of Overseas History*, 18 (2), 50–64.

—— (1996), "The transition from the Slave Trade to 'Legitimate' Commerce", *Studies in the World History of Slavery, Abolition and Emancipation*, I, 1, www2. h-net.msu.edu/slavery/essays.

—— (1997), *The Kingdom Of Allada*, Leiden: School of Asian, African, and Amerindian Studies.

Le Hérissé, A. (1911), *L'Ancien Royaume du Dahomey*, Paris.

Lovejoy, Paul E. (1983), *Transformations in slavery: A History of Slavery in West Africa*, Cambridge: Cambridge University Press.

—— (1989), "The impact of the Atlantic slave trade on Africa: a review of the literature", *Journal of African History*, 30, 365–394.

McLeod, John (1820/1971), *A Voyage to Africa: With Some Account of the Manners and Customs of the Dahomian People*, London: Cass.

Manning, Patrick (1982), *Slavery, Colonialism and Economic Growth in Dahomey, 1640–1960*, Cambridge: CUP.

Marshall, Ruth (1993), "'Power in the Name of Jesus': Social Transformation and Pentecostalism in Western Nigeria Revisited", in T. Ranger and O. Vaughan (eds), *Legitimacy and the State in Twentieth Century Africa*, London: Macmillan.

Martin, David (1990), *Tongues of Fire: The Explosion of Protestantism in Latin America*, Oxford: Blackwell.

Maupoil, Bernard (1943/reprinted 1981), *La Géomancie à l'ancienne Côte des Esclaves*, Paris: Institut d'Ethnologie.

Mayrargue, Cedric (1996), "'Le caméléon est remonté en haut de l'arbre': le retour au pouvoir de M. Kérékou au Bénin", *Politique Africaine*, 62, June, 124–131.

—— (1999), "Les élites béninoises au temps de Renouveau démocratique: Entre continuité et transformation", in J.-P. Daloz (ed.), *Le (non-) renouvellement des élites en Afrique subsaharienne*, Bordeaux: CEAN, 33–56.

—— (2001), "The Expansion of Pentecostalism in Benin: Individual Rationales and Transitional Dynamics", in A. Corten and R. Marshall (eds), *Betweeen Babel and Pentecost: Transnational Pentecostalism in Africa and Latin America*, Bloomington: Indiana University Press.

Mbembé, Achille (1988), *Afriques indociles: Christianisme, pouvoir et Etat en société post-coloniale*, Paris: Karthala.

—— (1993), "Proliferation du divin en Afrique subsahrienne", in G. Kepel (ed.), *Les politiques de Dieu*, Paris: Seuil.

—— (2000), "Esquisse d'une démocratie à l'Africaine", *Le Monde Diplomatioque*, October, 20–21, www.monde-diplomatique.fr/2000/10/MBEMBE/14296.

M'Bokolo, Elikia (1998), "The impact of the slave trade on Africa", *Le Monde Diplomatique*, www.monde-diplomatique.fr/en/04/02africa.

Mellier, Daniel (1982), "Marxisme et mission—Bénin", *SEDOS Bulletin*, 18, Rome, 352–357.

Miers, Suzanne and Koptyoff, Igor (1977), *Slavery in African: Historical and Anthropological Perspectives*, London: University of Wisconsin Press.

M'Nteba, Metena (1993), "Les Conférences Nationales et la figure politique de l'évêque président", *Zaire-Afrique*, 276, 361–372.

Monkotan, J.B. Kouassi (1991), "Une nouvelles voie d'accès au pluralisme politique: la Conférence nationale souveraine", *Afrique 2000*, 7, November, 41–53.

Morral, John B. (1980), *Political Thought in Mediaeval Times*, Toronto: UTP.

Morel, Yves (1992), "Démocratisation en Afrique noire: les conférences nationales", *Etudes*, June, 733–743.

Newbury, Colin W. (1961), *The West African Slave Coast and its Rulers: European Trade Administration among Yoruba and Adja Speaking People of Southwest Nigeria, Southern Dahomey and Togo*, Oxford: Greenwood Press.

Norris, Robert (1789/reprinted 1968), *Memoirs of the Reign of Bossa Ahadee, King of Dahomey*, London.

Nwajiaku, Katherine (1994), "The National Conferences in Benin and Togo Revisited", *The Journal of Modern African Studies*, 32, 3, 429–447.

Padilla, René (1999), "The future of Christiantiy in Latin America: Missiological Perspectives and Challlenges", *International Bulletin of Missionary Research*, 23 (3), 105–111.

Peel, J.D.Y. (1977), "Conversion and Tradition in two African societies: Ijebu and Buganda", *Past and Present*, 77.

—— (2000), *Religious Encounter and the Making of the Yoruba*, Indiana University Press.

Penoukou, Efoe-Julien (1984), *Eglises d'Afrique, proposition pour l'avenir*, Paris: Karthala.

Piqué, Francesca and Rainier, Leslie H. (1999), *Les Bas-reliefs d'Abomey: L'Histoire racontée sur les murs*, Cotonou: Les Editions du Flamboyant Paul Getty Trust.

Polanyi, Karl (1966), *Dahomey and the Slave Trade*, Seattle and London: University of Washington Press.

Quenum, Alphonse (1993), *Les Eglises chrétiennes et la traite atlantique du XVe au XIXe siècle*, Paris: Karthala.

Rassinoux, J. (2001), *Dictionnaire Français-Fon*, Madrid: Société des Missions Africaines.

Richardson, David (1989), "Slave exports from west and west-central Africa, 1700–1810: new estimates of volume and distribution", *Journal of African History*, XXX, I, 1–22.

Robinson, Pearl T. (1994), "The National Conference phenomenon in Francophone West Africa", *Comparative Studies in Society and History*, 36, 3, 574–610.

Ronen, Dov (1968), "Preliminary notes on the concept of regionalism in Dahomey", *Etudes Dahoméennes*, 12 (Numéro Spécial), 11–14.

—— (1968), "The Two Dahomeys", *Africa Report*, June.

—— (1975), *Dahomey: Between Tradition and Modernity*, London: Cornell University Press.

—— (1984), Ethnic *Ideology, and the military in the People's Republic of Benin*, Boston, MA: African-American Issues Center.

Ross, David (1983), "European models and West African History: further comments on the recent historiography of Dahomey", *History in Africa*, 10, 293–305.

Roussé-Grosseau, Christiane (1992), *Mission catholique et choc des modèles culturels en Afrique: l'exemple du Dahomey, 1861–1928*, Paris: L'Harmattan.

Salvaing, Bernard (1994), *Les missionnaires et la rencontre de l'Afrique au XIXe siècle: Côte des Esclaves et pays Yoruba*, Paris: L'Harmattan.

Sanneh, Lamin (1983), *West African Christianity: the Religious Impact*, London: Hurst.

Sastre, Robert and Dosseh, Robert (1956), "Propagande et vérité", in *Des Prêtres Noirs s'interrogent*, Paris: CERF/Présence Africaine, 137–153.

Saulnier, Pierre (2002), *Le Meurtre du Vodon Dan*, Madrid: SMA.

Segurola, B. and Rassinoux, J. (2000), *Dictionnaire Fon-Français*, Madrid: Société des Missions Africaines.
Skertchly, J.A. (1875), *Dahomey as it is; being a narrative of eight months residence in that country, with a full account of the notorious annual customs, and the social and religious institutions of the Ffons: also an appendix on the Ashantee, and a glossary of Dahomean words and titles. Ills and sketches by the author*, London: Chapman and Hall, 1875.
Snelgrave, William (1734/reprinted 1971), *A New Account of Some Parts of Guinea*, London.
Staniland, Martin (1973), "The three party system in Dahomey: I, 1946–56", *Journal of African History*, XIV, 2, 291–312.
Strandsbjerg, C. (2000), "Kérékou, God and the Ancestors: Religion and the conception of political power in Bénin", *African Affairs*, 99, 395–414.
Tevoedjre, Paul Martial, (2001), *Plus de 6000 Noirs Américains au Bénin: Pour Quoi Faire?* Porto Novo: CNPMS.
Toulabor, Comi (1989), "Monseigneur Dosseh, Archevêque de Lomé", *Politique Africaine*, 35, 68–76.
Trichet, Pierre (2001), "The Abiding of de Brésilliac to Dahomey", *Society of African Missions Bulletin*, 101.
Paul Vallely (ed.) (1998), *The New Politics: Catholic Social Teaching for the Twenty-First Century*, London: SCM.
Verger, Pierre (1976), *Flux et reflux de la traite des nègres entre le Golfe de Bénin et Bahia de Todos os Santos du XVIIᵉ au XIXᵉ siècle*, Ibadan, Nigeria: Ibadan University Press.
Vittin, Théophile. E. (1991), "Bénin du 'système Kérékou' au renouveau démocratique", in *Etats d'Afrique Noire: Formation, mécanisme et crise*, Paris: Karthala, 93–115.
Waterlot, George E. (1926), *Les bas-reliefs des bâtiments royaux d'Abomey (Dahomey)*, Paris: Institut d'Ethnologie.
Wilks, Ivor (1975), *Asante in the nineteenth century*, Cambridge: CUP.
—— (1996), *One Nation, Many Histories: Ghana Past and Present* (Aggrey-Fraser-Guggisberg Memorial Lectures 1995), Accra: Ghana Universities Press.
Wiseman, J. (ed.) (1995), *Democracy and Political Change in Sub-Saharan Africa*, London: Routledge.
Yoder, John C. (1974), "Fly and elephant parties: political polarisation in Dahomey, 1840–1870", *Journal of African History*, XV, iii, 417–432.

Unpublished theses, dissertations and miscellaneous academic materials

Aïdasso, Dorothé (2000), *Les Œuvres sociales de l'Eglise Catholique dans le Diocèse de Cotonou: 1958–1996*, Mémoire de Maîtrise, Université Nationale du Bénin.
Alladaye, Jérome C. (1978), *Les Missionnaires Catholiques au Dahomey à l'époque coloniale 1905–1957*, Thèse de Doctorat de 3ᵉ cycle, Université de Paris VII, sous la direction de Catherine Coquery-Vidrovitch.
Ali Baion, Sarate (1994), *Contribution à l'étude des rapprts historiques entre les Baribas et les Tchabé pednant lq période pré-coloniale*, Mémoire de maîtrise, Université Nationale du Bénin, FLASH, Cotonou.
Badufle, Guillaume (1999), *Dynamiques religieuses et urbanisation dans les campagnes de l'entre-deux villes Cotonou/Porot-Novo, Sud-Bénin (L'axe Djeregbé-Porto-Novo)*, Mémoire de maîtrise de géographie, sous la direction de Monique Bertrand, CRESO, Université de Caen (Centre de recherche sur les espaces et les sociétés).
Banégas, Richard (1998), *La démocratie "à pas de caméleon": transition et consolidation démocratique au Bénin*, Thèse présentée en vue de l'obtention du Doctrat de l'Institut d'Etudes Politiques de Paris, Directeur, Jean-François Leguil-Bayart.

Barbier, Jean-Claude (1999), *Les collines enchantées de Tchetti (Centre Bénin)*, unpub. ms at CBRST, Cotonou.
Claffey, Patrick (2000), *The churches, the National Conference and democratic transition in the Republic of Benin*, MA Thesis, University of London, School of Oriental and African Studies.
Codjo-Assogba, Luc M. (1996), *La Tradithérapie face à la médicine psychiatrique: analyse des méthodes thérapeutiques et nécessité d'une complementarité*, Mini-Mémoire en Philosophie (Psychologie), UNB, sous la direction de Dah-Lokonon Bodéhou Gbênoukpo.
Mayrargue, Cedric (1994), *Religions et changement politique au Bénin*, Mémoire de DEA "Etudes Africaines", CEAN, Bordeaux.
—— (1995), *Les nouveaux mouveaux religieux dans l'espace politique béninois*, rapport de mission.
Odjo, Ange (1990), *Messianismes Africains et dynamique sociale: la question du Christianisme Céleste au Bénin*, Mémoire de maîtrise de Sociologie-Anthropologie, UNB 1989–1990, sous la directon de Paulin Hountoundji.
Odouwo, Chogolou S.A. (2000), *Approche Sociologique du phénomène de la mobilité religieuse en milieu urbain: étude de cas de la ville de Cotonou*, Mémoire de Maîtrise, UNB.
Reid, John (1988), *Warrior Aristocrats in Crisis: The political effects of the transition from the slave trade to palm oil commerce in the nineteenth century Kingdom of Dahomey*, PhD thesis, University of Stirling.
Sodokin, Codjo (1984), *Les "Syncrétismes" Religieux Contemporains et la Société Béninoise (Le Cas du Christianisme Céleste)*, Thèse de doctorat de 3ᵉᵐᵉ Cycle en Histoire et Civilisations, Université de Lyon, sous la direction de Professeur Xavier de Montclos.
Staniland, Martin (1964), *Regionalism and the Political Parties of Dahomey*, MA thesis, University of Ghana.
de Surgy, Albert (ndg), *La Recherche de miracles dans les Eglises chrétiennes, en République du Bénin*, unpub. ms. CBRST Annexe, Département de Recherche en Sciences Huimaines et Sociales (DRSHS) de Porto Novo.

Primary sources and unpublished texts

Adimou, Mgr C. (1973), "Message de Noël", *Eglise de Cotonou*, vol. 14, 6, December, 161–165.
Adihou, A. (ed.) (1990), *L'Eglise, a-t-elle le droit de parler politique*, Cotonou: Imprimerie Notre Dame.
Aevoet, W. (1991), "Présence de l'Eglise dans le processus de démocratisation", *Vivant Univers*, September-October.
Agbononci, A. (1991), "Bénin: l'avancée d'un pays parmi les moins avancés vers la démocratie", *Perspectives Missionnaires*, 22, 31–44.
Akle, J. (1991), "L'Assemblée Nationale: Quel avenir pour le Bénin?", *La Sentinelle*, 1, 2, 6 (Methodist Bulletin).
Akodjetin, Christophe (ndg), *La Prière, L'Arme No. 1*, ECC pamphlet, Cotonou.
—— (ndg), *Pasteur Oschoffa, sa vie et son œuvre*, ECC pamphlet Cotonou.
Anon (1974), "Lettre de créance de S.E. Mgr. Wuestenberg, Pro-Nonce Apostolique au Dahomey" et "Réponse du Chef de l'Etat au discours de S.E. Mgr Wuestenberg", *Eglise de Cotonou*, vol. 14, 10 April, 240–245.
—— (1974), "Rencontre de Mgr Adimou avec le Chef de l'Etat: le 15 novembre 1974", *Eglise de Cotonou*, vol. 15, 4, December, 100–111.
—— (1989), "Devant des étudiants de divers pays, Jean-Paul II rappelle le sens du développement humain", *La Croix du Bénin*, 530: 12.

—— (1989), "Six mois d'application du programme d'ajustement structurel au Bénin. Quel bilan?", *La Croix du Bénin*, 530: 3.

—— (1990), "Association 'Chrétiens dans la vie publique'", *La Croix du Benin*, 539: 2

—— (1990), *Les Actes de la Conférence Nationale*, Cotonou: Editions ONEPI/ Fondation Friedrich Naumann.

—— (1991), *Les Evêques Africains dans la tourmente*, Paris: Dossiers du Bureau d'information missionnaire.

—— (1993), "Lettre circulaire du Ministre de l'intérieur à tous les responsables de cultes", *Eglise de Cotonou*, vol. 33, 6 June, pp. 14–15 (On inter-religious tensions).

—— (1994), *"Synthèse des résultats d'analyse"*. *Deuxième recensement général de la population et de l'habitation, février 1992*, Bureau Central du Recensement, Cotonou: Nations Unies.

—— (1998), *Politique macroéconomique au Bénin: Progrès, Limites et Perspectives*, (Document de Travail No. 98/001), Réalisé par la Cellule d'Analyse de Politique Economique (CAPE).

—— (1999), *Rapport sur l'état de l'Economie Nationale: développements récents et perspectives à moyen terme*, Réalisé par la cellule macroéconomique de la Présidence de la République (CAPE) en collaboration avec les Ministères.

—— (2000), *Bénin 2025, Alafia: Etudes Nationales de perspectives à long terme (stratégies de développement)*, Ministère d'Etat Chargé de la Coordination de l'Action Gouvernamentale, du Plan, du Développment et de la Promotion de l'Emploi en collaboration avec le Programmes des Nations Unies pour le Dével-oppement (PNUD).

—— (2000), "Benin: Me Sadikou Alao", *La Lettre du Continent*, 356, July (www. africaintelligence.fr).

—— (2000), "Benin: Kékékou, homme de paraboles", *La Lettre du Continent*, 356, July (www.africaintelligence.fr).

APIC (1989), "Bénin: rencontre des laïcs dans la perspective de l'assemblée spéciale du Synode des évêques consacrée à l'Afrique", *APIC KIPA*, 159, 5.

ARCEB (2000), *Leve-toi et Va*, Cotonou.

Aupiais, F., (1927), *"Les noirs, leurs aspirations, leur avenir"*, Paris: Comité National d'Etudes Sociale et politique (typescript and proceedings report), SMA Archives, Rome, 3H16.

—— (ndg), *Les Elites noires* (conférences), SMA Archives, Rome, 3H17.

—— (1929), *L'âme primitive*, intervention à la Société française de Philosophie, Paris: Sorbonne; SMA Archives, Rome, 3H19.

—— (1929), *Les besoins et les réalisations du service social en Afrique Noire*, conference typescript, SMA Archives, Rome 3H20.

—— (ndg), *Les missionnaires au service de la colonisation*, Semaines coloniales de Clermont, conference, SMA Archives, Rome, 3H21.

—— (1931), "Elites indigènes dans les pays de colonisation et les milieux fétich-istes", *Semaines Sociales de France*, 22ᵉ Session, Marseille, SMA Archives, Rome, 3H18.

Ayedoun, S. (1991a) "Revendication ou engagement syndical", *La Sentinelle*, 1, 2 (Methodist Bulletin).

—— (1991), "Le Président Soglo face aux syndicats", *La Sentinelle*, 2, 5 (Method-ist Bulletin).

Bernasko, Peter W. (1861), "Extract of a Letter from the Rev. Peter W. Bernasko, Native Assistant Missionary, dated Whydah, 29 November 1860", in *Wesleyan Missionary Notices*, 25 February.

Bonnke, Reinhard (2001), *Ibadan 2001: Countdown 2*, Advertising brochure for the CfaN Great Evangelistic campaign "Idaidan/Nigeria", 7–11 November 2001.

Borghero, Francesco (1864), "Relation sur l'établissment des missions", Ouidah, 8 December 1863, in *Annales de la Propagation de la Foi*, 1864, 420.

CEB (1960), "Au Clergé et aux fidèles de tout le Dahomey", *La Quinzaine Religieuse de Cotonou*, vol. 1, 9 August, (Episcopal message on the eve of independence).

—— (1974), "Nos suggestions et propositions pour l'élaboration d'une idéologie dahoméenne", *Eglise de Cotonou,* vol. 15, 4 December 105–111.

—— (1975), "Lettre au Président de la République Populaire", *Eglise de Cotonou*, 15 (numéro spécial), 1 April 10–13 (following death for treason passed on seven persons including Fr A. Quenum).

—— (1989), "Convertissez-vous et le Bénin vivra", (Lenten Pastoral Letter), Lokossa.

—— (1989), "Message des Evêques aux chrétiens et à tous les hommes de bonne volonté du Bénin", *La Croix du Bénin*, 530: 1; 10.

—— (1990), "Au Service du relèvement de notre pays" (Lenten Pastoral Letter), Lokossa, February.

—— (1990), "Béninoises et Béninois face au défi du Renouveau Démocratique" (Extraordinary Pastoral Letter), Cotonou, November.

—— (1992), "Exigences de la démocratie" (Extraordinary Pastoral Letter), Abomey 14 February.

—— (1996), "Pour un nouvel essor de notre pays" (Extraordinary Pastoral Letter), Cotonou 24 January.

—— (1999), "Message des évêques du Bénin à l'occasion de l'insécurité grandissante dans le pays", Natitingou.

CIEPB (1990), "Ethique chrétienne et politique dans le Bénin d'aujourd'hui: Colloque des 12 et 13 février 1990: Déclaration", Porto Novo, in *Perspectives Missionnaires*, 22: 44–50.

—— 'Bénin: l'évêque de Cotonou reprend son activité pastorale, chef de l'Etat pour une période de transition, *APIC*, 99, 9 April 1991: 4.

—— 'Nous nous posons des questions sur la démission de Mgr. Isidore de Souza du Haut Conseil de la République', *La Croix du Bénin*, 21 May 1993: 1; 7.

David-Gnahoui, E. (1991), "Mirabeau fût-il béninois", *La Sentinelle*, 1: 6 (Methodist Bulletin).

de Cuverville, Le Vice-Amiral (1900), *Le R.P. Dorgère au Dahomey*, Auxerre: Imprimerie de Chambon, SMA Archives, Rome, 3J33.

de Souza, Mgr I. (1990), "Pas question de se réfugier dans la sacristie", *Actualité Religieuse dans le Monde,* 15 September, 35–37.

—— (1990), "Mgr de Souza savait...", *Africa Report*, May–June, 32–33.

—— (1990), "In favore del popolo", (interview), *Nigrizia*, June, 45.

—— (1991), "Building a new Benin", *Africa Report*, May–June, 43–45.

—— (1991), "L'Eglise arbitre" (interview), *Croissance: Le Monde en Développement*, 336, Paris, 21.

—— (1991), "Je ne vois pas suffisamment de désintéressement et d'amour du pays", *Le Courrier*, 128, Paris, 21–22.

—— (1992), "L'Eglise au cœur des mutations politiques et sociales en Afrique" (interview with Vatican Radio, Africa Service), *Telena* 3–4, October–November, 31–33.

—— (1993), "Eglises Africaines au sein de l'Eglise Universelle dans un monde en mutation" (conference), *Revue de l'Institut Catholique de l'Afrique de l'Ouest*, 5–6 Abidjan, 65–71.

—— (1993), "Un prêtre ne doit pas faire de politique", (interview), *L'Osservatore Romano (French Edition)*, Rome, No. 13, 13 March 1993, 9.

—— (1993), "Lettre à mes frères", *Eglise de Cotonou*, vol. 33, 4, April, 1–5.

—— (1994), "Ayons le courage de la transparence, notre pays en sortira grandi", *La Croix du Bénin*, 30 December, 1, 6.

—— (1996), "L'Afrique est déçue par la démocratie" (interview), *Jeune Afrique* 1836, 13–19 March, 30.

de Surgy, Albert (ndg), *La recherche de miracles dans les Eglises chrétiennes, en République du Bénin*, unpub ms, Porto-Novo: CBRST.

Dedji, Rev. V. (1990), "Eglise et Société: Du colloque des Eglises Protestantes à la Conférence Nationale", *Informations, documentions*, 28, Eglise Protestante Méthodiste au Bénin.

Détchénou, A.R. (2000), "Il y a dix ans, la conférence nationale des forces vives de la nation", *La Croix du Bénin*, 11 February, 6.

Dossou-Yovo, G. (1992), "S. Exc. Mgr de Souza: 30 and de Vie Sacerdotale", *La Croix du Bénin*, 24 July, 9.

Echos des Missions Africaines, (1902), "Relations sur l'établissement des Mission au Dahomey", 112.

Eglise du Christianisme Céleste (1996), *Textes Fondamentaux de l'Eglise du Chrstianisme Céleste*, Saint Siège, Porto-Novo.

Fauré, C. (1991), "Mgr de Souza, la démocratie au cœur", *La Croix*, Paris, 5 April, 6.

Freeman, Thomas B. (1854), "Extract of a Letter from the Rev. Thomas B. Freeman, dated Cape-Coast, August 12th, 1854", in *Wesleyan Mission Notices*, November 1854, 175–176.

Gantin, Mgr B. (1960), "Face aux elections", *La Quinzaine Religieuse de Cotonou*, vol. 1, 15, November, 9–14 (Message before the elections from the Archbishop of Cotonou).

Guéry, Michel (1973), *Christianisme Céleste: Notes de travail*, unpublished ms, Akpakpa, Cotonou.

Guilcher R.-F. (1942), *L'activité pacificatrice d'un missionnaire*, Rome: SMA.

Hazoumé, M.L. (1989), "Un laïc chrétien s'interroge face à la crise", *La Croix du Bénin*, 530, 6, 12.

Hazoumé, Paul, (1942), *50 ans d'apostolat, Mgr Steinmetz* (érence du 13/03/1942), Typescript, SMA Archives, Rome 3J41, Lomé (Togo), Société des Missions Africaines Archives, Rome 4D6, republished in Cotonou in 2002 for a commemorative celebration.

Hegeman, B. (1999), PhD thesis in missiology, in preparation; typescript of chs 7, 10, 11 made available to the present writer by the author.

Hountondji, P. (2000), "Le chemin à parcourir reste énorme", *La Croix du Bénin*, 11 February, 7.

Hounvou, T. (1991), "Message du Secretaire Général de la Conférence Chrétienne pour la Paix au Bénin", *L'Héraut*, vol. 2, 3, 17–18.

Kérekou, M. (1990), "Je ne renie rien", *Africa International*, 229, 32.

Kouamouo, Théophile (2001), "Au départ de la 'Route des esclaves', le délicat débat sur l'indemnisation", *Le Monde*, 10 September, http://www.le.monde.fr/0.6063,221174,00.html.

Krabill, J.R. (ed.) (1996), *Nos racines racontée: récits historiques sur l'Eglise en Afrique de l'Ouest*, Abidjan: Presses Bibliques/Menonite Board of Mission.

Law, R. (2001), *Individualising the Transatlantic Slave Trade: the Biography of Mohammah Gardo Baquaqua of Djougou (1854)*, lecture to The Royal Historical Society, UCL, 30 March.

Lawson, V. and Hountoundji, P. (1991), interview: Ministre de la Santé et de l'Education Nationale', *Le Héraut*, vol. 2, 3 (Methodist Bulletin), 13–15.

Mellier, D. (1982), "Marxisme et Mission—Bénin", *SEDOS Bulletin*, 18, Rome, 352–357.

Mêtinhoue, P.G. (1993), "Monseigneur Christophe Adimou, un évêque au service de la vérité et du dialogue sous un régime marxiste-leniniste", *Eglise de Cotonou*, vol. 33, 7 (numéro spécial), July, 62–69.

Mununo, B. (ed.) (1998), *The Challenge of Justice and Peace: The Response of the Church in Africa Today, Symposium of the Pontifical Council for Justice and Peace, Harare, 29 July–1 August 1996.*

NDA (Sœurs de Notre Dames des Apôtres) (2002), "Sœurs enterrées en terre Béninoises", in *125 ans NDA au Bénin – 1877–2002*, Cotonou.

Nzamuto, F. (1992), "Evangile et développement", in *Société et éducation*, 5, Cotonou: Association 'Chrétiens dans la Vie Publique'/Internationales Institut, Konrad Adenauer Stiftung, 60.

Ofoegbu, Timothy Godwin (1999), *Skeleton of the Ancestors: Heal Your Family Tree*, Lagos: Flame Books.

Okponikpe Hubert O. (2002), "Le Président Kérékou donne le top: Journées Nationales des Béninois de l'Extérieur", *La Nation* no. 3035, 23 July.

Pompey, Fabienne (2001), "Durban: les descendants d'esclaves demandent réparation", *Le Monde*, 7 September, http://www.lemonde.fr.

Quenum, A. (1974), "Le programme national d'édification de l'Ecole Nouvelle", *Eglise de Cotonou*, vol. 15, 2 October, 31–41.

Sastre, Mgr R. (1987), "Le sous-développement enrichit les économies 'développées'", *La Semaine Africaine*, 1699, 15–16.

——— (1987), "Le sous-développement est culturel et spirituel", *La Semaine Africaine*, 1700, 8–9.

——— (1987), "Notre sous-développement culturel écartèle nos consciences religieuses", *La Semaine Africaine*, 1701: 6–7.

——— (1987), "Que faire?", *La Semaine Africaine*, 1703, 16–17.

——— (1987), "Oser des voies nouvelles de développement", *Construire Ensemble*, 6, 3–11.

——— (1987), "Evangélisation et développement", *La Croix du Bénin*, 501, 1, 6.

——— (1988), "Le Synode sur l'Apostolat des laïcs", *Eglise d'Abomey*, 3, 1–20.

——— (1989), "Evangiles et Forces Occultes: Quelle conscience chrétienne face à la conquête du pouvoir", *La Croix du Bénin*, 539, 2, 11.

——— (1990), "Lottare contro le injiustizie", *Nigrizia,* September, 43.

——— (1992), "Bien commun: définition et respect", in *Société et éducation*, 5, Cotonou: Association 'Chrétiens dans la Vie Publique'/Internationales Institut, Konrad Adenauer Stiftung, 18–30.

SCEAM (Symposium des Conférences épiscopales d'Afrique et de Madagascar) (1993), *Pensée et Action Sociale de l'Eglise en Afrique Francophone*, Actes de la rencontre du Conseil Pontifical Justice et Paix, Symposium des Conférences Episcopales d'Afrique et Madagascar, Yaoundé.

——— (2002), "L'Eglise-Famille de Dieu: lieu et sacrement de pardon, de reconciliation et de paix en Afrique", Port Louis, Mauritius 13–18 November 2001, *Documentation Catholique*, no. 2262, 20 January 2002, 64–86.

Smith, Stephen (2001), "Recontre avec Roger Botte, anthropologue et chercheur au CNRS sur la question de l'esclavage", *Le Monde*, 30 August, http:www.lemonde.fr.

Soglo, N. (1990), "Nicephore Soglo: après les tortures, le travail" (interview), *Africa International*, 229, 34–35.

Soglo, N. (1994), "Moralisation de la vie publique: où en est-on aujourd'hui?", *La Croix du Bénin*, 15 July, 1, 11.

Tevoedjre, A. (1990), "Rapport général de synthèse de la Conférence Nationale des Forces vives de la Nation", Annex in Boulaga (1993), 179–194.

Tohahide, J. (1991), "Programme d'action du Président de la République: Que retenir?", *La Sentinelle*, 2, 3 (Methodist Bulletin).

Tosso, C. (2000), "La bonne gouvernance n'a pas encore pion sur rue au Bénin", *La Croix du Bénin*, 11 February 7.

Union des Laïcs catholiques du Bénin (1989), "Alternance démocratique ou leurre", *La Croix du Bénin*, 530, 1–2, 7.

Villaça, Théophile (2002), *Mgr François Steinmetz, sa mort et ses onsèques à Ouidah* (Extrait du Bulletin de liaison SMA Frères d'Armes).
Villaça, Théophile (2002), *Hommage à Monseigneur François Steinmetz, le legendaire "Daga"*, Ouidah.
Wharton, Rev. Henry (1854–55), "Extract from a letter", *Wesleyan Missionary Notices*, vol. XIV, 172–175.

Roman Catholic official Vatican documents

Second Vatican Council (1965), *Ad Gentes, Decree on the Missionary Activity of the Church*, Rome.
—— (1965), *Nostra Aetate: Declaration on the Relationship of the Church to Non-Christian Religions*, Rome.
Paul VI (1975), *Evangelii Nuntiandi*, Encyclical on Missions, Rome.
John Paul II (1990), *Redemptoris Missio: On the Permanent Validity of the Church's Missionary Mandate*, Rome.
Congregation for the Doctrine of the Faith (2000), *Declaration "Dominus Iesus", on the unicity and salvific universality of Jesus Christ and the Church*, Rome.

Symposium of the Episcopal Conferences of Africa and Madascar (SECAM) documents

1992, *Les Nouveaux Mouvements Chrétiens en Afrique et Madagascar*.
1993, *Pensée et Action Sociale de l'Eglise en Afrique Francophone*, Actes de la rencontre du Conseil Pontifical Justice et Paix, Symposium des Conférences Episcopales d'Afrique et Madagascar, Yaoundé.

Interviews, personal communications and other sources

Adefarasin, Rev. Michael Adeymi, Pastor, Action Faith Ministries International, Cotonou, 11 August 2001.
Alladaye Jérôme, Lecturer in History, Université Nationale du Bénin, Cotonou, 21 August 2002.
Alokpo, Pastor Mikaël, Co-ordinator, Actions pour la recherche et la croissance des églises au Bénin (ARCEB), Cotonou, 26 June 2001.
Arigbe, Owei-Keye, J, Special Senior Apostle, General Secretary, Organisation of African Instituted Churches (OAIC), Nigeria Region, Benin City, Nigeria, 9 June 2001.
Assogba, Mgr N., Archbishop of Cotonou, written submission, received 15 August 2000.
—— Archbishop of Cotonou, interview 21 June 2002.
Asemota, S., Barrister and Constitutional Expert, Benin City, Nigeria, 5 June 2001.
Banégas, R., Editor, *Politique Africaine*, Sorbonne, Paris, 6 April 2000.
Bertello, Mgr Giuseppe, Papal Nuncio in Benin at the time of the National Conference, later Vatican Representative at the United Nations, Geneva, conversation, 8 December 2000.
Boukari, Bernard, Secretary in a printing firm and member of the UEEB, several interviews in June-August 2001 and information given during three years he spent working for us on language research and translation.
Brathier, Léon Editor-in-Chief, *La Nation*, Cotonou, 13 August 2002.
Dedji, Rev. V., Methodist Pastor, Theologian, Cambridge, March, April, June 2000; May, September 2001.

Dossou, Rev. Marcellin, Professor of Systematic Theology, Institute of Theology, Porto-Novo, interview, 11 July 2001.

Dossou, Rev. Simon, Moderator, Methodist Church of Benin (EPMB), Cotonou, 18 August 2001.

Dujarrier, Fr, M. Editor, *Mission d'Eglise*, former missionary, Paris, 16 March, 6 April 2000.

Durif, Fr J., Former Benin missionary (1948–1998), Lyon, 25 April 2000.

Eglise du Christianisme Céleste, ndg, *Lumière sur le Christinisme Céleste*. This is the fundamental document outlining the beliefs and practices of the church, as given by the Prophet Oschoffa, in detail. A photocopy was kindly provided to us by the church leasers at Akpakpa, Cotonou.

—— Sunday service, 8 July 2001.

—— interview with church leaders, including Mikaël Alakpo, Paroisse d'Akpakpa Centre, 9 July 2001.

—— interview with Sention Church authorities at the World See, Porto-Novo, 20 July 2001.

Faucher OCSO, Dom Charles, Prior, Cistercian Monastery, Koukoubou, Parakou, Benin, 25 July 2001.

Gantin, S.E. Bernardin Card., Former Archbishop of Cotonou, member of the Roman Curia, 5 and 19 April 2001.

Gbenonvi, Professeur Roger, President, Transparency International, interview, Cotonou, 28 July 2002.

Goudjo, Fr Raymond B., AIJP, Cotonou, interviews 30 June 2001, 14 July 2002.

Hartnett, Fr David, missionary in western Nigeria, Cotonou, 15 July 2001.

Hountoundji, Professor Paulin, Department of Philosophy, University of Benin, Vice President of the Methodist Church (Synod) of Benin, interview, Cotonou, 9 August 2001.

Jarret, Max (2001), *Racial Myths*, BBC World Service, 12 August 2001.

Konrad Adenauer Stiftung, http://www.kas.de, March 2000 for the following conferences:

Civic education in primary schools, Lokossa.

The Chair of Human Rights at the National University of Benin, Cotonou.

Administration and elections in Benin, Porto-Novo.

Political parties and elections, Porto-Novo.

Training of young commercials.

Workshop on television emission 'Entre Nous'.

Press conference with journalists of newspapers, radio and television in Benin, Cotonou.

Promotion of parliamentary elections in Benin, Cotonou.

Meeting between international donors and local NGOs for the preparation of parliamentary elections, Cotonou.

SOS—Civic education weeks, Benin.

Promotion of journalists (Le Héraut), Cotonou.

Promotion of young leaders, Parakou.

Journalists and national languages, Parakou.

Youth and democracy (I, II and III), Cotonou.

Radio and civic education, Cotonou.

Information and sensibilisation of the population about municipal elections.

Civil society and social control, Lokossa.

Civic education in barracks, Benin.

Further training in municipal leaders, Missérété.

Legendre, Fr P., Professor of Theology, Séminaire St; Gall, Ouidah, formerly in charge of lay movement in the Archdiocese of Cotonou, several interviews and conversations, Cotonou, June–August 2001.

Mabon, Fr A. Former Benin missionary (1951–1998), Montpellier, 8 April 2000.
Madougou, Pastor Ourou, Bible translator and pastor, UEEB, Parakou, 21 June 2001, and several other conversations in the course of our work on the Lokpa language 1987–1999.
Mahi, Fr M., former Benin missionary (1946–1998), Lyon, 25 April 2000.
Mangeot, Dom Jean Claude, OCSO, Monastère de Koukoubou, Parakou, Benin, letter of 26 September 2001, concerning the status of the Greek Orthodox Church in Benin.
Marco, Fr Rafael, SMA, Cotonou, concerning some details of the Borghero journals.
Motcho Marie, Services des Cultes, Ministère de l'Intérieur, interview, Cotonou, 21 August 2002.
Nyirabukeye Thérèse, Director, *Institut Pontifical Jean Paul II pour l'Afrique Francophone*, interview, Cotonou, 16 August 2002.
Quenum, Fr Alphonse, author of *Les Églises chrétiennes et la traite atlantique du XVe au XIXe siècle*, Rome, 19 April 2001.
Parrinder, Professor E.G., letters of 27 April and 25 September 2001.
Parke, Arthur, Northern Ireland Missionary, Financial Adminstrator, SIM Parakou, 18 July 2001.

Other material based on recall from personal observations, church publications, TV, radio, internet media,local press, and contacts with different ecclesiastical authorities in the course of my work over thirteen years in Benin (1987–1999) and during the course of my research.

Adoumou, Léandre (2002), "Les diables à l'Eglise catholique de Houèto: conflit entre chrétien catholiques et adeptes Zangbeto", *Fraternité*, no. 649, 26 July.
Adoun, Alain (2002), "Les critiques de Gbénonvi et Midiohouan: Festival International Gospel et Racines", *Fraternite*, no. 649, 26 July, 2.
Africa Intelligence (2000), "Kerekou, homme de paraboles", *Lettre du Continent*, 356, http://www.africaintelligence.fr.
Agbachi, Mgr Fidèle and Mgr Adjou Martin (2001), *Vous êtes la maison que Dieu Construit*, (Post Synodal Exhortation, pastoral and social orientation for the two dioceses of Parakou and N'dali), Bembereké.
Agbo-Ola, Bernard (1996), "Apôtre Docteur O.A. Joseph Abiodun: 'Je suis un serviteur de Dieu'", *La Sagesse*, no. 1, August.
Ahouanha, Constant Epiphane (1993), "Le Danxomé des Rois et son organisation politico-administrative au 17e, 18e, et 19e siècles", *La Voix de St Gall*, 64, 8–22 (Student publication of the Catholic Major Seminary of St Gall, Ouidah).
Akponikpe, Hubert O. (2002), "Mieux comprendre la décentralisation", *La Nation*, no. 3042, 2 August, 6.
Archidiocèse de Parakou (1999), *A l'Ecoute de l'Esprit*, Document de travail du Synode Diocésain.
Azifan, Reine, "Prolifération au Bénin des cabinets médicaux privés non-conformes: Les raisons d'une remise en ordre", *La Nation*, no. 3042, 2 August, 16.
Azonwakin, Alexis (2002), "Bénin: toujours l'immobilisme", *Fraternité*, no. 651, 30 July, 4.
Barbot, Jean (1688), "*Description des côtes d'Afrique*", unpublished ms, in Public Record Office, London: (Adm.7 830), II Partie, 136.
Ben, A. (1996), "L'Autorité spirituelle le devoir d'obéissance", *La Sagesse*, no. 1, August.
Binazon, Romuald (2002), "L'union défintivement scellée: Crise à l'Eglise du Christianisme Céleste", *La Nation*, no. 3044, 6 August.
Brathier, Léon (2002), "Religion, Pouvoir et Argent: Jusqu'où l'Eglise peut-elle aller?", *La Nation*, no. 3042, 2 August, 2.

CEB (2001), *Renforçons notre unité nationale* (extraordinary pastoral letter before the elections), Cotonou.

Djrèkpo, Charles (2002), Interview "…nous avons travaillé dans des conditions inhumaines…", *La Tribune*, no. 105, 18 April, 3.

Frenkiel, Olenka (2001), *The slave children*, Correspondent, BBC2 TV, broadcast Sunday 7 October 2001, Correspondent investigates the modern trade in child slaves which robs them of their childhood, reports from the West Coast of Africa.

Gohoungo, Andrée (1999), "Magie, sorcellerie ou religion? Le phénomène Bonnke: ce qui fait courir les Béninois", *Le Citoyen*, no. 648, 29 January.

Goudjo Raymond B. (ed.) (2000), *Discours Social des Evêques du Bénin de 1960 à 2000*, Cotonou: Editions Flamboyant (Collection Xwefa).

—— (ed.) (1998), *Identité ethniques et intégrité nationale*, Cotonou: Flamboyant (Collection Xwefa).

—— (ed.) (2000), *Le Chemin de la solidarité*, Cotonou: Flamboyant (Collection Xwefa).

—— (1999), *Ne plus s'endetter ou savoir s'endetter*, Cotonou: Flamboyant (Collection Xwefa).

—— (2001), "La Face Cachée de l'ONU: Questions sociales et familiales actuelles", *La Croix du Bénin,* published in four parts, July–August 2000; original ms provided by author.

Goudjo, Raymond B. (2002), *Eucharistie, Célébration du Devenir: Vers une culture de la communion pour une civilisation de la fraternité*, Cotonou: Editions du Flamboyant, Collection Xwefa.

Haute Autorité de l'Audiovisuel et de la Communication (HAAC), décision no. 01–011/HAAC, "Portant mise en demeure au Directeur Général de Radio Planète", Cotonou, 15 March 2001.

——, Décision no. 01–017/HAAC, "Portant mise en demeure au Directeur Général de Radio Carrefour", Cotonou, 20 March 2001.

Hounkoue, Adrien (1966), "Bientôt à Cotonou, un pasteur de 33 ans qui étonne", *Le Perroquet*, no. 6, 24 June.

Hounkpatin, Pius (2002), "Les Clarifications du Pasteur Dagbomey", *Liberté*, no. 799, 16 August.

Kérékou, Mathieu (2002), "Vaincre la pauvreté et conquérir la modernité" (Discours à l'occasion du 42e Anniversaire de l'Indépendance, *La Nation*, no. 3042, 2 August, 10.

Kinsou, José, T.L. (interview avec Léon Brathier) (2002), "A César ce qui est à César et à Dieu ce qui est à Dieu", *La Nation*, no. 3042, 2 August, 2.

Kouamouo, Théophile (2001), "Au Bénin, la campagne présidentielle conforte la démocratie", *Le Monde*, 3 March 2001, http://www.lemonde.fr.

—— (2001), "Au départ de la 'Route des esclaves', le délicat débat sur l'indemnisation", *Le Monde*, 10 September, http://www.le.monde.fr/0.6063,221174,00.html.

Latin American Independent Churches, http://www.clai.org.

La Nation, Le Premier Gouvernement du Président Matthieu Kérékou, 11 May 2001.

Le Républicain "Le Bénin classé 158ème pays selon le rapport IDH 2002 du PNUD", no. 406, 20 July 2002, 3.

Le Matin, "Le Pnud lance le débat sur 'politique et développement humain'", no. 1329, 29 July 2002, 2.

"Le Pasteur Agbaossi, seul capitaine du bateau: Dénouement de la Crise à l'Eglise du Christianisme Céleste", Les Echos du Jour, no. 1481, 17 August 2002, 3.

"Les christianistes célestes plus que jamais unis" (conférence de presse du Pasteur Marcellin Zannou), Le Béninois, no. 400, 16 August 2002, 2.

"Le Révérend Pasteur Dagbomè se défend: Soupçonné du décès du sous-préfet de Zagnanado", Le Béninois, no. 400, 16 August 2002, 4.

Massi, Maximin (1993), "Le Vodun et le pouvoir monarchique dans l'ancien royaume du Danxomæ", La voix de St Gall, no. 64, December, 23–34. (publication of the Catholic Major Seminary of St Gall, Ouidah).

Oschoffa, Samuel B.J. (1969/2000), interview given 1 January 1969 at Makoko, See of the Celestial Church of Christ, Diocese of Nigeria, translated and reproduced in *Contribution à l'Unité de l'Eglise du Christianisme Céleste: Spécial Millenaire*, ed. Tiburce Monteiro, Cotonou.

Panafrican News Agency (2001), "Campagne pour une présidentielle pacifique", Dakar, 12 January, www.allafrica.com/bénin.

—— (2001), "Les rois du Bénin appellent à voter Kérékou", Dakar, 12 January, www.allafrica.com/bénin.

—— (2001), "Décès du président du culte vodoun", Dakar, 12 January, www.allafrica.com/bénin.

—— (2001), "Benin adopts politicians good conduct code", Dakar, 12 January, www.allafrica.com/bénin.

—— (2001), "Les Evêques Appellent à un Scrutin Pacifique", Dakar, 7 February, www.allafrica.com/bénin.

—— (2001), "Bio-express du candidat Mathieu Kérékou", Dakar, 18 February, www.allafrica.com/bénin.

—— (2001), "Bio-express du candidat Nicéphone Soglo", Dakar, 18 February, www.allafrica.com/bénin.

—— (2001), "Bio-express du candidat Mathieu Kérékou", Dakar, 18 February, www.allafrica.com/bénin.

—— (2001), "Bio-express du candidat Bruno Amousou", Dakar, 18 February, www.allafrica.com/bénin.

—— (2001), "Bio-express du candidat Adrien Houngbedji", Dakar, 19 February, www.allafrica.com/bénin.

—— (2001), "Le défi du renouvellement de la classe politique", Dakar, 22 February, www.allafrica.com/bénin.

—— (2001), "Kérékou et Soglo arrivent en tête du premier tour", Dakar, 5 March, www.allafrica.com/bénin.

—— (2001), "Adrien Houngbédji plébiscité à Porto-Novo", Dakar, 5 March, www.allafrica.com/bénin.

—— (2001), "Difficile renouvellement de la classe politique", Dakar, 5 March, www.allafrica.com/bénin.

—— (2001), "Tractations pour les alliances au second tour", Dakar, 8 March, www.allafrica.com/bénin.

Penoukou, Efoé Julien (2002), "L'homme le plus imbecile est meilleur que l'or…", *La Nation*, no. 3042, 2 August, 3.

Sèdjro Félicien (1996), "Quelle éducation pour l'élévation de la conscience civique au Bénin", *La Croix du Bénin*, 6 September, 7.

Seidi, Mulero (2001), "Will Kérékou Win?", *Tempo*, Opinion and Analysis, Dakar, www.allafrica.com/bénin.

Sovide, Valentin (2002), "Bénin, l'autre visage de la pauvreté", *La Nation*, no. 3042, 2 August, 20.

UNESCO (1985), "Convention concerning the protection of the world cultural and natural heritage" (SC-85/CONF.0008/9 Paris, 2–6 December 1985).

INDEX